The Man of Independence

KENNIKAT PRESS SCHOLARLY REPRINTS

Dr. Ralph Adams Brown, Senior Editor

Series in
AMERICAN HISTORY AND CULTURE
IN THE TWENTIETH CENTURY
Under the General Editorial Supervision of
Dr. Donald R. McCoy
Professor of History, University of Kansas

THE MAN OF INDEPENDENCE

JONATHAN DANIELS

KENNIKAT PRESS
Port Washington, N. Y./London

THE MAN OF INDEPENDENCE

Copyright, 1950, by Jonathan Daniels
Reissued in 1971 by Kennikat Press by arrangement
Library of Congress Catalog Card No: 75-137969
ISBN 0-8046-1427-X

Manufactured by Taylor Publishing Company   Dallas, Texas

KENNIKAT SERIES ON AMERICAN HISTORY AND
CULTURE IN THE TWENTIETH CENTURY

For

Josephus Daniels
1862 — 1948

who devoted a life
half as long as the
Republic's to a fighting
faith in democracy's
fulfillment for all
the people.

CONTENTS

8 CONTENTS

SOURCES AND ACKNOWLEDGMENTS

THIS BOOK GREW from many sources, printed pages and living people. It is in no sense an authorized biography. Indeed, it is not meant to be a biography at all. I wanted to tell, in the concrete terms of a specific Ulysses, the Odyssey of the "everyday" American through our times. Truman was that "everyday man"; he remains his greatest symbol. His story is important at our midcentury though its meaning is as old as the Republic. The story actually began with Mr. Jefferson's instinctive understanding of the aspirations of the average human being. The fulfillment of those aspirations by the ordinary—"the everyday man" —was never more important than now when it is seriously proposed as a "revolutionary" doctrine that man may attain some of his hopes only by the admission of his entire incapacity for freedom. That is the book I meant to write. That is the thing I hope I have said.

It may be biography, nevertheless. The chief source must be set down as the President of the United States himself. He is responsible for none of the judgments expressed by me. Indeed, I am sure that in a number of cases he will disagree with my conclusions. I do not expect him to like all the new lines I have put upon his portrait. He was, however, generous with his time in my efforts to find my way to the facts. He told me much. Also, he cautioned me not to trust his memory but to check the facts where the facts were recorded. I think I have made the most thorough possible search for them.

Many people helped me. The book practically amounts to a collaboration between my wife, Lucy Cathcart Daniels, and myself. David Mearns, Donald Patterson, Robert Gooch of the Library of Congress helped me find my way to facts in the vast and infinitely detailed sources of that wonderful institution. Dr. Herman Kahn of the Franklin D. Roosevelt Library at Hyde Park put at my disposal the most significant documents in the

Roosevelt-Truman correspondence. I owe much to the staffs of the "morgues," or libraries, of *The St. Louis Post-Dispatch* and *The Kansas City Star,* particularly to John Doohan of *The Star.* Thomas H. Madden, of the Kansas City Title Insurance Company, traced the Truman story through the Truman and Young family land holdings in Jackson County during the last century.

William M. Reddig not only gave me basic help in his book, *Tom's Town,* but also other information, assistance, and advice. The same is true of Judge Henry A. Bundschu, Republican neighbor of the Trumans since childhood and author of *Harry S. Truman—The Missourian.*

Vivian and Mary Jane, the President's brother and sister, shared their memories with me. The President's cousins, Misses Ethel and Nellie Noland, told me much about the Truman background. There were old Truman friends who helped: the late Roger Sermon, Edgar G. Hinde, Henry P. Chiles, Colonel William Southern, Jr., and others, of Independence. I had a long talk with Spencer Salisbury, Truman's old home-town enemy.

I was surprised to discover the forgotten activities of the President in oil, mining, and the building and loan business. Great help was given me in these aspects of the President's story by David H. Morgan, of Eureka, Kansas, and J. K. Brelsford, of Topeka, Kansas. J. M. Slaughter, of Hickman Mills, Missouri, gave me new information about Truman as farmer and farm leader. Edward Jacobson told me much about the venture into haberdashery. Harry Jobes and Father L. Curtis Tiernan gave human emphasis to the story of the 129th Field Artillery in World War I which is carefully documented in *The Artilleryman* by the late Jay M. Lee, a book which promptly became a collectors' item after Truman became President.

I can only list the names of many whose help deserves much more space in appreciation: Dean Acheson, Barney Allis, John T. Barker, James M. Barnes, Hugh Bennett, Leslie Biffle, Thomas C. Blaisdell, Jr., Charles L. Blanton, William M. Boyle, Dr. W. L. Brandon, Charles F. Brannan, William Bray, Edgar Brown, Oscar Chapman, Mrs. Henry Clay Chiles, Clark Clifford, Ralph Coghlan, James V. Conran, Delmar Dail, Robert Dennison, Irving Dilliard, Jesse Donaldson, George Elsey, Tom L. Evans, Richard Farrington, Edward J. Flynn, Phil H. Graves, Gordon Gray, Dr. Paul Gross, Carl A. Hatch, Richard H. Hill, Edward

Keating, Edward J. Kelly, Ernest Kirschten, O. K. LaRoque, William D. Leahy, Mortimer B. Levy, Russell Lord, Max Lowenthal, Dr. Franc McCluer, Spencer McCulloch, Wesley McCune, Porter McKeever, Edward McKim, Victor Messall, Frank Monroe, Matt F. Morse, John W. Muir, Theodore O'Leary, Edwin Pauley, W. L. Powlison, Margaret Price, F. W. Reichelderfer, Roy Roberts, Dean Rusk, Alex Sachs, P. L. Shackelford, Duke Shoop, Forrest Smith, George Albert Smith, Merriman Smith, John Snyder, Margaret Truman, T. H. Van Sant, Harry Vaughan, Frank Walker, Jerome Walsh, Sam M. Wear.

JONATHAN DANIELS

The Man of Independence

CHAPTER I

American Plan

HARRY TRUMAN HITCHED up the buggy and drove down to the telegraph office in Grandview that summer of 1912, to find out what the news was from the convention in Baltimore. His father was eager for the nomination of Champ Clark, of Missouri, who had come as the Trumans had come from Kentucky. The younger Truman was for Woodrow Wilson. It was an exciting time. Men even said that old Champ Clark had gone to Baltimore with a pistol in his pocket for use on William Jennings Bryan. Bryan had successfully tied Clark's candidacy to his charge that "an effort was being made to sell the Democratic Party to the predatory interests of the country." Wilson was nominated on the forty-sixth ballot.

Harry Truman took the news home to his father. Both of them in the years before had been for Bryan. Harry Truman as a twelve-year-old boy had argued his Bryanism with the uncle for whom he was named, old Harrison Young, who snorted at Bryan and stood in the free silver years for gold and the ticket of the Gold Democrats. John A. Truman, Harry's father, had sat through every session when the still hopeful Democrats nominated Bryan for the second time in Kansas City in 1900. Sixteen-year-old Harry had been there, too, a boy listening to more than the combination of Bryan and pandemonium. Beside his father in the steaming, quickly built auditorium he had listened to a loud and gaslit part of the democratic debate. Now in 1912 it had been reopened and recharged with anger. And it mounted across the years, after Harry brought home the news from Grandview, until Wilson, torn from his efforts to repair democracy at home, made war a crusade for the safety of democracy in the world.

Democracy has not seemed safe since. Sometimes, indeed, Wilson's phrase has served only to make the word "democracy" seem frayed, futile and a little old-fashioned. It is difficult to think of anything more improbable than that the young man, hurrying home to the farm with news in 1912, should himself be the man who would be called upon to defend it and define it at American midcentury, when democracy was not only attacked across the earth but misunderstood at home. Even after he assumed that task Harry Truman seemed to many people an unlikely leader of the United States when the nation and its faith confronted their greatest danger. There have been no such external dangers in any of the years since Thomas Jefferson undertook to pull together in the Declaration the people's aspirations as a basis for an appeal to mankind.

Actually, at such a time it would have been impossible to find a man better qualified to embody and exemplify the democracy of America. There are, of course, Americans who believe that Roosevelt was only produced by a convulsion and who insisted as long as they could that Harry Truman was only an accident. Some of them have fashioned for themselves a fastidious faith that the widening concern of the American government for all the American people represents not the flow of the American tradition but only the unfortunate details of Roosevelt charm and Truman luck. At the other extreme there are those intellectuals who have been asking vaguely for a "new dynamic" in the American democracy to compete with communism. They miss the "old dynamic" and if they should find it, they might find it distastefully full of the determinations of ordinary and average Americans.

Neither of these groups was more surprised in 1948 than such men had been before. The Federalist merchants and preachers were appalled at the news of the election of Andrew Jackson in 1828. But there was more confidence in misinformation in 1948. There were more people educated in the misinterpretation of America. The outcome of the election, therefore, served not only American mass hope but also American mass humor which takes a loud and lingering enjoyment in the discomfiture of the distended.

Both the mistake and the laughter were revealing. Humor in the people confuses humorless intellectuals as it helps deflate methodical technicians who come into public affairs through the advertising business. Both Marxists and magnificos somehow ought to have at least the right to expect the masses to be grim. The American mixture of the fight and the frolic together can be baffling. That may help to explain why those who now are compelled to confess that they were wrong about that greatest post-war election have not yet recognized its meaning as the re-sounding re-emphasis of a continuing American revolution. It was not easy for them to see the new swing to the old native left, behind a President who could joke and damn from the same train platform. The truth is that the plain people are neither simple nor plain. It may be easiest to understand them in terms of the improbable person for whom they expressed their free democratic preference in the age of the greatest danger to democracy itself. They understood that what Harry Truman put to-gether in his 1948 campaign and the months before and after was not a political platform but an American philosophy. The man and the Americans understood that what he said was not merely "the Truman program" but the American plan.

There have been no new things in the Truman promises. After sixteen years and after five elections, it should have been clear at midcentury that both the New Deal and the Fair Deal were not the plans of Presidents but the directions of America. The New Deal long preceded and survived Franklin Roosevelt. And Harry Truman, who was described as he came into office as the embodiment of the ordinary American, emerged in his 1948 campaign as an American spokesman deemed by the electorate worthy of an ancient and continuing cause. That cause is more the embodiment of the spirit of the ordinary and extraordinary American than any one man could be, even an improbable man from Missouri. The important thing to remember is that the man on the rear platform of the campaign special and the people all amphitheatered behind it understood and made American directions together.

They had come the same way. Of course, Harry Truman is not the "average" or the "ordinary" American. Neither he nor any other American can be reduced to such statistical terms. Never-theless, the American direction through our times can be more clearly seen in the details of the case history of Harry Truman than in the story of any other American. It has been strangely neglected. There is a notion in Independence, Missouri, that every stone in his home town has been overturned and the micro-scope applied to the damp dark beneath them. The idea persists in Washington that our implacable press has not only denied his privacy as President, as is customary, but has scrutinized every part of his past. Not even his detractors have really dug into his story. Even his friends cling stubbornly to old mistakes about him.

Sometimes Harry Truman himself has served the malice of his enemies by an almost malignant modesty of his own. Some old teachers have built roomy Truman legends big enough to in-clude themselves. Old politicians have persuasive tales as to how they personally pushed him toward the Presidency. Jealousy and surprise work hand in hand with pride in any small town's tales about its greater sons. Harry Truman takes amusement for him-self from the story of the small-town man who became Postmaster General and who afterwards came home on an early morning train. Only the village half-wit was on hand at the station, so the great man asked him:

"What did people say when I was appointed Postmaster Gen-eral?"

The native half-wit spoke for the town. "They just laughed."

Such debunking is an essential part of the privileges of democ-racy, which nobody understands better than Truman. He is ready to take his share. He has certainly received it. No Presi-dent has ever had so much ill-fitting metaphor hung upon him. The sentimentalists will never make him a Tom Sawyer child in Mark Twain's Missouri. Neither will the detractors keep him only a haberdasher, a piano player and the political office boy of a political gorilla. Only the whole story can serve understanding of the man. And nobody has even tried to write the whole story. Anybody going over the piles of books and papers and pieces written about Harry Truman since he suddenly became Presi-dent must come to the truth that never has so little been so often rewritten by more men.

"I've been lied about, belittled, vilified and otherwise mis-treated in print," he told me. Also, like every other President, he has been petted and praised. Most important of all, he has been misunderstood at a time when world understanding of the choice of the American people in their President is the best possible image of the meaning of our democratic system to the world. He is certainly the most unaverage average man in America. The cliché of the ordinary American in the White House was a snob phrase first invented by those who, after Roosevelt's death, hoped to minimize the Presidency. Harry Truman's story is not average, but it is symbolic. It is unique in terms of the manner in which it has touched in personal problem and private pain all the difficulties of American life in our time.

Hardly any other President has so personally shared all the vicissitudes of all the people. The great Roosevelt was born—and died—with a golden spoon in his mouth. The one thing he shared in pain with the people—and shared gallantly—was susceptibly to a tragic disease. He and Jefferson were the patricians and the philosophers who understood the hungers of the people which Jefferson wrote to be remembered in the Declaration. Americans have remembered that the whole meaning of Independence, which Jefferson laid down and which Roosevelt translated into the rights which men, created equal, needed in our times, was that governments are instituted only for men and take the shape of their purposes and powers from men's consent.

The whole purpose of our being as a nation was written by Jefferson in four lines. It was the contract with the patriots. It was the pledge to "the opinions of mankind." They are remembered:

> "We hold these truths to be self-evident, that all men are created equal, that they are endowed by their Creator with certain inalienable Rights, that among these are Life, Liberty and the pursuit of Happiness. That to secure these rights, Governments are instituted among Men, deriving their just powers from the consent of the governed."

The American procession, delayed sometimes and diverted too often, has been the remembrance of those lines. Jackson and Truman emerged from the democratic stream of that remembrance. Jefferson and Jackson, Roosevelt and Truman are the analogies for our centuries. Each is essential in the combination, though there is a difference between Jefferson-Roosevelt and Jackson-Truman like that between velvet and leather. Americans felt leaderless when Roosevelt died. Truman taught them, as one of them, that their greatness lies in themselves.

No modern man has been so equipped in gifts and handicaps,

in his own failures and in his leadership, to teach that so well. His story has been ours and ours has been the advance of the United States to a power and eminence never equalled among nations. It has also been the story of democracy's burgeoning and its uneasiness, of the amassment of the refined gold and the processed uranium by a people who still understand that they can measure their security only by themselves.

Harry Truman's birth coincided with the closing of the frontier of free land in America. Karl Marx died the year before he was born. Harry Truman was an infant when the dynamite at the Haymarket labor rally in Chicago detonated the unrest in American cities and when the first central electric station sent out power to light Mr. Edison's lamps in New York. The Grand Army of the Republic still marched—and often marched as Republicans rather than as veterans—grandly and regardlessly past problems of people which were not solved at Appomattox. Yet, maybe a period came to an end two days before Harry Truman was born when Ulysses S. Grant was shamed in his sick old age by the disreputable failure of the brokerage firm of Grant and Ward. There were hard times that year. "The knaves have hurt the fools," said Henry Adams. That helped in the election of Grover Cleveland even if, as Adams also said, "the party behind him is ragged, timid, and stupid."

The scene is not less important than the time. Maybe its own orators have worn thin those phrases about the "heart of America" and "the crossroads of America," describing the place where the big north bend of the Missouri met the trails to the West. There is still a middleness about the Missouri-Kansas border country of Harry Truman. It is not only in the middle of America. It has been in the middle of every American quarrel and every American decision, too. Missouri has cast its vote with the American majority in every Presidential election in this century. The fight for one, free, enduring America was hand to hand and face to face there long before the Civil War. Missouri runs from the Mississippi to the prairie, Dred Scott to John Brown, and from Huckleberry Finn to Jesse James. It was a land where America learned about compromise, its possibilities and its definite limitations. That phrase "Show Me" which clings to its name and its character is not local in its meaning; it derives not from incredulity or curiosity but from an evident purpose not to be pushed around. There has been plenty of pushing. Truman's Missouri-Kansas country was a land where the American political differences involved mayhem, house-burnings, horse-whippings, theft and murder long before Tom Pendergast organized the comparatively puny later politics of Kansas City.

Not only did the West begin there; there also the door of the frontier swung shut with the biggest bang. And behind the shut door farm protest rose like the sound of a tornado carrying off a tin roof. The plows broke the plains and on the plains the money power, they said, broke the heart of the farmers. A woman cried on that border that it was time to raise less corn and more hell. And a young man named William Allen White, who had got his training on *The Kansas City Star*, bored with protest, asked what in the world was the matter with Kansas and, in effect, with America as well. Without editorial sarcasm men on the border have been asking that question ever since, with increasing insistence, and expecting answers.

For a long time out there Harry Truman knew a good deal more about the troubles than the answers. He was not only a bespectacled child; as a boy diphtheria left him totally paralyzed for a time. His eyes ended his West Point hope, but he saw the boy who studied with him, and did get to Annapolis, become not an admiral but an itinerant book agent. He not only served as American soldier at the front, he was also one of those who came home from war to see the unraveling of the safety of democracy for himself. He was one of the millions of farmers who moved to town and one of the small business men in town who discovered that ninety-cent wheat would not buy fifteen-dollar shirts. He saw his own store door shut up by his creditors. In 1940 when he was fighting for his political life, he saw his family farm foreclosed and his mother moved out with the furniture when she was eighty-eight years old. He was a small-town community leader who tried to save a local bank but saw it go down nevertheless and his neighbor, its president, settle his accounts with carbon monoxide from an automobile's exhaust. He saw the American thrift he helped to foster in a building and loan association confused by an ex-partner whom he had to help send to the penitentiary. In 1950 that ex-partner, who is the perfect man-who-hates-Harry in America, said, "Harry's the luckiest buzzard I ever knew, but I'll give him this: he's got plenty of guts."

Truman has needed them. He has taken his licks with speculative Americans as well as thrifty ones. He was, with most of us, the child not only of what he later called "the robust years" but also of what Mark Twain called "the gilded age" as well. His robust grandfather drove fifteen hundred head of cattle across the plain to California; but Truman's own father, who was "always ready," his son says, "to swap a needle or a threshing machine," hoped to get rich quick, in a pattern quite as expansive and American, in the futures of wheat on the Board of Trade.

Harry Truman inherited both his father's optimism and his financial bad luck. He put more money in than he took out of a zinc mine in Oklahoma. In Kansas, where he and his partners got only a dry hole in oil lands, they saw others bring in the gushers. Harry Truman liked the risk element of the oil business. He called it "hazard," his old-time oil partner says. Also, Truman seems a man optimistically unsure that any luck is bad. He wrote his partner years later about that oil well which did not come in, "Dave, maybe I wouldn't be President, if we'd hit." More recently he has been able to look back through the wreckage of the 1948 opinion polls and say, "The luckiest thing that ever happened to me was the Eightieth Congress."

He needed some such philosophy as he went along. He was bank clerk, promoter and salesman. He was politician. Of course, as every President must be, he still is. Yet, after twenty years in politics, he says, "I never in my life ran for a political office that I wanted." Maybe not, but he certainly fought for them all the way. Indeed, he was never elected to an office he did not have to fight for, tooth and nail, unless it was the nomination as Vice-President which he struggled to avoid. Even as a Mason, though he became Grand Master of Missouri, his enemies tried to stop him after his advancement had supposedly become automatic.

He was politician in the machine of Boss Tom Pendergast, and his personal loyalty to Pendergast followed the old Boss to the prison and the grave. It did not stop there. Even today Harry Truman says, "If he had died there that summer [in New York in 1936 where he was operated on for cancer] he would have

been remembered as the greatest boss this country ever had."
And after Potsdam, when he undertook to measure the strength
of Stalin, Truman said, "He was as near like Tom Pendergast as
any man I know." Yet old Tom Pendergast, by well-authenti-
cated report, regarded Harry Truman, who insisted on low road
bids even from Pendergast road contractors, as "the contrariest
cuss in Missouri."

From the beginning Truman brought power and did not
merely take it. He remembers with pride now that as county
leader "in any election I could deliver eleven thousand votes and
not steal a one. I looked out for my folks and they understood
my leadership. The vote-stealing in Kansas City was silly." He
was never merely politician. By the testimony of those who both
watched his work and relentlessly searched his record, he was
honest politician and honest and creative local public official.
It is only better remembered that in those days he was a member
of the Pendergast organization than it is that he was president of
the Greater Kansas City Plan Association and a member of the
board of directors of the National Conference on City Planning.

Pendergast or no Pendergast, he was beaten for political office
only once. That was in the midst of Pendergast power when the
Ku Klux Klan not only fought Truman in Jackson County but
also disrupted the national Democratic Party in Madison Square
Garden. That assured the election of Calvin Coolidge and the
return of the gilded age. When the gilded age cracked that second time, Harry Truman had some understanding of America.
So did other Americans who had come the same way. They were
going the same way together.

Nobody was ever more certain of that than Harry Truman in
1948. That accounts for his courage when not only all the commentators but most of his companions shook their heads over his
chances. He was not merely talking in that campaign about the
Eightieth Congress, but about the effectiveness of democracy. He
was never concerned only with the continuing items of failure
in one of the greatest periods of prosperity, or even with the
items which he counted as the parts of fulfillment: housing and
health, wages and farm prices, the human rights to human dignity, the prodding for production for plenty, the protections
from wild prices and wild prejudices, too. He is concerned with

them now only as details in the design for effective and meaning-
ful democracy in our time.

The American people understand that, intuitively, maybe,
but insistently, too. Enough of them, in 1948, understood and
in enough diversity to show not the power of pressure groups
but of people as Americans. No group or region could claim the
Truman victory of 1948. The vote of labor was effective only
because unexpected votes came from the supposedly anti-labor
farm country to join it. No minorities came to Truman with the
balance of power for victory from Harlem or The Bronx, Philadelphia or Detroit. He lost New York, but he carried Iowa. He
did not require the Solid South. He did not need such bosses as
Byrd or Crump or Talmadge to take their states. He could give
the extreme left to Henry Wallace. He could let Thurmond, of
South Carolina, carry off the last remnants of blatant Bourbon-
ism. He need not have been troubled by the reluctance of those
"liberals," who mistook their own departures from Washington
for the disappearance of liberalism in the United States. Harry
Truman's American purposes were more important than any
American powers.

"The Truman program," presented in the Truman speeches,
the documents, the messages and in the man himself, is easily
understood. It is the renewed and native expression of the
American's now firmly fixed faith that his government's function
is to help him have the security and decency of which his country is capable. Beyond the basic pledges of the Declaration, he
knows that his Constitution hangs upon a preamble pledging the
promotion of the general welfare. That American has seldom
heard of Marx except as a name for strange, foreign and wicked
ideas. Certainly in a time in which the word "state" has been
set up as one with which to frighten children and Republicans,
the "ordinary American," the "average American," turns to his
government with expectancy. His "state" does not terrify him.
He believes that he can both give it powers and keep his freedoms. He believes that it can guard his security without sapping
his strength. Above all, in an age in which socialization has new
terrors, he is willing to entrust his government with new social
responsibilities without fear of the totalitarian exercise of them.
He believes that he can make big government work for people

without the danger that people may be forced to work without freedom for government.

Fundamentally, his faith is the slowly grown and confidently grown free, democratic compromise for the modern world. It stands squarely between the irresponsible possessors of great power, whether they be the robber barons or the commissars, the gluttons of private privilege or the totalitarian masters of the instruments of the state. It is faith in big government in the hands of free men.

Of course, this is not merely a "Truman program." It did not grow merely from the New Deal even if its first clear development may have come with Franklin Roosevelt. Roosevelt certainly did not think up the New Deal suddenly or by himself. Its roots were strong in the American backcountry in such places as Kansas and Missouri before Roosevelt was out of Groton. It was not finally accomplished by Roosevelt. With the best luck Harry Truman will not completely accomplish its expected meaning for the American.

Actually, what he serves is the design for democracy in an age in which men more and more realize that political freedoms must be accompanied by social and economic assurances. Certainly, in a world beset by those who feel that hope must bypass freedom in order to find security, it has never been more important than now. It faces the crocodile promises of communism with the clear possibilities of democracy. The task in leadership was never greater than that given Harry Truman. He meets it. He is both the product and the embodiment of the American faith which is set up more clearly now than ever as a faith for the world. He speaks that faith in the language of his countrymen. He is separated from them by no abstract vocabulary of the overeducated or any half-baked techniques designed to count destiny like sales. Sometimes his vigorous vocabulary in private presents difficulties in polite translation for the historian. His language in public is understandable at the "whistle stops" of both politics and government. Moscow understands what he says, as well as Independence and Iowa, the steel towns, the Carolinas and Wall Street. What he has expressed are the determinations in hope of a nation and not merely the political phrases of a man.

Of course, it is revolution. The "business community," the "country club set," those political philosophers who quote the

words of Thomas Jefferson in order to serve the aims of Alexander Hamilton, those liberals who think that liberalism is made
of doctrines out of books and not purposes out of living may
find it distasteful. In many ways it is a rustic radicalism, lacking
the bookish beginnings upon which Marxists rely, sometimes
seeming tragi-comic as Bryan was after he was beaten and bald
and old. It can seem crude and countrified, even oddly old-
fashioned as it also seems brash. Of course, it is old-fashioned
and rustic in its origins as the nation's origins were largely rural,
too. (Even the cities now are filled with Americans who have
come to town.) It can be corn-fed and crackerbox. "Wall Street"
may seem a hoarse cry at a dead dog. It is also a stoutly service-
able label. Even intellectuals should understand the traditional
native protest against a political and economic system based
upon stuffing the horses in order that the sparrows may eat.
Maybe the prairie was easier than the forest. Perhaps we seek
a simpler security still. The strange thing may be that the
filling of the land, the crowding of the towns have not destroyed the faith in the abundance and the ability of America
to let a people created equal get with some equality to the fair
chance and the clean corn.

There are, of course, many who question the way to that best
hope and chance. America would scarcely seem America if it
ever emerged from its own long debate about its own directions.
Some of the labels are confusing. Some of the labels are designed
to confuse. Traditional American determination upon an America fashioned for the general welfare on the basis of the consent
of the governed is sometimes made to seem a strange and foreign
thing. Roosevelt betrayed his class, they said. Truman has betrayed the legend of a safe and solid middle America. The
managing editor of the conservative *Kansas City Star* described
the Truman who entered the White House as one who "has the
innate, instinctive conservatism in action of the Missouri-bred
countrymen." He still has. It is not Truman who is misunderstood but his countrymen. The purpose of such countrymen is
not only to conserve their ancient dream which was put clearly
into the first document of their independence. They believe that
only by such old-fashioned and hell-bent conservatism can the
hopes, the dignity and the personal liberties of men be preserved
anywhere on earth.

They are not confused, but it is not for lack of century-long and everyday effort to confuse them. They were provided with all the materials for the distortion of Roosevelt. It should have been easy for them to hate an aristocrat. Certainly in their own difficulties it should be easy for them to minimize a man who in so many things is one of themselves. It should be easy to be confused about the meaning of a man or even of America. I write as one who was confused about this man Truman. He had been a good Senator. But he had seemed to be a tragically inadequate substitute for Franklin Roosevelt that April night when he came to take his place.

It happened that I was the one of Roosevelt's Secretaries who was waiting the next, very empty-seeming morning of April 13, 1945, to put the essential papers of the Presidency on the big desk before Harry Truman. To me then, in that moment of actual succession, he seemed almost sacrilegiously small. The desk had been swept clean of the toys and bric-a-brac which Roosevelt had left there when he went off to Warm Springs. But his Hudson River prints still hung on the walls. It seemed still Roosevelt's desk and Roosevelt's room. It seemed to me, indeed, almost Roosevelt's sun which came in the wide south windows and touched Truman's thick glasses. I remember that his eyes were magnified by them. Also, I remember that he swung around in the President's chair as if he were testing it, more uncertain than even I was about its size.

I had opportunity to serve him for a short time after that. I had chances to meet him and talk to him after I had left Washington and the public service. I laughed at the jokes about him which followed the first almost indecent adulation of him. I remember particularly the cruel witty line out of Texas when post-war problems mounted after Roosevelt's death: "I wonder what Truman would do if he were alive." The most remarkable thing I saw was his unwillingness to let either the courtship or the cruelty shape his purposes. Some of his friends seemed strange; there is never anything unusual about odd people around the White House. Maybe Truman was foolhardy when, after the fall of Japan, he took to Congress a message which embodied the same program upon which he campaigned for the Presidency in 1948.

"That September the sixth speech," he told me, "was made

because I wanted to let the Hearsts and McCormicks know they were not going to take me into camp."

Perhaps then he moved too fast. Perhaps his too evident modesty did represent a too great uncertainty about his job. Maybe sometimes the polls were right when they counted his declining popularity. It is not easy to give full measure to a man by comparison with his predecessor or the vast new problems which grow around him. I think I first understood, however, that Truman was big enough for the chair behind the great desk at a time when, by all reports, he seemed smaller than ever. It was a Monday in October 1948, in the long Cabinet room at the White House. In June, it had seemed doubtful that he would be renominated. All the young Roosevelts and all the old reactionaries in the Democratic Party were against him. In October, it seemed incredible that he would be re-elected. The impression was given even that his own Administration, including his administrators, was somehow already separate from him. There were men at the table who thought that nothing less than dramatic, even desperate, measures would provide him with the possibility of re-election. I was one of them. That morning we talked about the Vinson Mission to Moscow. A speech had been written to announce it. And more had been told the radio people than should have been told them about it in advance. We hoped it was agreed upon. And Harry Truman went off to the communications room to discuss it with his Secretary of State, George Marshall, in Paris.

He came back and said, "No." Marshall felt that such a mission would be misunderstood and that it would make more difficult Marshall's work at the meeting of the Foreign Ministers in Paris. There were some about that table who felt—oh, yes, as politicians, of course—that the choice lay between making George Marshall's work more difficult and Harry Truman's aims impossible. They said so. Out of their partisanship they insisted that Marshall failed to understand that nothing was more important to the success even of his policy than the preservation of the Administration which had made that policy. The bi-partisan foreign policy had grown thin, men at that table felt, or had been captured by the Republicans. It was Truman's duty to show dramatically that he, Harry Truman, was President of the United States, the chief of its foreign policy, the leader of the

American aim for peace in the world. They talked to him as President and more sharply as candidate, too.

He listened. His magnified eyes seemed almost slate gray. Then he said very quietly, "I have heard enough. We won't do it."

He got up and went out of the glass-paned door to the terrace by the rose garden and walked alone—very much alone that day —back toward the White House itself. He was wrong, I thought, but he was strong, I knew. There were no dramatics about it. He never said that he would rather be right than be President. The next time we saw him he was laughing with the reporters, the politicians and the police as he got back on that long train which everyone seemed so sure was taking him nowhere. Only the crowds at the stations did not seem to understand that. The people in the halls seemed noisily misinformed. This man was going nowhere but home.

Home can seem strange, too. When Truman first came to the White House, the same conservative editor who stressed his Middle American conservatism summed up the transition in one phrase: "Power in America had shifted from the Hudson to the Missouri River." That seemed sheer gain. The American faith seemed safer home in Missouri. Yet, three years later, those who took hope from such river changes worked to shift power back to the same Hudson River, though not to the same point on its shore. It did not happen. There were enough citizens and voters who knew that their power was moving in no single valley but in the American main stream.

It can be big and muddy as the Missouri. It is still the American river of both remembrance and revolution. We shall find no clearer stream.

CHAPTER II

Son of the Middle Border

THE MISSOURI STORY of Harry Truman begins in the documents in 1844, the same year in which the Missouri River reached the greatest flood in the traditions of the Weather Bureau or the Indians. Where Kansas City now stands the flood was three miles wide. When late in June the waters fell, the chills and fever came in their most malignant form. Nobody was able to do any farming in the wet bottoms until late in July. But the corn was put in. Enough was raised. And on the fourth Saturday in August a note was made in the records of the Big Blue Baptist Church of Westport that Harry Truman's paternal grandmother had been received into membership by letter. That same month but earlier, on the eighth, his maternal grandfather had bought one hundred and sixty acres of land in the southern part of Jackson County from one Stephen Abston. Later the same year, on December 12, a clerk in the government land office at Clinton made an entry that this same grandfather had by preemption taken eighty acres of land in the same vicinity. He paid the United States eighty dollars for it.

The land had filled with people, too, like a flood. America was already old in 1844 when the documents mark the arrival of Harry Truman's kin in Missouri and their presence in the middle of the accelerating movement to fill a continent. It had taken five times as long for America to move from Jamestown, in Virginia, to Boonesboro, in Kentucky, as it would to push from Missouri to California. In Missouri, Truman's grandfathers served both the opening of the West and the settling of the middle land. They were there as speculator and settler, prairie caravan captain and corn planter. They were among the keepers of the thousands of horses and mules, cattle and sheep and swine which were already in Jackson County when the flood came. Be-

side such men were census takers to count the pioneers (and their
stock and slaves) almost as soon as they cut down the trees and
built their barns. There were politicians, too.

In the year after the flood, Senator Thomas Hart Benton
raised his high silk hat, which he regarded as part of a proper
costume for the country. Gesturing with it toward the levee
from which Kansas City grew, he said to those assembled about
him, "Gentlemen, this is the gateway to India." That put into
political and geographical poetry what the gentlemen had somehow been thinking all along. The statement still pleases Kansas
City. If India is no longer so dazzling a destination, the phrase
still speaks of an expansive destiny. It is still good politics, good
poetry and good sense. Old Benton knew that on that border
men liked the idea of the open gate and the feeling of the possibility of abundance for all, beyond it.

One of Truman's grandfathers could have heard Benton that
day. Solomon Young, Truman's maternal grandfather, had come
in 1841 to the country where the Missouri River meets the Kaw
and makes its big bend. He brought with him on the twin-
funneled, wood-burning steamboats down the Ohio, up the
Mississippi, westward as far as it goes west on the Missouri, his
wife Harriet Louisa Gregg and their two oldest children. Anderson Shippe Truman, the President's paternal grandfather, came
later, in 1846, but the force which moved him to Missouri, a girl
named Mary Jane Holmes, had arrived earlier. She came as an
already homesick young woman with her Kentucky tribe headed
by a grandam named Nancy (Ann Drusilla) Tyler Holmes. The
women in that movement were important not only as their presence proves the character of the country but because much of the
strength in Harry Truman's ancestry lies in them. Most of them
lived long and watched the changes in America both at ebb and
at flood.

The Trumans, the Holmeses, the Youngs and the Greggs make
a very native part of the American procession to and beyond
Missouri. It would be difficult to think of anybody better qualified to lead it than Nancy Tyler Holmes. She led her clan from
Kentucky carrying a huge sack of teacakes and a gentleman's
beaver hat in a leather hatbox. She had slaves to handle her
luggage. Two in particular, Marg and Hannah, have left their
names behind as her personal servants. ("Get Hannah a bonnet

suitable to wear to church.") Nancy Holmes supervised her three unmarried daughters (including Mary Jane) and the activities of a young man who accompanied them to marry one of the other daughters in Missouri. But Nancy Holmes herself paid particular attention to the hatbox and carried it wherever she went in the new opening American Middle Border for thirty-five more years.

The hat was not merely a relic of her husband, Captain Jesse Holmes, who had died in Shelby County, Kentucky, in 1840, on the eighth of May, which was to be the birthday of his presidential great-grandson forty-four years later. Nancy Holmes was the relict and the ruler, too. She wore, tradition says, an Indian's scalp mark from an earlier America, under her own lace cap. She held, among other strong views, that any woman once a widow should always be a widow. The hat and its box were the symbols not only of a dead man but of an indestructible tradition. Perhaps American history has been constantly modified by the frontier. The frontier, early and late, was also modified by characters like Nancy Tyler Holmes.

In 1840, when her husband died leaving her well off in lands and slaves, she was sixty years old. She was nine years older than the United States itself. She had been born in Daniel Boone's first Kentucky settlement when that frontier outpost was only five years old. The claim has been made that her brother was the first white child born in Kentucky. She had lived through the years in which Western ideas had been slipping back East, as people came West, to alter suffrage and other laws along the settled and stratified coast. The year in which her husband died such Western ideas—or at least emotions—had been oddly ratified when the Whig Party adopted the vocabulary of the Jacksonian democratic revolution to elect the first conservative President since 1796. But Nancy Holmes' West was no longer compounded of log cabins and hard cider. Her stoutly grown Kentucky individualism was not modified by any notions of complete equality. There is no suggestion that she saw any conflict between slavery and the Fourth of July freedoms.

There was no need for her to move. The crowding of Kentucky which had bothered Lincoln's footloose father, in 1816, need not have disturbed her, though in her lifetime she had seen Kentucky, which touches Missouri, become the sixth in population among the states in an America in which, in 1840, three of the six were west of the mountains. Captain Holmes had not only left her property; also, he left her the head of a family of seven daughters and three sons. The boys had been out and looked at the land where the Missouri meets the plains. They liked it.

When Nancy Tyler Holmes and her daughters arrived, Jackson County was a growing community with 6,245 white people and their 1,361 slaves already settled on the land. There were twenty-four dry goods and other stores. Her daughter, Mary Jane, however, had Kentucky on her mind. In 1845, or early in 1846, she persuaded her mother to put her in the care of one of the highly regarded steamboat captains for the trip back to Shelby County. The Truman family tradition is of a runaway marriage there. Harry Truman's first cousin, Miss Ethel Noland, of Independence, Missouri, who is unofficial keeper of the Truman family records, thinks that Nancy Tyler Holmes may have had some objection to Mary Jane's marriage to Anderson Shippe Truman "because the Trumans were not slaveholders." Harry Truman himself told the assembled citizens of Shelbyville, Kentucky, in the presidential campaign of 1948, that his grandfather "ran off" with Mary Jane and that the groom's father, William Truman, did not give formal approval to the marriage until years later when the son brought back the old man's first grandchild from Missouri to see him.

Anderson and Mary Jane certainly were not impetuous children. Perhaps Anderson should have gone all the way to Missouri to ask old Nancy for her daughter's hand, but he was thirty and Mary Jane was twenty-five when they were married on August 13, 1846. They were married with all propriety at the home of Mary Jane's sister, Catharine, who had stayed in Kentucky with her husband, Dr. James Clayton, of Christianburg. It seems doubtful that they had any trouble later placating stern old Nancy. She was one who stuck with her own. Their first child, a boy named after his Kentucky grandfather, was born before full spring in Missouri, on April 24, 1847. There were four other children, three girls and a boy named John Anderson. That boy, Harry Truman's father, was born on a farm in Jackson County, Missouri, on December 5, 1851.

The Holmes and Truman families had long been neighbors in

Kentucky. If the Trumans were not slaveholders, the Kentucky records indicate that Anderson Shippe Truman's father, William, was a prosperous farmer. Also, as a matter of fact, some years later he left a will, mentioning slaves and a landed estate, which was proved at Shelbyville in 1864. However, while Captain Jesse Holmes had been captain of a militia company, William Truman was only a private when he served in the Kentucky militia for a little over a month in the War of 1812. In 1857, long after his son had moved to Missouri, he was granted a land bounty for his services. Also, after William Truman's great-grandson became President of the United States, the Kentucky and Virginia genealogists traced a Truman genealogy matching anything that Nancy Holmes could claim including the Tylers of Virginia. (In it there is a lady with a name which sounds as if it might come straight out of a historical novel—Magdalin Monteith.) William Truman, who was born in Virginia in 1783, was in Kentucky before August 1807, when he married Emma Grant Shippe in Woodford County. He lived to be ninety and emphasized the biological fact of longevity which seems to come down every line to Harry Truman.

By any standards, young Anderson Shippe Truman and Mary Jane were a well-fixed young couple in Missouri. Nancy Holmes gave them slaves as a wedding present. They purchased a two-hundred-acre farm near Westport Landing. Anderson Shippe's education was sufficient to qualify him for the office of school director, which he later held for four years. (By 1850 the number of public schools in Jackson County had increased to thirty-two one-teacher schools with 1,195 pupils and, the U. S. Census reports, a total annual income of $708. I figure that at twenty-four dollars a year per teacher, counting nothing for chalk. There were also then five academies with seven teachers and 216 pupils.) Also, by the time their son, John Anderson Truman, was born there were fourteen churches in Jackson County with accommodations for 3,280 worshippers. The young Trumans joined the Holmeses in the Big Blue Baptist Church.

The romantic writers of the period generally missed the churches and the schoolhouses while they counted the Indians, the west-bound wagons, the saloons and the loaded pistols. The schools and churches were there. And the kind of people who build them. Anderson Shippe Truman was one. Apparently, having come to Missouri, he was never torn by any desire to join the surge of westing settlers, gold seekers, wagoners, tourists and traders which moved every year past his farm. Indeed, what he sought seems to have been not restless change but a continuity of the patterns of life in which he grew up in Kentucky. Perhaps a hundred years later it is too easy to read such a preference in the move he made in 1853. It took him from the west-mindedness of the wagon-train trade and hurly-burly of Jackson County to Platte County where a Southern plantation economy had grown up around slaves and tobacco and hemp. There is a quality of quietness about both Anderson Shippe and his wife. She died relatively young and seems to have lived long under the imperious shadow of old Nancy Holmes. From facts and memories he assumes the quality of a man of gentleness and humor, who liked the kind of grace and good living which transplanted Southerners in those years were fighting desperately to preserve—and which was already doomed in the conflict between righteously held rights of property and the indestructible idea of human freedom.

"There were no common people in Platte," Anderson Truman's daughter insisted until she died in 1948. That statement preserves an old lady's remembrance of years of grace and goodness in the Truman family tradition. Henry Clay died in 1852. Anderson Truman moved to Platte County just a year before Clay's Missouri Compromise was discarded for Stephen Douglas' doctrine of "squatter sovereignty." That meant that the battle of Boston and Charleston would be fought at Anderson Truman's door between the Beecher's-Bible abolitionists and the bowie-knife Southerners. He seems a very gentle character to be set down between the equally violent, equally determined Border Ruffians of the Slave South and the Redleg abolitionists who followed John Brown.

The Trumans moved to Platte County in the spring of 1853. Margaret Ellen, Harry Truman's aunt, was four in May that year. John, the President's father, was only one year old. But all their lives they had memories to count and memories handed down to them of good days in the supposedly so dark thirteen years of border war and civil war which they spent there. There were times when they kept the linen and the silver in the haystacks to save them from the Kansas Redlegs ("The Redlegs would steal anything"—and not merely a slave). There was a night of false alarm in which old Nancy Holmes fled into a field of high Indian corn with little John and a small Hinkle boy to escape a Redleg raid. In the cold cornfield she put them under her hoopskirts to keep them warm. Long afterwards there were in the family mildewed quilts, from the haystacks, which have been kept unlaundered for the warmth of remembering.

The memories say: "fine old families from hither and yon, most of them from Kentucky but also from surprising places, Major Hinkle from Pennsylvania, the Whites, the Faulkners, the Todds . . . a beautiful culture unsurpassed in Virginia, old stately houses, manners of the South." A romantic land is romantically remembered. There were tournaments in which young men rode on the finest horses to dislodge with their lances the ring and win the right of crowning a queen. There were always queens even if they reigned in a realm contested by the New England conscience and Southern honor, neither of which would balk at murder and house-burnings. There was the day, long remembered, when the circus went by the gate on the road from Pottsville to Platte City. Some circus proprietor obviously understood that there was business for him on that border, as well as for John Brown.

By Platte County the big muddy river runs between Missouri and Kansas, between different men who in those days seemed only able to meet in violence. But in southern Jackson County, where Harry Truman's Grandfather Young lived, a man or a wagon train could move without any stream's interruption into the West. That helped make Kansas City. It also helps point the distinction between Anderson Truman and Solomon Young. It is a distinction between grace and sweat, between a man with a riding crop at a tournament and one with a bull whip over a wagon train. Anybody looking for the middle nineteenth century model of the pioneer could satisfactorily settle on Solomon Young, who was a business man and not a pioneer at all.

Not much is known about the blood lines behind him except as he embodied them in his tough muscles and his tough mind. Indeed, he appears first almost like a boy emerging alone from the last Kentucky wilderness at the age of twelve, when he was already independently earning his way. After he died at seventy-seven, in the big homeplace he had built at Grandview, all his records, the Young family Bible, his business books, the records of his trips west, were destroyed in a fire caused by a Negro girl who was filling the lamps with coal oil and lit a match to see. But enough to measure him comes from the stories he told his children and from a grandchild's memory that when he was an old, well-to-do man he could still snap as much corn as any other two men in the field.

As a boy he made his money weighing hogs. He had some schooling. He had plenty of energy. He bought and sold stock. He acquired land in Kentucky and one or two slaves to work with him on the land. In the same years in which Lincoln was mighty with the ax, he worked at timbering too. They still tell the story that when he took a slave with him into the woods and cut a tree, he would afterwards measure with the ax handle to see how much he had cut and how much the slave. He measured but he also matched. He was twenty-three years old when he found a red-haired girl almost as alone in the world as he was himself.

We know more about Harriet Louisa Gregg. The Gregg Bible was not burned and the pages of the old book, brought over from Scotland where it was printed in Edinburgh by Adrian Watkins in 1752, can still be read. The Bible came with the family by way of Pennsylvania to Kentucky. Also, there is evidence about Harriet Louisa in the Will Books of Shelby and Jefferson counties, Kentucky. She inherited sums from her grandfather, William Scott. There is an item that her guardian and brother was allowed $4.25 for "Lewisa's" schooling. There are other items in the records. Her mother and father, Sally Scott and David Gregg, were married in Jefferson County in October 1795. Louisa, apparently the youngest of thirteen children, was born on October 15, 1818. Her mother died when she was five years old and her father when she was ten. Her brother, William Gregg, became the orphan's guardian.

He must have been a man of some means. Miss Mary Jane Truman, sister of the President, remembers her grandmother's story that she lived for a while as a girl in the famous old Rowan house called "Federal Hill" near Bardstown, Kentucky, where Henry Clay and others came to talk politics and play poker and where, according to a legend tenaciously held if historically discounted, Stephen Foster wrote "My Old Kentucky Home." William Gregg was building a turnpike through the area at the time and the lovely old house stood vacant, Louisa Gregg Young told her granddaughter, because the cholera had killed some of the Rowan children there. That would have been between the time when Louisa became an orphan in 1828 and when she married Solomon Young in 1838. The cholera hit Bardstown hard in 1832 and again in 1833. If Louisa was there in 1834, she was a girl of sixteen. She was nineteen when she married Solomon Young on January 9, 1838.

They had two children before they left their old Kentucky home forever in 1841. Martha Ellen Young, Harry Truman's mother, was not born until her parents had been settled in Missouri for more than a decade. They had acquired the first of their lands near Grandview then, but she was born November 25, 1852, when they still lived on a farm of one hundred sixty acres called the Parrish Place at what is now about Thirty-sixth and Prospect streets in Kansas City. She was the next to the youngest of six girls and three boys. One of the boys, Harrison, for whom Harry Truman is named, never married and another died young. The oldest boy and the second child, William, served in the Confederate Army under General Sterling Price. He perpetuated his Southern sentiments in a daughter named Winnie after Jefferson Davis' daughter.

Solomon Young apparently took his time after his arrival in Missouri before he settled on the lands in Washington Township in southern Jackson County, which across the years he acquired as a farm of plantation dimensions. The first records of purchase or entry are for the year 1844, the year of the flood. The government records show that between December 12, 1844, and December 26, 1860, he made nineteen government land acquisitions by pre-emption purchase and land warrant. Altogether they total 1,928.88 acres at a cost of $1,194.80 plus whatever he paid for the land warrants. Also, he bought and sold other lands during those years.

Some of the money he used in his land acquisitions he brought from Kentucky. More came from his wagon-trading and cattle-driving journeys to Utah, Colorado and California. Harry Truman says that his grandfather made such journeys between 1846 and 1854 and again between 1864 and 1870. The old man himself apparently approved a biographical statement that he also set out in the spring of 1854 with fifteen hundred head of cattle for California, lost five hundred on the way and was in the stock-raising business there until 1857. He made money and lost it and made more. But the first eighty acres which he acquired by government entry must have been the hardest for him and for Louisa, too.

In order to comply with the land laws "they had to stay there so many nights and cook so many meals," but, says Harry Truman's brother, Vivian, who lives on the farm today, Solomon for purposes of a home on the first homestead "just built a rail pen and threw brush over it." Then while Solomon rode to Clinton, seventy miles away, to enter his claim at the land office, Louisa stayed on the homestead. It must have been cold there in December in a log pen. It must have been lonely there, too. Also, 1844 was the winter of the sickness which followed the flood. It is possible, however, to overemphasize today the emptiness then of the rolling land. By 1850 more than a thousand people lived in Washington Township. There was the smoke of other chimneys in the sky.

It was lonely enough and long lonely. There was at least as much courage in Louisa's strong loneliness at home as there was in Solomon's continental trekking. He was not only gone year after year. He was also gone when James Henry Lane, the Kansan and Free-soiler, came on a raid and forced Louisa to cook hot biscuits for himself and his men while they stole and slaughtered all her pigs. Missourians like the Trumans and the Youngs always claimed that Lane was a soldier for "freedom" who would as soon steal a piano as steal a pig or free a slave. Years later when Harry Truman came home from a trip to Kansas, his mother asked him in humor but in hard memory, too, "Did you see your grandmother's silver?"

It is improbable that Solomon Young caught any romantic contagion about the West from the tumult and the hurly-burly of the crowds going through. It was as trader and business man who meant to come back that he first set out west in 1846, the same year in which Francis Parkman, who had "Injuns on his mind," came through on the romantic journey which he described in *The Oregon Trail*. Parkman was only out of Boston six months; Young worked the years. Solomon was thirty-one when he made the first trip west. Usually he left in May and came back the following spring. He knew men and mules, oxen and trade. Also, he left some legends and all of them are the legends of the business man, not the romantic adventurer.

One is that a herd of cattle which he drove to Colorado is still called "the Young herd" from the name of the man who brought the ancestral cattle across the plains. There may be such a herd but Truman's own Secretary of Agriculture was unable to find a trace of it. The other is that old Solomon, as Truman said in his 1948 campaign, once owned the land on which Sacramento was built. Sacramento was already growing before he got there. Undoubtedly, however, he made long trips and long trades. *The Deseret News* of Salt Lake City, on August 9, 1860, had a special story on his methods in the driving of one hundred thirty yoke of oxen and forty wagons across the West. There was an interesting meeting on that westing between the two Youngs, Solomon and Brigham. They met in Utah when Solomon arrived with a train of goods for the Army and the officer in charge refused to receive them. Solomon had the goods and no buyers. Brigham and his followers needed the goods and lacked the money with which to buy them. The two Youngs worked out a trade in trust which served both. The tradition is vouched for by George Albert Smith, president of The Church of Jesus Christ of Latter-Day Saints.

Both the Youngs and the Trumans seem to have escaped any major suffering in the Civil War. Undoubtedly, as Confederate sympathizers they were outraged by the famous, or infamous, Order No. 11 issued by the Union General Thomas E. Ewing. It was designed to clean out the Confederate guerrillas, but also it had the effect of driving many families out of their homes. But neither of Harry Truman's grandfathers served in that war. Solomon Young was forty-six; Anderson Truman was forty-five. Young John Truman was a boy of ten. When the war began, Anderson Truman hitched up his wagons and drove his slaves to Leavenworth, Kansas. Years later the family tried to locate some of them for old times' sake. They never found any trace of them again.

The two families did not escape change. Anderson moved his family back to Jackson County to a two-hundred-acre farm he owned in Washington Township near Solomon Young's place. He and his growing boys took over the cultivation of one hundred acres. That was in 1866, when a vaster movement was in progress all around him. That was the year in which Octave Chanute, who measured the flood stage of the 1844 flood from the high watermarks kept by old settlers like the Trumans and the Youngs, began to build the Hannibal Bridge across the Missouri at Kansas City. That first bridge meant the rolling up of a metropolis at Kansas City. The Civil War left a population of only 3,500 people there. But in the year of the completion of the Hannibal Bridge, 260,000 settlers passed through. The full flood had arrived in the West and in America.

It swept past Grandview. In 1867, Solomon bought for Louisa 398 acres from Thomas A. Smart and began building the big homeplace. He planted quick-growing soft maples about the house. He was beginning, beyond fifty, to be ready to stay home. Those were the Jesse James years and the boom years in that country. For the Youngs they were quiet and settled years, too. In 1868, emigrants, thinking of Kansas City and Jackson County, were told that "there are no lands near this point, in either Missouri or Kansas which can be pre-empted." By 1870, Missouri was the fifth state in population in the American Union. In 1881, both Anderson Truman and Solomon Young were included among the local personages described in a book called *A History of Jackson County*.

In the brief biographies, published apparently with their assistance and approval, Anderson Truman was described as "farmer—section 26, post office Hickman's Mills," and Solomon Young as "farmer and stock raiser—section 11, post office Hickman's Mills." Truman's acreage was two hundred; Young had two thousand. Truman, at sixty-five, was a widower (Mary Jane had died in February, 1879). His youngest daughter kept house for him and his boy, John A. Truman, then thirty years old, managed the farm. He was "an industrious and energetic young man that bids fair to make a success in life." He meant to be a success. He had ideas of his own. There is a story that old Anderson talked to his boys about what they wanted to do in life. He was answered.

"Be a horse dealer."

The father was taken aback but he smiled.

"Well," he said, "it is not always regarded as the highest calling in the world, but always tell the truth and nobody will believe you."

It was a calling which Solomon Young understood. And Martha Ellen, his next to youngest daughter, understood, too. She was twenty-nine in 1881 when, three days after Christmas, she and John Truman were married. They were a tiny couple. No one who remembers John Truman describes him as more than five feet, six inches high. He got his nickname "Peanuts" from his size. Martha Ellen was no taller. They had their picture taken together at that time. It seems now one of those photographs almost designed to show more of the photographer than his subjects. His flowered backdrop hangs down behind John and Martha Ellen, as well as between them and every usual characteristic of their lives. John sat in the Victorian chair with his left hand on his knee and his right hand just a little too elegantly at ease on the arm of the chair. He wore an ascot tie and a dark suit. His dark hair was plastered slick to the top of his flat skull. For some reason the artist had draped a rug over the arm of the chair, but in the chair John was the portrait of gentleman at ease. Martha Ellen stood beside and behind him with a braceleted left hand on his shoulder. She was sternly corseted in a dark dress with much tasseling. A matching silk petticoat peeped from under the dress. She must have made a nice silken noise when she walked that day. But both of them look as solemn as such couples were expected to look in albums. Indeed, in realization of the lively Missouri countryside behind them, they look almost less photographed than embalmed.

Fortunately, they were very much alive. John had both a lively humor and a violent temper. Martha Ellen had both an iron sense of duty and a wit which grew sharper as she grew older. She described herself in later years as "a lightfoot Baptist," who was one ready to dance and be undisturbed in dancing by any deacon's frowns. There must have been a gay time at Grandview with country Christmas and country wedding coming together. And afterwards they drove away, probably behind one of Solomon Young's fine teams.

The frontier was far behind them. Kansas City, up the road, had a population of fifty-five thousand people, and was claiming that on a per capita basis everybody in it was three times as rich as the people of St. Louis or Chicago: "the mission of Kansas

City is no longer problematical; it has become a matter of history." It is also a matter of history that John Truman and his bride moved not to the city but to the little village of Lamar, four counties south of Jackson, where among the farms, the horses and the cattle, John Truman began the career of trading, speculating, farming and uninterrupted addiction to Democratic politics. He and Martha Ellen set up housekeeping in a little story-and-a-half white house with a small square-columned porch and a bay window. The Ozarks were just a little further south. Kansas, Oklahoma and Arkansas were all within a hundred miles. The South and the West were both near at hand.

They had been married two and a half years when their first child, a boy was born. They named him Harry after Martha Ellen's brother, Harrison Young. And they gave him a middle initial "S" which is supposed to stand for nothing but which any grandfather who wanted to might think stood for Shippe or Solomon. The small-town doctor who delivered Harry S. Truman charged fifteen dollars for the job.

CHAPTER III

Beginning of the Trails

JOHN TRUMAN LIKED to mark his luck with good rural images. He nailed a mule shoe over the door of his house in Lamar to celebrate the birth of his first son. Also, he planted a seedling pine which, when he was thirty years dead and that son became President of the United States, was seventy straight feet tall. It seemed a lucky year. That was the year he won seventy-five dollars on Cleveland from a Republican lawyer in Lamar who believed in Blaine. Only an enthusiast would have made such a bet. No Democrat had been elected since Buchanan, and Cleveland could not have won then if, a few days before election, a Presbyterian preacher had not described the Democrats as the party of "Rum, Romanism and Rebellion." The epithet made it possible for John to collect his bet on a difference of 1,149 votes in New York. The victory seemed more important in Missouri than any conjunction of Confederates and Irishmen and liquor dealers in New York or even on the Middle Border. As a rebel by tradition John Truman had never even heard then of a devout Romanist named James Pendergast who that year opened a saloon at St. Louis Avenue and Mulberry Street in Kansas City. Win or lose, however, in any company John was a Democrat and a Democrat who believed in his luck.

Apparently it was a durable belief. Certainly there are few evidences that it paid off quickly except that one seventy-five dollars which is remembered while losses are forgotten. The mule business could not have been a bonanza in Lamar in those years. Indeed, it may have been part of John's luck that he had moved south from Jackson County at a time when good luck in Kansas City seemed a commodity available to everybody. While he traded mules in the two years after his elder son was born, trading in real estate in Kansas City jumped from $6,462,161 a year to $27,041,867. Out in the farm country such riches were becoming increasingly difficult to understand.

He did not get rich though he turned north toward the boom. When Harry was still an infant, John and Martha Ellen left Lamar for a farm southeast of the village of Belton, in Cass County (next to Jackson), where another boy, Vivian, was born on April 25, 1886. The next year, after five years of marriage, trading and hoping, they moved back to the place of their beginning together to live with her parents. That is not generally a sign of luck in Missouri or anywhere else, though years later it worked out well on a lifetime basis for their son, Harry. The third child, Mary Jane, was born on the Young homeplace on August 12, 1889. Years later their son, Harry, said that the move to Grandview was made at the request of old Solomon. At seventy-two he was still able, when he wished, to snap more corn than anybody else in the field. However, his unmarried son, Harrison, then in his thirties, was not a very consistent farmer. He liked the bedazzlements of the town and recurrently went to enjoy them. Solomon needed steadier help.

John and Martha Ellen stayed there three years. Solomon Young sold them forty acres of land. They bought eighty acres more near by. They farmed there long enough, with the emphasis of revisits to Grandview later, to give the children a sense of rural beginnings. It was time enough, also, for young Harry to share as a child the quality of strong old Solomon Young.

"My old grandfather took me in a cart with a strawberry roan horse and drove me six miles to the Cass County Fair at Belton. I went with him all six days, and sat with him in the judges' stand when the races were called."

He could not have been more than seven years old then, but the memory stood out like that one in his father's childhood when the elephants moved from Pottsville to Platte City. The more important event during those years was the death of John Truman's father, Anderson Shippe Truman, in 1887, at the age of seventy-one on his farm near by. Harry Truman was just three years old but he remembers well his Grandfather Truman's death. He was in the room when he died, heard one of his daughters say sadly, "He's gone," and ran himself to the bedside to tug at the old man's beard to wake him again. The country funeral brought Anderson's children together again. Also, it

must have emphasized that John belonged to the older generation in his line. He was pushing hard upon forty. It was time
for his luck, if he was ever going to have any. He inherited part
of his father's property, but there were four brothers and sisters
to share with him and the sharing of property has seemed almost
a standard basis for family differences in the lines behind Harry
Truman—and most of the rest of us. Americans who put high
hopes in the land had a strong sense of property. Certainly,
however, John Truman had enough money in 1890, three years
after his father's death, to buy a house in Independence.

Harry was only six when they moved from the farm at Grandview twenty miles to Independence, a distance which took as long
to travel then, he once said, as it did to drive from Kansas City
to St. Louis after the automobile came. He was deeply grieved
when his Grandfather Young died, in 1892, after they had moved
to town. Oddly enough, however, as often happens with children, the sad memory comes in conjunction with the triumphant
memory, too.

John Truman won again in 1892. And Harry Truman's triumphant memory is of his father climbing to the cupola on top
of the white house in Crysler Street, in Independence, to fix a
flag celebrating Cleveland's re-election. It would stay there, he
said, as long as the Democrats were in power. In America that
was going to be only four years in the next twenty. But the man
who was to secure approval of twenty years of uninterrupted
Democratic power in the next century, recalls the scene on that
bright November day as he watched his small, determined father
and the big flag he unfurled. The boy adored the little man of
quick pride who combined some shrewdness and much energy, a
torrential temper and great, almost secret, gentleness. He took
much from him. Long afterwards the son seemed so steadily
modest that the pride was almost secret in him. The temper was
controlled. Under every mask, however, he became a man who
could be quickly and deeply hurt. His memory of his father on
this proud occasion may be more vivid because it was about that
time that he began to see clearly through the thick spectacles
which made him look like a well-mixed combination of imp and
owl.

When John Truman bought the house from a Jewish merchant named Sam Blitz, in 1890, for $1,000 down and a purchase

money mortgage of $3,000, it is certain that he drove a bargain and believed that he got one. It was a comfortable house. It sat on Crysler Street, between Ruby and Haywood, across the near-by Missouri Pacific Railroad tracks from the courthouse square and other central parts of Independence. That made the house one from which his boys could better watch the passing of the trains. It was not on any social wrong side of the tracks. Across the street from it, in those days, were the big places of the Wilsons, the Proctors, the Woodsons, who stood for tradition and stability in Independence. The house itself was no mansion but it was big enough to hold John Truman's family. On the place, too, there was room for the family of the cook, Caroline Hunter ("as black as your hat"), three boys and a girl and a gardener husband, named Simpson, who, when Caroline took him, apparently never expected her to take his name.

The population of the place only started with the humans. As livestock dealer, John put a stout wire cattle fence around the big backyard. It was almost always, in combination and succession, full of horses and mules, cattle and goats. One year there were five hundred goats in the yard. Above and beside the animals John had one of the rare natural gas wells of the area and furnished fuel not only to his own house but to that of a neighbor as well. And somehow, safe from even the goats, there was a vegetable garden still memorable for a kind of yellow peach tomato that grew in it.

"We always had dogs and cats, pigeons and pet pigs," Harry Truman recalled years later. "Vivian had a team of red goats and a wagon. The harness was made for it by old man Rummell who beat me for county judge in 1924. My goat was bald with a black face."

Regardless of the price John Truman paid, the house on Crysler Street saw the best years of his life and the formative years of the life of his son. It was his crowded castle which he was every moment prepared to defend. He was ready always, indeed, in quick pride to defend everything that was his own.

"If anybody jumped on his kids," Harry Truman recalled grinning, "they were in for it."

The amused and affectionate memory of John Truman in Independence is that he was steadily ready to bring his small but effective physical powers to the defense of his politics, his character or his children. He was generally reticent, even to taciturnity, like his son Vivian who some say is his "spitting image." Sometimes he came home with the marks of fistic encounters on election days but with an evident conviction that he had given as good as he got. Wise men in Independence learned that it was not healthy to try to push him around. A few learned too slowly for their own good. Once, a big, domineering lawyer at the Independence bar undertook the cross-examination of John Truman as a witness in a lawsuit. He did not like John's answers. He shrugged his incredulity for the benefit of the jury. Then he said:

"Now, John, you know that's just a damn lie."

John Truman jumped out of the witness chair and chased the big lawyer all the way out of the courthouse. That broke up the lawsuit but it emphasized John Truman's character. He tended to his own business and he had plenty of that. Sometimes his concerns seemed as crowded as his house and his yard.

"When he sold a horse," his son in the White House said, "they knew it would be a good one."

Also, John was long active in the real estate business with a man named Oscar Mindrup, under the firm name of Mindrup and Truman, and they did very well. However, he did not always guess right even in real estate. He turned down a chance to buy forty acres at what is now Thirty-ninth Street and Troost Avenue in Kansas City, on the advice of friends who agreed that Kansas City would never get that far. He farmed rented lands all around the edges of Independence with the help of the Negro Simpson who married the Truman cook. It was not a part of John Truman's pride to be above using his own hands and his own muscles in that farming with Simpson. The sense of the dignity of agriculture remained in the years in which so many farmers felt cheated by it. (Racial relations were clear if not perfect. Solomon Young's widow once scolded a Negro preacher for coming to her front door but at the back door she gave him ten dollars. The Truman children kept Caroline Hunter's children as long as they lived. Only one, the daughter of Caroline, was alive in 1950. She was crippled and on a pension but she was remembered.)

During all the Independence years, John Truman was ready for any trade from a needle to a threshing machine, a goat, a horse or a house. He followed his hunches and he bet on his beliefs. His elder son is sure he was never a grocer in Independence, as was reported in his obituary when he died in 1915. He would have been quite ready if the opportunity had arisen to make a trade in food or feed. Indeed, some time during those years, he did begin buying wheat futures on the Board of Trade. He was a born speculator.

Harry Truman only understood that many years later. Indeed, most of his memories are sharpened by the lens of later understanding. Though his early memories are vivid, he knows now that many things were dimly seen and not merely in the character of his father but the character of the world around him as well. In some respects the things which he saw as a child may be less important than the things he could not see. In his development, his eyes were more important than the things before them.

Apparently no other member of his family connection had the kind of "flat eyeball" which caused limits on his vision beyond ordinary nearsightedness. As a child, of course, he did not know he was supposed to see better than he did when he ran after the hens or collected the eggs. His vision was quite sufficient for his needs in the nursery and in the farmyard of his Grandfather Young. The defect became apparent to his mother only when she undertook to point out the things a child should see as they rode in the buggy. Harry could not see them. That puzzled and then alarmed her. Glasses, in Missouri in those days, were generally aids to the aged. But before Harry was nine, he had put on spectacles which differentiated him from other boys and proclaimed the defect which in so many ways pushed him into himself.

He turned, even before they moved to Independence, from games and rough play to books. He could read, he says, when he was four. The recollection that he twice read through the big Truman family Bible may indicate less predilection for religion than an affection for the big type in which such Bibles were printed. Certainly, as he grew older, he read everything he could get his hands on.

The eye defect also turned him to his mother and, perhaps more important, his mother to him. Martha Ellen Truman was not one to be partial among her children. Vivian and Mary Jane had as much of her strong affection. Yet, nothing is clearer than that Harry seemed her special boy, just as Vivian, as a born horse trader, seemed in some respects his father's. By the time Vivian was twelve, his father gave him a check book to use as an already sharp partner in livestock trading. Some of Vivian's schoolmates still remember thinking that his mother gave him most of the hard work around the house.

Harry Truman was a sort of mama's boy, oddly more like a little old woman than a sissy child. He helped in the kitchen with neither reluctance nor boyish clumsiness. He learned to cook. When he was a little older he took with eagerness to the piano which Vivian rejected with disdain. (Vivian says: "Mama wanted me to take piano lessons but she couldn't get a lasso big enough.") Even when Harry was very young he learned to fix his sister Mary Jane's hair as well as her mother could. He rocked her to sleep, singing, and Mary Jane learned to demand his attention.

"Mama, make Harry bye-o."

He was always neat, as a boy of books instead of one of baseball bats. Yet, as a boy who was denied effective participation in active games, his incessant reading created in him a desire to be a man of action. That was not a strange juvenile compensation; it is almost standard for the frail child to fly the pirate's flag on his imaginary frigate. In Truman's case, however, his nearsightedness created a lasting need for proof of his powers in the field of action even if it took him decades to recognize politics as the satisfactory substitute for soldiering.

He hated a fight, however. He had, indeed, even on the playground some recognized gifts as a mediator. He took some teasing, his friends say, though he himself does not recall it, but he was never regarded as a sissy to be teased. There is no dispute, however, about the remembrance of respect for his mediation. One friend's memory of the time when he was called into a ball game as umpire and ended as player seems certainly credible. The addition, however, that he demonstrated that "he could holler louder, throw the ball harder and play just as rough as any kid on the lot" has the sound of post-presidential remembering. ("But it isn't!" Truman said.)

Undoubtedly, from the books his admirations and aspirations followed men of action—particularly soldiers. The story is that he read every book "including the encyclopedias" in the Independence Public Library. That was a very informal institution in those days which apparently began in a collection in a lawyer's office and then became the library of the high school. One special set of books of which he was fond was *Abbott's Lives*. Some millions of other boys liked them, too; and also the *Little Rollo* stories by the same author. They did not seem pompously pious to the children for whom they were written. Such didactic elevation was expected on the printed page. Harry Truman was older and the flag had already been run up over the house for Cleveland when Martha Ellen bought an ornately bound and printed set of books, published in 1894, called *Great Men and Famous Women*, edited by Charles F. Horne. It had separate volumes on *Soldiers and Sailors, Statesmen and Sages, Workmen and Heroes, Artists and Authors*. They ran from Nebuchadnezzar to Sarah Bernhardt. In all that range, it was a literature designed to impress the young with the virtues of the great and the good.

Apparently, history to young Harry was always men, not ideas. Indeed, all his life he has been better able to work from actual observation than from abstract reports about people or plans. The men who caught his imagination were more often the soldiers than the statesmen. The statesmen had made a bloody mess on the Middle Border; knightly soldiers fought the Civil War in Virginia. It was a period in education in which the worship of the hero, it was hoped, might lead to the emulation of the hero. There were Lee and Jackson, made alive not merely in the books but in the Confederate tradition. There was Napoleon and, almost immediately before him, the men of antiquity. Good and evil were personalized. Mark Twain remembered that his Missouri had been one in which good and evil men were very personal. Men, he wrote, "still cursed Benedict Arnold as if he were a personal friend who had broken faith but a week gone by." The heroes were just as close at hand.

There was no contradiction in Harry's piano-playing. Indeed, they were parts of the same pattern. The artist and the soldier met the needs of a boy who could not compete with the ball and the bat, who, indeed, was less skilled than Vivian in judging the value of a mule. Also, the piano-playing showed and developed a sensitiveness and an imagination which sometimes in later years seemed hidden under the hide of the politician. If the childhood of the young Trumans was crowded with dogs and cats, pigeons and pet pigs, Martha Ellen Truman insisted that there be room in the crowding also for books and music. In typical Missouri fashion, John Truman expected and supported his wife's determination upon culture. Even on the frontier there was an expectation that women would give some reality to the ideal. The American political past on the Middle Border was at least as much punctuated with classical illusions as pistol shots. John Truman had only had the schooling available around Grandview in the years after the Civil War. But Martha Ellen had gone to a Baptist Female College which educated young women in Lexington, Missouri, from the end of the Civil War until the 1890's. She studied music and art and could play the piano and draw very well, though she had little time for either after the children came. Long afterwards her schooling in Lexington sounds like the sort of education for elegance which matched the "tumor and wart" architecture of the period. Education and the arts in those years were largely female, though admired and honored by the most horny-handed husbands. Even when Harry Truman graduated from high school there were only eleven boys in a class of forty.

The bad eyes, the books, the piano and the mother are important. Undoubtedly, Martha Ellen did see something special in a boy who turned to books and—even in years which are usually regarded as savagely juvenile after the Tom Sawyer-Huck Finn fashion—quite willingly to the piano. It would be distorting the facts, however, to think of Martha Ellen Truman as a lady frustrated in the arts herself and imposing fuzzy artistic notions on her son. If she had confronted culture at the Baptist Female College, she was also old Solomon Young's daughter. She was at least as hard-headed as her husband, and as positive and partisan, too. To the end of her days she made little differentiation between a Republican in Missouri and a raiding Redleg from Kansas. She kept not only a piano for Harry but a switch for both her boys, and if Harry seldom needed it, it was still there if any need should arise. She was little, but tough-fibered and strongly gentle, too.

When Harry was ten and Vivian a little younger, diphtheria came to the Truman household in Independence. That was a year before Dr. William Welch, at Johns Hopkins, reported for the benefit of American doctors on the efficacy of the new antitoxins. Martha Ellen shipped Mary Jane off quickly to Grandmother Young at Grandview. But Harry and Vivian were very sick boys. Then, after they seemed well again under the ministrations of one of the Doctors Twyman (there have been five good Doctors Twyman in four generations around Independence) young Harry was drinking a glass of milk when his throat closed in a diphtheritic paralysis which quickly extended to a total paralysis of his whole body.

They had to carry him around in a baby carriage. Martha Ellen had black Caroline Hunter's help. Also, they called in Grandma Vaile ("a grand old lady," Harry Truman recalls), who was that day's best equivalent of a nurse. Harry Truman lay in the sun on her porch. He had to be lifted at home. I suggested once to Vivian Truman that his mother must have been greatly frightened. He smiled with humor and affection.

"She didn't scare easy," he said.

Harry recovered completely. He was in general the healthy child of healthy living in an American small town. Such living had great virtues even if it has sometimes been sentimentalized. While Harry Truman was a boy in Independence, Mark Twain said in India, "All that goes to make the *me* in me was in a Missourian village on the other side of the globe." The village product could be as diverse as Harry Truman and Huckleberry Finn who were "born" in the same year. Neither the village nor its products are simple. When Mark Twain spoke of himself as the village Missourian he was off lecturing as a literary man to pay the business debts he had acquired in the same sort of gaudy American dream of riches which he himself had satirized in *The Gilded Age*. Also, if time turned out both Huck and Harry in 1884, that was also the year in which E. W. Howe, not many miles from Independence, revised some idyllic American village notions in *The Story of a Country Town*.

Indeed, in Truman's childhood Independence had some American defects clear to all. Even cities seemed small towns then and in the Middle Border all seemed besieged by Populist angers and the cry for quick panaceas. Even Kansas City, William Allen White reported from his own youth in it, was only "consciously citified, like a country jake in his first store clothes." City and town had been hit by the economic collapse which had begun on the farms before the Trumans left them. Independence had a larger ratio of the mansions of the jigsaw architectural period to the "shabby and unpainted houses of the workers" than White saw in Kansas City. Also, the poor and the rich were closer together. There was a greater possibility of understanding the democracy of people in the small town, especially at a time when the towns seemed to be growing shabby, and not town boom but rural anger made the most noise in politics around the courthouse square. Independence, however, did not look shabby to young Harry Truman as he regarded it through his spectacles.

In November 1895, the Trumans moved to a new house at Waldo Street and River Boulevard, which brought the family close to the geography of Truman's childhood now best remembered. Martha Ellen had received property from the estate of her father who died in the winter of 1892. Also, the move paid tribute to John's ability as trader. He swapped the Crysler Street house, for which he had paid $4,000, and two adjacent lots which had cost him $600, for the Waldo Street property and received $5,400 in cash and good notes to boot. His luck seemed good.

The grounds ran back deep toward Oak Street. Near by, in those days, was Woodland College, run by Professor George S. Bryant who, when his college disintegrated as such "colleges" had a habit of doing in those days, became the principal of the Independence High School. Perhaps more important than Bryant's college was Bryant's pond, a block from the new Truman house, where the young people swam and skated with the seasons. (Today the old pond site is the basement of a public school.) There was also Bryant's pasture which was the baseball field. Across River Boulevard was Idlewild, a wooded area—the wood is thinner now, there are houses where the rabbits ran—in which most boys (but not Harry) hunted for small game. Harry did help shoot the neighbors' chickens when the boys were patriotically drilling as riflemen at the time of the Spanish-American War. Generally, however, Vivian was the young Truman with the gun and the dogs. Even then, no wilderness was at hand for the young. The last passenger pigeon was seen in Missouri in 1890, only a year or two before the arrival of the first automobile.

In the neighborhood there were new children who became old friends. Professor Bryant had a boy named Paul who became Harry's close friend. A Baptist preacher's son, Fielding Houchens, studied with Harry when one wanted to go to Annapolis, the other to West Point. Charles Ross, whose father was once jailer, who seemed more brilliant than Harry in school, and who later became the President's Press Secretary, was a tall, long-headed, lank fellow. There was Elmer Twyman of the family of doctors. At his house in a spontaneous burst of progressive education Harry helped build, while they were studying Latin, a replica of Caesar's bridge across the Rhine. He studied Latin with a girl, too, and nobody expected either of them to learn much from the studying. She was Elizabeth Virginia Wallace who lived two blocks from the Waldo Street house at 610 Delaware. That house was burned but a great oak which spread over it remains. Harry had met her at the Presbyterian Sunday School which he attended, though a Baptist, because a cordial Presbyterian preacher had given the Truman children particular welcome when they first came to town.

Harry's geography widened as he grew. It included the drugstore and the square where now the monuments stand attesting the fact that the Oregon and Santa Fe Trails both began in Independence. It included all of Independence which, long before, Prophet Joseph Smith had chosen as the Mormon Zion where the Lord's Temple would rise. Young Harry knew the Swope children in the formidable Swope mansion where later Missouri's most mysterious murder case had its scene. His geography extended outside of Independence in long buggy rides to the river, to Grandview, to the site of the old pioneer outpost at Osage. He went with his father to little farms to swap mules. Also, he went to greater places, like the Salisbury farm, big enough to be called plantations even in western Missouri.

The Salisbury farm was the home of Spencer Salisbury, who was his war comrade, his business partner, and at last the bitter and scornful man who hated Harry more than anyone else in the world. There was no hate around Harry's life then. He did have an uncle by marriage who hated some people a good deal and carried both a whip and the sobriquet "Jim Crow" Chiles. Young Truman knew the old Confederates who held the offices, the farmers who came to town, the loafers with brown-cornered mouths. In the vivid detail he saw through his glasses, he knew his town and the whole of eastern Jackson County. It was a county which he had to understand and which had to understand him in the years of his first political power.

He was definitely not thinking of politics as a career for himself then. In those days instead, he began to study piano under Miss Florence Burrus who lived next door to the Truman house on Waldo Street. His mother had taught him a little at home, but this was his first formal instruction. He remembers that "they had a system in those days of teaching with figures instead of notes." Then, when he was thirteen he started studying in "dead earnest" with Mrs. E. C. White. She was about Martha Ellen's age and was married to Professor White who was later superintendent of schools in Kansas City.

"She was a wonderful woman and a fine teacher," Truman says. She must have been something rather unusual in teachers even in Kansas City in those days. She had been a pupil of Fannie Bloomfield Zeisler and also of Zeisler's Viennese teacher, Theodor Leschetizky, who taught Paderewski, Rubinstein and Josef Lhevinne.

"I wanted to be a musician and she encouraged me. I would get up every morning and practice for two hours, and twice a week I went to Mrs. White," Truman says.

Yet, at the same time the desire to make a career as an Army officer grew and he studied also with that idea in his mind. There seems to have been nothing remarkable about his formal schooling. Though he lost some time because of his eyes and because of the difficult siege of diphtheria, he graduated in regular course with the class of his age. His school records were lost when the Independence High School building was burned in 1938. Some very fancy post-presidential reports in praise have been made about him by some of his old teachers. Yet, not even from those does he emerge in the image of the brightest boy in the class. He was punctual, he was dutiful, he did his work well. But even he realized, as West Point grew in his head, that he needed special coaching. He got it from Miss Margaret Phelps, his high school history teacher.

"She was my best teacher," he says. After school hours, and after he graduated with the class of 1901 when he was seventeen years old, he studied with Miss Phelps. He and Fielding Houchens worked together, and together compared their hopes and their preferences for West Point and Annapolis. Harry got no further than that. One day he decided to check his eyesight against the West Point standard. He went, he thinks, to the

Army Recruiting Station in Kansas City. They told him there that he did not have a chance. He went no further. No appointment was ever given him. He took it in good spirit when Fielding later did get his appointment from Congressman W. S. Cowherd, of Kansas City, who has often been credited with giving one to Harry. Fielding's record was brief: he was appointed a midshipman on 7 July 1904, as the Navy dates its documents, and his resignation was accepted on 6 February 1905, on account of deficiencies in studies—mechanical drawing and languages.

But much had happened to Harry before Fielding failed at Annapolis. He did not go to college. He did not immediately and earnestly go to work after he graduated from high school. A first job he had had, as a helper in the Clinton Drug Store at three dollars a week, was almost a small-town stereotype of the small-town boy's first job. But that was not a young man's job. In the 1937-38 issue of the *Missouri Manual,* Truman stated that that work was done when he was eleven, too young for any pharmaceutical notions to take shape in his mind.

His first real work was as a timekeeper for the L. J. Smith Construction Company in the summer of 1902. That spring the construction company had been awarded the contract by the Atchison, Topeka and Santa Fe Railroad to grade for double tracking its main line from Chicago to Kansas City on the section between Sheffield and Sibley, two small towns near Independence. The report is that he got thirty-five dollars a month and board. Also, a job on the railroad, even one checking the hours of such a rough gang as a grading crew, must have had a special appeal to a boy who took as much pleasure as young Harry had watching the Missouri Pacific trains go by when the Trumans first moved close to the tracks on Crysler Street. After he was President, a cousin who remembered asked him, "Harry, do you remember how much you loved the trains?"

"I still do," he said.

He liked that summertime railroad job. It put him into the company of tougher-talking men than he ever saw again until he took command of his Kansas City battery in France. The lean, bespectacled boy with the piano player's hands must have seemed strange among them. Sometimes he paid them off in the same saloon where they spent their earnings. He did his job well.

Also, he once said that on it he learned "all the cuss words in the English language—not by ear but by note." When he left, the tougher foreman of the tough crew, in language slightly translated here, pronounced him "all right—he's all right from his navel out in every direction."

There was nothing permanent about that job. It was over before the summer of 1902 was done. His next job in the mailing room of *The Kansas City Star* was of very brief duration. He may have worked at some time delivering *The Star* in Independence, but so far as the records of *The Star* show, he labored in its mailing room for just two weeks in August 1902. He made seven dollars one week and five dollars and forty cents the next.

With a year gone after high school, he was in no apparent hurry. Everything appeared to be going well on Waldo Street. The year he graduated seems, indeed, to have been an expansive year for his father. Not everything in business and politics pleased him, but enough did. The year before Harry had graduated, his father had sat through every session of the Democratic National Convention of 1900 in Kansas City, which renominated William Jennings Bryan. The convention hall had burned down not long before the Democrats were due to arrive and energetic Kansas City had rebuilt it in time for the gathering. It must have still smelled of fresh concrete above the smell of the stockyards. Young Harry went to some sessions and looked at the assembled Democrats of America for the first time. Both he and his father were pleased by Bryan's almost automatic renomination. And if also afterwards they were saddened in November, the convention had been a great occasion. John had sat through it as friend and equal in the box of William T. Kemper, who began as a shoe clerk and was going to be the richest banker in Kansas City. That could happen to anybody in America—as Populist furies subsided, it was still the American dream.

There seemed no reason for Harry to hurry to work. Indeed, in the summer of 1901, after he graduated from high school, he made his first real trip away from home to Murphysboro, in southern Illinois, where he visited his mother's youngest sister, Ada, Mrs. Joseph Van Clooster. Murphysboro is south of St. Louis and he stopped in St. Louis, on his way home, with relatives there. He was seventeen years old and he had eighteen silver dollars. With a cousin and three other young fellows he

went out to the horse races which were then going strong in St.
Louis. He had never been to such a race track before. He never
bet on a horse race again, though sometimes in later years he
had to go to the tracks in Kansas City to talk politics with Tom
Pendergast. That day they bet five dollars on a horse named
Claude. It rained just before the race and Claude not only came
in ahead; he paid twenty-five to one.

"I never had so much money in my life."

Then, when he came home, full of his story and with his
pockets sagging with his silver money, somebody asked him if it
had rained before the race. Then they laughed.

"No wonder you won. Claude is the best mud horse in the
United States."

The tougher the track the better Claude ran. Sometimes,
later, that has seemed a parable about Truman luck. It did not
seem particularly relevant then. He went on seriously with his
music under Mrs. White. After he found out the final truth
about his eyes and a military career, he might have gone on to
college. Charlie Ross and Elmer Twyman had gone. Even
bookish boys in those days, however, were not so apt to go to
college in Missouri. It was different in the East. Franklin
Roosevelt got his A.B. at Harvard the year Harry saw Fielding
Houchens off to Annapolis. Harry Truman did not have to
make any decision about it. It was provided for him.

John Truman became even more explosive abroad and, if
possible, even more gentle at home. The small, proud, taciturn
man, already past fifty, talked to Martha Ellen. The children
had to know; they were babies no longer. Actually Harry began
to be a member of the family council about the time Vivian got
the checkbook for horse-trading. Vivian was the trader, Harry
the manager and counselor. Instead of becoming rich, as he
had hoped, John Truman had lost everything he and Martha
Ellen had, in speculation on grain market futures.

"He got the notion he could get rich." That was not a strange
notion in America at that time or in the years before or since.
"Instead, he lost everything at one fell swoop and went completely broke."

He lost the hundred-and-sixty-acre farm which Martha Ellen
had inherited from old Solomon, her father. He lost also about
$30,000 or $40,000 in cash, stocks and other personal property.

They had to give up the house on Waldo Street and take one, not so good, at 2108 Park Avenue, in Kansas City. There, in 1903, John Truman was still listed in the city directory as a livestock dealer. But none of the children were able to join the mass movement of Missourians to St. Louis for the great Louisiana Purchase Exposition of 1904 commemorating the growth of middle America. That year, John Truman was listed in the directory as a watchman. Also in the directory, the listings showed that the boys—Harry, aged twenty; Vivian, aged eighteen —had gone to work as bank clerks. Only young Mary Jane went on with her music.

CHAPTER IV

Crossroads of America

CATASTROPHE IN AMERICA is always spectacle, too. People lined
the high shore that year, in which John Truman moved from his
broken expectations to Kansas City, to see the great flood of
1903. It arrived, predicted and measured day by day and then
hour by hour by government experts, just fifty-nine years after
the appalling and unexpected rise of 1844 which had coincided
with the appearance of the Trumans and the Youngs in the
documents of Missouri. On the crowded bluffs old Harriet
Louisa Gregg Young was one of the few who had watched that
earlier flood spread up the Missouri and the Kaw rivers like a
sea in the middle of America. That other time she had watched
the high waters as a red-haired, twenty-six-year-old mother in a
new country. In 1903, she was an old lady of eighty-four who
had come in from her farm near Grandview to visit her daughter
who must have seemed to her a child in trouble still.

The memory is that John Truman and Martha Ellen, the big
boys and young Mary Jane stood with Louisa Young on a bluff,
now cut away, where Grand Avenue ran down to the river.
There were all sorts of people there, some very sober and a few
a little drunk, women who laughed and men who chewed their
cigars, boys who spat as far as they could toward the flood. There
were other little family groups like the Trumans. It was not only
the calamity of that summer but the wonder, too. Parents
wanted their children to see it to remember it as old Louisa did.
And John Truman asked his mother-in-law the obvious question:
How did this flood compare with the one she had watched so
long before. Louisa answered him with the matter-of-fact quality which is a family characteristic. She was an old woman
stating facts, not undertaking parables.

61

"The waters are no higher," she said, "but there is so much more to destroy."

Many felt that way about the American stream and men's hopes beside it. John Truman, at a time when there was so much more to destroy, had already lost almost everything he had. Of course, that was nobody's fault but his own. As one of the sons of the firstcomers, he was also one of those who had had the longest chance. He had lost and that was too bad. Others had lost, too, in an American hazard not quite as simple as speculation on the Board of Trade—in a greater gambling involving the farm prices of corn and hogs, freight rates, monopoly, usury, as well as flood, grasshoppers and the burning lack of rain. That was also too bad. Some others had won in the rushing expansion and at least one of them, old Colonel Thomas H. Swope, said that was too good. He had kept some mudhole and hilltop lots which he could not sell until they were at the center of clamorous Kansas City. That was the only reason, he said, why he got rich. Somehow such a statement seemed more shocking than shouted socialism. Old man Swope must have been drunk, which would not have been incredible. Hardly anything was incredible in those years. Swope gave Kansas City its biggest park, and his death, many believed, was murder for his money, though the crime was never proved. The rich and the poor rose in numbers in Kansas City, in the Middle Border and in America like a flood. And even among the puzzled poor, as among the confidently righteous rich, there was a feeling of flood tide in the whole land.

It is simpler to describe what John Truman lost than the roaring gain around him in America and in Kansas City. Both were equally important in the youth of his son, Harry. The loss was very clear. It was pioneer land which went in 1902 and 1903 to pay John's debts. One piece of it was a part of the first land Solomon Young acquired after he moved to Missouri. He got it in August 1844, from Stephen Abston, when the great flood of that year had scarcely dried from the bottom lands. Another part he had bought in 1851 from Charles Younger, a relative of the famous Younger brothers who later rode with Jesse James. The land had been in the Young family for half a century when Martha Ellen let it go. It was good land, a very dark brown to black, deep, mellow silt of high fertility, which had fed old Solomon's cattle, nurtured his oxen, his mules and his high-stepping strawberry roan. It was not land easily to be let go even if old titles were swiftly changing in the Middle Border and elsewhere and pioneer patterns were slipping away sometimes in good luck and sometimes in bad.

There was no sense of loss in Kansas City to which Harry Truman came with his family in 1903. If a decade before it had seemed only an overgrown country town to young William Allen White, of Kansas, it already considered itself the crossroads of the continent. Much of America did come together there "where the elbow of the ice sheet protruded and the Missouri made its Great Bend to the east." That was locally regarded as only proper behavior by the ice sheet. No part of the United States felt any more "manifest destiny" as the nation moved beyond the turn of the century. Also, if America seemed rushing ahead in terms of both Bigness and Reform at the same time, Kansas City embodied both, and understood neither any better than most of the rest of America.

What was happening in America was as much around Harry Truman's youth as Bryant's pond, the goats in the backyard, the Missouri Pacific trains roaring by. J. P. Morgan celebrated the new century by putting together the first billion-dollar corporation (four fifths as much as the national debt of the United States). U. S. Steel was greeted with as much awe as anger even if it was followed by the emergence of the "muckrakers" who undertook the dissection of both politics and finance with startling results. In a strange way, Theodore Roosevelt, who roared a little at both Morgan and the muckrakers, embodied the attitudes of both, and advanced both ideas of Bigness and Reform at once and together. Somehow in his strenuous person he provided a sort of controlled release for the protest of America which had seemed after 1900 merely frustration behind Bryan. It was not odd that the first Roosevelt was the man who took Missouri out of Democratic regularity.

In Kansas City, where the patterns of people and power were little less complicated than in the country as a whole, Theodore Roosevelt made a special impression. His great supporter, Colonel William Rockhill Nelson, publisher of *The Kansas City Star*, wanted to make him a resident and an editor. *The Star* flung TR's progressive views across Kansas and Missouri. Also, as the champion of the finer things in life like boulevards, parks and art galleries, "Baron Bill" Nelson made his apostolate of perfection a part of his struggle for crude power.

The Star made rarely interrupted war upon the Democratic Pendergast bosses and brothers (first Jim, then Tom) who were in their initial city-wide power when the Trumans came to town. However, if the Pendergasts were made to seem only predatory anthropoids in plug hats in other parts of America which failed to remember their own bosses, at home they took part in a city progress which busied contractors and consumed concrete as it extended boulevards. It was the process which marked most American municipal improvements. Kansas City grew from the cooperation in combat of Nelson and the Pendergasts. They even looked alike. As that was the age in the United States of the first display of the Roosevelt teeth, it was also a time down below the White House when corpulence and power seemed inseparable. The great J. P. Morgan may be the model, but Nelson's fat face in the faded print which still hangs in the office of *The Star* makes him look almost hydrocephalic. The greatest American and Republican boss, Boise Penrose of Pennsylvania, weighed 350 pounds before he died. Tom Pendergast thickened and fattened as his power grew.

Nelson underpaid his help and demanded a more decent city for everybody. (The story that he left his paper to his employes is wholecloth lie; he did not even remember his personal servants in his will.) The Pendergasts fed the poor, got them jobs and collected their votes; and sometimes their henchmen found a good many more votes than there were men. One undertook to monopolize politics and the other the press, and both were ready to be rough in the process. Both were the inseparable and easily seen parts of power in the American city (not merely Kansas City) along with the bankers, the real estate men, the liquor and railroad boys, the corporation attorneys, the traction companies and the insurance people.

It was about the time the Trumans moved to the house on Park Avenue and the Pendergasts were rising to power in Kansas City that Lincoln Steffens came to Missouri to begin his disclosures in *The Shame of the Cities* in St. Louis. It was not a new story. James Bryce had written in *The American Commonwealth* years before that "there is no denying that the government of the cities is the one conspicuous failure of the United States." Later that other scholar of politics, Woodrow Wilson, was put into politics by Boss Jim Smith of New Jersey. Wilson broke with Smith only when Smith proposed that they disregard a senatorial primary in order to put Smith in the Senate. Wilson rejected it as an immoral suggestion. Pendergast, Truman has said many times, never asked him to do anything wrong and also that Pendergast knew Truman would not have done it if he had. Many politicians and their associates forget afterward their own relationships and indebtedness to the bosses. The classic case, of course, is that of TR's daughter, Alice Longworth, who in her memoirs was shocked by the Ohio Gang atmosphere under Harding, though her own aristocratic husband, Nicholas Longworth, had been sent to Congress from Ohio by George B. Cox, the corrupt, saloonkeeper Republican boss of Cincinnati. Other people's bosses are always the unpleasant ones.

Also the bosses are regarded only as the predatory chieftains of the venal poor. Yet the thing that Steffens emphasized in America and Missouri was that "the corruption of St. Louis came from the top"—from the corporations ready to swap swag for franchises. This was not merely the St. Louis but the American pattern. Nearly forty years later the fatal corruption of the Pendergast machine in Kansas City came not from the gangsters or gamblers, bootleggers or bookmakers, dope peddlers or prostitutes, but from bribery by the richest and most respectable fire insurance companies in the United States.

Missouri, which sentimentalized Jesse James, may have been less confused than the nation was by the differences between the big and the bad. After he got to the Senate, Truman was speaking in the images of his boyhood when he spoke once of the railroad financiers.

"Speaking of Rock Island," he said, "reminds me that the first railroad robbery was committed on the Rock Island in 1873 just east of Council Bluffs, Iowa. The man who committed that robbery used a gun and a horse, and got up early in the morning. He and his gang took a chance of being killed, and eventually most of them were killed. The loot was $3,000. That railroad robber's name was Jesse James. The same Jesse James held up the Missouri Pacific in 1876 and took the paltry sum of $17,000 from the express car. About thirty years after the Council Bluffs holdup, the Rock Island went through a looting by some gentlemen known as the tin-plate millionaires. They used no gun, but they ruined the railroad and got away with $70,000,000 or more. They did it by means of holding companies. Senators can see what 'pikers' Mr. James and his crowd were along side of some real artists."

One of the fascinating things about history is how close an unknown boy can be to such items in it. The Trumans in the house at 2108 Park Avenue, which they had bought with all that was left after John's debts were paid, must have seemed a long way from such men and patterns of power, political and financial. They were not joining the rich in Kansas City. Lean, diminutive John Truman, indeed, looked even before bad luck caught him almost the antithesis of the corpulent captains of his time. After his failure, there are few memories of the explosive qualities which he sometimes displayed in Independence. The sort of story which does come down is that when they were hard up he and Harry agreed to throw all their dimes into the tray of an old trunk until they had enough money to buy a "Booklovers' Edition" of Shakespeare's plays which was published in 1901.

"It was surprising how fast they accumulated," the son said.

Sometimes John read with Harry from their old red edition of *Plutarch's Lives*. The politics of Rome must not have seemed so strange in Kansas City or the United States. And John Truman never lost his interest in politics. As his boy Harry grew older it made a special bond between them which stock-trading had not been able to provide. John Truman was almost the perfect example of the Kansas City Democrat and he would not have objected to a definition written later by the editor of Colonel Nelson's *Star*.

"The central phalanx of the Unterrified Democrats of Kansas City," he wrote, "is made up of families with war traditions. For them to vote a Republican ticket would be to make a covenant with hell."

In John's case the inheritance was not all. He had been strenuously for Bryan even in the days when he had hoped to be rich. Also, he had come on Park Avenue to a point where the people of Bryan's resonant imperatives were not other fellows but himself. If fifty years later his son was still spoken of as an average man in the White House, John Truman much more clearly in

Kansas City met the inexact mathematics by which such a figure is produced. That figure was not unimportant at the beginning of this century despite the well-fed personages in the foreground. Mark Sullivan, the journalist who followed the Republicans from Theodore Roosevelt to Hoover, wrote before either Franklin Roosevelt or Harry Truman had made presidential appearances, "As democracy in America has expressed itself, the period of 1900-25 is unparalleled in the importance of the role played by the average man."

It is not always an exciting or satisfying role for the player. The story of the Trumans in that capacity is told with statistic-like starkness in the city directories of Kansas City:

> 1903—John A., live stock, r. 2108 Park
> Harry S., 2108 Park
>
> 1904—Harry S., clk Nat Bank Com, r. 2108 Park
> John A., watch Mo Elevator, r. 2108 Park
> J. Vivian, clk Nat Bank Com, r. 2108 Park
>
> 1905—Harry S., clk Union Nat Bank, rms. 2650 e 29th
>
> 1906—Harry S., clk Union Nat Bank, rms. 1314 Troost
>
> 1907—Vivian, clk, b. 1417 Locust

That is all. Yet, it tells it all pretty well. That first year after the money and the family farms were gone, old John (he was only fifty but he seemed already spent) listed himself as he had always thought of himself in all the years since he and Martha Ellen first went, young and hopeful, to Lamar to deal in the famous mules of Missouri. But when the second year came around it was not so simple. Vivian had gone first (as the one who had been in trade longer) and then Harry to the National Bank of Commerce and got jobs as clerks in the cage which was more affectionately called "the zoo." John had got the job as watchman. It was not exactly what he had been expecting a few years before when he sat at the Democratic National Convention in the box of William Kemper, who was his friend in the "grain business" and was to become not only Pendergast's police commissioner but also the richest banker in Kansas City. It was a job. If the banks with expanding deposits wanted boys, there were not too many opportunities for men of fifty who had been trained as stock traders and no longer had the capital for trade. A year or two before in Missouri *The St. Louis Post-Dispatch* had run a little advertisement for a watchman, who could give references, at fifteen dollars a week and had received seven hundred and fifty answers within twenty-four hours. There is no record of any such competition in John's case. Apparently it did not seem worth any such strenuous seeking. He stood it for one year—or less than that.

Then he swapped the house on Park Avenue for an eighty-acre farm near Clinton where Solomon Young had ridden to patent the first land he took from the United States. Martha Ellen and Mary Jane went with him. They never lived on the farm but in the town of Clinton itself. They were there only six months. Then they moved back to the old place at Grandview to live with Grandma Young and her bachelor son, Harrison. Vivian joined them there. But Harry stayed in town.

Those four years which he spent in Kansas City have ever since been insistently regarded by Harry Truman as an interlude only. In politics he has steadily stressed his geographical classification as that of "country boy" and small-town man. They were important years, nevertheless. He did not come to Kansas City with small-town eyes popping as young William Allen White had a dozen years before him. He did not imagine his arrival, as White had, as that of Childe Harold to the Dark Tower. There must have been dark fascinations about it to boys who came over from Kansas to "the gilded metropolis." Even Tammany politicians in the first years of the century told a *New York Tribune* reporter that they were "amazed" at the "wide-open" character of the town. The slot machines, they said, sat with Kansas City's pride in the lobby of the Midland Hotel which claimed the "finest and most expensive marble finishings of any hotel in America."

Lean, bespectacled, owlish-looking Harry Truman, who keeps from those days the capacity to get convulsively tickled like a boy, developed his immunities to the wicked and bedazzling city by easy stages. There was not a time in his memory when there were not some sort of trains running on regular schedule the nine miles from Independence to the metropolis. If it was a city wicked enough to bring Carry Nation (who had once lived in Belton, Missouri, where Harry spent part of his infancy) over from Kansas, he went swinging through it as a boy with his music in a case on his way to Mrs. White's for his piano lessons.

It did not disturb him or any other Trumans when the Kansas City judge sent bobbed-haired Carry back to Kansas with the declaration that Kansas City was "not a good place for short-haired women, long-haired men, and whistling girls." There was discipline but not Puritanism in the Truman heritage.

"Between the time I was about sixteen to twenty," he says, "I used to go to every vaudeville show that came to Kansas City at the old Orpheum and at the Grand Theater."

At one of them he got a Saturday afternoon job as usher which made it possible for him to see the show for nothing. He remembered particularly Eva Tanguay and "The Four Cohans," starring George M. Cohan who made the American flag a standard prop of his vaudeville and musical comedy career. Also, Truman recalled years later that he saw not only the shows but heard the hardening conversation of other older and more sophisticated young men. One story, which made him laugh later at his innocence then, was that the race problem in America would solve itself because mulattoes were as infertile as mules and gradually by a process of miscegenation the last vestige of the African would disappear. It seemed logical enough at the time to the son of a mule trader. It emphasizes now the same sort of eager innocence of the well-brought-up small-town boy which William Allen White described in gentle self-derision in his own case many years later. What White wrote of himself could be substituted almost unchanged for the innocence of Harry Truman in those days. He saw a lot through those thick lenses, but he seems to have been an almost aseptically good boy. Martha Ellen knew what kind of boy she was sending off to town. She was with him the first two years he lived there. During that time he joined the Benton Boulevard Baptist Church. Also, in those Kansas City years, he was in love with that girl in Independence. The year Harry's father failed, Bess Wallace lost her own father very suddenly. As often as he could, Harry went back to see her in Independence at the house of her grandmother, the Gates mansion, to which she had moved with her mother.

He stayed on at the Union National Bank (to which he had moved from the National Bank of Commerce for better pay) when his mother and father moved to Clinton. He lived first with his Aunt Emma, Mrs. Rochester Colgan, at 2650 East Twenty-ninth, and for a longer time at Mrs. Trow's boarding house at 1314 Troost Avenue. The latter is better remembered. It seems in the memories like one of those boarding houses in America in which O. Henry in those days was placing so many of his comic and sentimental stories. Harry played the piano for two young ladies who sound across the years almost like a team of long-skirted and starched-shirtwaisted working girls of the time—Miss Casby Bailey and Miss Ida Trow. They went on picnics sometimes. They had fun. In the "joyous crudity" of those Kansas City times, the Victorian period and Victorian manners made less noise but they still remained. (The Victorian period, precisely, ended on January 22, 1901, just eight months before Theodore Roosevelt became President of the United States.) A young fellow from Kansas named Arthur Eisenhower, who became a banker while his brother was becoming a general, lived in the house and remembered those days.

"Harry and I only had a dollar a week left over for riotous living," he said.

The important thing perhaps was that Harry was in the midst of the long period it took him to make up his mind as to what he wanted to do. He was doing very well at the bank. One old banker, after he was President, said he deserved no medals for his work in "the zoo," but one bank was willing to raise his salary to get him from another. The man at the recruiting station had cleanly finished his hopes for a career as an Army officer. And one day with almost equal dispatch, Harry put an end to his own early ideas about a career as a pianist.

"I decided it was sissy," he said. The impression he gives in remembrance is almost of a young man stopping suddenly on the street and abruptly making up his mind. There seems to have been no long conscious inner struggle about it. He was not without promise as a pianist. (Long afterwards when his only practice for years had been playing for his own pleasure, Conductor Emeritus Serge Koussevitzky, of the Boston Symphony Orchestra, said after leaving the White House, "We all know that he plays much better than he talks about it.") Certainly an ambition to be a concert pianist could have seemed sissy to the sort of associates he had in a bank cage, even among the ushers at the vaudeville theaters, or the boys and girls at the boarding house. It was nice to be able to play but it seemed an odd way to hope to make a living in a town which talked about art but was much more seriously concerned about cattle and wheat and those who bought and sold them.

He was not intimidated by any meat-and-bread-town prejudices. The best evidence seems to suggest that he really did not, after the West Point hope disappeared, know what he wanted to do. He developed early enough in aptitude but he appears to have been one of those men who come late to maturity in purpose. He went to work in the bank because it was necessary that he have a job. He did not dislike it. He did well. He became a good farmer but only because he was needed on the farm. There was undoubtedly toughness in Martha Ellen's apron strings. That does not seem a satisfactory explanation of the fact that he never really seemed to know what he wanted to do until he was nearly forty years old.

Certainly, however, in those Kansas City years and after, he was not a frustrated artist in a bank bookkeeper's cage. He was not only geographically but spiritually native to Kansas City. He liked to walk in those days, as in his later years. He knew every part of the big sprawling and, when the wind blew wrong from the stockyards, stinking town. (Upton Sinclair made the American stockyards sensitive about dirt and smell only in 1906, when he published *The Jungle,* the year Harry went to the farm.) Sometimes Harry dreamed of himself as a rich man, as unquestionably he dreamed of himself in the patterns of the great soldiers and great musicians. He was sometimes bored by being a bank clerk.

One certain thing is that he was not alone in not knowing what he wanted to be. Neither did Kansas City, nor America. Kansas City clung to its oldest and crudest wide-open ways which it hoped pleased those who came to sell the cows, while it cried, with *The Star* leading the chorus, for boulevards, art galleries and parks. *The Star*'s editor said, after Truman had made up his mind on a political career, that in Kansas City "the civilization of the go-getter tempered by houn' dawg is still in combat with the civilization of beauty." Such conflict was not limited to Kansas City. Indeed, nothing is more characteristic of the Middle Border than that the people, whose hard folk wisdom underlay the contemptuous economics of Thorstein Veblen (who taught at the University of Missouri while Harry was a farmer), also indulged themselves in dreaming beyond difficulties. Harry

Truman grew up while Americans were reading Edward Bella-my's *Looking Backward,* which pictured a year 2000 of socialistic perfection. Indeed, more of them read it than had read any other novel since *Uncle Tom's Cabin.* It did not seem out of place by the books of hard and practical protest. By neat—and purely personal—coincidence in the same year that John Tru-man went broke on grain futures there appeared Frank Norris' *The Pit,* about men on the grain exchange and wheat in the commerce of the world. Decision was not simple in America. While Harry Truman was making up his mind the United States swung like a pendulum in its preferences from Theodore Roose-velt to Taft to Wilson to Harding. That last time it seemed more than ever sure.

Harry did not find it easy to be sure either. While he was working at the National Bank of Commerce he met a young Jewish boy named Eddie Jacobson with whom he was to go later into the men's furnishing business, but he had neither the inclination nor the capital for such a venture in the early Kansas City days. He did indulge his old military aspirations by becom-ing a charter member of the newly formed Battery B of the Missouri National Guard on Flag Day in 1905, and in August of that year went to his first encampment across the state at Cape Girardeau. In September 1906, he was made a corporal. He was twenty-two years old. His old schoolmates were getting settled. Charlie Ross had a job on *The St. Louis Post-Dispatch* and in a couple of years would be a professor of journalism. Elmer Twyman was a doctor.

Harry did not really have to make a decision. He was needed on the farm at Grandview. John and Martha Ellen, with young Mary Jane, had moved there in October 1905. Grandmother Young was eighty-seven years old and her bachelor son, Harrison, was ready to be released from farm responsibility. Harrison Young lived in town part of the time after the John Trumans came. This was "a strictly business deal" between Harrison and John and his boys. It is not improbable, however, that Martha Ellen's mother and brother had been troubled about the difficul-ties that had followed Martha Ellen and John. Certainly old Louisa would be happy to have them at home. John and Vivian operated the farm until 1906, but that was only for a winter and spring before Harry came. Vivian, according to the Kansas

City directory, was back in Kansas City working as a clerk in 1907. In the other years he was on the farm until he married and moved away in 1911.

When Harry came to the farm in 1906, it was the first real farming in his life. He had been only six years old when they left the farm for Independence. He had visited the farm in the years after that and sometimes helped with the work. He was familiar with stock from a boyhood in which animals always filled the backyard. But he had a banker's hands and there were some who suggested that he would be the sort of farmer who would like to sit on the porch and read a book in the shade. Such a suggestion can rouse Harry Truman still.

"My father would not have let me get away with that. I'd get up and start the binder by the time the sun was up. I worked on the farm and then came in and helped mother get the meals."

Yet there were questions when he turned to farming.

"There were all sorts of bets that I wouldn't stay on the farm. I was getting a hundred and twenty-five dollars a month in the bank, which was a lot of money in those days."

It was beautiful farm country. The surface soil of Summit silt loam ranged from fifteen to eighteen inches deep. The dark prairie soil was well adapted to corn, wheat cover, and especially favorable to blue grass. It was almost ideal for livestock production including Missouri mules, which nobody could judge better than John. It was Harry Truman's native country, farm and town. The homeplace sat upon a broad ridge of gently rolling prairie land extending from Independence to Grandview, which is the western edge of the prairie plateau. And from Grandview there was—and is—a fine view across the valley of the Big Blue River.

It was home. The maples Solomon Young had planted were high over the house. They were good years. Father and son planted the crops and talked Democratic politics in the evening. Harry drove sometimes over to Independence, though it was a long way by buggy. They seem slow years in the life of a man who was to be President of the United States. None of the family were getting any younger. Grandma Young died in 1909 not quite two months after she was ninety-one years old, sixty-five years after she had stayed on the land with the children that December when Solomon had ridden to Clinton to patent their first government land grant. In 1912, Harry hitched up the buggy and drove into Grandview to find out at the telegraph office what was happening to Champ Clark and Woodrow Wilson at Baltimore. In 1912, also, the President for whom John Truman voted was elected—the first since Cleveland. But at sixty-two he was a little old to be fixing flags on the top of his house. He himself was an office holder in his old age, having been appointed by the county court of Jackson County as road overseer. It was not a great honor. It did not pay very much, but he gave it conscientious labor. And it cost him his life.

He seemed, as most men do, to become a smaller man as he grew older, but his determinations were as big as ever. He never underestimated his powers at work or anything else. As road overseer, he undertook to lift a very big rock and injured himself. He was not able to hide the pain in his side, but he refused to do anything about it and developed an intestinal block. He never weighed more than one hundred and forty pounds in his life, and now the weight slipped away from his slight frame. Even then he declined to be operated on, but at last they took him to the Swedish Hospital in Kansas City where an operation was performed. A week later he was home. It was early in November and the crops had been put by. The maples were still bright red outside the window.

"I was with him," Harry Truman remembers. "I had been sitting with him and watching a long time. I nodded off. When I woke up he was dead."

CHAPTER V

Contour Plowing

THE CONVENTIONAL STORY of Harry Truman's farm years grows from that proud phrase of his mother's that he could plow the straightest furrow that could be found in the county, in Missouri, or maybe in the world. Old Martha Ellen till she died kept the images in her lively language close to the Missouri earth. She could describe a President, who was her boy, in words that were still simple and good in a world which hungered for some signs of simplicity and goodness.

Unfortunately, the straight furrow is not generally regarded as a good and simple image any more. Many of those which were plowed across the prairie soil let the water run off carrying the fertility. Harry Truman thinks now that he guarded against that on the level lands at Grandview. Certainly, even if he could "plant the straightest row of corn in the whole country," the straight furrow is not his story. Contour plowing in America, up grade, down dale, over the hill, around the outcrops of the limestone, matches better than any straight furrow the story of his farm years.

Undoubtedly, as recalled, the first years do seem almost as good as a city man's nostalgia for the soil which never stirred his sweat. Indeed, when old John Truman died that November in 1914 he could look out across the lands through his sickness with the certainty that he left in security the family which he had made poor when he hoped to get rich. The son beside him was a good farmer. Old John had taught him.

"My father was a stickler for doing things correctly on the farm," Truman told me. "As senior partner in the firm of John Truman and Sons, farmers, he talked always about clean fence corners, cleaning fence rows and killing weeds along the roads bordering the farm. When it rained and we couldn't plow or harvest, we'd take down the old scythe—and we had a dozen of them—and cut weeds in the fence corners and along the fences bordering the roads."

He remembered the work: "When it came to planting time after the fields were plowed, harrowed and put into proper shape, it was my job to drive the corn planter or the drill if wheat or oats were to be sown. We had a couple of lively horses for the corn planter and the object was to make them walk fast and straight ahead so that the first row would be a straight one. My father told me to adjust the planter before starting, have the horses well in hand and under control, pick out an object on the other side of the field usually a quarter or a half mile away, point the tongue of the planter at that object and keep it there, letting the horses step out at a lively gait. I became expert in laying out the corn rows. When I drove the drill for a field of wheat the rows of the drill were as straight as the corn rows and there was never a bend or a skipped place in the field—and sometimes that field would be a half mile square—a hundred and sixty acres.

"It really was a feat," he smiled in remembrance, "and one to keep me on my toes, because if a crooked row or a blank space showed in the cornfield or the wheat, I'd hear of it for a year. I finally became an expert at planting and that's where the reputation for driving the straightest row came from. It had nothing to do with 'plowing' because if you plant them straight, you have to plow them that way."

He worked out a plowing system, nevertheless: "In those days we had what we called a gang plow, two twelve-inch plows on the same frame with three wheels on it, and the locomotive power was four horses, or four mules, or three mules and a horse, or whatever you could get to pull it. It moved at a rate where it turned over a two-foot furrow, and you could count the revolutions of the big wheel from which you could tell how long it would take to plow an acre or to plow a field."

An old man dying, while he watched his son from the porch, could almost figure the future. The years just before John Truman died, from 1909 to 1914, had been pretty good years for farmers and for businesses depending directly upon farmers having money. Indeed, the biographer of an American agriculturist who was a freshman at Iowa State when Harry Truman moved to the farm and with whom he had to deal later as President, has pointed that out for the Wallaces of Iowa as well as the Trumans of Missouri. Those were the years of the "parity" period which farm relief acts were later to seek to re-establish in terms of farm prices and farm-buying. In those days when Harry Truman took a bushel of wheat to Belton he could expect to bring home a bushel-of-wheat's worth of goods.

That was not all, so far as the security in which John left his family was concerned. Louisa Young had left all her lands to Martha Ellen Truman and her bachelor brother, Harrison Young. The Trumans counted their expectations from that estate at $150,000. Harry Truman has said that in good farm years the family made as much as $15,000 a year on the Grandview farm. Perhaps the best evidence of well-being is that in 1913, when there were only 38,140 automobiles in Missouri, he bought a dark, four-cylinder Stafford automobile, said to have been the thirteenth off the assembly line in the Kansas City plant.

The Stafford Motor Company was only in business in Kansas City from 1911 to 1913. As in other such industries a few big companies were already growing from the many small companies that had begun. At that time the Stafford Company manufactured a four-door touring car which sold at $2,350 and a roadster for $2,250. That makes Harry Truman seem better off than even he thought he was.

"Terry Stafford started out in Topeka in 1910 or 1911," Truman remembers. "He had an improved overhead cam, valve-in-the-head motor. He built about one hundred cars in Topeka and about one hundred in Kansas City. They were excellent cars. I got mine—one of the 1910 or 1911 models—second-hand for six hundred dollars. I bought it in 1913 and took it with me to Fort Sill when I went to war and left it there. It would go sixty miles an hour—a touring car with high brass windshield and Prest-O-Lite lamps."

It made a lot easier his trips to Independence to see Bess Wallace. Also, his other interests were expanding beyond the straight or turning furrows. In December, 1909, he joined the Masonic Lodge in the near-by village of Belton, in Cass County. He took his Masonry seriously and it played an important part in his political life. Both his grandfathers had been Masons, old Solomon at Raytown and Anderson Truman at Westport. (John

Truman said he had always meant to be a Mason but "somehow never got around to it.") Also, about that time Harry Truman began to be interested in the organization of the Farm Bureau which was just beginning in Missouri. He was one of those who, in 1913, paid one dollar membership.

J. M. Slaughter, executive vice-president of the Hickman Mills Bank (Hickman Mills is a village up the road toward Kansas City) had taken on the job of secretary in the Farm Bureau's organization. He recalls: "Mr. E. A. Ikenberry was our County Agent, at that time called a Farm Adviser much to the disgust of many farmers, and through his direction and cooperation our local work was carried on. In 1914, when time came for the annual election of township officers, Mr. Ikenberry advised us to seek out a progressive farmer who was also a good farmer and one who would also have some political support with the County Court of Jackson County as the Farm Bureau work received much of its support from the County Court. Harry S. Truman was elected."

Ikenberry, who in 1950 was an independent orchardist in Independence, and Banker Slaughter, of Hickman Mills, were apparently the first to recognize any political influence on the part of Harry Truman. His father had been road overseer, a position in which Harry succeeded him, for four years before he died. Also, John had been, from the time he moved back to Grandview, a judge of elections in the precinct. The influence which Ikenberry recognized, however, Harry Truman thinks amounted only to the fact that Robert Mize, who was then the Eastern Jackson County Judge on the County Court—the job to which he himself was to be elected in 1922—was "a political friend of my father's and of mine." It is clear, however, that he was being recognized, even before his father died. (The year after John's death he served as postmaster of Grandview from February 27 to August 31, 1915, and received total pay of $297.38 which he passed on to a woman assistant who needed it more than he did.)

He was no boy any longer. He was thirty when his father died. At that time Alben Barkley and Sam Rayburn were already in Congress. Franklin Roosevelt was Assistant Secretary of the Navy. Herbert Hoover, aged forty, was in Europe representing the Panama-Pacific International Exposition. But Harry

Truman was doing well in Jackson County. He was riding along in that Stafford and in his life. The Truman world looked good not only to old John who was leaving it. The war in Europe seemed in Missouri just one of those European wars. It is a good thing that before they buried John Truman in the Forest Hills Cemetery in South Kansas City, the row ahead looked straight to him. That made it easier for them all.

The contours are worth examining, nevertheless. Not even progressive farmers paid much attention to them then. Few thought much about soil conservation in those days. Harry Truman seemed a little odd even to his neighbors when he took the waste straw from a pile at which cattle had been feeding, baled it and dumped the bales into gullies which erosion had made. When the rains coated the bales with the washed soil, Harry sowed the mass with timothy. "A sodded watercourse," the neighbors called it.

"The planting that I had to do was on level ground," Truman explained to me, "and required no soil conservation methods."

That was at least fifteen years before one of the first two soil erosion laboratories in America was established in Missouri in 1929—a year in which more things than top soil seemed draining away in America. "Not ten per cent of the people of Missouri knew what soil erosion was, or had heard of contours as a protection at that time," says J. E. Noll of the Erosion Experiment Farm at Bethany, Missouri. The man with the longest straight furrow was still considered the best farmer by old Martha Ellen and everybody else. And not all departures from the straight and simple line turned out well. Certainly that was true with Harry Truman. Some he could not avoid. And some, in terms of old John's heritage as both hard worker and eager speculator, he could not resist.

When old Louisa Young had left her lands to Martha Ellen and Harrison, she cut off in the same testament four other daughters and one other son with only five dollars each. That was not altogether pleasing to all the other relatives and heirs.

"Nearly all the sons-in-law previous to father had been paid out of debts by Solomon Young," Harry Truman says. There had also apparently been advances by the old man to his eldest son, William. John Truman's failure had come ten years after

Solomon Young's death. "When Grandmother Young died she felt that Uncle Harrison and Mother had not got their rightful shares so she left her property to them."

It was a sizeable estate. Solomon Young had given his wife, Louisa, the homeplace of 398 acres when they acquired it in 1867. She had taken a child's share when Solomon's lands were partitioned after his death. So she left more than 518 good acres to the children who had stayed closest to home. Then when Harrison died at Grandview in August 1916, he left his half of Louisa's estate and his own lands, amounting to three hundred acres, to Martha Ellen and her children, Harry, Vivian and Mary Jane. They had a feeling of riches but, as Vivian Truman says, "The lawyers got most of it—all we got was debts." Certainly the years after were filled with a complicated procession of claims and debts. Even before John Truman died, Martha Ellen had found it necessary to put a $7,500 mortgage on her land. It is interesting now as a matter of history that this was the same land which stayed under almost constant mortgage until the place was foreclosed over old Martha Ellen's head by the Jackson County sheriff for the Jackson County school board twenty-six years later, in 1940 while her son was making perhaps his most desperate political fight for re-election to the Senate. It dogged them, irritated family relationships, and was steadily used for the political harassment of Harry all the way.

Harry had had to take over the full management of the farm during the long illness before his father died. Also, in the summer before his father died, he had leased Harrison Young's adjacent three hundred acres. It was a lot of land, particularly for a farmer who undertook to keep systematic records of production, to follow a crop rotation plan, to raise and increase his per acre production of wheat and oats and corn, and to raise Hampshire hogs, black Angus cattle and keep dairy cattle, too.

Anyone studying the record of those years must come to the conclusion, however, that the farm was not enough. It did not satisfy all his energies or his aims. Also, at that time both his energies and his aims may have been stirred and lifted by the increasing success of the long courtship he had been carrying on in Independence. He had continued in the National Guard, which required him to go into Kansas City every week for drill. But at least as early as 1916 he was occupied not only in farming

but in zinc mining and oil speculation as well. They were interests which extended into Kansas, Oklahoma and Texas.

Apparently the zinc and lead mining came first. He had a
friend in those days who was from near-by Harrisonville, where
John Truman once farmed and where Mary Jane was born,
named Jerry Culbertson. With him and another man named
Tom Hughes, Harry took an interest in a zinc mine at Commerce, Oklahoma, an old mining village about one hundred and
fifty miles south of Grandview and just across the Oklahoma line.
They thought they had found a new vein in an old mine. There
were plenty of old mines there, and in the war years, 1917-18,
some of them shared a boom. But that boom was still in the
future when Harry went down on week ends in those pre-war
years.

"Each of us lost about $7,500," he remembers.

He went with Culbertson into the oil business, too. On September 25, 1916, he signed with Culbertson and David H. Morgan a contract for the purchase of a third interest in the firm of
Morgan and Company which was engaged in "a general brokerage business, buying and selling oil lands, leases, production
stocks and securities and any and all other investments of
whatever nature on a commission basis or otherwise." Under
the terms of the contract, Truman paid $5,000 in cash and gave
five notes for $1,000 each all due in ten months "which notes
shall also be signed by Martha E. Truman, the mother of said
Harry S. Truman." The contract established Truman as treasurer, Culbertson as secretary, and Morgan as president and
provided that each of them "will devote his entire time and
attention to the interest of this partnership firm." Morgan, now
oil man in Eureka, Kansas, remembers, however, that it was
understood that Truman would continue to do "most of the
supervision on the Truman 600-acre farm near Grandview while
he was more or less engaged in performing the duties incident to
his official capacity as 'Treasurer' of our company, etc."

Obviously, however, he was much in town. J. K. Brelsford,
now a certified public accountant in Topeka, Kansas, came from
Colorado to be bookkeeper of the company and he remembers
the far-from-rustic Truman of those days. "Truman was surrounded with people, people, people. Salesmen, lease men, lease
owners, scouts and what-have-you. Morgan had his duties, but

he shoved quite a burden of seeing people over to Mr. Truman."

Farmer Truman was city man, too, outside the office as well as in it. He was, Brelsford says, "What I might call a western gourmet." Others might call it a man about town. Truman introduced the young bookkeeper to places where "the cooking of western food could not be excelled." Mr. Brelsford, in later years, ceased to share Truman's political ideas but he kept a bright memory of his company.

"It was a treat for him," Brelsford remembers, "to take a new visitor to Kansas City to such places, and he could certainly describe what you were going to get to eat in such a way that your anticipation was great. When the realization was as great as the anticipation, which it was at such places as 'Johnston's' and 'Valerius',' each of which featured special steak sauces and other accompaniments, and you had Harry S. Truman as a dinner companion, then you really were living."

(Frank Valerius in those days had three cafés in the downtown nighttime loop. One on West Eighth was a couple of blocks from the Jefferson Hotel, Tom Pendergast's headquarters at the time. The others were on Walnut and Tenth streets. Johnston's Café was at 1010 Walnut, three blocks from Pendergast's three-door saloon at Twelfth and Main.)

Truman's friend Culbertson sold out his interest in the company to J. S. Mullen of Ardmore, Oklahoma, described by the company as the "largest individual farm landowner in Oklahoma" and "one of the largest oil men in the Mid-Continent field." Harry, however, remained to sponsor with Morgan the incorporation of the Morgan Oil and Refining Company in a large advertisement in *The Kansas City Star,* on Sunday, April 1, 1917. Others who sponsored the new company were: J. J. Hurd, of Chanute, Kansas; Earl S. Ridge, of Kansas City; W. H. Lynn, of Wetmore, Kansas; E. B. DeLoe, of Coffeyville, Kansas; M. M. Jackson, of Muskogee, Oklahoma; and Dr. C. H. Washburn, "chemist and refiner of national reputation," of Chanute, Kansas, formerly of St. Louis.

The company advertised that it controlled twenty thousand acres "on structures in Kansas and approved by geologists," owned its own refinery, owned in fee simple 1,500 acres of probable oil and gas territory in Oklahoma and had holdings of ten thousand acres in Texas. The investing public was invited to

purchase ten thousand of its sixty thousand no par value shares
at twenty-five dollars a share. Its offices, like the offices of Morgan
and Company, were located at 702 New Ridge Arcade in
Kansas City. As its treasurer, Harry Truman was only described
as "native of Jackson County, Missouri; widely known in Kansas
City."

The advertisement concluded: "In the event this country is
unfortunately brought to war, the absolute necessity of gasoline
and other by-products of crude petroleum are bound to come to
such an urgent demand that the price will soar beyond all expectations and an investment in the shares of any oil company
that has production and large holdings of proven properties,
with its thousands of acres of probable oil producing territory,
with its own refinery for the refining of the crude product ready
for the market such as are held and owned by the MORGAN
OIL & REFINING COMPANY, is beyond question an investment of rare opportunity."

In retrospect it is clear that that was not an improbable
prophecy even in an oil advertisement. War would mean a new,
rare opportunity for riveters, stock salesmen and steelmakers.
It came just five days after the advertisement but the quality of
the rare opportunity so far as Harry Truman was concerned
altered.

"Harry," says his old partner, David Morgan, "was greatly
interested in the oil development business. He liked the element
of chance (he called it 'Hazard'), and had it not been for World
War I he would have continued in our oil operations and would
have made the same great success in that as he has done in
politics. We had the properties to develop and were in the
process of doing just that."

Years later Truman, in his own hand, wrote Morgan who had
sent him a copy of the old contract between them:

> Dave:
> This is an interesting document. As you will remember we
> had leases in Greenwood Co., Ks. and Bowie County, Tex—
> both if I remember correctly afterward produced immense
> quantities of oil. I went to war and things happened over
> which we had no control.
> Maybe I wouldn't be Pres if we'd hit.
> HST

Morgan was an Indiana-born man, just a year older than Harry, who had got his L.L.B. at the University of Kansas and practiced law in Muskogee, Oklahoma, where he "became thoroughly inoculated with the 'Oil Fever.'" He moved first to Tulsa and then to Kansas City, where he formed the partnership with Culbertson, known as Morgan and Company. (The name of the company first appears in the Kansas City directories in 1916, the same year Truman entered it. In 1918 the company had an advertisement on the front of the directory itself.) Not even a war apparently shook the "oil fever" out of Morgan.

"I have opened numerous oil pools," he wrote in 1949, "in which I had a minor interest or perhaps just a fee. I have personally been responsible for untold millions of barrels of crude oil being produced and have made millions of dollars for other folks, and, have been ushered aside by Fate from numerous other then unborn fields such as the 'Teter Field' here in Greenwood County.

"I can state very definitely, however," he went on, "that I am about ready to retire from active work in the oil fields. I do have a couple of properties which I am going to bring up to a stage of development that will insure myself and family of a substantial annuity over the years to come. I might even transfer a substantial interest to Harry. I certainly would if he needs it. I might include a few of his friends who seem to think they still need to make some more money, why, I wouldn't know. Personally, I have all I need and will continue to carry on just for the love of my work."

Neither he nor Truman has always been so philosophical. Both remember the big chance which they missed by a few feet of drilling. Morgan recalls: "In early 1917 the firm of Morgan and Company procured several thousand acres of oil leases, on a development contract, in the northwest portion of Greenwood County, Kansas, and a test well for oil was commenced at a location on said Block of Leases in Section 21, Twp. 23, Range 9 being the J. J. Morris lease of 1,900 acres and this well was drilling at about 1,500 feet when, due to World War emergencies, loss of operating personnel and with Harry Truman enlisted and in training at Fort Sill, Oklahoma, it was decided to sell and dispose of the Morris No. 1 well and equipment together with all the several thousand acres of leases owned by the firm in this area.

"Yes," Morgan said, "it is nice to be able to sit around in the twilight and ponder on what might have been had we just drilled that Morris No. 1 well on down another nine hundred feet and opened up the 'Teter Oil Field' instead of waiting to see the Empire Company (Cities Service Oil Co. now) do the trick with the rig we had purchased down in Arkansas and shipped to Phillipsburg, Phillips County, Kansas, where Morgan and Company had leased over 240,000 acres in Phillips, Rooks, Graham and Norton counties. Yes, we were going to drill here in 1918, but we decided to reship the rig to Eureka and moved it out on the Morris lease and then the Empire moved in again over on 'Jim Teter's land' in Section 16 just north of the Morris in Section 21 where we had 1,500 ft. hole made with casing set etc. Yes, the Empire moved our rig to the Jim Teter land and they completed the first producing well at 2,400 ft. in the Bartlesville Sand and the 'TETER OIL FIELD' was born and Greenwood County's greatest Oil Field was in the making."

The Morgan company drilled a well in Louisiana in an offset location to a well that was producing one thousand barrels a day for Standard Oil and "when completed made some of the finest salt water in the entire area." The company drilled a dry hole in the Bowie County, Texas, block of leases.

"It just was not in the cards," Morgan said, "for Harry S. Truman to hit the jackpot in the oil business, so, when the war was over and he returned home in 1919, it was agreed to dissolve the firm."

Apparently, he lost no money, however. The five notes for $1,000 each which his mother signed with him were, Morgan says, "soon paid off from the profits accruing to the one third interest which Harry had purchased." They certainly did not get rich. And neither did any of the people who bought the stock advertised in *The Star* five days before war began. The President's old partner Morgan, however, is a philosopher as well as an oil man.

"After all," he says, "it isn't the money which one accumulates which counts so much. No Siree. It is the friends which one makes and keeps down through the years that really counts. That is the way Harry Truman and Dave Morgan would have it, just old friends and BUT GOOD."

More and more of the actual farming behind the plow at

Grandview must have been left to others. It was not hard in those days to pick up hired hands in Grandview or Kansas City. Harry's sister, Mary Jane, had farm-management sense. There were farm hands of dependability and long tenure as well as the ones who came quickly and stayed briefly. Even in those days, however, Harry Truman had the gifts of delegating authority. He was already running a wide and diverse show. The zinc and lead mining down in Oklahoma took time even if only on week ends. He was courting Bess Wallace in Independence, and that took time, too, even if very pleasant time. Problems of the settlement of the estate hung on. The mortgage on Martha Ellen's lands was re-arranged at $25,000 at the Bank of Belton in February 1917. The last quitclaim deed from the other heirs whom Louisa Young had cut off with five dollars each was not recorded until after Harry went into active service as an artilleryman and there was an encompassing sense of urgency about that.

The years were certainly not simply bucolic. There can, however, be no question of the memories from some of those years of the man plowing all day and day after day. The memory of early rising then (4:30 A.M. in the summer, 6:30 A.M. in the winter) is the habit now. He stretched and stapled his fences to hold the hogs and the cattle. He castrated the pigs, and not only farmers remember but also some politicians have noted the phrase from those times that "when Harry sharpens his knife the pigs run out of the pasture." He bucket-fed the weaning calves. He drove the horses from the barn lot and once got a broken leg from the kick of a fractious heifer. He nailed the shingles on the barn and moved the privy. He watched the weather. He hauled the hay. He combed the mules. He could still help his mother with the cooking.

"It was on the farm," she said as an old lady, "that Harry got his common sense. He didn't get it in town."

Yet, obviously, there was pull in the town. There were the people whom a gregarious man needed in his life. There was chance in the town. There was that "hazard" which bound him both to the town and to his father, and which was as important in his life as the sharp, witty common sense which Martha Ellen saw best in her boy perhaps because she gave it to him. Also, those were the years when, not waiting for the end of the war, the movement to town in America was already in full swing.

This was the decade in which urban population in America for the first time passed the total of the people in the rural regions. It had taken more than a century and a quarter to accomplish the change since the first counting in 1790. It was a significant transition in the American story of Independence. Indeed, Mr. Jefferson had feared that when Americans got "piled upon one another in large cities, we shall become corrupt as in Europe, and go to eating one another as they do there." Too little has been understood about it.

The American proportion had shifted: "Generally speaking," Jefferson said, "the proportion which the aggregate of other classes of citizens bears in any State to that of its husbandmen, is the proportion of its unsound to its healthy parts, and is a good enough barometer whereby to measure its degree of corruption."

Actually it was not cities themselves which disturbed Jefferson, as he later pointed out, but the condition of workers in cities "with whom the want of food and clothing necessary to sustain life, has begotten a depravity of morals, a dependence and corruption, which renders them an undesirable accession to a country whose morals are sound." Desperate conditions among men, which produced depravity was his fear. That has continued to be the concern of men who fix their faith firmly in democracy—in the cities and on the land, too. What Jefferson meant was his fear of slums. He would not have confused his faith in the yeomanry with carelessness about the condition of men on the land who later followed or hoped to follow the pursuit of happiness into the towns. He believed in the possibility of democracy where the dignity, the independence, the decency of people were preserved.

The separation between good and evil, independence and corruption, was never clearly drawn at town lines and city limits. Even men in the country were nearer to the towns when Harry Truman moved from the one to the other. When he left his Stafford at Fort Sill there were already six million automobiles in America. Their drivers were increasingly conscious of the roads to town. Certainly, when Harry Truman went to war, though he may not have known it or admitted it, he left the farm forever.

Mary Jane Truman, then a young woman of twenty-eight, took over the operation of the farm in the war years as so many other young women did. Harry came back from war in the spring of

1919, but in the fall they had a sale and sold off all the stock and the farm machinery. It would take another generation—a second World War—to put the Trumans back as farmers on the land. It might have shocked old John Truman even then to see his grandsons, Vivian's boys, farming skillfully in Missouri without a mule or any other work animal on the land. Behind the tractors, however, they plowed the land in careful contours to save the soil.

CHAPTER VI

Safe for Democracy

HARRY TRUMAN HAD been so busy between the farm at Grand-view and the offices of Morgan & Company, oil investments, in the New Ridge Arcade that he got himself excused from service on the Mexican Border. But, on April 7, 1917, when Congress declared war, he went to work with Major John L. Miles and others as an old B Battery enlisted man to build a Field Artillery regiment out of a couple of undermanned batteries in the Missouri National Guard. Miles, a Republican, later became the symbol of the strength of Truman's ties to his comrades in arms. That spring he was only one of those who built the 129th. They went out recruiting while Harry Jobes, a Republican also, and Captain of the Supply Company, stayed in the old convention hall in which Bryan had been nominated and which had been turned quickly into an armory.

At his desk in the big empty hall Jobes cursed continually and audibly at the situation. In those first days after war was declared, the National Guard (and also the Army) seemed almost as empty as the resounding convention hall. In the whole military establishment including the Regular Army and the National Guard, there had been when Congress declared war only 8,990 officers and 185,192 men. The Kansas City regiment was in approximately the same shape. It had only two organized batteries and though they had served on the Mexican Border expiration of enlistments had greatly reduced their membership. A few men came in to talk or enlist. Jobes went on with his work and his cursing. A young priest with a face like Ireland in the sunshine came in. Jobes acknowledged his presence and then went on with his work and with his cursing which represented habit as well as harassment. But by-and-by he remembered his manners.

"Priest," he said, "excuse my cursing."

Young Father L. Curtis Tiernan smiled. No apology was required of the young Protestant captain. He could recognize that the cursing did not come from the heart. Also, he had come to say that, if his Bishop would let him, he would like to be chaplain of the new Field Artillery regiment. At that moment the regiment seemed even to the oathful Captain Jobes to need not only cursing but prayers if it was to be able to help Mr. Wilson make democracy safe on earth—or even to do just some matter-of-fact fighting. Most of all it needed men. A few came in like Father Tiernan. Harry helped round up more. Indeed, Truman did so well that he frankly told his officers that he thought he ought to be a sergeant. He was surprised, however, when Battery F was organized and he was chosen as a lieutenant instead.

If afterwards it became, as the 129th Field Artillery, a famous regiment around its most famous member, that member seemed an unlikely soldier when Major Miles personally examined him and qualified him as a first lieutenant. Undoubtedly he had wanted a military career, but he had the same eyes that had kept him from it. He was thirty-three years old. So far as the record shows he was the first soldier in the direct line of his family since his great-grandfathers served briefly and far from any battles in the War of 1812. The oil company which he hoped would make him rich had just put its big advertisement in *The Star*. He had plenty to do on the farm. Also, he was a son who, despite their understanding elasticity, had never in his whole life been very far from his mother's apron strings. Nobody would have expected him to go. The Middle Border was a long way from Europe. Within a month before the declaration, Missouri's senior Senator, who for years had carried the Democratic Party in Missouri in something resembling the hollow of his hand, had taken his place among Wilson's "little group of wilful men" by opposing the arming of merchant ships. After war was declared, Champ Clark, of Missouri, got out of his high seat as Speaker of the House of Representatives to oppose the draft.

Looking back now, it is easy to see that Harry Truman's decision to go into service was the one which made his whole career.

"My whole political career," he knows, "is based upon my war service and war associates."

What is less easily seen is that his whole career before the war summed up to make him the soldier that he was. Not many generals in that war had behind them such an intent eager reading of military tactics and military history. The farmer and the livestock dealer's son was qualified to understand the horses which pulled the 75mm. guns in the forests and mountains of France. It was because he had been bank clerk and company treasurer that he could do a job which first got him the attention of his superior officers. His political career later was based upon the unexpected skill which he then brought to the handling of lively, tumultuous, sometimes unruly but eager-to-be-led young men.

He was in early enough to assist in the organization of the regiment. Though Captain Jobes went on with his automatic cursing, the convention hall filled up with men—and men in uniforms which very nearly fit them. They marched in the parks and in the streets with increasing pride. They were a regiment of neighbors in the pattern of those days, who would fight as neighbors side by side and come home together to remember together. Also, they had home contentions in the regiment itself. It began with the contest between Kansas City men and the Independence men over the election of their colonel. Independence wanted Edward M. Stayton, who later was to help Truman build dependable and non-political highways for Jackson County. In a Kansas City company, Harry Truman stood with the Kansas City men who wanted and got Colonel Karl D. Klemm. He learned that an American does not always like the man he helps to elect. They went off to war proudly behind their chosen colonel, nevertheless, even if Kansas City's cheering departure was all but drowned out by a pouring rain.

The historians and the veterans always have very different stories to tell of the wars. Generally it is the story of the historian which survives for ardent but nearsighted boys, such as Harry Truman once was, to read. The veteran's recollection may be more essentially accurate, nevertheless, even when it is loud and laughing, rough and profane. A war is never merely the sum of the tactics of staff officers, the logistics of supply, the competitive promises of combatant statesmen. Certainly, it is also —and history in any country may afterwards be shaped by it—the total of the adventure, the comradeship and the escapade of ordinary men. In the United States the memory of the last fight is generally mixed up with the recollection of the great frolic. That is so of the 129th. The war was bad but the comradeship was good. It is celebrated long afterwards not merely in cemeteries but in crowded, smoky hotel rooms and in political campaigns.

The historian's story of that first World War and that first lieutenant who left Kansas City for Camp Doniphan on the Fort Sill reservation in Oklahoma is simply stated. He worked hard at Doniphan, both in the science of field fire and the business of running the regimental canteen. He was one of ten officers and a hundred men, detached to be sent ahead for training, who arrived in France on the S.S. *George Washington* (which was to ferry Woodrow Wilson back and forth to the Peace Conference) on April 13, 1918. That voyage was not only the first time he had crossed an ocean, it was the first time he had seen one. The day of his landing was exactly twenty-seven years before his first day as President of the United States. On April 23, 1918, he was promoted to captain. He attended the Second Corps School, Chatillon-sur-Seine, from April 27 to June 5, when he rejoined the 129th Field Artillery at Camp Coetquidan in Brittany as adjutant of the 2nd Battalion. A month later, on July 11, he was given the command of Battery D of the 129th Field Artillery. It saw service in the Gerardmer Sector from August 20 to September 2. From September 12 to September 16, it was in reserve of the American First Army during the St. Mihiel offensive. From September 21, to September 25, the regiment was in the Grange le Comte defensive sector, and from September 26 to October 3, and from October 15 to the Armistice, in the Meuse-Argonne offensive. Truman returned with his regiment to the United States, April 20, 1919, on the S.S. *Zeppelin,* and was honorably discharged at Camp Funston, Kansas, on May 6, 1919.

The history is undoubtedly all there but scarcely any of the story. Meuse-Argonne, St. Mihiel, Gerardmer, Grange le Comte are words in the record of the world but the story of the war for Harry Truman breaks down into more obscure but no less important items: the spectacular mercantile success of the canteen at Camp Doniphan; the demonstration that he could control and lead rambunctious Battery D; the acquisition of both a picaresque vocabulary and a strong respect for and from men of other origins and religions; the Battle of Who Run; and the interminable poker game which began in the woods back of Verdun in November 1918, and continued in the villages around Le Mans until April 1919. More important than any of these and perhaps the sum of them all was the phalanx of friends whom he made in that war and in most cases kept ever afterwards.

It would be difficult to think of a milder-seeming young man than the one who peers through his spectacles diffidently from the photograph of Harry Truman, Lieutenant in the Missouri National Guard. Obviously a National Guard barber had cut his hair and cut it high. What remained on the top was plastered down flat and dark. The mouth, the nose and the chin are strong to a suggestion of stubbornness under the bashfulness in his mild eyes. It looks like the photograph of bank clerk or bookkeeper in uniform. Even without knowledge of his experience, it would be easy to understand his selection as a dependable man to put in charge of the canteen which the regimental authorities set up soon after arrival at Camp Doniphan. They picked Lieutenant Truman, and Lieutenant Truman picked as his assistant Sergeant Edward Jacobson.

Eddie Jacobson, who had enlisted in the 129th about the same time Truman was commissioned, was a young Jew whom Truman had first known when he was a clerk in the National Bank of Commerce and Jacobson in his teens was already working in a men's furnishing store at Eighth and Walnut streets. He was seven years younger than Truman but had ten years of experience in merchandising. Indeed, he had almost a hereditary experience. He was born in New York in 1891, the son of a Jewish shoemaker who moved to Leavenworth, Kansas, entered the clothing business and later went to Kansas City. Eddie was one of six children. He was a good Jew who went regularly to the synagogue.

Neither one of them had ever seen a canteen before they organized that one at Camp Doniphan. Truman had never in his life sold anything but farm products and some oil stock. They had, however, in Kansas City built up a mess fund for Battery F when, at Jacobson's suggestion, they gave a dance and showed a movie of Battery B in action on the Mexican Border. They made $2,600, Jacobson recalls. It is not strange that after that it seemed a good idea to put the regimental canteen "under the responsible supervision of Lieutenant Truman with Jacobson as exchange steward." They were already a team. On the funds from the batteries which they collected to stock and start the canteen ($2 a man) in six months, according to the regimental historian, they paid dividends of $15,000 or 666 per cent. It was commended at the time as the most businesslike and efficiently managed canteen in the division. Also, undoubtedly, its success even then put post-war ideas into Harry Truman's head.

They had their troubles. There were some in the regiment who would have pushed Eddie around if Lieutenant Truman had not stood steadily with him. One captain tried to get Jacobson to pay him his battery's dividends in cash. There were other incidents. Indeed, the meeting of Harry Truman with one of the most controversial friends of his presidential years took place while Brigadier General Lucien G. Berry, of the 60th Field Artillery Brigade, was giving Truman a big-brass blowing up for some such detail as trash on the floor of the canteen. He was interrupted by a noisy arrival which became familiar later in Washington. With loud talk, wisecrack and laughter, Second Lieutenant Harry Hawkins Vaughan of the 130th Field Artillery trooped up the walk with some friends and threw open the door. He both drowned out the General and took the heat off Harry. Berry turned upon the new offender.

"How long have you been an officer?" he demanded.

"One week, sir."

"I hope you'll learn to be a better one."

"I hope so, sir," said Vaughan.

The General departed in a brassy disgust. Undoubtedly, however, the success of the canteen had much to do with the selection of Truman as one of the officers and men selected to go to France ahead of the regiment for training. That record entered into his promotion to a captaincy before he began the special training in France at the beautiful town of Chatillon-sur-Seine in the department of Côte-d'Or. It was probably responsible for his selection as commanding officer of Battery D.

It was already Dizzy D. Also, its members were called "Teasley's Hackdrivers" from both the quality of the men and a first lieutenant named Walter Teasley who had been in charge before Truman took command. It was composed of Kansas City boys, a high percentage of whom were Irish Catholics. The suggestion has grown across the years that they were the tough Irish of section-hand, hack-driver, and rough-neighborhood status. Actually, from the point of view of discipline they may have been tougher than that. A good many of them were college boys with more intelligence than docility. They had been recruited from the neighborhood of Rockhurst College, a Jesuit school in Kansas City. The battery certainly had a bad name for lack of discipline. Indeed, by the time Truman took command it was pretty clear that it took a lively pride in its mustang reputation. It had been too much for three captains who preceded Truman to command. It figured that it could have more fun with a bespectacled fourth. It has been stated that Colonel Klemm was contemplating breaking up the battery and shifting its men to others but that Truman persuaded him to let him try his hand at its command.

"I always tried to do every job I got better than anybody had ever done it before," Truman once said of his captaincy of Battery D.

"When I first took command of the battery I called all the sergeants and corporals together. I told them I knew they had been making trouble for the previous commanders. I said, 'I didn't come over here to get along with you. You've got to get along with me. And if there are any of you who can't, speak up right now and I'll bust you right back now.'"

In terms of both his jaw and the gray eyes through those glasses, it was apparent that he meant it.

"We got along," Truman said.

Indeed, he took command on July 11, and when the regiment moved out toward the front on August 17 and 18, the official historian of the 129th Field Artillery has noted that "the R.T.O. at Guer officially advised D Battery that its time of loading, 48 minutes, was the best record up to that date." The final test did not come, however, until that event which, not in the records but in the recollections of the 129th, is known as the Battle of Who Run. It occurred in the Gerardmer Sector, a "quiet sector" in Alsace where D Battery was in position high on Mount Herrenberg in the Vosges Mountains. There, on the evening of August 29, 1918, the 129th let loose a barrage of gas shells, "the liveliest thing that had occurred in that sector for some time," and got a quick German retaliation. D Battery particularly was subjected to a combined high explosive and gas shell fire and in the midst of it occurred the Battle of Who Run.

Its official description is as follows: "While withdrawing from its temporary firing position after the barrage, D Battery had four horses killed, and on account of the mud it was not possible to move two of the pieces with the horses remaining. Officers and men joined in running one gun back under cover, and the other was camouflaged with branches, and both were left until they could be returned for with sufficient horses the following evening, and safely removed back to the old position. . . . For their cool courage on this occasion Privates John Gordon, William O'Hare and Glenn Woods of 'D' Battery were later cited in General Orders."

Harry Truman tells the story more vividly.

"It was a serious thing when it happened," he said. "Our regular battery positions were in the Herrenberg forests in the Vosges Mountains. Somebody took a notion to fire three thousand rounds of gas at the Germans. So we had to move to another position and put the batteries into place to fire five hundred rounds at seven o'clock. The horses were sent back. As soon as the last round was fired they were to come with the horses. They were twenty or twenty-five minutes late. I got on a horse to see what was going on. He fell in a shellhole and rolled over on me. The German batteries began to fire on us. The sergeant gave the men by the wrong flank and two of our guns got stuck in the mud. While we were working to release them the Germans fired very close to us and this sergeant hollered, 'Run, boys, they got a bracket on us.'"

Years later Truman's mouth hardened as he recalled that moment.

"I got up and called them everything I knew." It was, by that time, quite a lot. Missouri males may not use a vernacular which is unintelligible to males in other parts of America, but the language of rural Missouri and Kansas City combined is sometimes strong enough to shock the stranger. At the big bend of the Missouri the combination is the collected profanity brought in by the mule men, the cattle men, the corn and oil men, the Missouri River boatmen, the houn' dog Southerners, and the muscular-minded Irish. In the hands of an expert it is a merger which combines the best features of them all. It is an instrument suited alike to anger and hilarity. By the time he got to the Vosges, Harry Truman was a master of its use, and that night in the Herrenberg forest must have been a classic example of Middle Border and Kansas City cussing by a master. His shouts on that mountainside were a thunder of imprecations upon the maternity of the Irish and the courage of the Irish, neither of which are to be lightly referred to. He gave them everything he had ever heard, with flourishes.

"Pretty soon they came sneaking back," Truman said.

That night the Irish boys apparently were as fascinated as they were frightened. Today Truman is a tired, tough man even when he tells about it.

"The Major and the Colonel wanted me to court-martial the sergeant. I didn't but I busted him and afterwards I had to transfer him to another battery. Later in the war, he stood firm under the fiercest fire.

"I didn't care for court-martials," he said. "I'd get myself back of a table and I'd look as mean as I could. Then I'd tell them, 'You can have a court-martial or, if you prefer, you can take what I give you.' That worked."

It was a battery of high morale, swearing by its captain, which got the news of the Armistice in its position on a rocky hillside just east of Verdun. More remarkable, it kept its morale in the five more senseless-seeming months in which it waited in muddy camp behind Verdun and then in crowded villages around Le Mans before it received orders to head home. Truman, whose men had watched the sharpness of his eyes behind the spectacles in spotting enemy batteries and in reconnaissance far ahead of the batteries, watched his men in both discipline and consideration. Stories remain of offers of loans along with leave to Irish boys who still had relatives on the Old Island. He looked at France in peace, too, and remembered the planting of the trees along its roads when he began the building of highways later in Jackson County. He saw many things in France which rose out of his memory later. A man realized how much there was to see in the good silence after the last gun.

"I can remember," Truman said when another war came, "that on November 10, 1918, we'd got our orders to move down the following afternoon into the valley of Verdun. That next morning some units did move down. Some men I knew and that I thought a lot of got killed that morning. If we had moved down that morning some of us would have got it."

The living were lucky. Indeed, considering its combat record it was a lucky war for D Battery. Not a man in it was afterwards listed by the regimental historian as having been "killed in action," though the deaths of four in France and one on the ship coming home were listed as deaths in line of duty. In addition to them only two men were listed as wounded in action. Not all the living were so lucky. It was in the first days after the last firing that Truman saw his first Russians. There was a big camp of Russian soldiers, who had been German prisoners, just west of the camp of the 129th Field Artillery at Verdun. The revolution in Russia left them both homesick and homeless. They hung about the camp of the 129th and sought any possible remnants of the American rations.

"They were great big, fine-looking fellows," Truman recalled later, "and they were virtually starving. As people they made a good impression on all of us. They were like shepherd dogs, so grateful that it was pitiful."

It was a homesick time even for Americans. Yet, it was a time in which the swift associations of war were firmly fixed. Major John Miles, commanding officer of the First Battalion, and Harry Jobes, whose steady profanity that winter seemed quite as appropriate as it had seemed in the empty convention hall at the war's beginning, remained Truman's friends. (Jobes served in the RFC after Truman became President.) Father Tiernan, who was gassed in that war beside the troops, joined his friend President Truman at Potsdam after World War II in which Father Tiernan served as Chief of Army Chaplains in the European Theater. James M. Pendergast, son of Mike and nephew of Tom, who ran the politics of Kansas City and Jackson County, was a second lieutenant. First Lieutenant Edgar G. Hinde became postmaster of Independence. Captain Roger T. Sermon, regimental adjutant, was to be mayor of Independence, candidate for Governor, and Truman's assistant in some of his toughest political fights. There were other friends of the years ahead like Theodore Marks, the English tailor who became an American captain. There was a private in the company whom Truman made study law and later got appointed as a Federal judge. There was a sergeant in his battery who was to be with him in Washington on the night when Truman first admitted that Roosevelt's declining health meant that he would become President of the United States. Also, among friends then was Captain Spencer Salisbury of Battery E, who would become Truman's business associate and then his most bitter enemy.

Not many of them nor any other people in the world had noted the prophetic phrase in Pershing's order which had come, on November 11, in the woods of Verdun: "Every emphasis will be laid on the fact that the arrangement is an armistice only and not a peace." The Peace Conference opened at Paris before the 129th got its orders to move out of the muddy camp in the woods. The regiment came to its new and more habitable billet-ing station in the Le Mans area on the day before Wilson won from the Peace Conference an agreement that the League of Nations would be an integral part of the peace treaty. The 129th Field Artillery could be very little help in shaping that peace. While they waited, Senator James A. Reed, of Missouri, was already fighting Wilson in the Senate. Colonel Klemm got his orders to leave the regiment and go home for other duty on February second: "every man amongst you has always performed his full duty." He was lucky to be one of the first to be going home. The peace did not seem a time in which he would commit suicide, but he did. A new colonel took over. The batteries were kept alert and shining for such occasions as the regiment's review, in a pouring rain, by General Pershing and the Prince of Wales. Not much could be done about a Kansas City Irish-man who cracked loud enough for his battery commander, if not the Prince, to hear, "Hey, Captain Truman! What did the little so-and-so say about freeing Ireland?" The waiting was not any easier on the officers.

"To keep from going crazy," said Roger Sermon, "we had an almost continuous poker game."

Truman and Sermon lived, after the regiment moved from Verdun, with other officers in a small chateau near Courcemont. Salisbury, whose battery had acquired the name "Carranza and His Forty Thieves" from its Mexican service, with his soldier's skill in looking out for himself, had found pleasant and private quarters on the second floor of a house occupied by two old maids in a village near by. It was a good place to play the long game. Salisbury's sergeant knew how to find the right kind of wine. It was not their business that the peace was not being made. They played poker and not even very serious poker, though Missourians can make poker a very serious enterprise. The problem was passing time. Once the game went on far into the night. It not only seemed too far to leave the game and the house; also, at the time it seemed a great joke to use the windows. It did not seem funny, however, to the old maids, or to the Colonel when they reported it to him in a long letter reciting their Gallic indignation. In the stern discipline which necessarily had to be maintained all the other players listened in stony silence while Regimental Adjutant Sermon, who had started it all, read solemnly the Colonel's reprimand to Captain Salisbury on the basis of the old maids' complaint.

The 129th was only part of an army and a country which slipped from unity of purpose into private prank and a juvenile lack of concern for any future except each individual's own. Slow as it seemed in France, American disbandment moved faster than after any earlier great war. By February 15, 1919, men mustered out totaled 1,246,218 as compared with the 640,806 Union soldiers released during exactly the same interval after Appomattox. By January, 1920, the Army was down to a peacetime low of 130,000 men. The men coming out had plenty of problems of their own. A few remembered the problem of the peace, but not enough. Senator James A. Reed, who had helped kill Wilson's peace, was re-elected by Missouri after the war though not with Harry Truman's consent.

"I never liked Reed," he said later. "I hated his guts after the way he treated Wilson. I supported him the first two times he ran, but the third time I was against him."

He added with a wry pride: "He was opposed to me every time I ran for anything."

Harry Truman was not running for anything that winter after the Armistice. He was coming home and planning ahead for the long delayed home-coming. He was to be married on June 28, 1919, six weeks after he returned to Missouri. He was not going back to the farm. The oil business was in process of dissolution.

"I didn't know what I wanted to do," he said later. "I had $15,000 or $20,000 and eighty acres of land which I had inherited from my uncle."

There was a lot of angry talk in those days about mounting distinctions between officers and enlisted men. But Harry Truman remembered Sergeant Eddie Jacobson and their success in the canteen at Camp Doniphan. Though he was in another battery he saw Jacobson occasionally in France. They came home together on the S.S. *Zeppelin* and were both discharged at Camp Funston, Kansas, on May 6, two days before Truman's thirty-fifth birthday. He still was not certain what he wanted to do except marry Bess Wallace and stay at home with her. It was after they were married that he met Jacobson again one day in Kansas City in July. They talked long and seriously.

"We'll have a partnership again," Truman said.

They began planning, working, buying then, but it was fall before they opened the store on Twelfth Street just across from the entrance of the new Muehlebach and around the corner from the older and famous Baltimore Hotel.

CHAPTER VII

Any Number Can Play

WHEAT SOLD FOR $2.15 that year.

And before Christmas in 1919 Harry Truman was a partner in his own business and a happily married man. Probably there never was a busier, happier six months in his whole life than those between the spring in which he came home and the autumn in which he and Eddie opened their haberdashery store near the corner of Twelfth and Baltimore streets in Kansas City.

It took them time to find and fix and stock the store near that corner which did seem at the very crossroads of America. As a matter of fact either Twelfth or Baltimore could probably have better qualified as American Main Street than the mean stretch of pavement in Gopher Prairie upon the description of which Sinclair Lewis was working that year. The Muehlebach and Baltimore hotels brought to that corner the congregation of the Main Streets of the prairies and the Panhandle, of the corn country and the wheat lands, the cattle ranges and the oil fields. The South drawled there. The North traded there. In those days there were as many big Western hats, black, tan and putty-colored, as any others on that corner.

The people, who crowded that crossing in those days and made Truman & Jacobson's rent high and apparently worth it, were not much worried by the sharp suggestions of Sinclair Lewis that the American promise had turned sour in drabness and regimentation. ("Standardization" by business sickened the intellectuals before "regimentation" by government disturbed the business men.) Oddly enough, the little business man, who seemed so vacuous and vulgar to the satirists in such cities then, was the Free Enterprise which seemed so important later. Undoubtedly, however, there was a standard, if materialistic, hope for the glittering plumbing, the new cars, the bright shirts, which seemed to the satirists less the signs of hope for a new standard of living than the stigmata of a land become futile, complacent and dull, though loud in them all.

Harry Truman made no noise that summer of 1919. He fitted snugly into the picture of the returning soldier trying with as little ado as possible to adjust himself to normal civilian life and not into any special "normalcy" of the early twenties. In later years it was sometimes fastidiously suggested that haberdashery was not quite appropriate in the past of a President. Lincoln had been a storekeeper who failed, but "gents' furnishings" seemed even less dignified than Andrew Johnson's tailoring. It was a descent from heroic soldier, great musician, oil millionaire, even farmer. The simple explanation is that it promised security (they had made 666 per cent at Doniphan) at a time when that was more important than anything else in the world—or ever before in the world.

Within less than two months after he came home he was married to a woman whose reticences about her personal life are remarkable. On June 28, 1919, when he and Elizabeth Virginia Wallace were married in the diminutive Trinity Episcopal Church by the Reverend John W. Plunkett, each was thirty-five years old. Ted Marks, recently Captain of C Battery of the 129th, was best man and as tailor-returned-to-his-shears made the wedding suits for both the groom and himself. When Harry and Bess came home from their brief honeymoon, they settled for the rest of their lives in the big Wallace-Gates house at 219 North Delaware Street in Independence. Mrs. Truman has been as close as possible to his work and as far as possible from his publicity in all the years since. Even in the White House their lives have been kept separate from his politics.

That has not always been easy. In the publicity of the Presidency, their story as childhood sweethearts has been repeatedly stirred and sweetened by the sentimental and the merely curious. And the question has been repeatedly asked, why, if they were sweethearts all their lives, did they wait until they were practically middle-aged before they married. Both were the eldest children of widowed mothers. Harry had been slow in settling into the career which satisfied him. Undoubtedly, also, he had much competition in his courtship. The only proper answer to such questions was given by Harry's mother before she died.

"Maybe," she said, "Bess wouldn't have him."

Everybody who knows them is agreed that so far as Harry Truman was concerned there never was any other girl except Bess Wallace. There is equal unanimity about the fact that no girl in Independence had more beaux than Bess. There was considerable difference between them as children. If Harry was an almost womanish little boy, Bess Wallace was a tomboy who grew into an athletic girl. One of her schoolmates has unkindly remembered that she "was the first girl I ever knew who could whistle through her teeth." She could beat all the boys at mumbly-peg. With his eyes, Harry could not hope to join her at tennis. (There is a story in Independence that at least one of her other beaux lost out because, though not as good a player as Bess, he always shouted to her that he would get the ball when they were playing doubles together.) There were similarities in the lives of Harry and Bess, nevertheless. The Wallaces like the Trumans had come from Kentucky. The year in which the Trumans moved to Kansas City after the failure of Harry's father, Bess Wallace's father died. He had been a precocious citizen. According to the 1881 *History of Jackson County,* he was assistant docket clerk of the Missouri State Senate when he was fourteen. At thirty-one he was Eminent Commander of the Knights Templar of Missouri. He had held a number of public offices including that of county treasurer. Also, he was "the handsomest man in town." But he left little property when he died. Bess moved with her widowed mother to live with her Grandmother Gates.

That house at 219 North Delaware is impressive in Independence. It was built by Bess Truman's grandfather, George P. Gates, whose father had come to Independence from Vermont after the Civil War. George Gates was one of the founders of the Waggoner-Gates Milling Company which still makes "Queen of the Pantry Flour." George Gates was a stalwart Presbyterian and even his English-born wife, Elizabeth Emery, went with him to his Calvinistic church. That is how Episcopalian Bess Wallace happened to be in the Presbyterian Sunday School when the little Baptist Truman children accepted the minister's invitation to attend when they moved to Independence. It was after George Gates' death that the Church of England tradition of

Grandmother Gates took Bess and her mother back into the Episcopal Church.

The legend that the Wallaces were of higher social position and greater riches than the Trumans and that that delayed the marriage still persists. It does not bother the President, but some of his Truman kin have been restive under its repetition. Neither the Wallaces nor the Trumans, however, could have been counted as rich in 1919 when Harry Truman and Bess Wallace were married.

Truman's memory is that he had $15,000 or $20,000 and eighty acres of land, which he had inherited from his Uncle Harrison, when he came home from war. It seems clear, however, from a study of the records and transfers of the Solomon and Louisa Young lands that he took his share of that estate in cash for his business ventures. The month before he entered the oil business, with his mother's help in 1916, he gave her a quitclaim deed to all his rights in his Uncle Harrison's estate. Also, in the fall of 1919, when he was going into the haberdashery business with Jacobson, he was active in getting for his mother a quitclaim deed from the last of Louisa's other heirs. Harry also gave his mother, Mary Jane and Vivian a quitclaim deed for all his interests in the farm. Martha Ellen, Vivian and Mary Jane divided up the Young lands with Harry taking no share. Soon afterwards Martha Ellen, Vivian and Mary Jane all gave mortgages on their lands.

The store opened in the fall. It took money to stock it. As after all wars, there was a huge mass-buying of clothing by the returning soldiers though they were a little surprised, despite letters from home, by the new prices. One joke of the demobilized was: "A man without a dollar is fifty cents better off that he used to be." Those were the days of the fifteen-dollar silk shirt. But people who were getting $2.15 for wheat, and working at town jobs in the Middle Border on the basis of that sort of agricultural support, were ready to buy them. It was at such levels that Truman and Jacobson put in their stock. Eddie, out of his experience, served as buyer and mark-up man. Truman's popularity was a basis of the store's good will and he served as salesman of neckties, shirts, belts, socks and hats.

"We opened the store at eight in the morning and closed at nine at night," Jacobson recalls. "Twelfth Street was in its hey-

day and our war buddies and the Twelfth Street boys and girls
were our customers. Those were the days when the boys wore
silk underwear and silk shirts. We sold shirts at sixteen dollars.
Our business was all cash. No credit. Harry and I worked re-
verse shifts and we had a clerk all the time. Harry did the book-
keeping and I did the buying. We both did the selling."

There was easy money on Twelfth Street in those days. It was
the real "whiteway" of a wide-open Kansas City and Middle
America around it. In 1950 the Phillips Hotel entrance opened
where the store was in 1919. The Muehlebach remained across
the street. But the famous old Baltimore was gone. In those
old days in the Dixon Hotel on another corner, two wide-open
gambling houses operated, one upstairs and one in the basement. "Craps," Jacobson remembers, was the principal game.
There were always women hustling on the street. The side-
walks were crowded long after dark and Truman & Jacobson
stayed open every night to get the trade. By the autumn of 1920,
however, the price of wheat had dropped from $2.15 to $1.44 a
bushel. The girls on the street, the men in the gambling houses
and people who sold neckties noticed a difference.

Warren Harding, who passed through Kansas City not long
before he was nominated in the well-known smoke-filled room
at Chicago, defined "normalcy" in a campaign speech in July
1920. Less than a year later farm prices had tumbled forty per
cent. People on farms netted only $3,795,000,000 in 1921—com-
pared with $8,368,000,000 in 1920. In the towns in 1919, there
were 6,451 mercantile and industrial insolvencies with liabilities
of $113,291,237; in 1921, there were 19,652 with liabilities of
$627,401,883. Something of the same sort was happening on the
farms—at Grandview and elsewhere in the Middle Border.
Harding's Secretary of Agriculture, who was the father of Roosevelt's Secretary of Agriculture, reported that from 1920 to 1923
nearly ten per cent of the farmers of Missouri had lost their
farms or held them only through the leniency of creditors. Old
Martha Ellen never seemed like a statistic but she probably
belonged in that last one.

It is hard to see that swift, destructive depression (which was
not actually so swift in passing in the farm country) through the
darkness of the Depression we spell with a capital "D," which
did not hit Harry as hard as the earlier one. The sense of im-

potence and frustration was certainly greater when dependence
was on Harding rather than Roosevelt. That same Wallace who
was Secretary of Agriculture under Harding has left a clear
picture of the farmer's situation:

"In times such as these the problems of farm management on
most farms are reduced to the simplest terms and can be stated
very briefly. For example: produce as much as you can and as
cheaply as you can of what you can produce best; spend as little
as you can; do without everything you can; work as hard as you
can; make your wife and children work as hard as they can.
Having done this, take what comfort you can in the thought that
if you succeed in doing what you set out to do, and if most
other farmers also succeed, you will have provided larger crops
than can be sold at a profit and you will still be under the
harrow. Nevertheless, the average farmer is forced by unhappy
circumstance to adopt exactly that policy. It is not good for the
farmer, not good for the farmer's wife and children, not good
for the nation."

It duplicated, however, the situation that faced Harry Truman and Eddie Jacobson. Having made their contracts and
put in their inventories at the level of $2.15 wheat, they were
only energetically losing when they labored to sell shirts and
socks and ties at the prices to which they had been forced to
mark them down. Measuring by that wheat price, Truman &
Jacobson not only failed in 1922 exactly twenty years after John
Truman bet wrong on wheat futures on the Board of Trade;
also, they failed for approximately the same cause. Not all the
gambling was on the Board of Trade, in Legion crap games, or
even in the big open gambling houses on the other side of the
corner. The widow on the farm, the small haberdasher, the
worker and the harvester were in the same game. Any number
could play.

"We did a remarkable business the first couple of years until
old Mellon got in his licks," Truman said years afterwards.
"Then we saw an inventory of $30,000 or $40,000 drop down to
about $10,000 value." In 1945, he wrote from the office of the
Vice-President when Jacobson was going into business for himself again: "Don't let them catch you on an inflation squeeze
as they did us before."

That was not merely an alibi afterwards. William Allen White in his *Autobiography* says that the national directors of the Federal Reserve Bank in New York decided by formal resolution in 1921 to deflate the currency: "After the war, labor troubles broke out all over the country. The high wages which prevailed during the war, wages symbolized by silk shirts on workers and a great herd of new and secondhand Fords stampeding over the country, persuaded the American banking interests that their job as viceregent of God in the United States required them to do something about labor. They felt that deflation would take the crimp out of arrogant labor leaders and help Harding restore the country to normalcy. But they made a bad guess. Deflation did not hit labor but it did hit the American farmer, and it hit especially hard the cattlemen of the Middle West."

It hit Harry Truman. Years later he figured that he "lost about $28,000 in this business." He refused to take bankruptcy. As late as 1934 there was an unsatisfied judgment of $8,944.78 against him in favor of the Security State Bank of Kansas City. Across the years he settled such claims on the basis of the best settlement he could get, but they hung heavy on him even after he was Senator, more than a decade later. In January 1922, as a part of the failure he transferred to the Security State Bank a 160-acre farm in Johnson County, Kansas, for which just six months before he had paid $5,000 and assumed a mortgage of $8,800 which was on it. Truman's memory is that he got it by "swapping a flat in Kansas City for it." That farm is an interesting item in the story of inflated values in the Middle Border. Just twelve years before Truman thought it was worth $13,800, it had sold in July 1909, mortgage free, for $2,250.

In the case of neither Truman nor Jacobson is it possible to figure the total losses from the partnership. Each lost all he invested in it as well as the debts acquired in the business. Jacobson's bankruptcy petition in February 1925, however, shows total debts still unpaid of $10,058.50, of which the two largest debts were $5,600 to the Commerce Trust Company (when it failed, its paper was transferred to the Security State Bank) and $3,900 due Louis Oppenstein, their landlord, on the remainder of the lease for the store which still had some months to go when they failed. Other smaller debts were owed a cloak and suit company and Cluett, Peabody & Company for shirts, which seemed the symbol of the inflation and deflation of the times.

Jacobson listed all his assets as $507 (including $28 cash on hand) and claimed that the whole $507 was exempt from his debts under the law. Later, when Truman settled claims against him, Jacobson insisted on reimbursing Truman for his part. Also, after the failure and after Truman was a county official, they met one day for lunch and Truman saw how frayed were the clothes of his old partner in "gents' furnishings." He went into his own not very full pocket and brought out some money.

"Don't spend it," he told Jacobson, "on anything but clothes." And probably he called him then the standard term of endearment which Jacobson as old friend and old comrade understands and appreciates, "You bald-headed so-and-so." A sentimental man like Eddie Jacobson will never forget the incident. His heart warms to the phrase.

The whole world looked a little frayed in the late winter and early spring of 1922. Then, one day the big Locomobile of Michael J. Pendergast rolled up Twelfth Street and stopped at the curb. Truman had known Mike as a man interested in the politics of Jackson County. Also, he knew him better as the father of his war associate, Lieutenant Jim Pendergast.

"I was in the store one day just when we were going broke," Truman recalls. "I had had a job offered me with an insurance and building and loan company. But I was standing behind the counter feeling fairly blue when Mike Pendergast came in.

" 'How'd you like to be county judge?'

" 'I don't know,' I told him.

" 'If you would, you can have it,' he said."

That is the most simple and direct story of the entrance of Harry Truman into politics. Mike was the older, but subordinate, brother of Thomas J. Pendergast, head of the Kansas City Democratic organization. Mike, himself, in Kansas City was boss of the Tenth Ward—the old "Bloody Tenth" which had been bloody even before the Pendergasts organized it—and presided over its destinies at the Tenth Ward Democratic Club, Inc., of which he was permanent chairman. Also, under his brother Tom, he exercised a special supervision over county affairs outside of Kansas City.

Others tell different stories. Spencer Salisbury, who was a Pendergast follower long before Truman, says that Truman had wanted to run for county judge from Eastern Jackson County in

1920. It should be stated here immediately and clearly that in Missouri a county judge is not a "judge" in the usually accepted judicial meaning of that term. It is a peculiarly Missourian term for a county administrative officer who is called county commissioner in most other American states. Salisbury says that he took Truman down that year to see Tom Pendergast about it. Pendergast's office then was in a cubbyhole off the lobby of his Jefferson Hotel at Sixth and Wyandotte streets. Pendergast, says Salisbury, told Truman then that he had already promised his support to Jim Gilday.

"Come around next time," Salisbury says Tom told Truman.

Salisbury's recollection seems to be inaccurate. Truman and Salisbury were friends then, but Truman was doing very well in the haberdashery business in 1920, and his wife, Bess, like a good many other ladies in Missouri and elsewhere, had no very high opinion of politics as a career. (Sometimes she gives the impression of feeling that way still.) Also, in that year Truman for the only time in his life scratched the Democratic ticket to vote for Major John L. Miles as marshal of Jackson County.

A more familiar story is that of Colonel William M. Southern, Jr., editor of *The Independence Examiner,* who is well known in Missouri as the writer of a syndicated Sunday School column. In 1922, he says, Truman came into his office and said that he was going to run for county judge. Southern, whose daughter later married Bess Truman's brother, says that he advised Truman not to run. He has told the story often, perhaps never more vividly than in the version he gave to Edward R. Schauffler, well-known Kansas City newspaperman.

"Look, Harry," the Colonel told Schauffler that he said, "I know you're discouraged over your business failure and I'm sorry. But there's no reason to be as downhearted as that. Don't mess up your whole life by going into politics. It's no disgrace to have failed in business. Many good men have done that. You'll make good at some other business. Cheer up, Harry."

That was not all: "I abused him like a pickpocket for an hour. I told him all the bad effects a life of chronic campaigning could have on a man. I told him how poor were its rewards, how will-o'-the-wisp its promises, how undermining the constant need for popular approval could be to a man's character. I told him how hard it was on a man's family to have him in politics. Still he smiled and shook his head, and repeated he intended to make a career in politics."

Colonel Southern, who liked to keep a little thumbnail-size piece of tobacco under his lip, must have preached a sermon. He was not only undoubtedly sincere about his advice to Harry. Also, the anti-Pendergast faction in Eastern Jackson County counted on him not to back Truman because it had supported Colonel Southern's brother, Allen Carriger Southern, for circuit judge. However, Harry's eagerness shook him. He agreed to go in his behalf to see Nick Phelps, Mike Pendergast's lieutenant in Eastern Jackson County.

" 'Who the hell is Harry Truman?' " Southern says Phelps said to him. It was a question due to be repeated on several occasions in later years. The Washington correspondent of *The Kansas City Journal-Post* asked Congressman Joseph Shannon that, in 1934 when Shannon decided not to run for the Senate and came back to Washington with the news that Truman would. Also, in July 1944, as Franklin Roosevelt's train headed west from Chicago toward a "West Coast Naval Base," he told Admiral William D. Leahy that the vice-presidential nominee would be Senator Truman.

The Admiral, who was to become one of Truman's most devoted advisers in later years, put down his glass. "Who the hell is Harry Truman?" he asked.

Usually the answer was known but it was more than a rhetorical question when Nick Phelps asked it. It gave Colonel Southern an opportunity to describe Harry as his candidate. And Phelps listened skeptically but solemnly. The Colonel warmed to his task. Years later Truman threw some light upon Nick's solemnity by describing what actually happened after Mike Pendergast drove up in his Locomobile and offered him the job, there at the counter in the lingering but failing store of Truman & Jacobson.

"So Nick Phelps came to see me," Truman related later. "He said, 'Now, Harry, I want you to help me play some slick politics.' Nick had told Southern that if he would suggest a good man, he could get Mike Pendergast to support him. So we worked it out that Southern suggested me."

Colonel Southern has been proud of his suggestion ever since. Undoubtedly, also, Nick Phelps thought as long as he lived that

as Pendergast's lieutenant he had slickly got Colonel Southern's
support for Harry Truman though the Colonel's brother had
been made a judge by the anti-Pendergast faction. Actually, the
picture is not completely clear from either the Southern or the
Phelps point of view. There is a Truman modesty involved
which sometimes—not often—confuses Truman himself.

When Mike Pendergast came into Truman & Jacobson's haberdashery in 1922 and told Truman he could be county judge if
he wanted to be, his offer may have seemed as substantial as big
Mike himself or his long Locomobile parked at the door. Actually, though Mike would have denied it with loud Irish blustering, that day he was not offering but asking. That is not the
customary view of the scene in the store. Generally it is looked
back upon across the horrid Humpty-Dumptiness of Boss Tom
Pendergast's great fall before the sudden-seeming disclosure of
his physical, moral and political disintegration on Good Friday
in 1939. In such retrospect, full Pendergast power appears par-
allel with the modern history of Kansas City and much of Missouri, including the whole of the first and second phases of the
political career of Harry Truman.

The clear truth is that when Mike walked heavily back to his
Locomobile and headed up Twelfth Street in the general direction of the battered bronze statue of his brother, Jim, who had
founded the Pendergast dynasty, he knew that, if Truman
agreed, Truman and the Pendergasts together would have a hard
time winning that election. The Pendergasts had rivals within
the Democratic Party. There was the shrewd Joseph Shannon
who was a troublesome terrier at the Pendergast heels for three
decades. Also, at that time there was a brightly dressed and
strutting little politician named Miles Bulger. They had completely euchred the Pendergasts out of the county courthouse
into which Mike had just confidently promised to put Harry.
Bulger had announced, while Tom Pendergast was suffering
from a mastoid infection, that he meant to take over as boss.
It was not an impossible impudence. The Ku Klux Klan, which
did not like the Irish or the Italians or the Negroes of the Kansas City constituency—and particularly did not like Tom Pendergast—was rising in Jackson County as in the United States.
There was one other detail: The Pendergasts, who offered the job
of judge from Eastern Jackson County to Harry, had previously

entered into an agreement allotting that job, in a division of political spoils, to the Shannon faction. With good reason, the Pendergasts thought, they were running out of that agreement, but it would take some running. In Jackson County the Pendergast situation looked a little sick and not merely behind Tom's ear.

Truman had more to offer the Pendergasts than the Pendergasts had to offer him. In the area of their greatest danger, he was a member of one of the oldest families in Eastern Jackson County, which contains both Independence and Grandview. There was, in 1922, no veteran in Jackson County who, in his hard luck at so central a location as well as in his continuing comradeship, served better as a rallying point for those veterans whose solidarity in America sometimes increased as the bright promises of the peace seemed personally more and more dull. Some of those veterans had been talking in the store about politics. Harry was a Baptist. He brought his increasing prominence as a Mason to the ticket of the Irish Catholic bosses. And, as county candidate for the city politicians, he was still well known as a farmer and farm organization man. In later years he clung sometimes almost comically to his "country boy" status. Indeed, in that state politician's handbook, the *Official Manual, State of Missouri,* for 1937-38, he skipped over the post-war, hard-luck Kansas City years and put after his war record, "Went back to the farm." It was only for a visit. He was at home, country or town. He had a gift for listening to people. Also, while he lacked his mother's sometimes sardonic wit, he had an almost convulsive appreciation of other people's jokes. He was no public speaker but his lack of oratorical powers apparently made him seem a man and neighbor who was not a politician at all.

Most of that Harry Truman knew the day when Mike came into the store, and a good deal of it Mike knew that Harry knew. Truman never mentioned any of it to Mike. Somehow at last Truman had come to a decision about his career. It was not made in response to Mike's offer. It had, indeed, taken him thirty-eight years to reach it. That day in the store and always afterwards he was as appreciative to Mike as Harry Truman can be. And Mike loved Truman all his days. Indeed, it is Mike, who died in 1929, to whom Truman in remembrance gives the real warmth of his affection. He has loyal admiration for Tom

Pendergast, whom he never met until after he was elected in 1922, but whose later disintegration, Truman thinks, was the tragic close of an impressive career. But old, combative, blustering Mike was Harry's friend, sometimes even against Tom.

"I went to Mike's meeting at his Tenth Ward Democratic Club at Twenty-sixth and Prospect streets about June," Truman reported years later. "Mike got up and said to the meeting, 'Now I'm going to tell you who you are going to be for for county judge.'"

Truman smiled, "He told them just like that. I could see one fellow preening himself to receive Mike's selection. But Mike said, 'It's Harry Truman. He's got a fine war record. He comes from a fine family. He'll make a fine judge.'"

Harry Truman was in politics. Also, from an evaluation of all the stories about his entrance it seems probable that the man who put him into politics was Harry Truman. His determinations probably began among his comrades before one of them, Jim Pendergast, took their plans and succeeded in turning them into his father's offer. It was time for a decision by Harry. Nobody was more conscious than he that up to that time he had failed at almost everything he had tried—zinc, oil, haberdashery. Even the farm, in 1922, was heavily mortgaged. In February, Martha Ellen subdivided some of her land to sell it off in lots.

A quarter of a century later he said, "I never ran for a political job in my life that I wanted."

The price of wheat in September 1922 was eighty-eight cents.

CHAPTER VIII

Comrades and Klansmen

THE CRUELEST LIBEL in Truman's whole story is that one about a frayed major of artillery about to become both insolvent and unemployed who was put into politics by a corrupt political boss. It is a very familiar story, and comes plausibly from those times. It was in the spring of Truman's decision to enter American politics that Edward L. Doheny and Harry F. Sinclair secured the leases for the Elk Hill and Teapot Dome oil reserves. And Harding's Secretary of Interior received a loan of $100,000 brought to him in small bills in an inconspicuous satchel. When the time came for the expression of the American wrath, the country was concerned instead with the furies and counterfuries aroused by the Ku Klux Klan. Also, the boom had begun. It was an improbable time for a Democrat, though a major in the reserves to which Truman had been promoted on January 10, 1920, to begin a political progress toward the Presidency of the United States.

Harry Truman sometimes wore his oak leaves on ceremonial occasions. But fewer and fewer occasions were ceremonial. He was an unsuccessful civilian going back and forth from his insolvent store on Twelfth Street to his mother-in-law's house in Independence. The only dramatic thing about the man and the store was that they made a center for a good many young fellows at loose ends who congregated in common recollections of dramatic times together in camp and in war.

Such gathering places of the bored and the disappointed have served good and bad causes. After the Civil War, the Ku Klux Klan was founded in such a place more to combat boredom than Yankees or freedmen. In such places in Munich, in April 1922, veterans were listening to an ex-non-com named Hitler. It is almost forgotten that the hates he preached were loudly talked in little rooms and some great halls in America in 1922. The old hates sharpened against Negroes, Catholics and Jews, and foreigners. But the sharpest hates and fears were against the new Reds. On one government transport, 249 alleged revolutionaries were shipped to Russia. The New York Legislature refused to seat five Socialists elected to the Assembly from New York City. It was perhaps not odd that the strongest protest against that came from Alfred E. Smith who was to feel the sharpest sting of prejudice in 1928.

"Although I am unalterably opposed to the fundamental principles of the Socialist Party," he said, "it is inconceivable that a minority party, duly constituted and legally organized, should be deprived of its right to expression so long as it has honestly, by lawful methods of education and propaganda, succeeded in securing representation, unless the chosen representatives are unfit as individuals."

There was no sympathy for Reds but also no preoccupation with hates among the Irish Catholic boys who gathered at the store of the Baptist and the Jew on Twelfth Street. Instead, that place was store, unemployment agency, schoolroom, small loan center, confession booth and club. As time went on it seemed to become more of the others than the store.

"My whole political career is based on my war service and war associates," Truman said.

That political career was not off to a precipitate start. As in other states, veterans in Missouri let the politicians know they were home. In August 1921, just before the American Legion came to Kansas City to establish its reputation for boisterousness in its third national convention, Missouri had voted a bonus for every veteran. Harry Truman at that time was not the only veteran who needed help or thought he did. Perhaps the fact that hard times were already knocking on the door of the haberdashery then made him a supporter of bonus legislation throughout his career even when it was practically his only opposition to the policies of Roosevelt. But in the first years after the war, Truman watched other veterans turn to politics.

Indeed, not the politically famous 129th Field Artillery but the 140th U. S. Infantry (which grew from the 6th Missouri) made the first pattern of the soldier in politics in Missouri. The 140th Infantry brought together Colonel Bennett Champ Clark, of St. Louis, who had been nursed in American politics by his father, Speaker Champ Clark, and Captain Jacob L. ("Tuck") Milligan, of Richmond in Ray County adjacent to Jackson. They were the big veterans in politics. Truman was just a war veteran then, though later he was to defeat one of them and surprisingly outstrip the other.

Milligan, a twice-cited hero of the Argonne, was one of the first veterans to be elected to Congress after the war. On a pro-League platform he had been elected to fill a vacancy early in 1920 in a district next door to the Kansas City stronghold of League-fighting and Wilson-hating United States Senator James A. Reed. Milligan's friend and fellow officer, Colonel Clark, was on the other side of the state and the League issue. They remained friends and friendly politicians. Clark helped organize the American Legion in Paris, became one of its national commanders, and, against the opposition of Pendergast but with the help of Senator Reed, was elected United States Senator in 1932. Veterans Clark and Milligan were the ones who were headed toward the top in Missouri and American politics. Their records in the 140th Infantry were behind them and the 129th Field Artillery was just a body of the demobilized who dropped in occasionally for talk, company and comfort at a haberdashery store.

They had votes for a fellow veteran, however. Truman in 1920 even crossed the line into the Republican Party, to help elect as county marshal Major John L. Miles, of Independence and the 129th Field Artillery. It would be difficult to find a better measure of the strength of the ties which bound that group of veterans together. Miles was not only a Republican, he was, in that election, the rural Jackson County champion of Arthur M. Hyde, who won the Republican nomination for Governor that year—and the election, too—with Pendergastism as one of his chief targets. (It was Hyde whom Senator Reed, speaking for the Pendergasts, described as a "steam whistle on a fertilizer factory.") Miles was not only a respected soldier. Like Hyde, he was also a Fundamentalist and a reformer. He fought crime as Republican marshal, sheriff, and Kansas City chief of police. He failed in the American twenties which began with the angry Ku Klux and ended with the agile gangsters. In recent years he has been living in semi-retirement.

But in 1918 Truman had tested his quality as comrade in arms in the 129th. On election day in 1920, which brought Hyde and Harding and Miles into office, and which brought women for the first time to the polls, Truman took his mother with him and in Miles' case got her to cast her vote with his for a Republican. Old John Truman must have turned over in his grave in Forest Hill Cemetery. In 1922, though the Pendergasts did not mind, some other Democrats remembered well enough to pull an explanation from Truman.

"You have heard it said that I voted for John Miles for county marshal," he told a Democratic campaign picnic. "I'll have to plead guilty to that charge along with some five thousand other ex-soldiers. I was closer to John Miles than a brother. I have seen him in places that made hell look like a playground. I have seen him stick to his guns when Frenchmen were falling back. I have seen him hold the American line when only John Miles and his three batteries were between the Germans and a successful counterattack. He was of the right stuff, and a man who wouldn't vote for his comrade under circumstances such as these would be untrue to his country. I know that every soldier understands it. I have no apology to make for it."

Apparently that explanation sufficed. The charge did not plague Truman in other elections. Five thousand soldier voters were a lot of voters in Jackson County in those days, before the vote in Kansas City began to rise in an eccentric relationship to the population. The soldiers were not to be sneezed at—not in practical American politics. There were 143,571 of them, out of 166,000 who had been in service from Missouri, who had applied for the bonus from the state at the time when Truman was running for his first county office. The veterans had power and it could be seen. It was shown in Kansas City. The American Legion, which Truman had joined early and helped to organize in Missouri, staged its greatest demonstration up to that time on the corner by Truman & Jacobson's store in its third annual convention, in October 1921. Apparently the Legion established its hell-raising convention tradition in Kansas City, which seemed appropriate in that town so often called sinful. One historian of Legion history speaks of it as "the dawn of hilarity" in that organization's annual affairs. And if later,

Legion hilarity disappeared with Legionnaires' hair, both are worth remembering.

Truman & Jacobson's store was ready and waiting for the convention. Lieutenant James M. Pendergast, who was back in politics with his father and uncle, dropped in. Albert A. Ridge, ex-D Battery private, later to become a Federal Judge, studied his lessons as a law student there. Truman was insisting, too, that former Sergeant Edward McKim study for his examination as Field Artillery Reserve officer. Certainly, in late October 1921, it was at the center of the whole American veteran swarm when the Legion came to the hotels around that corner. The records show that General Foch, Admiral Beatty and Calvin Coolidge were at the convention. Madame Schumann-Heink, who had had sons in both the American and the German armies, sang "The Star-Spangled Banner." There were some unemployed veterans in the throng. There were veterans who became Ku Kluxers and veterans who became gangsters. Harry Truman was there who became President of the United States. He enjoyed himself even if for a year the price of wheat had been tumbling steadily downward along with the prices of corn, and beef and hogs, neckties and shirts. Madame Schumann-Heink was getting old but the Legion was still very young.

"That was when we took the Baltimore Hotel to pieces," General Harry Vaughan remembered years later. General Vaughan was not yet a significant detail in history, but historians have recorded the Texas steer that was driven into the lobby of the Hotel Baltimore and the unidentified veterans who walked in lock-step across the stages of theaters. There was a tremendous crap game at one time on the Twelfth and Baltimore corner which stopped traffic and could only be viewed satisfactorily from the high windows of the hotels. Also, the Legionnaires played a kind of trash can and taxi cab polo at the corner, the winner being the Legionnaire driver of the cab which could hit the can and drive it beyond the line of the intersection at the Crossroads of America. Actually, not much damage was done except to the cans. Truman & Jacobson, despite their joint preoccupation with the convention, sold some extra shirts. But not enough, and not at a profit.

That Legion hilarity, like the high jinks in mental self-defense in France between the fighting and the sailing for home, could be a loud thing. The politics of veterans was not a comradeship based upon solemnity. The haberdashery on Twelfth Street, even as it sagged, often sounded loud with masculine laughter. Truman still liked on occasion to lead a group of the old boys to restaurants where the best Kansas City steaks could be found. While in his whole life he has never been more than a moderate drinker, on some late afternoons even in prohibition times some of the fellows would find a bottle of good stuff. His choice, when he could get it, was a drink of bourbon straight.

Clearly, however, he has the greatest gift for sociability, and upon it many of the friendships of politics have been made before and since the comradeship of the 129th. He could sometimes stand some pretty commonplace company. Indeed, he has had all his life a liking for people even when they seem to have very little social grace or intellectual stimulation to offer. Nobody has run over him even in sociability, but often he has seemed to enjoy more than anybody else an amusing joke at his own expense. Perhaps a typical one was the ceremony made after the famous stud poker hand at Camp Ripley, in Minnesota, during one of the regular periods of training as an artillery colonel in the Reserve Corps. Harry Truman had a pair of fives showing and an officer named Jeff Henderson showed a pair of deuces. Harry Vaughan showed an ace and a king. McKim had a king showing and a buried ace. It was the biggest pot of the training period. Harry Truman looked at the cards and the faces of the players above them. Then he threw in his cards. Henderson pulled out, too. McKim beat Vaughan only because his fifth card was higher. And afterwards they fixed up the "Military Order of the Flying Coattails" and presented it to Colonel Harry at the encampment banquet. Nobody enjoyed the ceremony more than he.

Yet, sometimes when the recreation hall was empty he sat down alone at the piano. Sometimes when he came home he would play by himself—or for Bess—Beethoven's "Sonata in C Minor" or Mozart's "Sonata IX." He laughed when the boys found big books on artillery or military history in the counters under the shirts. But he was ready to play rollicking soldier songs with easy swinging shoulders when they found a piano at a convention. He was the easiest man to know in the world and yet, older than most of his Army comrades, a little strange at the same time. He was always in the world of his companions but the shrewdest among them realized that he had other concerns not easily shared or seen. Not even the shrewdest among them apparently saw any sign of the politician in him at first. He surprised most of them when he decided to be one.

One story, which Truman says he does not remember but which others do, may indicate the surprise. Edgar G. Hinde, who in 1950 was postmaster of Independence, had been a second lieutenant in the 129th Field Artillery. In 1922, however, he was doing the best he could running a small garage on Maple Avenue in Independence. He was at work one day when Harry Truman came in grinning broadly. Hinde looked up waiting for the joke.

"What do you think I've done?" Truman asked him.

Hinde had no idea.

Truman told him: "I have filed for judge of the Eastern district. What do you think of that?"

"I think you're crazy," said Hinde.

"I might be," Truman agreed, "but I have to eat."

That last phrase gives a false impression. Truman's troubles never got him to any such pass as that. He had an opportunity at the time to go into a building and loan and insurance job. There is nothing improbable, however, about Hinde's reply.

"If that is the case," he said, "go ahead and we'll see what can be done."

The "we" is important. Hinde, in his small garage, was not accustomed to using either the editorial or the imperial "we." He was talking about his friends and Harry's, particularly that cohesive company of country boys and Kansas City Irish Catholics who have never permitted the demobilization of the comradeship of the 129th. Already, even then, the bespectacled major who could outcuss cowardice had become the real leader of the regiment's affection and remembrance.

The importance of the 129th Field Artillery in Harry Truman's first election can be mathematically demonstrated. It meant a political base in local elections not possible after World War II. In the second great war, after one or two old National Guard companies had been wiped out in the Pacific in such a way as practically to destroy the young manhood of the small towns from which they came, War Department policy was changed to eliminate home-town companies. Truman's war associates went from Jackson County to fight and came back to Jackson County to vote. A total of 2,269 officers and men were attached to the regiment from August 5, 1917, to May 6, 1919. Some were killed, some moved away, some disappeared. Those who remained, however, had a fellow-feeling with other local veterans. When the election was held in the summer of 1922, Truman, as the Pendergast-supported, country, Baptist, Mason, farmer candidate, won by only 282 votes over Emmett Montgomery, a prominent banker from the town of Blue Springs. He would not have won then, according to local historians, if the 129th in the person of a highly nervous ex-private with a very large .45 calibre automatic had not been on guard at the ballot box in a precinct at Mount Washington in the Intercity district.

That incident put the election of Major John Miles and that of Major Harry Truman together again in the annals of the 129th. Marshal Miles staffed the thin line between Truman and successful counterattack. What happened was that in the afternoon of election day some of Truman's friends who were Miles' friends, too, heard that Joe Shannon's anti-Pendergast faction would attempt to steal the election box in the Mount Washington precinct. Miles sent his brother, George Miles, and a young ex-soldier to preserve the peace. Judge Henry Bundschu, Republican friend of Truman's and the affectionate chronicler of Eastern Jackson County history, says the young soldier was John Gibson of the 129th. The roster of the 129th lists a Private John W. Gibson, Jr., who served in Battery C but who did not go to France with the regiment. Apparently his one engagement was in Mount Washington that day.

Gibson and his companion had hardly stationed themselves on the porch of the cottage which served as the polling place, he told Bundschu, when three or four taxicabs pulled up in front. A group of tough-looking fellows emerged. Gibson was scared, but he pulled his .45 from its holster, stuck it into the stomach of the man who seemed to be in charge. That man quickly diagnosed both Gibson's nervousness and his determination. He turned pale, flung up his hands and shouted, "Come on, boys, let's go." The taxicabs left with the dust high behind them.

Later, Gibson, walking across the square in Independence,

saw the man whose stomach he had prodded. He asked who it was and was told, "Why, that is Joe Shannon." Years later, Judge Bundschu met Shannon, then a Congressman, on a Chicago-Kansas City train and asked him about it, but the only reply he could get was, "Where is that man Gibson? I want to see him. I want to talk to him." Otherwise Shannon would only say that the Republicans were to blame for everything and that, if they had stayed out of the primary, Montgomery would have been elected and that Montgomery was far better qualified to hold the position of judge of the Eastern district than Harry Truman.

What Harry Truman got from his associates in arms during World War I itself was more important than any help he got from them after it. Their post-war energies and loyalties helped him win that first election in 1922. It was more important that their variety as men in the common experience of war fixed his faith forever in the worthiness of their variety and made him ready to take, on that faith, the chance which cost him defeat in 1924. Jacobson taught him some of that faith at Camp Doniphan and after. The good wild Irishmen of D Battery taught him more. The Missouri determination not to be pushed around included also an unwillingness to see underdogs kicked around either. If his mother had strong prejudices against Kansans and Republicans and particularly the combination of the two, she certainly wore no masks over them. His politically combative father taught him that cruelty to either animals or men was a sin against his heritage. His reading had given him a young faith in the American liberties but there never was anything theoretical, constitutional, or abstract about his consideration for all kinds of people. His war service turned a natural spirit into a basic faith.

It was a coincidence that the Ku Klux began to burn torches on a hill near Lee's Summit, east of Grandview and south of Independence, at the same time that Truman began to ride the roads in a battered Dodge as an office-seeker. Other Klan coincidences were more important. Its growth coincided with the scandals of the Harding Administration in America. It was the Klan fight in the Democratic National Convention of 1924 which diverted national indignation from those scandals and postponed still longer the social reforms which seemed to come very suddenly in an American vacuum of need for them in the New Deal.

Klan membership in the United States went up like the stock market, from 100,000 in 1921 to 5,000,000 in 1924. It was definitely not a movement limited to the South. In 1923, William Allen White came home to Kansas from Europe to discover that the Klan had captured the city hall of his Emporia. Perhaps its greatest excesses were in Indiana. It grew in Missouri. In Jackson County, William M. Reddig, the ablest historian of its politics has reported, "The Klansmen in this region were not the ordinary one-hundred-per-cent Americans who were the Klan ideal. They were two-hundred-per-cent Americans, so aptly described in a popular joke of the period. They didn't hate just Catholics, Jews and Negroes. They hated everybody."

Nobody paid much attention to them at first in Jackson County. The best evidence is that Harry Truman's political judgment was to duck the Klan issue—to be neither Klan nor anti-Klan but to get elected county judge. Apparently he was successful in doing that for a while. As the campaign advanced and warmed, however, Edgar Hinde, who heard talk of the Klan among patrons of his little garage, and other friends of Truman figured that it would be good politics for him to join it. An organizer of the Klan suggested to them that the Klan would be glad to support him as a member.

"I put it up to Truman," Edgar Hinde, of Independence, has reported, "and he gave me ten dollars for an entrance fee—cash. I took it down and then the organizer asked for a conference in the Hotel Baltimore in Kansas City. There he met Harry and said: 'You've got to promise us you won't give a Catholic a job if you belong to us and we support you.'

" 'I won't agree to anything like that,' Harry said. 'I had a Catholic battery in the war and if any of those boys need help I'm going to give them a job.'

"The organizer said, 'We can't take you then,' and he gave back the ten dollars, and that was the end of that."

Hinde's memory checks with Truman's. It checks with the logic of the situation of a man in politics who had not only commanded an Irish Catholic battery but was at that moment the candidate of an Irish Catholic boss. Yet, twenty-two years later the Hearst newspapers published, a few days before the election in which he was a candidate for Vice-President, that he had joined the Klan. Spencer Salisbury says that the Hearst papers were right.

"I was there when he joined," Salisbury says. "I joined with him."

Fortunately, the record is very clear that in 1924 the Klan and the anti-Pendergast Democrats joined to defeat Truman in the general election. In some respects it was a comic defeat. He was no longer an unknown in politics. He had done a good job as county judge. *The Kansas City Star,* which was never a partisan of the Pendergast machine, said in June 1924, that the county court of which Truman was a member had in less than a full term "reduced a deficit of $1,200,000, left by the plundering Bulger machine, approximately one half and have in the county treasury besides a balance of $270,000." *The Star*'s morning edition, *The Times,* called Truman "a faithful and economical public servant" deserving of re-election. Truman himself, with new confidence, spoke near home at Grandview to "nail lie after lie" of his angry opponents. He was easily renominated.

However, the Republicans also held a primary that spring. On the last day of filing, Truman's Republican friend, Major Miles, called up that other Republican friend of Truman's, Judge Bundschu. Miles said that no Republican had filed as candidate for county judge in Eastern Jackson County and asked Bundschu what to do. They decided to get one of Miles' deputy marshals to file with the understanding that he would withdraw as soon as Miles could find some other Republican better qualified for the place. The deputy was Henry Rummell, the harness maker who years before had made the harness for Vivian Truman's team of red goats.

"So without saying anything to Rummell about it," says Bundschu, "I went to the courthouse and paid the five dollar filing fee for him for the Republican nomination for county judge against Harry Truman."

Later Miles went to Rummell and suggested that he withdraw, but, Bundschu says, Rummell had made an agreement with Joseph Shannon, head of the anti-Pendergast Democrats, and Todd George, reputed leader of the Jackson County Klansmen, to vote for him in the general election.

"Here I was," says Bundschu, "a Catholic who hated the Klan, used to work an injustice on a friend of mine, Harry Truman. And old man Rummell never did pay me that five dollars back!"

It did not seem comic at the time.

"They threatened to kill me," Truman said later of the Klan. "And I went out to one of their meetings and dared them to try. This was a meeting of Todd George's 'Independents' at Lee's Summit. I poured it into them. Then I came down from the platform and walked through them to my car. There I met my gang with a load of shotguns in a car. It was a good thing they did not come earlier. If they had met, there would have been trouble."

Fortunately for history, *The Kansas City Star* made a contemporary record of the Klan opposition to Truman. It published an anti-Truman statement ("We are unalterably opposed to Harry Truman") by Todd George, who described himself as president of the Independent Democrats of Rural Jackson County. *The Star* stated that "the 'Independents' are known as an organization of the Ku Klux Klan" and added that in 1924 such Independents "centered their attack on Judge Truman."

Rummell was elected in November. Truman was without a job again. But what happened to him was, as on so many other occasions in his life, only an item in the greater history around him, though a dramatic and revealing item.

Tom Pendergast and Joseph Shannon, as was the custom of their complicated Democratic rivalry, both went as delegates to the Democratic National Convention in New York in June. Harding was dead, and the Republican Party seemed mortally wounded. The scandals of the Harding Administration, however, turned out to be entirely irrelevant at the great and long battle of the Democratic Party in Madison Square Garden. The American wrath that year was trampled from entirely different grapes. And in the trampling the same thing happened to Harry Truman that happened to the Democratic Party and, as it turned out, in a very real sense to the American people. So far as the record of that convention goes, Tom Pendergast had not a word to say. Joseph Shannon made some very vigorous remarks about honor in politics: "We decline to be delivered even if we were sold." Pendergast was often absent when his name was called. But all the Democrats were gathered in confidence that they were there to nominate the next President of the United States.

The disappointment did not come after the long balloting—103 ballots to secure a nominee. It came on the night of the fifth day of the convention. The Democrats preferred to be timid on the issue of the League. But the real end of hope came when the Democrats voted as to whether or not the Ku Klux Klan should be condemned by name in the platform. The vote was one of the closest in American political history and perhaps once the bitter debate had begun the party's hopes would have been broken whichever way it went. By a vote of $543\frac{3}{20}$ to $542\frac{7}{20}$ the convention decided not to name the Klan. As soon as the chairman could hammer a little crevice of quietness out of the tumult, he recognized a handsome young man on crutches. He swung himself to the speaker's stand and spoke into the new radio.

"Mr. Chairman, it is now nearly two o'clock in the morning of the Sabbath Day. I move, Mr. Chairman, that the Convention do now adjourn."

There were a few cries of "No" at Franklin Roosevelt, but most of the Democrats were already headed for the doors and the night.

CHAPTER IX

The Gilded Age

HARRY TRUMAN HAD walked out of the courthouse that January in 1925 without any uncertainty about what to do with his life. If his political career was interrupted, his life as a man in business or politics, surrounded by people and sought by people, was fully underway. The veterans had not come to the haberdashery merely because it was at a center and a crossroads. Even back in the old oil company days, Truman's associate and bookkeeper remembered the "people, people, people" who were always around him. Later they had learned to crowd the courthouse. They followed him out of it. When, in mid-term of his services as county judge, he and Bess had known that Margaret was on her way and he had decided to study law and had enrolled in the Kansas City Law School with the class of 1927, the people interrupted even those evenings. All sorts of people followed him to school; they came into the law library to talk to him about personal matters and county matters.

"They just made me quit," he said.

The crowding continued after the Ku Klux made him quit as county judge, too. In a period in which the combination of sales and contacts promised a glittering America, the crowding was reassuring. The exact date of his final departure from law school is not quite clear. As member or ex-member of the class he made the speech at the banquet in the Muehlebach Hotel on February 21, 1925. Margaret had just celebrated a big-eyed first birthday. When he went to the Muehlebach banquet the site of the old haberdashery seemed much further away than the other side of the street. His subject was that of an ex-county official who meant to be an official again, "Honor and Government." He spoke without oratory but he was very serious about his subject.

He did not wait in idleness for a political return. If a man of forty with a wife and a one-year-old daughter had to be unemployed, it would be difficult to think of a time when men like Harry Truman felt less that they needed to be troubled about it. It was long afterwards, in the case of most Americans, before they realized that they had been moving in the most hazardous years of their lives. Always optimistic, Harry Truman certainly had no sense of hazard. He did not feel exactly twenty years from the Presidency of the United States, but he was as aware as others around him of the return of the gilded age in America. They did not call it that. Indeed, the gilded age is never at hand. Ten years before Truman was born, when his father was just old enough to be doing his first serious and confident mule-swapping, Mark Twain and Charles Dudley Warner, in their boisterous satirization of *The Gilded Age* in America, suggested that their story even then came out of a remote past, even from an imaginary realm. It bore a remarkable resemblance, however, to those times in which every man hoped to be his own robber baron or at least to be the beneficiary of some resource which the nation had not nailed down.

The America of January 1925, in which Harry Truman returned to free enterprise, would have been recognized as familiar by Mark Twain's Colonel Beriah Sellers ("there's whole Atlantic Oceans of cash in it, gulfs and bays thrown in"). Babbitt, whose portrait as the small and highly hopeful realtor in a metropolis not unlike Kansas City had recently been drawn by Sinclair Lewis, seemed a less lusty figure than the Colonel. But they would have understood each other even if neither ever realized that the real suckers were themselves. That was not apparent to many Americans in 1926. As Calvin Coolidge began his first full term, in 1925, the high tide of the industrial and commercial boom of the twenties was rolling in. Even Democrats were gay. When Coolidge was nominated, Franklin Roosevelt was on a cruise on the houseboat *Larooco* among the Florida Keys. In the log he noted, with a thrift of which later he was not much suspected, that the gasoline he could buy for twenty-six cents in Maine cost him thirty-four cents in Florida. But nobody was much concerned about prices. Everything seemed very happily headed upward. Oddly enough, one of the few who suspected a "sordid decade" very early was that loyal but often troubled

Republican, William Allen White, of the Middle Border, who later wrote Coolidge's biography. If Coolidge had listened carefully to that tide of prosperity rolling in, he wrote, "he might have heard the moan of an undertow.

"In the agricultural West," he wrote of that spring when Coolidge was inaugurated and Harry Truman became independent business man again, "the farmer had become a free hand soil despoiler and the lumberman a freebooter. Western grain lands were showing a constantly decreasing yield per acre. Pastures were shriveling; forests disappearing. The water level in the Mississippi Valley was steadily receding in the wells, in the creeks, in the rivers. Great floods, uncontrolled, were tearing their disastrous way through the valleys. Mortgages were increasing. Tenantry was on the rise. People were moving restlessly about the land seeking to better unhappy conditions. Migratory labor had begun to work in the wheat harvests, in the citrus country, in the fruit orchards, in the lumber camps, on the docks. . . . Swifter and more powerfully ran the vortex current of bank expansion through all the Coolidge years. Money in terms of hundreds of millions, even billions, was coming from all over the continent into the speculative orgy of stock selling."

It cannot be said that a hundred miles away from White's Emporia, Kansas, in Independence, Missouri, Harry Truman heard the undertow either. These were good years for him, but they were also years in which without knowing it he was occasionally closer to danger than in almost any other years of his life. His business career in this two-year interval has been neglected in both research and memory, but he was clearly then a business man of the new gilded age. One of his principal business associates was the president of the Kansas City Chamber of Commerce at that time. His life-long friend and political supporter, Tom Evans, was beginning to build his big Crown Drug Company chain of stores after an unimpressive start in 1923. Also, Truman was dangerously close to some who played the swift times too fast and too loose. Like the rest of America, Harry Truman, who had been broke in the American deflation two years before, was out to make some money. With varying luck, that involved him in selling auto club memberships, organizing a building and loan company, and trying to save a looted bank. Both his good luck and good sense held even in the company of Spencer Salisbury.

Salisbury suggests that he was waiting in helpfulness to Truman as his partner in several enterprises in the years after old man Rummell, the harness maker, walked in with his certificate of election and took Truman's place as county judge. Perhaps it was essential in a career like Harry Truman's, in which one man made so many friends, that the time had to come when he would find an enemy waiting for him, too.

Some of Truman's critics who later questioned the quality of some of his friends would get no denial from him about at least one. He was as clearly mistaken in the twenties about a man, as he and other Americans were about the times. American prosperity seemed permanent at last. The lean, self-assured Salisbury did not look like an adversary. He was an energetic politician, a lively business man, a fellow who knew how to get things done. This old Captain of E Battery was as different as any man could possibly be from Truman. Sometimes in the war and at the front it had irritated the steady, careful Truman when Salisbury got his battery into action before Truman figured out the range. "The job is to hit the target, lay them down on it, isn't it?" Truman once demanded. But Salisbury would put the range 1,000 meters ahead and then begin firing before he worked out the actual range. "Ninety per cent of the Field Artillery," Salisbury figured, "is the moral effect on your own troops." Salisbury had other quick ideas. When his own E Battery needed horses and new horses were allotted only to Battery F and had "F's" cut into their coats, he figured that it did not require much ingenuity with a pair of shears to cut an "F" into an "E." He had unquestionably been a good soldier with a graceless grin even if above his lips his eyes met the requirements of the nickname, "Snake Eye." He was to be Truman's companion in the go-getter business of America's gilded age.

"Truman had to get into something," said Eddie Jacobson, the earlier and dependable partner who was then out selling wholesale the shirts he and Truman had not been able successfully to sell at retail. "That was the only reason he teamed up with Spencer Salisbury."

That does not seem quite correct. If Truman and other members of the 129th Field Artillery had had their troubles with

Salisbury and his E Battery as "Carranza and His Forty Thieves"
in the Army, Salisbury afterwards had both effectiveness and flair.
Whether or not, as Salisbury claims, he introduced Truman to
Tom Pendergast in 1920, it seems clear that he did work for
Truman's election in 1922 even if Truman would not go along
with him into the Ku Klux Klan. Their later association makes
it improbable that Salisbury went along with the Klan against
Truman in 1924.

By all Independence standards Salisbury was a gentleman born.
His people were well-to-do, though the family had been broken
when his mother and father were divorced while he was at war.
His mother was at one time state regent of the DAR in Missouri.
It was she, Salisbury says, who in 1926 made Truman president
of the National Old Trails Association to which he later gave so
much energy and interest. Even years later when he had lost
wealth and position, Salisbury still collected antiques. In 1940,
just before he was sent to prison, he offered a twenty-five dollar
reward for the return of a 1669 cannon which had been stolen
from his front porch.

In 1949, after he had been many years out of prison, Salisbury
had become a devout convert to the Catholic Church and was a
professional bondsman who operated a small tavern on week
ends, his considered judgment was: "Harry is a no good buzzard
if there ever was one." The opinion was fully returned in kind
by Truman. Theirs was no swift political row. When Father
Tiernan, the old chaplain of the 129th Field Artillery, went at
Salisbury's sister's request to ask a final Federal pardon for him
from the President of the United States, Harry Truman's mouth
was hard and he shook his head. Truman has no memory that
his entrance into business or earlier into politics waited upon the
good will of Salisbury. It was he who gave the jobs to Salisbury.

Truman, as citizen and business man in 1925, took offices in
the Board of Trade Building in Kansas City. That was not only
just twenty years before he became President; it was also just
twenty-two years since his father had lost all he and his mother
had on the futures of wheat on the Board of Trade. Truman
himself was not gambling. He was selling in the age of the
idealization of the salesman. It was no gamble then to sell the
memberships in the Kansas City Automobile Club which apparently is the only activity of those years which until now has been

recalled. In 1925, more passenger automobiles were produced than ever before. In the five years before that, more automobiles came off the assembly lines than in the whole history of the industry up to that time. The K.C.A.C., now consolidated with the Automobile Club of Missouri, has no records about the salesmen of its memberships at that time. Apparently, Truman not only sold memberships himself but had a staff of other men working with him on the job. After he was President, when he was given an engraved gold certificate as honorary member of the board of governors of the club, he said, "I once personally sold 1,500 members in a membership campaign for them."

Also, in later years he told me: "I set up an organization at the auto club headquarters at Tenth and Central. I got a percentage of the initiation fees. As I remember it, we got about fourteen or fifteen dollars a head of which the salesman got five dollars. I made five or six thousand dollars. I thought in those days about the consolidation of the Kansas City and the Missouri auto associations and if I'd done that I would have made much more."

It was a nice start but it was makeshift and temporary work. He was seeking something more substantial and found it in the building and loan field. There again, he got in at a good time. The post-war building boom was at its peak in 1925, the index of residential building was at 211.4 in 1925 based upon 100 in 1921. New subdivisions were being opened all around Kansas City. People were building new houses in Independence and putting modern improvements into old ones. There was as much demand for home mortgages as for autos bought on the installment plan. But Truman entered the building and loan business and the Salisbury story at approximately the same time.

Salisbury says that he helped Truman in his automobile club membership campaign when he, then a deputy internal revenue collector in Kansas City, told him to go to the income tax list to find prospects. Salisbury was employed by the U. S. Bureau of Internal Revenue as a division deputy in Kansas City at $1,500 a year on November 10, 1919. He resigned on February 28, 1926, when he was a deputy collector at $3,000. His and Truman's first clear association was after that in the Community Savings and Loan Association of Independence. Salisbury says he got Truman into that, too, after Truman had spent close to a year in the automobile association work. Salisbury's story is that he bought the Southwest Building and Loan and moved it to Independence.

"I organized it from taw," Truman told me of the association, using the terminology of the shooting line in a game of marbles.

Truman seems clearly to have been the organizer. The Kansas City directory for 1926 lists Harry S. Truman as the general manager of the association with his office in the Board of Trade Building in Kansas City and with another office at 1300 Union Avenue. As is generally the case with city directories, their listings are often after the fact and cover a year before. The association was organized at Independence, on October 13, 1924, just before Truman was defeated for county judge. Salisbury does not appear in the directory listings of the association until the directory of 1927, when he was treasurer, and a friend of his, Arthur S. Metzger, was secretary. Truman was president and general manager. At that time the main office was at 204 North Liberty Street, in Independence. The facts seem to be that Truman sold the stock and organized the association from the same Board of Trade Building offices in Kansas City from which he sold the auto club memberships and then moved his offices to Independence. The one fact about which there is no dispute is that they did very well. Everybody was building. (That is everybody but Truman. Years later, when he was in the Senate, Roger Sermon took him to see a house he was building. "You make me jealous," he recalled that Truman told him. "I never owned a house of my own and I probably never will.")

In addition to their association in the building and loan, Truman and Salisbury went side by side into another venture which came very close to causing the final financial destruction of both of them in their efforts to save a tottering local bank, half a decade before banks were bursting like firecrackers in small towns and big towns throughout the United States. Early in 1926, Truman, Salisbury, Metzger and General Stayton bought the control of the Citizens Security Bank of Englewood, a tiny community near Independence. They settled on Truman's friend, Lou E. Holland, a well-to-do engraver who lived in Englewood and was at that time president of the Kansas City Chamber of Commerce and later its executive secretary, as president of the bank. (In 1949 he was elected president of the

American Automobile Association.) Holland accepted with the proviso that the five of them make their own personal examination of all assets and liabilities. They spent a Sunday in February 1926, looking at them.

They found the bank loaded with very doubtful paper, insisted upon the cashier substituting dependable assets for it, and reported the matter to the cashier's bonding company. Also, and promptly, they got out of the banking business. A few months later the bank failed and carried one of Truman's neighbors down with it. He was B. M. Houchens, the brother of Fielding Houchens with whom Truman had studied when he was hoping to go to West Point. B. M. Houchens became president of the bank after Truman's withdrawal. Those other officials, whom Truman and his friends forced to clean up the bank, had later loaded it with bad paper again. A bank examiner forced the two officers who had caused the trouble to get out. In August, *The Kansas City Star* reported: "But Houchens remained to hold the sack. His father-in-law, John W. Clements, Independence lawyer, came to his rescue with $12,000 and Houchens mortgaged and sold everything he had accumulated. . . . All disclosures have tended to vindicate Houchens from any responsibility for the bank's condition other than that he allowed himself to be blindfolded and made president of the bank in name only. But to offset that misstep, Houchens has protected the depositors and stockholders with his own personal fortune and much of his health." And after that *Star* story was written he went into his garage and killed himself. Not everything was golden in the gilded age.

"I got into the bank before it failed," Truman told me, "only as a community enterprise. Houchens and the others bought our stock."

It was a close shave, nevertheless.

"I told the damn fool he'd better get out of it," Salisbury, who was as lucky as Truman in getting out, said of Truman later. "But he's a happy-go-lucky fellow—the luckiest buzzard I ever knew."

That was long after the fact. They were friends that late summer of 1926 when the bank closed. In the building and loan, Truman was depending more than ever on Salisbury. Truman was already a candidate for presiding judge of the Jackson

County court. He remained as president of the building and loan company after he was elected, though its actual management passed into Salisbury's hands. When they began to fall out in both business and politics is not easy to say. Truman was still president in 1930, but he was out even as a director when the institution was converted to a Federal savings and loan association on July 10, 1934, four days after Truman had officially opened his campaign for the United States Senate. And that year Salisbury was Eastern Jackson County manager for Tuck Milligan, late of the 140th Infantry, who was one of Truman's opponents in the Democratic primary. Salisbury made a violent campaign against Truman in his home town, their home town in which they had grown up and been business men together.

"In the early thirties," Truman remembers, "Salisbury, using proxies, got his own directors elected, throwing out my friends and me. His associate was Arthur Metzger, a big fat man who died young of diabetes. He had succeeded Salisbury as constable and he was also attorney for the building and loan. Salisbury was mismanaging the association. There was not anything I could do when I found out what Salisbury was doing but report it to the Federal authorities."

Salisbury tells a very different story of their break. "The building and loan was doing OK," he said. "Then Harry ran for presiding judge [in 1926] and we got him elected and he gave me a job as purchasing agent outside of Kansas City for the county. But Mike [Pendergast] didn't like it, so Harry canned me and gave me a job to collect interest due on county school funds held by the county court and I got a little rough making 'em pay so he canned me, but I had made a contract so he paid me $3,000 to quit. I got rid of Harry in the building and loan in 1932 when he tried to turn things over to Jimmy Pendergast—when he wanted to give him a list of all the stockholders so he could consolidate with the building and loan in Kansas City which Jim Pendergast had."

(James M. Pendergast was president of the North American Savings and Loan Association of Missouri from 1928 to 1938. In terms of its assets at that time it was a smaller association than the Community Building and Loan of Independence. It was still in operation in Kansas City in 1950.)

Salisbury did very well. He inherited part of an estate from his mother which was sufficiently large to require him to put up a $30,000 bond as trustee. In the 1930's he added an oil business to his activities in the building and loan which had, when he converted it from a state to a Federal institution in 1934, assets totalling $451,096. He made this conversion very much against the advice of his attorney, the same amiable Republican, Judge Henry Bundschu.

The trouble began after the conversion. The record shows that Salisbury resigned as president of the association in December 1939. Truman, as Senator, after a visit to Independence had wired the governor of the Federal Home Loan Bank System in August 1939, urging a complete investigation of the association and the manager. In that same month Salisbury, who once stated that he had been a Pendergast man since 1910, was declaring, as president of the James A. Reed Democratic Association, that "we're mighty tired out in this part of the county of being dominated by Pendergast appointees in the courthouse." (Pendergast himself was already in prison. Reed had already bolted the Democratic Party to vote against Franklin Roosevelt in 1936.) Salisbury invited Governor Stark, who opposed Truman in 1940, to come to Truman's home town to speak.

Six months after Salisbury resigned he filed suit for $75,000 against the building and loan association saying that refusal to give him a letter stating the true cause of his resignation had humiliated him and reduced his income from $450 to $100 per month. (At his trial his attorney said he had lost the wealth he had once had; when he was sentenced he was a lieutenant colonel in the Field Artillery Reserve.) In February 1941, he was sentenced, after a plea of guilty, to fifteen months in prison on the charge that he made an affidavit in 1939 saying no lawsuits were then pending against the association. He was not convicted on another count that he had deceived the examiners by a false appraisal of the Premium Petroleum Company which he operated "in order to make certain loans in connection with the association," as the prosecutor said. He was sentenced by the same Judge Reeves who conducted grand jury investigations which led to the fall of Pendergast. Before he was sentenced, old comrades of the 129th Field Artillery filed before the judge in character testimony: Colonel (then Major General) Stayton, Cap-

tain Roger Sermon, Captain Harry Jobes, others. Harry Truman
was not among them.

"They sold off all the good assets," Salisbury said of the liqui-
dators of the association later, "and still paid $1.08 on the
dollar."

He pulled out of his pocket a frayed clipping from *The Kansas
City Star* which said that depositors had received $1.075 on the
dollar in the liquidation. That fact is verified by Federal Savings and Loan Insurance Corporation records.

That takes the story far forward, jumping important years.
But the mark of the gilded age and the anger of the enmity are
in all the years forward. Actually, those two years of private
business, 1925-26, made no golden age for either Harry or many
other Americans. William Allen White realized that, even if
Calvin Coolidge could not hear the undertow for the surf and
the tide. Truman was not getting rich. He had debts which
were still not paid. He made the sort of living the average manager of a building and loan association in the average small
town like Independence made in those years when prices were
high even if the stock market went higher and higher, too. Also,
the political fever remained in his blood.

In 1926 Truman did go to see Tom Pendergast. From his
small office at 1908 Main Street in Kansas City Pendergast ruled
in dull-seeming casualness the widening area of his power across
Missouri. There he talked to the stream of callers, mendicants
and petitioners, whose hopes lay in his words—hopes for the
governorship or a job in the stockyards or the gas house. It was
the only time Truman ever directly asked him for his support
for a job. He did not get it. Truman, with debts still over his
head, wanted to run for the office of county collector which paid
about $25,000 a year, including salary and fees.

"No," said Tom Pendergast. He had already offered his support for that post to another man. He would be glad to support
Harry for the job of presiding judge of the county court—a
promotion in dignity and power but none in salary from the post
he had held before. Truman went to see Mike Pendergast and
told him his disappointment. Mike was disappointed, too. Tom
made his brother mad sometimes.

"Run," he said. "I'll support you regardless of Tom."

Truman smiled gratefully at the combative, affectionate Mike, but he took Tom's offer. The county court job would not give him enough money to pay the debts which remained. It was a good job still. In three years the gilded age of the twenties would be over. Debts would hang not only over a man but over America. In three years, also, Mike Pendergast would be dead and Truman would be the leader in the county. But he could not count those things as he could at that time count on Tom Pendergast. He rode back to Independence to tell Bess what he had done. Next time maybe Tom would let him have a shot at the collector's office and the collector's salary. He could wait a little while longer.

CHAPTER X

Planning and People

A LITTLE GIRL of snow and taffy, Margaret was big enough to ride with her father that fall of 1926 after he had been elected presiding judge of the county court. He took her to the zoo in Swope Park. She rode on the seat beside him down the highway to Grandview to see her grandmother on the farm. Truman and Bess and Margaret drove a great deal about the county that fall and sometimes he got out of the car and stamped on the edges of the old, crumbly macadam. He shook his head when it cracked beneath his feet. He climbed down the banks at the roadsides and looked into clogged culverts. Margaret and her mother picked bunches of bittersweet and carried the red and orange berries home to Delaware Street. Her mother and father talked a lot about roads. It was fun for Margaret. It was also a planning for people.

They saw less of him after January when he moved into his office in the courthouse, at Missouri Avenue and Locust Street, with its splintered, oil-soaked wooden floors, its rattletrap elevators and its generally dilapidated air of government and gloom. The old building rose to pointed towers in a tortured stone pile which corresponded to the jigsaw residential architecture of the 1880's and 1890's. It was the sort of building which made the new, strange thing called "planning" in government seem strange and new indeed. Yet, the familiar story is that very suddenly a plan appeared there and performance followed in the life of an American county and particularly in the life of a man.

The impression of swift, if not abrupt, development in Harry Truman's life is important, nevertheless. One day he was a man in the building and loan business, who just missed becoming involved in the disreputable collapse of a bank. He was still,

140

when Margaret listened or when there was a piano and men and voices around it, something of the boy who wanted to be a pianist. He was a reserve officer who had once wanted to be a West Pointer. He was the farmer who had not found quite enough to satisfy him on the farm, the oil man who just missed, and the haberdasher who failed, the county judge who did not get re-elected. Then, suddenly, as presiding judge from January 1927, onward, he was an American public official who succeeded better than anyone expected at every job he assumed. Out of that old grim courthouse emerged a modern politician. He made the older and bigger politicians around him seem as out-of-date as the courthouse which he replaced with a modern set-back soaring building. He kept old Andrew Jackson in bronze still on guard at its door.

The apparent speed in which a man, who had seemed at so many loose ends so long, became a local government official who did the best job at home and was recognized for it in Missouri and beyond still puzzles even some who know him best. Some of them are puzzled still, too, by his combination of creative honesty to people and his continuing loyalty to Pendergast in a county become notorious for political corruption. The smear is clear—too clear. Few have recognized his undisputed honesty and efficiency in a political miasma as a political miracle performed by a man. Apparently that just happened. It has steadily been emphasized but never adequately explained. The explanation may be the best measure of the man.

While it is completely clear that, in 1922, the Pendergasts needed Truman the veteran and farmer, as a candidate more than he needed them, it is insistently forgotten that Pendergast backed Truman in that campaign in the very program of good roads honestly built which was the basis of his record after 1927. This represented no Pendergast idealism. Miles Bulger, the factional enemy the Pendergasts were after, controlled not only the courthouse but the contracts. In that campaign, whatever may have been their own sins before or since, the Pendergasts loudly shared the indignation over "Bulgerism" (which took its name from the lively little Miles) in county affairs. "Bulgerism," both the Pendergasts and *The Kansas City Star* agreed, was plundering the county treasury and running up county deficits in the building of "pie crust" roads. Truman fitted into that campaign like a strong hand into a stout glove.

His father's death had come from overstrenuous devotion to his work as road overseer. Harry had succeeded him and worked hard at the job himself with a farmer's understanding of the need. He had a rural roadside understanding of the Miles Bulger system whereby Bulger would call on each overseer for one hundred dollars cash to him, then he would order and pay county funds to the overseers for hundred dollar culverts with no notion or expectation that any culverts would be built. Harry knew Jackson County roads from much riding of them. At the very beginning of his career in 1922, Truman made the fight, not only to get the Pendergasts back into the courthouse, but for the people in the honest building of their roads. He never changed that platform. It was not new in 1927. If some Pendergast contractors were surprised in 1928 and 1929 to learn that he was serious about it, it was not for lack of warning.

He gave that to everybody at a Saturday political picnic at the little town of Oak Grove, in his campaign for nomination in 1922. "He received," said *The Kansas City Star,* "a flattering reception and he talked to the point." He wanted road-spending put on a sound financial budget basis. If road funds had been spent on a budget basis, he said, "with a certain amount per mile for upkeep on dirt roads and a certain amount per mile for upkeep on rock roads, and then what was left had been used for building permanent highways, we might have all been benefited.

"I am not," he said, "in favor of spending the county's money for water-bound macadam roads. They will not stand up under the heavy traffic of the present day."

Then he added: "I want men for road overseers who know roads and who want to work—men who will do a day's work for a day's pay, who will work for the county as they would for themselves. I would rather have forty men for overseers who are willing to work than to have sixty politicians who care nothing about work."

Pendergast politicians thinking of Bulger and Shannon road overseers must have cheered that. They may also have cheered the final sentence from that published speech.

"I believe that honest work for the county," said Truman, "is the best politics today.

Truman had never seen Tom Pendergast when he made that campaign. It was his own campaign even if it fitted Tom's purpose at the time. He saw big Tom first only after he was elected and he and Tom went together to a conference with Joseph Shannon about the division of the jobs under the county court. As an honest Jacksonian Democrat, Truman's belief in honest government never caused him to disagree with either Tom Pendergast or Andrew Jackson about the idea that the political victor should have the political jobs.

Tom Pendergast then was fifty years old and veteran of three decades in politics. He had succeeded his big brother, James, the founder of the dynasty, in 1911 when James was already dying in his fifties of Bright's disease which kept him looking healthy almost until he died. The day Truman met him, Tom already was the gross image of the American political boss which Nast had imposed upon the American mind in his cartoons of Boss Tweed. He wore a derby hat cocked a little to one side on his massive head above his thick neck and bull-like body. It was easy to understand that his hairy fists were those which had knocked out the only man who ever knocked out Jack Dempsey. He was not pretty but he was impressive and his beef did not hide the great intelligence which even his critics have agreed was the basis of his political power. It was not any easier then to see the weaknesses in the great strength, which pulled him down in a procession of mastoiditis, thrombosis, cancer and general decay, than to suspect the time bomb, in his intelligence, of maniac betting on the horses which made him a fool before disease made him a corpse.

Big Tom looked at the neat, bespectacled, smiling Harry Truman. No record of his impression of the new official in his county organization has been handed down. What he said, however, was surprising to Truman.

"Look here, Harry. They tell me you're a pretty hot-headed fellow. When we get in this meeting now I don't want any fighting."

County Judge Truman blinked behind his glasses. Nothing could have been further in the world from his intention than going into the meeting and starting a row. He promised solemnly that he would not. In the meeting, however, the discussion had not gone far forward before the huge Pendergast and the wily Shannon were again joined in their ancient intra-mural Democratic debate. Pendergast was letting loose a verbal blast at Shannon which seemed the certain prelude to physical violence when suddenly his eyes fell on Truman. His new county judge was grinning at him. It was not customary for Pendergast's political subordinates to grin at him. Truman was frankly amused, and slowly Tom, remembering what he had said to Truman, began grinning, too. Shannon probably never understood. The grins may have saved him from an unequal encounter. They probably did not save him any more jobs for his followers in the courthouse in which Pendergast officials then had control. But this was the beginning of the strange and enduring political relationship between Pendergast and Truman which neither of them quite clearly understood. As Pendergast grew older his vanity in his power mounted with his fatuous notion that he could pick the right horses. Certainly, as Truman grew older his modesty combined with his loyalty to make him blind sometimes to the insensate selfishness which, with gambling, grew in Pendergast like a disease.

"Pendergast," Truman said years later after Tom was both disgraced and dead, "would stay with his friends straight or crooked, but when he found a man who was honest he would stand by him."

That statement as the moral of another and perhaps more important meeting between Truman and Pendergast requires examination. The meeting took place in the famous 1908 Main Street office. Judging from related events it must have been held around July 1928. It included not only Truman and Pendergast but also such Pendergast friends and friendly contractors as John J. Pryor, William D. Boyle and W. A. Ross. It was convened casually, as such meetings were, by a telephone call from the Boss.

"Harry," he said. "I'm in trouble. I wish you'd come over."

Usually Pendergast, whose courtesy in his relationships Truman remembers, would not summon his associates. He would phone, "Harry, would it be convenient for me to come to see you?"

It was always, as he expected, more convenient for Truman or anybody else in Kansas City to insist in answer that he would come to see Tom. The formula was important and it was preserved.

On this occasion Truman must have had an idea of what the Boss wanted to see him about. It was the road story. The preliminaries to the meeting require some recounting. Truman had been easily re-elected county judge by a reunited Jackson County Democracy. Old Joe Shannon had done perhaps a more thorough job than he had intended in 1924, when his friends and the Klan ganged-up on Harry Truman and other Pendergast candidates. They had succeeded in electing an entire Republican ticket. Realism brought Shannon and Pendergast together in 1926. The Klan was disintegrating. Pendergast, who had supported a reform city manager movement for Kansas City, had his own city manager in control. His power, like Coolidge's prosperity, was at rising tide though Pendergast power was to last longer. Under the genial supervision of Tom's brother Mike, Truman was becoming his county man.

Also, Truman was an enthusiastic official. In the same month that he was elected, Truman, as president of the National Old Trails Association, which sought good national highways following the historic American trails, headed a delegation from Kansas City to talk with the Governor of Kansas. As soon as he took office in January 1927, he got his old friend and associate, Colonel Edward M. Stayton, and a younger Republican engineer, N. T. Veatch, Jr., to make a bi-partisan study of the road needs of Jackson County. He must have talked with Pendergast about their appointment. Pendergast liked to be kept informed about such matters. Also, it is certain, that some time before May 1928, he had an agreement with Pendergast about roads and how he meant to build them.

"When Kansas City came on, in 1928, with a bond issue," Truman says, "I suggested to Tom Pendergast a county bond issue for a new courthouse and two hundred and fifty miles of roads.

"Tom said, 'You can't do it. They'll say I'm going to steal it. Bulger tried it and every other presiding judge for twenty years.'

"I told him I could. That I would tell the people what I meant to do and they would vote the bonds.

"Tom said, 'Go tell the voters anything you want to.'"

While that seems hardly an enthusiastic directive, to Truman it meant, "So I got authority from him," and in advance. There was a good deal to Tom Pendergast's pessimism. In a report on progress, published years later, the Kansas City Chamber of Commerce reported that, in the whole decade of the twenties, of seventy-one bond proposals by Kansas City and Jackson County only fourteen carried. Of $116,410,000 asked, $83,760,000 was turned down by the reluctant and suspicious taxpayers. Most of this had already occurred when Harry Truman came to office in January 1927. The need remained. His bi-partisan engineers, who had public confidence, presented Truman's program in a way which got public understanding. They said:

"It is quite evident from inspection, as well as admitted facts, that the hard roads in Jackson County were not built according to best practice, even for 'water-bound macadam' roads. Also that the location of many of the roads was determined by political preference rather than by good engineering location. . . . As a result of conditions stated, the County is confronted with what is practically an impossible situation. There are some 350 miles of what has been aptly termed 'pie crust' roads, clearly inadequate to stand the demands of modern traffic. The cost of maintaining these roads even in fair condition is almost an impossibility and certainly financially undesirable, as it is quite evident that the amount required to properly maintain them will soon exceed the amount that can be raised by taxes."

They proposed the construction of 224 miles of roads at a cost of $6,407,838.

"I had an agreement with Pendergast," Truman says. "I told the voters we would let the contracts to low bidders and build under the supervision of these bi-partisan engineers."

The people voted Truman the $6,500,000 for roads, though they turned him down on his courthouse until 1931. In the same election, however, the voters rejected practically all the bond issues proposed for Kansas City.

"After they approved," Truman says, "we let $400,000 at the first crack and we awarded it to the American Road Building Company of South Dakota."

That was in July 1928. It was not many days before Tom Pendergast summoned him to his office. Even in the days of his greatest power it was a tawdry office on the second floor of a two story yellow building which also housed a wholesale linen store and a café. Pendergast's Jackson County Democratic Club occupied three rooms on the second floor. Pendergast sat at a business man's desk. Truman knew his way there by 1928.

"I went," he recalls, "and there were all the crooked contractors that caused the scandals under Bulger: Boyle and Pryor and Ross.

"Tom said, 'These boys tell me that you won't give them contracts.'

" 'They can get them,' I said, 'if they are low bidders, but they won't get paid for them unless they come up to specifications.' "

Truman smiles when he remembers Pendergast's reply.

" 'Didn't I tell you boys,' he said, 'he's the contrariest cuss in Missouri?'

"After they left," Truman remembers, "Pendergast told me to go ahead. He had the two other judges on the county court and they could have outvoted me if he'd told them to." And he repeated the statement: "Pendergast would stay with his friends straight or crooked but when he found a man who was honest, he would stand by him."

Harry Truman is loyal to Tom Pendergast but Pendergast's decision at that meeting deserves some discussion. In the first place, he had agreed to the terms under which Truman submitted the bonds to the people. He shared the almost superstitious insistence of political bosses that they keep their word. Also, he had given his word in the presence of some other people. He had let the Truman pledge, obviously made with his approval, stand through the elections. A good deal more, probably, entered into Tom's decision at that meeting, though he was certainly not as disinterested a boss and umpire as Truman at that meeting believed.

Tom Pendergast, despite the driven greediness of his last years when as a gambler he was entitled to be called "America's No. 1 sucker," was not in his own eyes or the eyes of his friends a crooked politician. He was almost the epitome of the business man boss. He was the master of "honest graft" brought to him from such enterprises as the Ready-Mixed Concrete Company whose trucks carried his name to every job. Critics miss the meaning of the man who see only the wide-open character of

Kansas City and the shake-down of gambling houses, brothels and racket centers. He was big in the wholesale liquor business before prohibition and after. As boss of Kansas City, he cannot escape responsibility for crime there during the years of his power. He was close to some of the racketeers, particularly after they took the control of Little Italy away from Mike Ross, the contractor and politician, in the same election in which most of the city bonds were defeated and Truman's road bonds were approved. It is, however, to minimize the malignancy of the Pendergast-type politician in the American democracy to remember him only as a ward heeler with his hand out behind a brothel. Kansas City always apparently wanted to be wicked. Tammany politicians were shocked by its slot machines as early as 1900. From the beginning, its lively wickedness was a part of its appeal as an exciting metropolis of a not always puritanical West. Wide open was good business. And business was politics —in Kansas City and other American cities, too.

Pendergast was no more a figure in American politics than in American business. His position as boss was that of broker for corporations as well as saloonkeepers. His associates were not only in the city hall but in the Chamber of Commerce. As chief employment agent for the whole community, he sent job applicants with his little notes in red pencil to the power company as directly as to the city hall. They were legal tender for a job under the Kansas City system in both places. A Missourian who was once Assistant Secretary of Commerce has testified that Pendergast worked "hand-in-glove with the public utilities in Kansas City." Former Attorney General of Missouri, John T. Barker, wrote in his memoirs that "he had a close alliance with the big utility interests." The only newspaper which gave steady support to his organization was the late *Kansas City Journal-Post* which was the voice of Henry L. Doherty, head of the Cities Service Company. Some of the most important of his political conferences were held in the office of William T. Kemper, chairman of the Commerce Trust Company. Pendergast was a business man. He put his name on the wagons as a man in business with whom it might be profitable to do business.

"I live here, am in business here, own property here, pay all my taxes here," he said. "Does any man say I have not a right to try to make a living here? My business right now is selling

Ready-Mixed Concrete. I am selling all of it I can to anybody I can induce to buy it, and in that particular I am exactly like the maker of sewer pipe, or vitrified brick, or tiling or any other material. They all hustle for business. . . .

"I am for more and better and bigger business, from Ready-Mixed Concrete to ice cream cones."

He could not have been in a better town for his business. One of the many wonderful things about Kansas City was that its greatest antagonists, Pendergast and *The Kansas City Star,* fought steadily together for the municipal improvements—parks, boulevards, aqueducts, traffic ways—which required contractors and concrete. It is interesting, also, that when the one Boss lost his monopolistic power, *The Kansas City Star* had become, with its morning edition *The Times,* the one daily newspaper voice for the whole city and much of Missouri and Kansas as well. It had the biggest radio station, too.

Even as presiding county judge, Harry Truman was a small man in the company of Kansas City business men and politicians who made the complex body of the simple-seeming Pendergast power. He was an insolvent veteran when, with Pendergast backing, he ran for office in 1922. It could not have been within his knowledge that perhaps even then the fight with Miles Bulger was a business man's war as much as a politician's. Bulger was a contractor, too. He was out of the way when Truman began building roads on the low-bid, high-specification basis which brought him the call to the Boss' office.

The chief contractor among them all in the office may have been Tom Pendergast himself. District Attorney Maurice Milligan, who sent him to prison, has reported that his investigations showed that Pendergast "owned and controlled" the W. A. Ross Construction Company. Truman thinks that is not true. The partnership of the Ross family and the Pendergasts was in the Ready-Mixed Concrete Company which made no contracts to build roads though it was glad to furnish a good grade of concrete. The interlocking business and political relationships of Pendergast, Boyle, Pryor and Ross made a maze that day. It is still bewildering. It may mean that in that meeting, Pendergast stood with Truman not only against the trio of contractors but against himself as well, in approving recognition of an honest man. As he was always more intelligent than his merely muscular associates, however, he undoubtedly realized, even as a business man interested in contracts, that Truman had found the way to break the reluctance of the people against bond issues, which meant more building. Low-bid building was building still. Also, from the time Harry Truman grinned at him at that first meeting with Shannon, Pendergast must have understood that he was dealing with no ordinary politician. He stood by him. Also, afterwards he was never in a great hurry to shower Harry Truman with favors in spite of the legend of the later years.

Truman built the roads. With his two special engineers, Colonel Stayton and Mr. Veatch, he traveled over every foot of the 350 miles of supposedly hard-surfaced road in the county, most of it laid out for wagon traffic and much of it modernized only with a Bulger "pie crust." Truman not only wanted good engineering. As farm-trained man he insisted that no Jackson County farmer be left more than two and a half miles from a concrete slab road. Also, as veteran he remembered the green roads in France along which his battery had moved its guns. He planted rows of elms and poplars beside the roads—seven thousand of them—with the idea that when the swift growing poplars died the long-lasting elms would have attained their growth. That turned out to be too aesthetic a notion for the Missourian. Farmers mowed down the seedlings and today the only ones which remain are those which have been carefully tended by the Truman farm.

In that road-building Truman promised that consideration would be given "only to practical needs—not political." And afterwards he was able to say that "this county plan was based on *practical* needs; it was carried out along *practical* lines; its effect will be for the *practical* benefit of every citizen!" In each case it was he who italicized the word "practical." Yet, nothing is so clear as that in everything he did he gave emphasis to the beauty of Jackson County in the roads which he ran through it. After most of the work was done, he published a booklet about it filled with pictures of the roadsides and the farms, the country places, the streams and the parks beside which the highways passed. He was thinking not merely of roads. Long before the New Deal made such words familiar, his planning included parks and recreation grounds, the development of the

streams, the preservation of the forests. Above all, it was planning for people by imaginative, intelligent and honest government in a county which included the men of the metropolis and
of the farms as well.

"Here were hundreds of square miles," he said in the booklet of his report called "Results of County Planning—Jackson
County, Missouri." "Hundreds of thousands of people . . . *each
dependent on the other* . . . and only a plan and a determined
spirit needed to develop these opportunities and make each
available and understanding of the other!

"The plan was developed—*and inaugurated.*"

The certain thing is that the "determined spirit" was named
Harry Truman. Out of the $6,500,000 bond issue, $200,000 was
saved and more miles of road were built than the original estimate called for. Actually improved were 166 miles of concrete
roads and 52 miles of secondary roads. *The Kansas City Times*
declared that the road system represented a "distinct achievement
that would be creditable to any county in the United States."
And added: "That is a situation reflecting the excellent service
of the county court under the leadership of Judge Truman and
of the consulting engineers, Colonel Stayton and Mr. Veatch."
The Star spoke of Truman as "extraordinarily efficient" and
declared that there was "not a suspicion of graft" in the entire
program.

More and more Jackson County, Kansas City and Missouri
were aware of him. His office in the gloomy old courthouse
stayed crowded all day long. On September 3, 1929, Mike Pendergast died. It is a date well remembered in Kansas City because that was the night, also, when thieves broke into Tom
Pendergast's great mansion and emphasized both his wealth and
the crime which was increasing in his town. For Truman, Mike's
death meant that at last he was the chief of the organization
in the county. It was, perhaps, ironical that he succeeded to it
just a little less than two months before the collapse of the stock
market was to signal change not only in American economic
ideas, governmental ideas, but profound alteration in the people
and political organization throughout the United States. The
amazing, forgotten thing is the readiness of Harry Truman for
the change itself.

No story of his efficient public service should be allowed to obscure the fact that Harry Truman was always a politician and found no conflict in his life between public service and politics. He was serious about it, though he always carried a sense of humor into it, too. His "Harpie Club," in Independence, combined poker, politics and conviviality. It was named, the late Mayor Roger Sermon of Independence said, from its spontaneous origin at a hilarious harmonica-playing contest arranged for an Independence town character who imagined himself an artist on that instrument. It became, however, the county club of the Pendergast people.

"I controlled the Democratic Party in Eastern Jackson County when I was county judge," Truman said. "Mike turned it over to me. In any election I could deliver eleven thousand votes and not steal a one. It was not necessary. I looked out for the people and they understood my leadership. The vote-stealing in Kansas City was silly."

In January 1930, the county judge, whose clearly stated plan for the people had resulted in their approval of his road bond issue when most of the Kansas City bond proposals were rejected, was elected president of the Greater Kansas City Plan Association which proposed the extension of the planning he had done for Jackson County to two other Missouri counties and three counties just across the line in Kansas. In June 1930, he was made a director of the National Conference on City Planning. In road-building, he learned, only Westchester County, New York, in the whole United States had done a greater job. The "public approval and public confidence" which *The Star* said was based upon his "extraordinary record" spread into the knowledge of the state. People recognized him in the halls of the Capitol at Jefferson City. He had more and more friends in the county seats.

The politics and public service were never separate. He regarded himself as a politician and as an organization Democrat. In September 1930, when he was making his own easy campaign for re-election, he followed the organization line in support of an old foe. At a big tent meeting at Grandview, he presented Joseph Shannon, who at sixty-three was being eliminated by elevation to Congress. Shannon won, but as low man, while Truman ran far ahead of the ticket. After the election *The Odessa Democrat* gave its small-town Missouri opinion that the state might go farther and do worse than pick Harry Truman for Governor in 1932.

On May 26, 1931, the voters gave Truman, as head of the county government, $7,950,000 more in bonds for more roads, a new courthouse in place of the old stone rookery, and other county improvements. That was the county's part of a much-publicized Kansas City Ten-Year Plan which meant work and jobs at a time when the idea that the end of the depression was just around the corner was becoming grimly humorous in America. The Truman demonstration of the possibility of planning for people and of honesty in building for people had a large part to do with the approval of the Ten-Year program.

In Emporia, Kansas, William Allen White almost lyrically praised the program. Here were "jobs at useful and beautiful public improvements" instead of soup kitchens maintained by charity to feed the idle. *The St. Louis Post-Dispatch,* which seemed so often to regard Kansas City as the special subject for its superior chiding, regarded it as "a striking object lesson for the national government." "While the administration," it said, "is coasting along puerilely hoping the depression will solve itself, a middle-western city is shrewd and progressive enough to launch an offensive against it."

Immediately following the election, Judge Truman announced plans to go ahead with road-building and the construction of a new courthouse. The same sort of bi-partisan board of architects would design and supervise the construction of the new county building. As he had personally gone over the road system, however, he set out on a big automobile swing to see other courthouses before building a new one for Kansas City. He found his model at Shreveport, Louisiana, in the Caddo Parish Courthouse which had been built by an architect named Edward F. Neild in 1926. He hired Neild to help design the building. Truman himself saw that it went up financially straight to the top of its tower.

They were busy years. He had watched almost every stone go into the courthouse. He had certainly watched every bill that was paid. He had checked with Stayton and Veatch on the new roads being added to the county system. He had found time to go to Jefferson City and other places in Missouri urging local government reforms, the hope of enactment of which seem even more fantastic than his later hopes for an effective United Nations. He proposed that Missouri cut the number of its counties from one hundred and fourteen to thirty or forty. No American politician in any American state can propose anything more sensible, or so improbable of fulfilment. One world is simpler than fewer counties.

"My grandfather lived twenty miles from the county seat at Independence," he said, "and it took him as long to make the trip then as it takes me now to ride from Independence to St. Louis."

He moved—occasionally speeding—on those roads from town to town. The county seats listened but they remained county seats and remain county seats still. He had time, also, to ride, as he had ridden looking at courthouses, to Nashville and New Orleans talking his ideas to Charles L. Keck, who was shaping the Jackson statue. In addition to his continuing job as county judge, he had assumed without pay, late in 1933, the position of Re-Employment Director for Missouri. Yet, he continued to have *The Star's* appreciation for his "enthusiastic devotion to county affairs." Already, also, he was moving up the chairs in Masonry in the Grand Lodge of Missouri. Apparently all that was not enough. He also accepted appointment by Governor Guy B. Park as chairman of a committee to support a $10,000,-000 bond issue for the rehabilitation of state eleemosynary and penal institutions.

He was enthusiastic, optimistic, close to the details and full of expansive ideas. In general, however, he seemed to be doing a great deal better in public service than in either his personal politics or his private affairs. It is a detail as important as a skyscraper in that period that, on April 30, 1929, after he had let $6,500,000 in road contracts, a judgment by default for $8,944.78 was entered against him for the old Truman & Jacobson debts. He had still not been able to pay it in July 1934. That was particularly interesting in view of the fact that, in October 1929 and April 1930, Jackson County took strips one hundred feet wide for highway rights of way through the Truman homeplace. Truman declined to let the county pay his family for it.

Obviously, he could not stay county judge all his life at $6,000. It began to look essential that he go forward in politics or get out of politics again. In 1931, *The Star* reported that Truman's friends were already campaigning for him for Governor in a sort of trial heat in the hope that Pendergast would give him his support. Pendergast did not. He nominated another man in 1932, and when that man died before the general election selected still another. Truman apparently he did not consider at all. In 1933, when the Legislature was undertaking to re-district Missouri for Congressional seats, Truman went to Jefferson City and worked for the establishment of a district for Eastern Jackson County which he hoped to represent. He got the district established. He had every prospect of being elected from it. Then Pendergast gave his support for the new seat to C. Jasper Bell, who had served as city councilman and circuit judge. Later, some little talk was revived that Truman might get the well-paid job of county collector which Pendergast had declined to let him have when he had asked for it in 1926. He did not get it. "And did not want it," he said.

It was not Truman's view, but there are good grounds for believing that the explanation of Pendergast's reluctance to support Truman in these cases was that though he went along with him, Truman's stubborn honesty sometimes seemed too uncompromising. Truman's explanation is that Pendergast had bigger plans for him.

On the eighth of May, 1934, he was fifty years old. He was not tired but he was working hard. He took off time to play with Margaret and to be with Bess. Sometimes he played long and peacefully on the piano. Whether he was getting anywhere or not, there were many things to do. About the middle of May, he drove up to Sedalia, Missouri, to speak in connection with the campaign for the improvement of state institutions which he was leading. Frank Monroe, a real estate man and chairman of the campaign in that county, had a little dinner for him.

At dinner he told Monroe that James P. Aylward, Pendergast lawyer and Democratic State Chairman, and James M. Pendergast had been trying to get him on the phone all day. He gave Monroe the impression that he had been dodging the call. Both he and Monroe understood the situation which had been described in *The Star* on Truman's birthday: "The big problem now of the Kansas City machine, backed in a corner, is to find a man who can defeat J. L. (Tuck) Milligan, of Richmond, supported for the Senatorial nomination by Senator Bennett C. Clark."

Somewhere that night or the day after, Truman took the telephone call. All right, he told them, he would meet them at the Bothwell Hotel. He hung up the receiver and walked out to his car. Years later he said, "I never did run for a political job that I wanted." He had a feeling as he went to meet Pendergast and Aylward that he was headed again in that direction that May.

CHAPTER XI

End of the "Robust Years"

"LET THE RIVER take its course," Tom Pendergast used to say in his more imperious moments. Somehow that carried the sense that he was the river, as important in Kansas City as the Missouri beside it. In many ways he was. It was the essence of his business always to seem to be. He could say where the sewers would run and how much concrete must be bought from him. He could make a man an official. He could, as some said he did, even say that he made a Senator half as a joke and half as a gesture of his power.

The truth, clear in the evidence, is that when Pendergast turned to Harry Truman as his candidate for Senator he had very little more free choice than the Missouri River did in its big sweep around the end of the glacial ice cap. He was in trouble in Missouri. In his business, things had been changing since the stock market cracked and Franklin Roosevelt first used the phrase "New Deal" to delighted Democrats in Chicago. Pendergast was puzzled, and in the American political procession he was late. The selection of Truman was almost the only course open to him. More important, it is now clear that of all those considered and solicited as his candidate that year by Tom Pendergast, Harry Truman was the only man in the course of his times.

That may seem only interpretation after the fact. It is based on a clear and consecutive story, nevertheless. The best way to begin it may be to go back to that New Year's Day in 1931, when Truman's mother came with Bess and other members of his family to see Truman sworn in once more as presiding judge of the county court. It was at a significant time in America. Martha Ellen then was more than half as old as the Republic, which had sometimes seemed pretty shaky since the fall of 1929.

Ninety-one banks in Missouri were already tottering toward their failure that year. Not only had the free land like that her father had taken when she was a child been long gone; in 1931, one farmer out of four in Missouri was a tenant. Martha Ellen had not a single unmortgaged acre of her own. The whole land had changed in her lifetime. The fifteen million acres of forest in Missouri had, by the lumber companies' policy of "cut out and get out," been reduced to 250,000 acres. Not long before Martha Ellen was born, Francis Parkman had been nervous about the painted Indians and white men loaded with both guns and whiskey; now the murder rate in Kansas City had run up with that of Chicago. There were problems for pioneers on the Middle Border still.

Her boy, Harry, in the gloomy courthouse was only briefly solemn as he swore. He grinned then at his mother and his friends. Even in that year he was an optimist. The deepening hard times outside the courthouse were his public, but not his personal, concern. This was not Truman's depression. He had had his with Eddie Jacobson and others who were caught, quickly and hard, long before Wall Street discovered the depression. This time he was on a regular payroll. Indeed, it was at Christmas in 1932, the last presidential Christmas of Hoover and before, as the satirists said, Santa Claus came with Roosevelt, that Truman bought eight-year-old Margaret a shiny baby grand piano. Margaret was a little disappointed then not to get electric trains. It took her some years to understand the excitement of her father for whom it was probably the most expensive purchase he had ever made in his life. It was also one of the most important.

He came eagerly home every day to the big Gates house. Green Delaware Street showed few signs of the depression. Some of the substantial houses needed a little paint. It was the sort of small-town street which could leave all its lawns to the tending of one such colored man as Moses Menefee, who in 1950 tended it still—even though some Republican neighbors suggested he paid too much attention to one presidential lawn. In hard times, as in good ones, people spoke across its quietness from their doorsteps to neighbors who were known in fixed, dependable (or well-known undependable) relationships. It was a street which seemed as remote as possible from any of the brutal images of hard times in America, though sometimes it decorously covered difficulty and even tragedy. Harry Truman was a man who matched that street.

Also, as one who had been the victim of hard times before, he understood the needs of other men on the roads and on the grimmer streets. As a realist he knew the need of jobs for men. As both politician and official, he found people in trouble lined up at his office door. Also, as an optimist determined upon realism, he had begun, before the bonds for a new courthouse were voted, to look at the best new courthouses all over the country. Characteristically in that enterprise he counted upon his own best judgment and on a politician upon whom he could depend even in the tight places. His driver and companion on that trip was not an architect or technician but Fred Canfil, who across the decades was to be Truman's energetically devoted man Friday. He is a short, ugly man with the personality of a baited bear, but with a primitive bearlike loyalty, too. They drove over 24,000 miles. It was a trip which let Truman see more of America than he had ever seen before and at a time when America was critically looking at itself.

The journey ran south to include Oklahoma and Arkansas, where already the tractors were moving onto the plantations and the Okies and the Arkies were being made ready to hit the road to California, which had altered some since Solomon Young's day. There were already Hoovervilles near the larger cities in the South and Southwest. The various courthouses which Truman visited all had lines of people in them inquiring about relief. Truman made such a study of courthouses as has hardly ever preceded the building of any other one. And, unintentionally he made a study of his country when its problems were people in trouble.

(That trip South was only one lap of the courthouse quest. He went to look at buildings in Buffalo and Brooklyn, at a Sun Life Assurance Company building in Canada. He examined city halls and courthouses and capitols in Denver, Milwaukee, Racine and Chicago. He met architects and remembered years later that Bertram Grosvenor Goodhue, designer of the State Capitol at Lincoln, Nebraska, once told him that the time would come when the only three recognized periods and types of architecture would be "Greek, Gothic and Goodhue.")

Truman came back to find the lines of people in trouble lengthening at the courthouse door in Jackson County, too, at the city hall and at Tom Pendergast's office at 1908 Main. While he planned and campaigned for the courthouse, he tried also, like officials everywhere in a country in which trouble was still dependent upon local resources only, to protect such local government resources as there were. He tried to meet the situation with pay cuts, enforced vacations, an end of allowances for automobiles. Yet, he defended at the same time county workers; there were no more deadheads on public payrolls, he said, than on private ones. More people needed help; jobs were more and more precious; people grumbled and complained. Some charged that he favored old neighbors at Grandview in giving road jobs.

"This is not a Red meeting," their spokesman said. "This is a blue meeting. There are men, women and children in his district who are hungry. We must have jobs or food."

There were other things in those years which were not easy. Those were the years upon which rest the big memory of his close political association with the Pendergast machine. It was close. Tom Pendergast was having troubles, too. There were more men asking for jobs than were available even to those armed with notes from Pendergast in his characteristic red pencil. Tom helped Truman. He approved Truman's employment of good men who had no claim on the organization politically like Alex F. Sachs, the able Jew whom Truman made his new highway engineer. Pendergast never, Truman always remembered, asked Truman even in the toughest times to do any dishonest thing. He expected political loyalty and from Harry Truman he got it. There was nothing in political loyalty, however, to require Truman enthusiasm about every one of Pendergast's political enterprises.

In March 1932, Truman was one of five thousand Pendergast men whom Tom poured by special train upon St. Louis for the Democratic State Convention at which Pendergast sought (and did not quite get) a delegation to the National Convention instructed for James Reed for President. Truman was never enthusiastic about Jim Reed. After Reed had helped Republican isolationists kill the League of Nations, Truman was close to Woodrow Wilson's judgment of Reed as a man "incapable of sustained allegiance to any person or cause." Also, in following Pendergast in support of Reed, Truman was called into service to help bind the Democratic Party to the most reactionary aspects of its past.

Reed was Tom Pendergast's almost romantic project. He had tried to get him the Democratic nomination in 1928. He was even more eager to help him in 1932. That year many Democrats were ragged; some may have seemed stupid; but few were timid. It was Reed's romantic judgment that they would want a man who wanted the government to be less concerned about their welfare, not more. Pendergast agreed out of adoration for Reed.

Truman was also one of the hundreds of Missouri Democrats who went with Pendergast to the convention in Chicago in June. He was a loyal but not a happy man.

"I was at the 1932 convention in Chicago as a spectator at a couple of sessions," Truman told me later as if he were trying to minimize his presence there. "I never liked Jim Reed after his disloyal treatment of Wilson."

As organization partisan he was in his place. And his presence put him in bulk if not in belief behind the opposition to the very sort of imaginative governmental planning for people in which he believed and which Roosevelt embodied. He did not attend all the sessions, but he must have been among the listening when the Pendergast case for Reed was stated by Missouri orators in phrases which have become the standard epithets flung against the New Deal and the Truman Fair Deal, too: "paternalism," "experimentation," "socialistic," "a swarm of taxeaters, snoopers and spies," "devour the substance of our people," "frightening every man with a dollar," "the already overburdened people," and "encroachment of Federal authority." Pendergast and the three of his loyal Missourians who nominated Reed did the best they could. But even Missouri was reluctant. The best Reed got was 27½ votes on the third ballot—never even the whole vote of Missouri. After Roosevelt was nominated, Reed himself took the floor to speak the philosophy which out of faith in him Tom Pendergast had followed.

"It is the highest duty of the Democratic Party," he said in that prosecutor's voice which combined arrogance, violence and velvet, "to get back the old principles and old methods. There has been no improvement on the policies of George Washington in regard to international affairs, and there never will be an improvement. There has been no improvement on the philosophy of Thomas Jefferson, and there never will be an improvement. There has been no improvement on the philosophy—the economic philosophy of John Stuart Mill, and there never will be an improvement. What we want is to recognize that government cannot take care of the people, that the people must take care of government."

It was, as usual, a fine speech. Harry Truman's father had listened to that voice in 1900. Even as a street superintendent years before, Tom Pendergast had melted to that music which combined the lute or the whistle and the sound of the ax biting into the block. Harry Truman could listen to it with no stirring along his spine. He was probably less surprised than Tom Pendergast when Reed supported the anti-Pendergast candidate for the Senate that same summer. Reed had, of course, the persuasive excuse that that candidate, Bennett Champ Clark, of St. Louis, was the son of the great Speaker Champ Clark whom he had nominated for the Presidency at Baltimore in 1912. Harry Truman went down the line for Tom's candidate for the Senate, Charles M. Howell, who had been Jim Reed's own former law partner. Clark's election was classed as an upset. It was the beginning of some upsetting times for Tom Pendergast.

There were few other overt signs of trouble in the Pendergast organization, however. Harry Truman was not aware of any. Indeed, with the exception of Clark's victory, the 1932 election in Missouri seemed the apex of Pendergast power. The failure of the Legislature to re-district the state after the 1930 census had meant that every Congressman had had to run at large in the whole state. They came in a procession to ask for the support of Pendergast and his huge Kansas City and Jackson County vote. Afterwards some of them seemed awkward in the procession. It included one of the two Milligan brothers, who ran against Truman for the Senate, one in 1934 and the other in 1940, both on strong anti-Pendergast grounds. It also included John Cochran, of St. Louis, who ran against him in 1934 on similar grounds. Lloyd Crow Stark, who seemed to hope in 1940 to become either Vice-President or Senator for his anti-Pendergast crusade, came to ask Pendergast support for the governorship for the first time. He did not get it until his second visit and second request in 1936. In Missouri at least, Pendergast support did not seem tainted in 1932.

The truth is that the word "Pendergast" only began to be dramatically offensive on a heroic scale after 1932. Indeed, no real crimes were proved against the organization until after the election of 1936 in which Stark was elected Governor, and investigation showed almost prodigious election irregularities which swelled the vote in almost whimsical disregard of the population. Pendergast himself was caught in a maze of bribe-taking and tax-dodging only in 1939, though his own associates had been appalled by the gambling mania which had already begun to possess him in 1934.

On the morning of June 17, 1933, however, just two days before Truman let the contract for the new Kansas City court-house, the news flashed across Kansas City of the Union Station Massacre in which five persons were killed. Slowly afterwards the gossip spread that the public enemies who had tried to free a killer named Frank Nash from local and Federal officers had received help and hiding from Kansas City racketeers who were also Pendergast political lieutenants. It was not proved. Truman believed that the massacre was an outside job and happened there only because Kansas City was the place where train change was necessary. However, some suspicion was directed at John Lazia, of the North Side, who was himself murdered not long after. It was public knowledge, however, that the rackets flourished under Lazia. He had pushed Pendergast's old Irish lieutenant out of the Fifth Ward and taken his place, receiving Pendergast's acceptance and blessing. Perhaps, as some old residents said, "wide open" in Kansas City was not anything new there even at a time when the American annual crime bill, according to the Wickersham Commission, was $1,000,000,000 (half the total receipts of the United States government then). Crime certainly was not restricted to Kansas City. Al Capone, who contributed along with Samuel Insull to the Republican machine in Chicago, had been sent to Federal prison just a year before the Union Station Massacre in Kansas City. The situation in Kansas City was not such as to stir local pride, nevertheless. It helped get some of the citizens fighting mad.

The city election of March 27, 1934, provided the basis for even greater indignation. Here was no mere suspicion of ties between racketeers and politicians, here was a clear and inescapable demonstration of connection between balloting and brutality. The Pendergast opposition was smashed, but only after four people had been killed and eleven severely injured. Pendergast got a victory but his organization also roused a new hue and a louder cry. Furthermore, the violence of that election seemed almost suicidally designed to serve a more serious setback to Pendergast's power in Missouri.

Looking back, any student must wonder whether the Pendergast intelligence had not already begun to slip in the gambling obsession which overtook him. As early as 1932, his support of Reed showed a lack of political realism. Those like Truman, who followed him silently on that enterprise, apparently looked at his iron physique and missed the dimensions of inner stresses and strains on an overextended Irishman. There were strains. In Kansas City, while the old, tough, combative, sometimes criminal Irish had been familiar to him, the newer Italians even in their protestations of loyalty were strange. There were other strange things. He was a business man in an age of changing ideas about business. Also, as the big-hearted boss and friend of the poor he lived to see the basket of groceries and the scuttle of coal transferred socially, statistically and politically from the ward to Washington. There was, a little later, nothing new or strange about his understanding that the place for a crooked politician to hold out his hand was not behind a brothel but in the sanctum of the law firm of many of the leading fire insurance companies of America. He did not recognize that there were new cops in the world who never walked a beat or accepted a free beer but who, in order to collect a tax, could trace a bribe from Missouri to the passenger list of the *Queen Mary*. Some of those things must have worried Tom Pendergast before even his associates knew he had reason to worry about them. Long before his almost panic preoccupation with the horse races, he was gambling for larger and larger stakes on narrower and narrower margins. Some psychiatrist later may dissect the Pendergast legend to discover that in his last years he turned to the

sharp, single alternative of gambling as some other men turn
to drink. Early in 1934, he did not move against the dangers
to his power with any such skill as people then and later attributed to him.

In February, before the rough city victory of March, Senator
Clark announced almost gaily that he meant to secure the Democratic nomination of Congressman Tuck Milligan as his companion in the United States Senate. That, in effect, not only
meant that Clark would have both Senators. Also, since the
Missouri custom is to have one Senator from the west and the
other from the east, it meant the capture of the Senator from
Pendergast's western section of the state. In a year of pistol
shots, the two veterans of the 140th Infantry, Clark and Milligan, seemed to suggest that the only weapon needed against Pendergast was a thumb at the nose. And when the state-wide
indignation rose after the Kansas City elections in March, it
looked as if they might be right.

Pendergast had much to give, of course, in Kansas City. Also
at the time, as afterwards, the tag of the Pendergast machine was
a burden for any candidate to bear in the state. It seems odd
that no commentator has compared his situation in that Senate
race with his situation in the county in 1922, when his brother,
Mike, went into Truman & Jacobson's store and told Harry that
he "could be county judge if he wanted to be." Mike was dead
now and Tom apparently did not see the similarity. Indeed,
nothing is so clear as that Tom, seeking a candidate, moved
slowly, awkwardly, and with an out-of-date understanding of his
needs in Missouri and America which were living in the first
fascination of the New Deal.

Apparently Pendergast did not even notice Truman in his
first search for a Senator. Truman that year was doing his job
in such a way as to require no special attention. He was, however, doing it in such a way that more and more Missourians
were aware of him. After twelve years in politics, not one real
criticism was in the record against his name. It was his clear
intention that there should not be any grounds for any. A year
before, when the cloudhead of indignation was forming against
Pendergast in Kansas City, a grand jury began looking into affairs which disturbed many citizens. It had hardly begun its
labors before it got a letter from County Judge Truman:

"There have been large expenditures of money for public purposes during the period of my services as presiding judge.

"If there is any investigation of the activities of the court, I should be more than glad to appear before the grand jury, waiving immunity if you desire it, and furnish you with any information you desire. . . .

"I am inviting the closest investigation because I am proud of the county court."

The grand jury found nothing to censure. The county affairs were handled to the satisfaction of a community which had ceased to be silent on most other governmental subjects. Furthermore, Judge Truman was giving effective attention to other matters in which a very great many Kansas City and Missouri citizens were almost desperately concerned. In October 1933, he accepted, to serve without pay, national appointment as Federal Re-employment Director for Missouri. His boss was Harry Hopkins, who conferred with him in Kansas City within a week after his appointment. They were engaged, as Robert Sherwood, Hopkins' biographer, has said, not in any completely worked out system of relief but in "a series of remarkable improvisations impelled by the character of the myriad problems that were discovered from day to day." Apparently Hopkins approved of his Missouri man. Truman approved of Hopkins. They talked, Truman recalls, of ways of getting wholesale employment and Truman told him that he thought the plans which were taking shape in Hopkins' mind, which later led to the WPA, were practical if he could get the funds.

"I always liked Hopkins," Truman said long after the relief days and after Hopkins had gone to Russia as his emissary.

With Hopkins, Truman was one of those anxious for measures equal to the problem. Perhaps once it had been a good idea for the people to take care of the government and not the government take care of the people. Truman was working with people every day who were, through no fault of their own, no longer able to take care of themselves. He was running for no job in January 1934 when he spoke at Columbia, the Missouri university town. He was talking about the desperate needs of people.

"If it is necessary to cut each working day to two hours to give everybody a job," Truman said, "then let's cut it to two hours and give the same wage we used to earn for a ten-hour day. In place of permitting two or three men to get all the profit by the use of machines, we are going to distribute it over the entire community. I think that is in accord with the President's idea of the situation.

"We are now going about the job," he continued, "of redistributing wealth that was amassed in the robust years, but, thank heaven, we are going about it more peacefully than was done in Russia, Italy and Germany."

That was four months before Pendergast got around to Harry Truman in his search for a candidate for the United States Senate. It seemed, also, at least four centuries beyond the Reed-Pendergast position at Chicago. Truman told me that Pendergast suggested that he run for the Senate before he asked three other men in succession but that Truman then declined. Others who were offered Pendergast's support were not aware of this fact. According to William P. Helm, who was then the Washington correspondent of *The Kansas City Journal-Post,* Pendergast first turned to Jim Reed who had helped create this Clark menace against him two years before. *The New York Times* reported the expectation that Reed would run. Helm gives as his authority Joseph Shannon, who was working in close harmony with Pendergast at the time.

"Jim Reed is an able man," Helm says Shannon told him. "And one of the most difficult; I've heard that he can't even get along with himself at times. He's a good vote-getter and I think he could win, if any Democrat could. But he's getting old. And he's comfortable. I don't think he'll run."

He did not. Then Shannon told Helm—and the Missouri papers at the time carried a statement by Shannon verifying it—that "Pendergast has asked me to take the nomination for the Senate." One of the reasons which entered into Shannon's decision not to run, according to Helm, was that Shannon was as unsympathetic with the Roosevelt Administration as Reed was. Shannon was also getting old and he was also comfortable as a Congressman making speeches about Thomas Jefferson and talking behind his hand about Franklin Roosevelt.

Then Pendergast turned to the chief lawyer of his organization, James P. Aylward, of Kansas City, who was that year also Democratic State Chairman. (Maybe some limitation on the

Pendergast mind after he had grown to state power is shown by
the fact that all his hopes were men in Jackson County.) On the
seventh day of May, Aylward made a public statement taking
himself out of consideration. That was the same day that *The
Star* said that Pendergast was "backed in a corner" in his efforts
to find an opponent for Clark's Milligan. In Washington, Joe
Shannon seemed to share *The Star*'s opinion. The number of
those able and willing to make the race for Tom Pendergast
that year was limited.

"You know, Brother Helm," Shannon told the newspaperman,
"Tom hasn't got a field of world-beaters to choose from."

In that same conversation Shannon mentioned that Pendergast
was "talking about Judge Truman."

"And who," Helm asked Shannon, "is Judge Truman?"

It was no such rhetorical question as Nick Phelps had asked
twelve years before. Helm, who was not a Missourian, actually
did not know. He had never seen Truman speaking in the outstate counties with that strangely effective, almost conversational
persuasiveness which he was using at that time to raise money
for better state institutions. He spoke in Sedalia, Moberly and
Warsaw. And in Warsaw he took the phone call about the conference in the Bothwell Hotel.

It was not a jubilant occasion for Harry Truman. Not even
his old comrade Jim Pendergast could have come to that hotel
room happily confident that he was about to make Harry United
States Senator. It must have been in some regards an embarrass-
ing session for Jim Aylward, who had turned the offer down
himself. The two Jims had in that room not the pleasure of
a presentation but the job of selling Truman a support which
had already been turned down two or three times before. If it
was a smoke-filled room, none of the smoke came from non-
smoking Truman. They promised him "98 per cent" of the
organization support in Kansas City. They told him that influ-
ential Democrats in St. Louis could be counted upon to help.

Truman told them that he was in no financial position to
make the race. He said that he was afraid that he was not well
enough known in the state. All three of them did a good deal of
carpet-pacing in that room. It is doubtful that Truman mentioned the fact that within two years he had been turned down
at 1908 Main for Governor and for Congressman. He had been

passed over when the lucrative office of collector had been considered again, though this last time he had not asked for it.
The one thing that was most clear in that hotel room at Sedalia
was that Tom Pendergast, with Bennett Clark pushing him for
power in Missouri, was "backed into a corner." That entered
largely into the Truman decision to run.

The Star headlined the news: "Truman Widely Known—As
Federal Re-employment Head He Has Traveled The State."
And it added the obvious: "He is aligned with the Pendergast
organization and is its leader in Eastern Jackson County." Actually, he was more widely known than even newspapermen
generally understood, and known where it counted. There were
people who could speak for him and who were ready to speak.
Early in the 1934 campaign, Truman was in Maryville, in the
northwest corner of the state, when a big convention of preachers
and Sunday School teachers was in progress. There was little
sympathy for Tom Pendergast in that crowd. Truman was introduced to the assembly by Colonel Southern, who had a part
in Truman's first entry into politics and whose friends in Missouri regard him as "the greatest Bible teacher of them all." He
took Truman by the hand and told the crowd:

"Here is my boy. I vouch for him, and don't pay any attention to what others may say about him."

Truman had Missouri friends in politics as well as the Sunday
Schools. By the time he ran for the Senate he had been a county
judge over a period of a dozen years.

"There was a county judges' association in Missouri," Truman
recalls, "with 114 counties and three judges in each. They appointed the judges and clerks of election. So when I ran for
the Senate there was not a precinct in Missouri in which I did
not have at least one friend at the polls."

He was going to need them. Even before he filed for the race
at Jefferson City on May 17, Senator Bennett Clark hit at him
hard in a demand to Secretary of Labor Frances Perkins that
Truman resign immediately as Missouri Re-employment Director.

"The Senator is just two days late," said Truman. He had
already resigned. The Pendergast connection was flung at him
by his opponents quickly with particular reference to the killings
in the recent rough election in Kansas City.

"Those can't be pinned on me," Truman said. "I live in Independence, not Kansas City. I've never voted in Kansas City in my life."

If he had the Pendergast support, he had the Pendergast smear at his heels all the time. He did not reject it. At Joplin, in July, he declared, "Jackson County has the greatest Democratic organization west of New York, I am proud of it." Both Milligan and Congressman John J. Cochran, of St. Louis, who had entered the race a few days after Truman with the kindly feelings of *The St. Louis Post-Dispatch* and the St. Louis machine politicians, hammered at Pendergast more and more. (In the campaign, old Joe Shannon called Cochran "ranting John," "the office boy of *The St. Louis Post-Dispatch.*") Milligan called Truman the "Münchausen of Politics." Senator Clark declared that "Mr. Truman has been conducting a campaign of mendacity and imbecility unparalleled in the history of Missouri." *The Star* reported that all county employes in Jackson County were to be assessed ten per cent for campaign funds, mostly for Truman. Old friend and new enemy, Spencer Salisbury, charged that Federal employment officials in Independence were using their offices to help Truman. This election apparently first publicized their new enmity.

The Pendergast organization fought for Truman and its statewide power with everything it had in Kansas City and in "Uncle Tom's Cabin" at Jefferson City, too. Early in July, Tom Pendergast staged one of the Kansas City outpourings like that one to St. Louis when he was seeking an instructed delegation for Jim Reed from the State Democratic Convention. This time the trains ran to the college town of Columbia in the center of the state. Apparently Tom himself was not in attendance, but his Governor Guy B. Park introduced Truman. Martha Ellen Truman, at eighty-six, sat on the platform among the politicians.

"Kansas City just about took over Columbia," said *The Star*.

Harry Truman read his speech, which was broadcast throughout the state. He pointed out that both Milligan and Cochran had made their pilgrimages to 1908 Main Street in 1932 to ask for Pendergast's support. Both had got it. He was not ashamed to have it, he said. But he emphasized that he himself was not a Kansas City man: "I know the farmers' problems, having been a dirt farmer for twelve years."

Truman had begun his campaign with the declaration, "I am heart and soul for Roosevelt." He continued it and concluded it with declarations like the one at a rally at a little community called Pleasant Hill: "Two words are all any Democratic candidate for the Senate or Congress needs—'Back Roosevelt.' "

He hammered at that. He moved from county seat to county seat hammering it. He slept while his campaign chauffeur, Hunter Allen, drove in the mornings, late at night, throughout July. He spoke bare-headed and sweating in the sun at Clinton and Webster Groves, Cape Girardeau, Kennett, Caruthersville, Kirksville, Pleasant Hill, Joplin, cities and towns and wide places in the road. And the Pendergast organization, which had just two years before given Jim Reed all its strength in his fight to stop Roosevelt, followed and applauded. It has been suggested that Pendergast was trying to get back into the graces of Washington. But Truman was talking Roosevelt when Pendergast was asking Reed and urging Aylward. Neither of the other candidates was opposing Roosevelt. His coattails had already become a substantial platform for all Democrats, but Truman was more insistently pro-Roosevelt than any man in the race. It was a race. *The Kansas City Times* declared that "in the whole of Missouri history there have been few such spirited contests within a party." Obviously it was a contest not merely between the candidates but for control of the Democratic organization in Missouri.

Captain Roger Sermon of the 129th, who acted as treasurer in the campaign, reported expenses of $12,280. Members of the Pendergast family put up $1,400. John Truman's old banker friend, William T. Kemper, who was then Democratic National Committeeman by Pendergast dispensation, gave $1,000. Joseph J. McGee gave $1,000, too. Various Aylwards contributed $270. The names of Shannon and Reed do not appear. There were contributions from Pendergast office-holders like Mayor Bryce B. Smith and City Manager McElroy. Also Colonel E. M. Stayton, the Democratic half of Judge Truman's bi-partisan road engineers, and the architects of the new courthouse contributed. The primary ended, Sermon said, with a deficit of $3,335.43. Since he won, nobody worried very much about that.

On July 29, *The Kansas City Star* reported "even money on Truman" by St. Louis betting commissioners. On primary day, the voting in Kansas City was quiet and orderly compared to the riotous election in the spring. But no commentator has missed the fact that Tom Pendergast's men rolled up 137,529 votes for Truman in Kansas City and surrounding Jackson County, while 8,912 went to Milligan and 1,525 to Cochran. Cyril Clemens, who makes a relationship to Mark Twain the foundation of an energetic literary life in Missouri, said, in the first quick biography of Truman after he became President, that Pendergast in his eagerness had increased the Kansas City vote for Truman by approximately 39,000 over what he had given Howell when Howell was running against Clark in 1932.

One item to which Truman is entitled is steadily overlooked, however. It is that on the other side of the state, where *The St. Louis Post-Dispatch* was so shocked by boss power after the election, Cochran in the city of St. Louis got 104,265 votes while Milligan got only 6,670 and Truman just 3,742. The essential item which has never been emphasized is that if every vote from both of the big cities of the big city bosses had been thrown out in that primary election and only the "outstate counties" counted, Truman would have still won the nomination. Once again he had given Tom Pendergast what Tom Pendergast desperately needed—support among the people who were not under the paw of his power.

Truman was Senator but something else, also. It is not certain who invented the "Pendergast office boy" phrase. William Hirth, veteran head of the Missouri Farmers' Association, who was later to seek the gubernatorial nomination on an anti-Pendergast platform, referred to Truman as a "bellhop." Jacob Milligan came to Kansas City in the campaign to say that Truman as Senator would get "calluses on his ears listening on the long distance telephone to his boss."

But the scream that was heard around the country was that of *The St. Louis Post-Dispatch*. At that time Truman's old schoolmate and later Presidential Secretary, Charles Ross, was high on *The Post-Dispatch* staff, moving that year from Washington correspondent to editor of its editorial page. *The Post-Dispatch* declared after the election that "an obscure man . . . scarcely known outside the confines of Jackson County" had been put into the Senate by the boss. "The result demonstrates the power of machine politics.

"County Judge Truman," it declared, "is the nominee of the

Democratic Party for the United States Senate because Tom Pendergast willed it so.

"Shades of Benton and Blair, Cockrell and Vest, Stone and Jim Reed!"

The Post-Dispatch blast was more widely read and remembered than the statement of the strongly anti-Pendergast *Kansas City Star* that "Jackson County has found him a capable and honest public official," and "a man of unimpeachable character and integrity." It added after the election in November, in which the voters of Missouri gave no sign of revulsion against the nomination: "With Judge Truman in the Senate Missouri can expect that its interests will be safeguarded and advanced from a national standpoint." That may not have suggested world statesmanship; it did indicate home faith from even a Republican newspaper. *The Star,* however, saw the meaning of the election as making Tom Pendergast the undisputed boss of the Democratic Party in Missouri. That was the main thing the boys cheered at 1908 Main Street. It was the main thing remembered in America.

Truman himself went straight back to his work as county judge in the old courthouse. He was tired at the end of long driving days from county seat to county seat, from rally to hotel room conferences. The frame of the new high courthouse and the stone which sheathed it were rising between Twelfth and Thirteenth and Oak and Locust streets. It was good to look up at it and the workmen high in the air. After that election, however, Truman was a little more than tired. The papers recorded one of the rare, brief illnesses of his life which caused him to cancel a trip to Washington to look over the new ground. The one certain thing is that that campaign hurt Truman as much as it gave him the elation of victory—perhaps more. He was made to seem on a Missouri-wide and even an American-wide scale the puppet of a disreputable machine. He kept his temper to the end of that campaign. He had made the point in the presence of his opponents during the campaign that he had attacked only their public records. But he was the son of old John Truman whose election angers were a part of both Harry's youth and his inheritance. He missed the relief John sometimes got with his fists or even with his own blackened eye. It was an odd thing to become at once sickened and a Senator.

Even some men within the loyalties of his own political organization seemed to belittle him to build the Boss. Years afterwards, a *Post-Dispatch* writer, Spencer McCulloch, said that Pendergast himself had told him of that 1934 campaign, that he had noticed there were Senators who represented oil and steel, utilities and railroads, so he decided to send his "office boy" to represent Pendergast. Harry Truman never believed Pendergast said any such thing. He told me that Pendergast really told McCulloch that steel, railroads, utilities had Senators; his candidate represented the people. If Pendergast ever spoke the McCulloch version it was another item in the disintegration of the intelligent boss. It was a story which, nevertheless, was repeated by some supposed friends and open enemies and spread and grew. And sometimes the modesty of Truman seemed to thicken like a scar over the hurt and over his loyalties, too. And sometimes that modesty served the story's growth. He called himself, with apparently increasingly insistent humility, a "country boy," and that seemed to prove that he was just an "office boy," too.

The courthouse rose. There was, under his careful handling, the money left over for the statue of Andrew Jackson for whom the county was named. The statue and the tall building behind it and the graceful remodeled courthouse in Independence were items in his pride which nobody could hurt. Certainly, the completion of the high courthouse in Kansas City capped the story of his planning and his building for Jackson County. Its dedication closed those years. It seemed afterwards an odd thing that old Justice Pierce Butler, the rich conservative opponent of the New Deal, should have been asked to make the speech dedicating the new Truman courthouse in the second year of Roosevelt, on December 27, 1934. Perhaps the builder and the speaker there together that day appropriately emphasized the past before Roosevelt and the future beyond him. Butler's speech is not remembered. The great moment for Truman and for Bess and for old Martha Ellen there on the platform was when the Jackson statue was unveiled by a group of ten-year-old girls led by slender and large-eyed Margaret.

She had wept when her father was elected and her mother told her they were moving to Washington.

"What's a Senator?" she had demanded.

Her father was going to find out. He was not as happy about it as he had expected to be.

CHAPTER XII

The Gentleman from Pendergast

"I ALWAYS LIKED HOPKINS. He was one of the few people who were kind to me when I first came to Washington."

In those sentences Harry Truman spoke not only about a man but about a mood and a time. Nothing is quite so clear in the whole Truman story as that when he came to Washington after his election to the Senate, he was no brash newcomer. He was not merely modest then as always. The impression is that somehow this was almost the low point of his pride.

"I was under a cloud," he told me years later. "I did not see Roosevelt alone until I had been in Washington for six months."

Actually he had no notion of the dimensions of the threat in the cloud above his head. Not until four years afterwards did he learn with other Americans how serious was the situation in the Pendergast organization which everybody regarded him as representing, when he walked up the Senate aisle dressed in unaccustomed tail coat and striped pants and on the unfamiliar arm of Bennett Clark. His war comrade, political friend and old Mike's son, James M. Pendergast sat in the Senate gallery. There were other smiling friends, and Bess and eleven-year-old Margaret. None of them had any inkling that in the same month in which Truman took his oath, Tom Pendergast, in one of those Chicago hotel rooms which recur in American history, would make a bargain which would turn him into a convict and threaten the careers of all, including Truman, who had had political association with him.

Truman was the Gentleman from Pendergast. Not only was it accepted that Pendergast had sent him as his Senator; also, he arrived from Missouri with a reputation prepared for him by the blurted contempt of such a paper as *The Post-Dispatch*. Even without such marks against him a new Democratic Senator

175

could not have counted upon tumultuous welcome in New Deal Washington that year. There were thirteen new Democrats. They did not seem particularly precious at a time when the Republican minority was weaker than at any session since the Civil War. There were so many Democrats, new and old, that Harry Hopkins, who took time to be kind to Truman, could say to some of his fellow social reformers on their way to a race track, "Boys, this is our hour."

It was not quite that. That was probably the year of the beginning of the conservative coalition of some Southern Democrats and all Republicans which presented a problem in party government in the United States in the following years. It was not a new phenomenon. Party government in the Republican twenties was marked by recurrent revolt of those "wild jackasses" the progressive Republican Senators. Wilson had faced it on the eve and in the aftermath of war. It seems almost standard in any American party government which has been long or seems firmly entrenched in power. Hopkins misread the clock of history.

It definitely was not Truman's hour. From the day of his election, his mood had appeared to be that of a man intent upon minimizing both himself and the office to which he had been elected. His purpose may have been to placate his opponents after an angry party division. His modesty, however, seemed to prove the insignificance with which his critics charged him.

He would, he said, not be one of the great Missouri Senators. ("Shades of Benton and Blair!") "But I'll do my best and keep my feet on the ground. That's one of the hardest things for a Senator to do, it seems. All this precedence and other hooey accorded a Senator isn't very good for a Republic. A Senator should be a dignified person when he's seated on the Senate floor, but after that, he should keep in mind he's no more or no better than any other person. There isn't going to be any splurge when I get to Washington."

There was not. He went first, in December, to look for a house or an apartment. He was appalled by the rents. He felt poor not only in spirit but in purse: "I am undoubtedly the poorest Senator financially in Washington." Senator Clark presented him and State Chairman Aylward to President Roosevelt.

Apparently it was an entirely perfunctory call. Also with Aylward that month, he went to the dinner of the Gridiron Club which brings together the great and the near-great of American politics for semi-annual lampoonings. He and Aylward went to the newspapermen's club banquet with Republican Roy Roberts of *The Kansas City Star.* Truman's old friend Charlie Ross sat at another table.

Truman's announcement in the fall that he planned to study law at night school at Georgetown University suggested a renewed sense of the inadequacy of his formal education and a lack of understanding of how much work he would have to do as Senator. There is hardly a record or a memory of that time which does not reflect a humility which went beyond modesty almost to apology. On that visit to Washington he seemed almost pathetically eager to please. When he called on the correspondent of *The Kansas City Journal-Post,* which was almost the only paper friendly to him, to "pay his respects," he was "grinning like two Chessie cats." Yet, he stressed his own insignificance as "only an humble member of the next Senate, green as grass and ignorant as a fool about practically everything worth knowing." That could have been "country boy" shrewdness which perhaps paid off later. At the time it served the city papers which were stressing the impression of both his insignificance and his subserviency.

He had been in Missouri politics long enough to grow a skin tough enough to take the epithets designed to remove the hide as well as the hopes. He had taken his share. He had perhaps too much immunity to belief in charges regularly and carelessly flung about in elections. Indeed, it is clear that that immunity made it difficult for him to believe, until they were admitted in the court, the charges which sent Tom Pendergast to prison. Among so many charges even the non-partisan on the Middle Border developed a high degree of incredulity. Indeed, Kansas City's own best historian of these years has said, "Kansas Citians had been accustomed to hearing of election thieves for fifty years." One thing, however, got under Harry Truman's skin. He was loyal to Pendergast, but never subservient to him. The suggestion that he was left a scar.

Like every other Senator, however, he had plenty of office-boy work to do—for the people of Missouri and for the Pendergast organization. Some of his non-legislative work must have seemed too important for an office boy to Tom Pendergast. It would be difficult to think of an emptier suggestion than the one that Pendergast had picked Truman without much regard for merit because he was not concerned about national affairs. A year earlier Pendergast himself had taken up directly with James A. Farley a tax case like the one in which he himself was finally caught. To the end Pendergast declined to praise Roosevelt, but he needed in his business close ties with his Administration. Washington and Kansas City relations even between Democrats, however, seemed on a cold war basis when Truman went to Washington.

The interest of the Department of Justice in Kansas City and a possible connection there between crime and politics may have been originally sharpened by the fact that one of the men killed in the Union Station Massacre was an unarmed F.B.I. agent. (They only began to go armed after that killing.) Maurice Milligan, the United States District Attorney, who later conducted the case against Pendergast and then made a Senate race against Truman, has written that before he was appointed on February 3, 1934, Roosevelt's Attorney General Homer Cummings had made certain that he had no connection with the Pendergast organization and told him that Kansas City was one of the three worst crime centers in the United States.

Milligan also said, "Mine was no routine appointment to pay a political debt." Pendergast men who had supported Reed against Roosevelt understood that no great debt was due them. Some of them, including Harry Truman, however, noted that Milligan was endorsed by Senator Bennett Clark in the same month in which Clark had announced his support of Maurice Milligan's brother, Tuck, for the Senate in an anti-Pendergast drive for power in Missouri. It was not easy for Pendergast partisans to divest themselves of political fears. It was also not easy for Washington to separate Truman from the Pendergast support.

Within two weeks after he was sworn in, *The Star* reported that Truman and other Missourians hoped to see Roosevelt and Farley about generally closer relations between the Administration and the Kansas City organization and not merely about, as *The Star* put it, the "harassment and investigations of its members." When the conference finally came off it was not with Roosevelt but with Cummings, and Truman attended along with Congressman Jasper Bell and old Joe Shannon. Apparently there was not too much to worry about at the time. It was more than a year later that Treasury agents stumbled on the first clue which led to the Pendergast tax case. It was a little over a year before Joe Shannon himself, having resumed intramural strife with Pendergast in the Kansas City Democracy, raised again and finally the charges of ghost voting in the Middle Border metropolis.

Meanwhile there was a period of peace or at least surface quiet in the politics of Missouri. The ghost vote cry was not raised until after the 1936 election. In the quietude in Washington Harry Truman was already Senator, voting in consistent support of the New Deal (except on soldiers' bonus legislation) and sitting silent in the back rows. More dramatic than his voting on national measures, however, was his clear effort from the beginning to divest himself of the Pendergast "office boy" label. In June, a news story in *The Star* quoted Truman as saying that Pendergast often sent him telegrams urging him to vote one way or another on certain matters before Congress.

"I don't follow his advice on legislation," Truman is quoted as saying, "I vote the way I believe Missourians as a whole would want me to vote."

Some smiled at that in Kansas City, and some smiled also in Washington. The smiles were not quite such smirks after he voted for the Public Utility Holding Company Act of 1935. A mammoth lobby had been assembled to fight it but, more important so far as Truman was concerned, a big cog in that lobby organization was *The Kansas City Journal-Post* in which Henry L. Doherty, president of the Cities Service Company, owned a large interest. It provided the only newspaper support of the Pendergast organization. Truman voted for the bill and afterwards the paper editorially flayed him alive.

The classic case of his independence of Pendergast, however, was one matter in which he opposed Roosevelt. Despite the story in *The Star* about Pendergast's telegrams Truman says that this was the only time that Pendergast ever called him with any request. Pendergast never made any suggestions to him about legislation, Truman told me. This one case in which he did call was the Roosevelt fight to elect Alben Barkley as Democratic leader of the Senate after the death of Senator Joseph T. Robinson, of Arkansas. Truman had already promised his vote to Pat Harrison, of Mississippi. Jim Aylward phoned him. Then Tom Pendergast phoned him and asked him to vote for Barkley. The White House had called Pendergast and asked him to phone Truman.

"I just can't do it, Tom," Truman said, "and I'll tell you why. I've given my word to Pat Harrison."

At the other end of the line Pendergast did not seem disturbed, but when Truman put down the receiver he was mad. He resented the White House idea that Pendergast could tell him what to do.

"I'm tired of being pushed around," he told a newspaperman at the time, "tired of having the President treat me like an office boy." And he called the White House and sent just that message to FDR. He was United States Senator Harry S. Truman and not the office boy of anybody in the world and that included Tom Pendergast of Kansas City.

He was already beginning to feel not only his independence but his adequacy as a Senator when, in 1936, he drove from Washington to Philadelphia for the Democratic National Convention. At that convention, however, he was not treated with any high consideration by the Democratic organization of Missouri. He was not named on any of the important committees of the convention to which, as Senator, after Missouri custom, he went as delegate-at-large. He got only empty honor as one of the forty-eight honorary vice-presidents of the convention. It was an historic time for both Harry Truman and Tom Pendergast, nevertheless.

Tom Pendergast and his wife had arrived in the United States on the *Queen Mary,* making her gala maiden voyage, on June 1. Cunard White Star Line publicity men played their names high on the list of notable passengers. Missourians had become accustomed to read of Tom's sumptuous European travels year after year. ("Distance makes the heart grow fonder," he wrote home one year to 1908 Main.) In 1936, his arrival up the harbor was also noted with interest, as it was learned later, by Treasury agents who were trying to trace a mysterious $100,500 which they had noticed in the examination of the estate of a lawyer in

Chicago. The Pendergasts went to the Waldorf where they took elaborate quarters on the twenty-ninth floor. Pendergast came down to Philadelphia to assume command of the Missouri delegation. It was there that he had the upset which was the first sign of the succession of illnesses which attended his last years. Truman did not know how ill he was when he put him on the train to go back to New York where a long siege in Roosevelt Hospital awaited him.

Gala maiden voyages seemed fated for Pendergast. The year before he had sailed amid the whistling tugs, the confetti, and the publicity when the *Normandie* departed on her first eastway voyage. Truman came to New York to see him that summer, too —that time with Senator Clark and Lloyd C. Stark.

The Waldorf suite was a more elaborate scene for a political conference than was customary for men who did their business in the small, bare office at 1908 Main Street in Kansas City. Pendergast paid by the day more than the high rent Truman paid by the month in Washington. As a rich man himself, Stark was undoubtedly less impressed, but he was eager. As a big-jawed, ambitious man he was impressed with Pendergast power. Since Pendergast had denied his request for support in 1932, he had courted Tom's friends. He had supported Truman in 1934. (His name does not, however, appear in the list of Truman campaign contributors that year, though he was—and is—one of the wealthiest nurserymen in the United States.)

"In 1935," Truman told me, "Bennett Clark and I took Stark up to New York to see Pendergast and urge him to support him for Governor.

"Pendergast kept saying to me, 'He won't do, Harry,' 'I don't like the so-and-so,' 'He's a no-good.' "

Truman smiled when he talked about it years later in admiration of the judgment of old Tom.

"But finally," he said, "he agreed that if Stark would get some country support he would support him, too. The old man had better judgment than I did."

A year later, in 1936, when Stark ran, Pendergast was in the hospital during the primary. He did not get back to Missouri to vote for him or to vote for anybody in that 1936 election which was followed by the ghost vote charges. Afterwards his own recollection, which he recited to the press after Stark, as he believed, had turned ingrate on him to tear him down, was that he had agreed in his office in Kansas City to support Stark. The formal agreement may have been there after the meeting in New York. Pendergast in reciting his agreement to support Stark mentioned that "outstanding Democrats" had urged him to support him. Truman, to his own regret later, was certainly one of them.

"I lined up the country and T.J., too!" he said.

The two New York visits of Pendergast seem successive scenes in a drama of disintegration. On one of them he reluctantly agreed to support Stark who was to help destroy him. During the other he was stricken by the illnesses which cut his great strength. Perhaps his judgment slipped at the meeting in 1935 (though Truman's memory of Pendergast is of a man often betrayed by those who asked for his support). Certainly his vigor as boss must have been weakened by the illness and operation of 1936. Truman's remembrance of Pendergast in New York and Philadelphia in 1936 is of the top of the great divide in Pendergast's life between rising power and hastening disintegration. It was also the divide in Truman's life between the times when Pendergast's power could help him upward and the days when the Pendergast association was the weight which all but pulled him down.

"If he had died there in New York," Truman said, "he would be remembered as the greatest boss this country ever had."

The signs of disintegration were piling up. Even before 1936, newspapermen noticed that Pendergast was "heavier and grayer and his eyes carried a sick look." Age was visible on him though he still weighed 240 pounds and was only sixty-four. What had seemed only a stomach upset when he went down to the convention in Philadelphia was diagnosed as coronary thrombosis when he got back to New York. Then after examination, it became apparent that "an intestinal obstruction" would have to be removed. It was a malignancy and its removal required the closing of his rectum and the use of a tube in his side for the rest of his life. At that time in New York, he had already received $430,000 of the $750,000 bribe from the insurance companies for his part in the settlement of Missouri rate refunds worth more than seven million dollars to them. Part of it Pendergast shared with the others involved.

("Corruption begins at the top," Lincoln Steffens had written of crooked politics in Missouri in 1902.)

Almost like a fresh start, Harry Truman's effective senatorial career began in the fall of 1936. After a year and a half of silence and inconspicuousness in the Senate, he began to feel his way and show his force. All the record of service which he himself related, at the end of his first term, in the *Missouri Manual* began after that time. He put it down in elliptical sentences: "Was chairman of the sub-committee which wrote the Civil Aeronautics Act of 1937; acted as vice-chairman of the Senate Committee on Interstate Commerce, which conducted hearings on railroad finance, the result of which hearings was made the basis of the Transportation Act of 1940. With Senator Wheeler of Montana he was co-author of this act."

Like some other history it leaves out much of the story. That story is of a man who seemed an almost eccentric student among Senators. He showed, also, the same thoroughness which went into his road-building. As a politician, he was aware of the necessity for sociability in politics. Some of Truman's friends are to blame for the fact that too many of the stories of those Senate years relate to poker chip companionship. The Senate is a club, and during the Vice-Presidency of John Nance Garner, Truman enjoyed gathering in Garner's sanctum with other Senators to "strike a blow for liberty" from the private stock in Garner's cabinet. Some of the same group met over a green table in the evenings, occasionally long into the night. However, Truman never attended any of those night sessions. He never played poker with Garner, indeed, but twice—once on a deer hunt in Pennsylvania and once on a trip to South Carolina. Garner won from him on the Pennsylvania trip but Truman retaliated "with interest" on the trip to South Carolina. The combination of hard work and conviviality in American politics is at least as old as Webster and Clay. Sometimes the evaluation of men across a poker table has been a more important part of the game than the immediate business of the evaluation of the hands they held.

The forgotten figure in the Truman story in the Senate, however, is the almost eccentrically studious Senator. His office was piled with documents, reports, briefs. He took books home to his apartment at night. He made up for his lack of speeches on the floor by his work on committees, and particularly by the vast amount of reading and studying he did about the problems before the committees—especially problems of transportation by highway, railroad and air.

In years since, some older Senators—like old schoolteachers in Independence—have taken much credit to themselves for "breaking me in," as Truman puts it, in the Senate. Some of these stories got a little tiresome to Truman, particularly when they were used to suggest that he was ungrateful to his teachers.

The man, however, from whom—or under whom—he learned the most was Senator Burton K. Wheeler of Montana. Early in Truman's term, Wheeler, as chairman of the Interstate Commerce Committee, put Truman on a sub-committee with another Democrat and Senator Warren Austin of Vermont as the minority member. The Democrat who was his senior never showed up and Truman conducted the hearings. From these hearings and some fancy fighting on that and other committees finally emerged the Civil Aeronautics Act of 1937.

"I kept the bill as the President wanted it," Truman recalls.

The important hearings in his first senatorial term, however, and those which both expressed and developed the ideas which were important when he became President were the investigations of railroad finance. Years later, two reporters who were familiar with the hearings and the period wrote that "the public's indifference to the railroad hearings was simply deafening." They become dramatic now both in terms of Truman's ideas and the skill which he then demonstrated in senatorial investigations. Also, they emphasized the courage and increasing independence of the junior Senator from Missouri.

A self-effacing but ubiquitous man named Max Lowenthal had written a book on corporate reorganization methods at that time, using as paramount illustration the Chicago, Milwaukee & St. Paul Railway reorganization of 1925-28. It aroused Wheeler's interest and he set up a special investigation of railroad finances. Wheeler made himself chairman of the sub-committee to do the job. Truman was added only after another member resigned. Then it turned out that nobody but himself and Wheeler were interested in the investigation. The committee held its first hearing in December 1936, with Wheeler presiding. It was apparent even then that the Senator from Missouri had been boring through all the available documents on the subject.

The investigation proceeded through the spring in unequal competition for public attention with the great Supreme Court battle of that year. Wheeler fought the so-called "court packing" proposal. Truman supported Roosevelt. When the fight ended, Wheeler went home to Montana for a rest. And Truman slipped, without any perceptible acclaim, into the chairman's seat just as the hearings about his big home railroad, which had roared past his childhood on Crysler Street—the Missouri Pacific —came up.

Max Lowenthal and other members of the staff of the sub-committee were a little disturbed about this unexpected coincidence of a Missouri railroad and a Missouri Senator. They pointed out to Truman that some of the things which would come out in the investigation might embarrass him at home.

No, Truman told them. He would not be embarrassed.

"Then," said Lowenthal, "some of the lawyers told Truman that some of the exhibits were pretty hot stuff and it would be possible to just put them into the record without bringing them out in the hearing."

"No," Truman told them. "Treat this just as you would any other hearing."

The messages and telephone calls, telegrams and letters began pouring in from Missouri asking him, first: to stop the hearings on the Missouri Pacific; and, second: to go easy on it.

"Treat this like any other hearing," Truman told them again. Lowenthal, who had had the image of the Pendergast office boy in his mind when Truman had assumed the chairmanship, was impressed. He began to watch this Senator from Missouri. Un-noticed then, his methods in investigation were the same which made his Truman Committee later so effective in the war effort. He combined the politician's ease with the public servant's determination.

"There were not half a dozen Senators then who would have withstood the pressure he took," Lowenthal said.

Casually one day, but with the secret feeling of a man offering a well-earned accolade, Lowenthal suggested to Truman that he would like to take him to see his friend Justice Louis D. Brandeis. Brandeis was over eighty then and had become, with

Oliver Wendell Holmes, one of the two great judges of the American liberal tradition. Brandeis' California Street apartment had become a Washington institution when Lowenthal invited Truman to go with him there. Truman regarded him very seriously.

"I'm not used to meeting people like that," he said.

It was true. Most of his growth and studying had been free from great intellectual companionship, as his voracious reading as a small-town boy had been largely self-directed. Before he went to Washington he had met practically no intellectuals or theoretical students. His companions were small-town business men and politicians. He had no such feeling then as Arthur Meier Schlesinger, Jr., expressed after his election in 1948: "The conceptions of the intellectual are at last beginning to catch up with the instincts of the democratic politician." Truman was aware only of how much he had to learn.

After his first meeting with Brandeis, he went often to California Street, almost every other week, to the open houses which the Justice held for his selected friends. It was during that time, with the help of Lowenthal and probably with the influence of Brandeis' talk, that Truman made a speech which was completely and comfortably forgotten by hopeful conservatives when he succeeded Roosevelt in the White House in 1945.

It was a broadside against concentrated wealth and the bankers and lawyers in its service. The railroad investigations, he said, had shown that such great law firms as Davis, Polk, Wardwell, Gardner and Reed, of New York; Winston, Strawn and Shaw, of Chicago; and Cravath, De Gersdorff, Swaine and Wood, of New York, resorted "to tricks that would make an ambulance chaser in a coroner's court blush with shame." Against such lawyers, he said, the "ordinary mine-run bureaucratic lawyer" is no more a match than "the ordinary lamb is a match for a butcher." He not only attacked the lawyers of great wealth. He even suspected great charities. The Carnegie libraries, he said, were "steeped in the blood of the Homestead steel workers." The Rockefeller Foundation was "founded on the dead miners of the Colorado Fuel & Iron Co., and a dozen other similar performances."

Beyond sharp attack he stated a philosophy in terms of American preferences: "I believe that a thousand insurance companies, with $4,000,000 each in assets, would be just a thousand times better for the country than the Metropolitan Life, with $4,000,000,000 in assets. . . . I also say that a thousand county-seat towns of 7,000 people each are a thousand times more important to this Republic than one city of 7,000,000 people."

After that speech, the old gray Justice, who had written *The Curse of Bigness,* gave special welcome to the Senator from Missouri.

"The old man would back me into a corner," Truman said in affectionate memory of Brandeis, "and pay no attention to anybody else while he talked transportation to me. He was very much against the control of financial credit—hipped on a few insurance companies controlling too much of the country's credit."

That apartment of Louis Brandeis at 2205 California Street was a new world to Truman. He met there people unlike those he had been accustomed to knowing in the politics and the public service of Missouri. His old world remained, however; he had no wish to escape from the practical political world in which he had grown. Indeed, within two months after that speech which pleased Brandeis, he made the most vigorous pro-Pendergast speech of his whole career in the Senate in opposition to the reappointment of Maurice Milligan as United States District Attorney for the Western District of Missouri. He never seemed more the Gentleman from Pendergast than at that time.

The speech not only emphasized his personal loyalty to Pendergast. As a part of his Senate service it underscored the two aspects of Truman's stubborn loyalties. He stood by his associates in politics, sometimes most vigorously when they were assailed, sometimes too long, after they were properly criticized. In opposing Milligan he was not departing from his loyalty to the New Deal. It was a part of the pattern of his working faith in party organization and party government as a means of getting democratic results. He voted with Roosevelt as a man elected to help carry out a party program. He stood by Pendergast not merely in personal gratitude but in political loyalty. Always, apparently, he stood with the Pendergast organization on patronage and with the Roosevelt Administration on policy. That was a clear political distinction. Also, it was one which involved Truman in one case which has not been much publicized but about which he might be legitimately criticized.

Not long after the conference with Cummings on better relations between the Administration and Missouri, the administration did name Matthew S. Murray on his recommendation as Director of the WPA in Missouri. He defended the appointment of Murray, who was a Pendergast lieutenant and Director of Public Works in Kansas City, when it was opposed by Emily Newell Blair, former Democratic National Committeewoman from Missouri. Shortly after Pendergast, Murray was sentenced to two years in prison for tax evasion on $90,000, part of which he said had come to him as non-taxable gifts from Pendergast and Contractor Mike Ross. Truman never believed that he was guilty and gave him a full pardon in that faith after he became President.

Since Truman had seen Pendergast in the summer of 1936, the Treasury agents had been implacably following Pendergast's trail. Also, since the 1936 elections, in which Stark had advanced to the Governorship with the reluctantly given support of Pendergast, Milligan had been pressing the vote fraud cases against the Pendergast organization in Kansas City. Soon after the election, Stark had broken with Pendergast and joined the crusade which moved on several fronts against him. Oddly enough, though almost automatically it had seemed at the time, "the first to cry fraud," according to William Reddig in *Tom's Town*, "was not *The Star* or District Attorney Milligan but Congressman Shannon"—after a candidate he supported for the State Supreme Court had been demolished in the primary election of 1936.

In Kansas City that was only what Shannon would be expected to say after any election he had lost, but after this particular cry District Attorney Milligan and Federal District Judges Albert L. Reeves and Merrill E. Otis moved with a vigor which had been lacking after such cries in the past. Their disclosures showed that they were amply justified. There were between fifty and sixty thousand illegal votes counted in Kansas City in the election of November, 1936. Oddly enough, however, none of those who were at that time greatly concerned about the interference of big government in local matters noted that the cases were conducted under a Reconstruction statute. It permitted Federal interference in local elections to protect Negroes in the South—and, as Democrats then charged, to ensure Republican victories in the pattern of the Hayes-Tilden election of 1876.

Truman's opposition to the reappointment of Milligan involved, undoubtedly, the fact that the vote fraud cry had been raised so long and so often by defeated politicians that it was regarded as standard opposition politics. Moreover, the appointment of Milligan, against Truman's wishes in 1938, represented not merely a threat to Pendergast but almost a deliberate affront to Truman as a Democratic Senator who had supported the Administration in its toughest fights. Clark had been stripped of his rights to patronage after he fought Roosevelt on the Court bill. Truman had supported Roosevelt in that fight and almost every other one. Yet, a year after the Court fight, his desires were dismissed and his protests rejected in connection with a position in his own county normally regarded as his proper patronage. Whatever Milligan's reappointment may have meant in the political morals of Missouri, in the American political system the appointment approximated an almost direct assault on Truman's senatorial rights, privileges and pride. He was an angry man, and in the accepted standards of the American system of party government, he had a right to be.

That was not the picture which emerged. His opposition to Milligan made him seem not the opponent of Milligan but the defender of fraud. His colleagues listened. Only a few of them spoke. But he must have seen even on their faces that he was the Senator from Pendergast again. He had protested the renomination of Milligan to the Attorney General. He had taken his protest to the President. He got nowhere. Apparently the Administration's mind had been made up on the reappointment in the fall, long before Truman spoke against it in the Senate. Attorney General Cummings wrote, on November 1, 1937, in response to a memorandum from Roosevelt, that he had "heard indirectly that there is a good deal of opposition to him [Milligan] amongst the powers that be in Missouri."

"Answering your question specifically," he told Roosevelt, however, "I can say that I have not heard one word from either Senator on the subject, or from any other person in authority adverse to Mr. Milligan."

Who prompted Roosevelt's question is not known. It would have been a little odd for him to take up the question of opposition to a re-appointment so far in advance unless some special thing or person had suggested it to him. However, he told Cummings in a memorandum from Hyde Park, November 3, 1937:

"Thank you for the information about Milligan. I have very good reason to believe that he ought to be reappointed, and I think if you and I from now on take the position that we have heard no valid reason against his reappointment, it will help him to be confirmed next February.

". . . If either of the Missouri Senators were to oppose Milligan it is my judgment that it would hurt them and the Democratic Party in the same way."

Lloyd Stark, as Governor of Missouri and an Annapolis graduate, went fairly often to the White House in those days. He may have put the bee about Milligan in FDR's ample bonnet. How long after it was that Truman finally saw Roosevelt is not clear. Somewhere along the line, however, Truman had agreed that he would not make the point in the club of the Senate that Milligan was personally objectionable to him—a point which normally in the Senate is a bar to any candidate's confirmation.

He made his speech, however, and he left the record:

"My opposition to Mr. Milligan began long before vote frauds were brought to light in Kansas City. His morals and his political thinking never appealed to me."

Truman declared that Milligan had been made a hero by *The Star* and *The Post-Dispatch* and "the implication has been that any capable lawyer I would recommend for District Attorney in Western Missouri would not do his duty in regard to the vote fraud prosecutions."

A Republican Senator demanded whether Truman thought that Milligan should be penalized for doing his duty in the vote fraud case.

"No," Truman answered, "I do not. I have never asked that he be penalized. I asked that he be made a special prosecutor to continue these prosecutions, and that a District Attorney be appointed in Kansas City who was agreeable to the Democrats in that community."

Also, he said, "There are certain people in connection with the vote frauds who are guilty and who ought to be punished to the fullest extent. But there are people being railroaded in these wholesale convictions who are no more guilty than the members of this august legislative body."

He had an impossible case. He stood in an indefensible position. The "Democrats in that community" seemed clearly that February the Pendergast machine. The Pendergast machine had produced the vote frauds. Milligan had properly prosecuted them. But Truman went on, badgered and very much alone. He said that not Milligan but his deputies had done the real work in uncovering the ghost voters. He struck at Milligan with earnest fury.

"Mr. Milligan has accepted emoluments in the form of fees in bankruptcy proceedings in the Federal Court of Western Missouri. In fact, he has received more money in fees in one case than his salary has been from the Federal Treasury for a whole year. The Federal Court at Kansas City is presided over by two as violently partisan judges as have ever sat on a Federal bench since the Federalist judges of Jefferson's Administration. They are Merrill E. Otis and Albert L. Reeves. Mr. Reeves was appointed by that great advocate of clean non-partisan government, Warren G. Harding, and Mr. Otis was appointed by that other progressive non-partisan, Calvin Coolidge."

He summed it up:

"I say, Mr. President, that a Jackson County, Missouri, Democrat has as much chance of a fair trial in the Federal District Court of Western Missouri as a Jew would have in a Hitler Court or a Trotzky follower before Stalin."

Truman himself cast the only vote against Milligan's confirmation for the second term. And out in Kansas City Judge Reeves, who had declared himself corruptly counted out when he had run for Congress in 1918, answered the Truman speech with the barbed declaration that the Senator's protest had been the "speech of a man nominated by ghost votes, elected with ghost votes, and whose speeches are probably written by ghost writers."

Oddly enough that answer by Judge Reeves seems almost the only evidence to justify Truman's charge of rabid partisanship in the cases. As a student of the situation the judge should have known that in both the primary and general elections in 1934, Truman would have been nominated and elected even if the votes from the big cities of the big bosses had not been considered.

The trials were valuable for sanitation in democracy. If they disclosed no new crimes in American political history, they emphasized evils that needed to be cleaned up and evils not restricted to Kansas City. Also, they emphasized that in American politics, not all the evil is accomplished by racketeers and roughnecks. There were some tough customers among the defendants. Yet, William Reddig reports: "Most of these people were individuals from small homes who supported themselves in little jobs and were regarded as good citizens before their involvement in the vote fraud prosecutions." A pattern along the Middle Border, at least as old as the hot partisanship and corrupt politics of "squatter sovereignty," was revealed as not a tradition but a crime. And little people were caught in it.

Harry Truman himself seemed a very small man then, convicted among many of his own colleagues of guilt by association. He never had voted in Kansas City and never had been an election official there. There were not even any charges brought against election officials in the precincts in Jackson County, which made his bailiwick and, in effect, his wards. Hardly anybody noticed that. Few Senators came up to speak to him after that speech. He was very much alone when he went home to the apartment and Margaret and Bess.

There were other troubles that year. Not only were the cases and the clamor against Pendergast politicians reaching him and his reputation in Congress, also at home the long-growing debt on his mother's farm reached its high point almost at the same time that he rose against Milligan. Two months later, on April 2, 1938, Martha Ellen Truman rearranged the indebtedness on the old Grandview homeplace and gave a mortgage to Jackson County for a $35,000 loan from its school board funds. Her son, Vivian, and Harry Truman's political factotum and campaign chauffeur, Fred Canfil, signed the mortgage and endorsed the indebtedness with her. Harry, back in Washington, had nothing to do with the loan but it subjected him to criticism in the years ahead.

"While I was in Washington," he told me, "Buck Purcell and the other judges suggested the loan to Vivian as a good one for the county. I didn't know anything about it."

There was a question as to whether Vivian Truman and Canfil were sufficiently wealthy to be acceptable as endorsers. Vivian was sharing trouble on the land with his mother. His lands were under mortgage to the Kansas City Life Insurance Company. Canfil, who always made himself as mysterious as he was loyal to Truman, at one time owned a plantation in Louisiana and possibly some other lands in Kansas. At this time he was director of buildings at the courthouse which Truman had left when he went to Washington. The loan, however, was publicly made. It was also made at a time when farmers in Missouri and other Middle Border states were still suffering from the results of the droughts of 1934 and 1935. (Ernie Pyle, the great war reporter, who was then as little known as Truman, drove east while the dust blew from Colorado to Missouri in those years and saw "the saddest land I had ever seen.")

Truman had been a member of the Appropriations Committee when the tail end of a dust storm reaching Washington out of the West had helped secure approval of funds for soil conservation. He was in no position to help at home. His Senate salary was not getting any bigger. He declined to follow other members of Congress into the lecture business. He was still financially one of the poorest men in the Senate. Indeed, as his salary remained the same and taxes rose in later years, he felt justified in putting Bess on his Senate payroll at $4,500 a year. She worked for her salary, he insisted. The truth is that she had to work to help him in all the years before the salary began. There was, of course—there still is—a question about the propriety of employing her. Truman himself had rather sharply questioned Tuck Milligan about relatives on the payroll in 1934.

He was still poor and, despite all the hard committee work and his studiousness in doing his work, he still seemed perhaps more than ever—the Gentleman from Pendergast. Fortunately, he was less lonely in Washington and in the Senate. He had more and more friends. An old county judge had told him before he went to Washington—and James Hamilton Lewis had repeated to him after he got there—a piece of comic wisdom about the Senate: At first he would sit in the Senate and wonder how he got there; then he would begin to wonder how the others got there. Certainly Senators around him became men of both understood worth and understood weakness. Some were friends. There were men with whom he had come to the Senate as a freshman: Schwellenbach, of Washington; Hatch, of New Mexico; Minton, of Indiana. Despite the Milligan reappointment—and particularly after it—Roosevelt began to show him in little ways his appreciation.

"He always did what I asked," Truman told me. In most cases, if not in the most important ones, that may be correct.

Garner, whom Roosevelt was not sorry to see leave for Texas in 1941, was Truman's friend and not merely the companion of off hours. Alben Barkley, whom Truman had opposed for majority leader, gave him his respect. He had the respect of Senators whom he did not regard as close personal friends. Old Senator George Norris, of Nebraska, the fighting Progressive who became the father of the Tennessee Valley Authority, was one of them.

"He came into public life with somewhat of a cloud," Norris wrote later in a personal letter to Henry Wallace, "because he was probably first elected to the Senate by the influence of the noted Boss Péndergast. I watched him in the public service more than I otherwise would, and I must say that in all the time I knew him, I never knew of an instance, I knew of no time that the bosses or the machine controlled his official work. I think he has done some very good work."

There were some others who seemed to be friends. After that trip to New York, Governor Stark always came into Truman's office when he was in Washington to express his gratitude. Truman recalls that one day Stark came in with the usual friendliness, but in the course of his conversation mentioned a new subject.

Stark laughed. "Some people out home are trying to get me to run for the Senate against you, Harry. You needn't worry. I'm going back and tell them off."

When he had left Truman looked at the door out of which he had gone. Then he called in his secretary, Victor Messall, a slight, long-headed man from southwest Missouri who had developed both political wisdom and stomach ulcers as a secretary in the offices of Missouri members of Congress before Truman came to Washington.

"Vic," said Truman. "That so-and-so is fixing to run against me."

There were times when Truman himself had not been so sure he wanted to come back to the Senate. Life in apartments was not as pleasant as in Independence which Bess and Margaret both loved so much. Living certainly was no cheaper. Undoubtedly, however, though he may not have realized it then, before Stark, still in the role of his grateful friend, left his office, he had stubbornly made up his mind. That was months before the primary or even before Stark's announcement that he would enter it if he were drafted. It must have been before the cloud over the Gentleman from Pendergast began to become almost night dark with developments in Kansas City.

Obviously, if Tom Pendergast ever needed an office boy, an ambassador, or a private Senator he needed them in the first months of 1939. Yet, whether from the growing reluctance of Truman or the desperation of Pendergast, the evidence is that the case for Pendergast was not left in Truman's hands in those days. Pendergast was sending a variety of emissaries back to Washington to party leaders. One envoy, definitely extraordinary, was the Kansas City police director, who spent a week in Washington trying desperately and futilely to see Roosevelt. Such ambassadors got nowhere while the gossip came in greater volume from the Federal courtrooms and the evidence increased that Roosevelt was sympathetic with Governor Stark and District Attorney Milligan in the anti-Pendergast crusade.

The well-dressed officials of the fire insurance companies came to Kansas City and disappeared into the District Attorney's offices. After "three long days" in which they emphatically denied that they had any notion that the $460,000, which Milligan says they had raised, would be used for any improper purpose, they agreed to persuade the man who had handled the money to tell the whole story. By dramatic coincidence, United States Attorney General Frank Murphy and J. Edgar Hoover arrived in Kansas City by plane on April 4. The insurance men went back to Chicago, New York and Hartford. They were busy men and that year they were worried about what was happening to the government under the New Deal. Pendergast was indicted on April 7.

Harry Truman was in Kansas City during that Holy Week of 1939, when Pendergast realized that his tenure in power was coming swiftly to an end. Boss Tom still seemed a tough man that early spring though he had lived with a tube in his side since the summer of 1936. How much Pendergast told his associates and even that late is uncertain. It came out afterwards that he had gone to elaborate precautions to fool not only the tax authorities but his own family too. District Attorney Milligan says that when the news came of Pendergast's indictment on Good Friday, his "followers were stunned." They were even more shocked when, on May 22, old Tom, who had always been ready for a fight to the finish, went into court and pleaded guilty to the evasion of income taxes on the cash the insurance companies had delivered to him.

Truman had left Kansas City before the news came. It seems unlikely that he would have left if he had had any realization of the proportions of Tom's trouble. His own innocence in the whole business is unquestionable. District Attorney Milligan, who has no love for Truman, has stated, "At no time did the finger of suspicion ever point in the direction of Harry Truman." His ignorance appears to have been almost as complete as his innocence.

Truman customarily kept his foot hard down on the accelerator on those long drives across Illinois, Indiana, Ohio, Maryland on the way to Washington. He could leave Kansas City in the early morning and make dinner the next day in Washington, half way across a continent. Somewhere along the way on this trip he got the news of Pendergast's indictment. He was aware of the meaning of the Pendergast indictment to himself as the Gentleman from Pendergast. It cut the cord of Pendergast support, yet bound him to the Pendergast story. His reaction was automatic and instinctive: "Pendergast has been my friend when I needed it. I am not one to desert a ship when it starts to go down."

He had made a choice. Pendergast was gone, but by his code Harry Truman was a gentleman still. At that time in the politics of America and Missouri it did not appear likely that Pendergast would go down alone.

CHAPTER XIII

You Can't Win, Harry

LATE IN 1939 Franklin Roosevelt sent a message to Harry Truman. The President did not think that Truman had any chance of renomination in Missouri the next year and he suggested that he would be glad to appoint him to the Interstate Commerce Commission. It could not have been a message which warmed Truman with any sense of personal gratitude. Just a week before Pendergast was indicted in April 1939, *The St. Louis Post-Dispatch* had printed a story stating that Roosevelt was backing Stark in the fight on the Pendergast machine. Some of Stark's friends had been busily spreading the suggestion that Roosevelt would like to see Stark in Truman's seat in the Senate. Some of them later, including Stark himself, carried their enthusiasm to the point of belief that Roosevelt would like to have Stark as his vice-presidential running mate in the third term enterprise of 1940.

"I sent him word," Truman told me, "that I would run if I only got one vote—mine."

That was a black winter. If World War II still seemed, as Hitler waited, only a phony war, the attack on Truman in Missouri was already clearly determined upon his political death. At the end of the year, Tom Pendergast had been seven months in Leavenworth Penitentiary. His organization was scattered and his name in Missouri was being used as a synonym for a political corruption which fouled all it touched, including particularly Harry Truman. That was not all. In the month after Pendergast had gone to prison, Truman in Kansas City was clearly troubled about the mortgage on his mother's farm.

"We are having difficulty," Truman told a reporter. "You know how it is when you seem to owe more than you can pay."

Apparently a Kansas City reporter did. A good many people

have shared the same troubles as Truman, but that year and the next it would have been difficult to find any man in a tighter corner. He would have sent that sharp message to Roosevelt if the words had been his last. He had said one week after Pendergast had walked steadily into the prison gate at Leavenworth that he would beat Stark if he ran. Yet, when John Snyder, old companion as reserve officer who came to Washington early in 1940 as executive vice-president of the new Defense Plants Corporation, dropped into Truman's office, he found no such brash pretense. Truman did not even have money to pay for the stamps to write to people to ask for their support. Snyder said that on the street outside the Senate Office Building he got Horace Deal, St. Louis contractor, to write a check for $1,000 using as a desk the fender of a car. The money was paid back after the primary campaign.

Such letters as Truman could send were bringing in no encouraging response. Missouri papers, in December, carried an announcement that he would run again, but there was a tentative quality about it. Then, on January 28, 1940, Curtis A. Betts of *The Post-Dispatch* wrote that Truman was coming home for conferences and would announce afterwards whether or not he would run. The meeting was held in St. Louis on a Saturday afternoon at the Hotel Statler.

"It was not easy to get the boys to the meeting," Roger Sermon told me. Only about half of those who were invited came. Most of those who did come had reasons why they could not be active in his primary campaign. There were, however, about twenty-five men there. Truman remembers Sermon, Snyder, Philip J. Welch, Harry Vaughan, James K. Vardaman, Jr., Roy Harper.

"All of them said I couldn't win," he remembered.

Sermon put it more emphatically: "Harry, I don't think you can win, and that's not merely my personal opinion but after inquiry around." He added later, "I'd a whole lot rather slapped him on the back and told him he could. 'Of course,' I said, 'if you do run, I'll be for you come hell or high water.' "

That was as much encouragement as he got from any of them, all the doleful way around the room. Truman listened. He had come to find out what his friends thought. He gave them his decision.

"Old Mr. Gloom," he said to Sermon, "I'm going to file. I

wouldn't have the guts to go home and face my people if I ran out."

He did file on February 3. Stark was already in the race. Then Maurice Milligan came in. Sermon said that Milligan had telephoned him before he went to the Truman meeting in St. Louis. Milligan had found out about the Truman meeting and wanted to talk to Sermon before he went. He asked Sermon to support him for Senator. Sermon told him that he would be for Truman if Truman ran, but that otherwise he would be for Milligan against Stark. He got the impression that Milligan would not run if Truman did.

"'One Milligan got his tail beat by Truman,'" Sermon quoted him as saying, "'and I'm not going to run if Truman files.'"

There were, indeed, rumors that the remnants of the Pendergast organization, which hated Stark as ingrate more than Milligan as prosecutor, might make a trade to support Milligan in order to be sure to beat Stark. James V. Conran, lawyer of New Madrid, Missouri, heard so much of the rumors that he asked Truman about them. Conran was one of those who felt that no chance could be taken on letting Stark win.

"Conran," Truman told him, "I'm getting damn tired of everybody talking about beating Stark. I want somebody to talk about electing Truman."

The rumors were serious enough to prompt Truman's secretary, Victor Messall, who claims to have been the one man besides Truman who thought he could be renominated, to go from the meeting in St. Louis to Kansas City to see Jim Pendergast. He met him in the echoing emptiness of Tom's old office at 1908 Main. Messall asked him if he would support Truman. Later he remembered that Jim took his cigarette out of his mouth and leaned back in his chair.

"You can tell Harry Truman," he said, "that if he gets only two votes in the primary one will be mine and the other will be my wife's."

That at least was that. Nobody early in 1940 knew, however, how many more votes than those two Jim Pendergast could deliver. Then Milligan, despite what he had said to Roger Sermon, did announce his candidacy.

"There was more hope when Milligan came in," Sermon said. Not all Truman's friends agreed to that. Even after the election some thought that Truman would have done better in a race with Stark alone. The general opinion, however, was that Milligan's entry meant that at least two candidates would be dividing the anti-Pendergast votes. All the same, as Truman had pointed out to Conran, there had to be votes for Harry as well as the votes to be divided by his opponents. The great need at the moment was for some demonstration that somebody wanted Harry Truman to stay in the Senate. Demonstrations, in the absence of spontaneous outbursts, cost money and at that point Truman had even less money than hope of votes. Nobody showed much disposition to raise any. They tried to get two old Truman friends (and later Truman friends, too) to serve as managers in eastern and western Missouri. They tried to get an old Truman friend to be treasurer. He turned up in the Milligan camp. The wife of one man, who did help Truman and who later was richly rewarded for it, refused to let her house be used for a Truman meeting.

"We wanted somebody for treasurer and somebody with a name or title," said Messall, who acted as chairman of the campaign, "so we hit on Harry Vaughan, who had the title of Colonel and was then selling loose-leaf book equipment in Illinois and wasn't worried about any political repercussions in Missouri."

Sermon, who until he died wore his apron as grocer in the mornings and sat at his desk as mayor of Independence in the afternoons, agreed to take on the job of chairman of the finance committee. He scraped the bottom of their empty barrel. It took all they could beg or borrow to open headquarters and stage the campaign-opening demonstration for Truman in Sedalia on June 15. It did not seem then an important event in history. The day before the German troops had marched into Paris. Hitler had ended the phony stages of the war on May 8, when Truman celebrated his fifty-sixth birthday. Sedalia, a quiet town of twenty thousand people in the center of the state, certainly did not seem the center of the world that day. It was the center of such hopes as Harry Truman had, nevertheless.

The community was friendly to him. (Or it seemed so: Stark carried the county in the primary.) There were industrial elements there which promised to swell the crowd, and crowd was what was needed. The meeting was not such a show as Tom Pen-

dergast had been able to put on for Truman at Columbia when
he ran in 1934, but it provided the first mass indication that
somebody was for Truman. Not everybody even at the meeting,
however, was for him. Stark supporters, driven over from the
capital at Jefferson City, scouted the meeting as coaches scout a
game. They helped swell the numbers. Messall and his assistants
had made certain that there were representatives present from all
parts of the state. Sam M. Wear, who later got Milligan's job as
District Attorney, presided. Senator Lewis B. Schwellenbach, of
Washington, had come to speak of Truman's service in the Senate. Colonel Stayton, of Independence, was there to speak of
the war they had fought and the roads they had built together.
Two representatives of big unions spoke.

Perhaps the most important person present was Martha Ellen
Truman. She was almost eighty-eight years old then. In two
months the old Young farm would be sold over her head. As
the crowd gathered, her son stayed on the lawn level and shook
as many hands as possible. He sent his mother with T. H. Van
Sant, banker of Fulton, to a seat on the front row of the platform. She sat there, meeting people, not merely an old lady
but a keen partisan watching all that went on. She asked Van
Sant about all those who came up to meet her.

"Is he our friend?"

Van Sant told her as best he could. Of some whom he identi-
fied as friends, she readily agreed. But there were a number of
cases in which she said, "I do not think so."

"I think," said Van Sant later, "that she missed not a single
one. Her instinctive judgment was uncanny."

Truman made his speech. The crowd liked it and altogether
the occasion was a success. One of those who was Truman's
friend and supporter in that campaign, however, Dr. W. L. Brandon, of Poplar Bluff, in southeast Missouri, says that in that
campaign Truman was "such a bad speaker that it was pitiful."
It was a remark which was echoed among his critics and his
friends, too, as late as the campaign of 1948. The strange thing
in both campaigns was the appeal which his speeches had for the
people. Also, if Truman made no pretenses as an orator, in that
campaign he already had confident ideas about the kind of
speeches people want. Van Sant relates that one day during the
campaign, Truman stopped briefly in his incessant riding at Ful-

ton, on a day when Larry McDaniel, candidate for Governor, was there to speak. Truman told McDaniel quickly that he was just passing through and would move right on since it was McDaniel's day. However, he took occasion to tell McDaniel that he was losing ground in the campaign because he talked too much. He told McDaniel that he was slipping into the error of adding a new paragraph to his speech to answer every new criticism made by his opponents.

"Larry," Van Sant remembers Truman telling him, "you can win this nomination if you can make a twenty or twenty-five minute speech. I understand that your speech has now grown to one hour and forty-five minutes which is too long and you answer too many things. You did not ask for my advice but I am going to volunteer it. Cut your speech to twenty-five minutes, shake hands with as many people as you can for a little while. Afterwards, even if you have time left, leave. If you have no place to go, you can always pull off the road and take a nap."

That advice did not help McDaniel. He went immediately from the conversation and spoke for an hour and forty-five minutes and had, Van Sant says, a fifty per cent walk-away. He was nominated, nevertheless, but, apparently still talking, was the only Democratic nominee who lost in November.

Whether or not it was good advice to McDaniel, it is a good description of the Truman campaign that year. He went everywhere, sometimes with Fred Canfil driving him, sometimes with Vaughan or Messall or some other supporter, often driving alone. Sometimes in that and other campaigns he went only to show himself: "I just wanted to come down and show you that I don't have horns and a tail just because I am from Jackson County." That often did more good than even twenty-five minutes of talk. He did not, however, win by either talking or state-wide handshaking.

"I wasn't worried," he said long afterwards of the dark early days of that campaign, "I knew my record was all right."

The record was rolled into line. Alben Barkley, Schwellenbach, Hatch and Minton came out to Missouri to testify to it. But the record itself was more important than the testimony about it. Down in the cotton country of southeast Missouri, which is more Southern than Virginia, his support of the farm program had strengthened him long before he started campaigning. He had strong Negro supporters in St. Louis. There were 244,386 Negroes in Missouri. In that campaign he made a speech to them, the reading of which would enlighten some Negroes and many Southerners on his civil rights' program later. The railroad hearings and his attitude toward railroad and other labor brought to him one of the most vigorous campaigns ever made by organized labor in America. Labor knew him well long before the Democratic Convention of 1944.

The railroad hearings of the Interstate Commerce Committee had brought him directly into contact with the various railroad brotherhoods. Also, his work there with Wheeler took him into a major fight between the railroads and the labor organizations about wages. Not long after the railroad unions had secured a wage increase of approximately five cents an hour in 1937, there came the slump which was labeled the "recession." The railroads sought a reduction and the unions opposed it. Eventually the difference was brought before a presidential emergency board. As the contest was drawing to a close, some of the labor people felt that they needed to put a punch into the final testimony. Edward Keating, editor of *Labor,* the newspaper of the railroad workers, and Max Lowenthal called Senator Wheeler, who was vacationing in Montana. He came. Harry Truman came with him and made a strong statement against the cut. The presidential board unanimously turned down the request for a wage reduction. Truman had not stopped with his statement at the hearings. In St. Louis he had put his feelings about railroad finance and railroad wages together in a speech to the Chamber of Commerce: "Banker management ought not to be allowed to sacrifice railroad labor because of its inability to control a situation of their own creation."

The unions did not forget. Furthermore, Lowenthal took no chances on their forgetting. He got the first contribution for Truman from A. F. Whitney, president of the Trainmen, who was one of those Truman later castigated in the threatened strike of 1946. That gift was only an initial detail in a greater labor campaign. All the chiefs of the railroad brotherhoods endorsed him and sent word to their members in Missouri. "Committees for Truman" were organized at all the railroad terminals in the state.

Labor leaders who were working for Truman did their best

to extract an endorsement from Roosevelt but failed. All they got was a telegram from Presidential Secretary Stephen Early. He wired: "The President asks me to explain to you personally that while Senator Truman is an old and trusted friend the President's invariable practice has been not to take part in primary contests. This is because in contests of this character among members of his own party the President must stand aloof regardless of any personal preference he might have."

The railroad unions went on working. They worked with other unions. They made and collected campaign contributions. Then, at the right moment, about ten days before the primary election they blanketed the state with a special Truman edition of *Labor*. It went not only to every union man but to every rural free delivery box in the state—about 250,000 of them. Altogether between 500,000 and 750,000 copies of the edition were distributed. It carefully did not overemphasize his labor record. There was, indeed, a special emphasis on his support of the New Deal farm program. The paper was loaded with statements from his colleagues in the Senate: Barkley, Wagner, Wheeler, Pat Harrison, Thomas, of Oklahoma, Connally, Donahey, of Ohio. Senator Byrnes' tribute said that Truman "is worthy of the support of any Democrat who appreciates intelligent, efficient and loyal public service."

That and other support was the result of the work in the Senate. But Truman also expected and he got help from a Stark mistake. Stark was an able man but one described by a newspaperman who reported his career as "a severe, humorless man with the eyes of a zealot and the mouth of a Puritan." By the time he ran for the Senate he had antagonized a good many Missouri Democrats who were not connected with the Pendergast organization. Probably, however, at the last it was his humorless ambition which gave the necessary break in the campaign to Truman. Truman understood how to handle him.

Van Sant recalled that before the primary began Truman gave him his evaluation of Stark at a dinner at the New Willard Hotel in Washington.

"You fellows know," he remembered Truman saying "that Nero was a great Roman politician and for a long time was very successful. I have studied his career very closely, and for a long time wondered why, having started out as he did, he should have come down in ruin at the end. I think I located the place in his history where he began to take his friends for granted and tried to buy his enemies and at that point I think his road to ruin began."

The politics he had studied as a boy in those old red leather volumes of *Plutarch's Lives* seemed a long way from 1940, but he went on:

"I believe Lloyd Stark has already been guilty of that same error. I further believe that any campaign he makes will be highly personal, and that he will overclaim on his part in the Kansas City affairs, for everybody really knows that it was the Treasury Department and the Department of Justice which broke those cases and not Stark. I think if I do not mention him, he will do everything he can to get me into a personal controversy on the stump and, though he will fail to do that, he will be led into making enough errors to give me a definite opportunity."

Truman stuck to his part of that plan. Indeed, his failure to make a personal attack on Stark sometimes puzzled his supporters. Editor Keating remembers a conversation on the subject when he and Truman were talking about the special edition of *Labor*.

"Why," Truman asked, "should Stark denounce me for accepting Mr. Pendergast's support, when he solicited that support and was so grateful for it that he wrote me a letter, thanking me for introducing him to Mr. Pendergast?"

"I suppose you have that letter?" Keating asked.

"Certainly."

"And, of course," Keating said, "you will use it in the campaign?"

"I am not sure I should do that," Truman said. "I am not sure it would be the right thing to do."

"I respect your scruples," Keating told him, "but if I were in your place, I would certainly slam him with that letter."

It was not necessary. Stark produced the error which Truman had been counting on all the time. The campaign had only three weeks to go when the Democratic National Convention of 1940 opened in Chicago. At that convention Stark set himself up as a candidate for Vice-President, gave away Stark Delicious Apples to delegates and seemed to be running for both the Vice-

Presidency and the Senate at the same time. Truman's friends controlled the delegation; he himself was the Missouri member on the important Resolutions Committee. At the State Convention in Kansas City some of Truman's friends had considered trying to keep Stark from even going to the National Convention as a delegate. They thought they had the votes to do it. Truman himself had put a halt to that and others agreed that such action might make a martyr of Stark. Instead he made a spectacle of himself or so they tried to convince Missourians. At a press conference he announced his candidacy for the Vice-Presidency. He opened headquarters for the distribution of his apples. He even staged a small demonstration on the convention floor, but one of Truman's women supporters, Mrs. Mary Chinn Chiles, a combative lady over six feet tall, carried a Truman-for-Senator banner into the Stark-for-Vice-President parade. Stark drew from Bennett Clark the comment that he was a man trying to ride two horses at the same time. Before the actual balloting he withdrew from the race. Only he and two of his friends voted for Henry Wallace whom Roosevelt had requested. Harry Truman and the rest of the delegation voted for William B. Bankhead. Truman did not owe anything to Roosevelt that year. In later years some of Truman's friends debated how much Stark's vice-presidential illusions helped Truman. They were no help to Stark. Still, he seemed in the public reports, as the campaign moved toward the election, to be the best bet for the nomination.

There was plenty of fighting behind the scenes. If the Pendergast organization was an uncertain quantity in Kansas City, the organization of Mayor Bernard F. Dickmann and a policeman's son named Robert E. Hannegan in St. Louis seemed to be increasing in power. If Pendergast in prison and later on parole left a vacuum in Missouri politics, they were ready to fill it and, in terms of their willingness to take over the state Capitol as well as the St. Louis city hall, they had launched the campaign of the talkative McDaniel. They wanted to win, and they were interested in trading for whatever remained of the big bloc of Jackson County votes which Pendergast had shoved onto the scales of state politics so long. Truman seemed to have the inside track in trading. Also, he had unexpected strength in southeast Missouri which went into the trading, too. It was, however, as the campaign proceeded, an uneasy bargaining. If old Tom

Pendergast's word stayed given once Tom had given it, some of Truman's friends were less confident about Dickmann and Hannegan. Stark and Milligan were, *The Post-Dispatch* reported in June, "vying" for Dickmann's aid. Apparently, indeed, the St. Louis men had some early bargain with Stark. After Hannegan's death in 1949, *The Post-Dispatch,* in reviewing his career, stated that "the Dickmann-Hannegan machine had favored Stark, but made a last minute election-eve switch to Truman." That paper, which records the history of that city, raised the question: "Why did Hannegan send out word to the ward bosses to drop Stark for Truman?" It added, "The answer is not known."

It is not a secret though the details are still confused. One of the stories, which Truman men tell, is that toward the end of the campaign Bennett Clark "got hold of Hannegan and lined up St. Louis committeemen for Truman." Clark had been slow in moving. He and Truman got along very well in the Senate. Indeed, sometime before 1940, Truman had joined Tom Pendergast in suggesting Clark for President before Roosevelt had made up his mind on a third term. (Clark, in commenting on their suggestion, had quoted a statement by Speaker Thomas B. Reed under similar circumstances to his father: "Why, Champ, I think they might go farther and fare worse and I think they will.") In the early part of the 1940 primary campaign, however, Clark was taking no part. One night Campaign Chairman Messall was back in his own secretarial haunts in Washington, feeling desperately blue about the whole business. His stomach ulcers kept him from taking a drink but in the Carroll Arms Hotel on Capitol Hill he ran into Bennett Clark who was under no such disability. He asked Clark why he did not make some speeches for Truman.

"Why in hell should I make any speeches for him? He never made any for me."

The depressed Messall told Clark he was mistaken and that he could give the dates and places. They talked a while and then went up to Clark's office in the Senate Office Building where Messall made no more progress. After a while Clark lay down on one of the Congress' special black leather couches and went to sleep. Messall went back to the Carroll Arms. There he ran into Senator Hatch.

"My gosh," said Hatch, "you look like you've lost your last
friend."

Messall told him about his unsuccessful talk with Clark. Hatch
took up where he had left off and came back with the declaration
that Clark would speak for Truman.

"I had merely helped to straighten out a situation which was
not generally understood," Hatch thought later. "Anyway, Vic
was advised that Clark would publicly come to the support of
Truman in that campaign which he did. I went out to Missouri
in an effort to be of assistance to Truman. While in the state I
found the prevailing sentiment to be that Truman practically
had no chance. His friends were greatly discouraged and his
enemies were sure that Truman would finish last in the three-
man campaign.

"The situation there," Hatch remembered later, "was just as
blue and discouraging as it was in the summer of 1948 when
some of his friends were trying to get him to withdraw and not
be a candidate for re-election as President. But in 1940, as in
1948, Truman himself gave every evidence of confidence."

There was not much to base it on. Clark did go to the Mayfair
Hotel in St. Louis and, as Messall puts it, "called up everybody
he knew in Missouri." Undoubtedly Hannegan, as chairman of
the St. Louis City Democratic Committee, was among them.
Mayor Dickmann seemed clearly committed to Stark.

Dr. W. L. Brandon remembers speaking to Truman about
both Dickmann and Hannegan in that campaign.

"The so-and-sos," Truman told him, "just want to be sure they
are on the winning side."

Certainly, in the early days of the campaign, there was not
much reason to think that that was the Truman side. Yet the
Truman men seemed to be going for the St. Louis candidate,
McDaniel. Truman's friend Conran, of New Madrid, remembers
that he was astounded at the big campaign kick-off at Sedalia to
hear the Truman people shouting, "Hurrah for McDaniel" without, he was sure, getting a return pledge from the St. Louis
people to take Truman.

"It was necessary," he says, "to start a quiet movement over
the state to hold back on McDaniel endorsements until St. Louis
came out for Truman."

Political bossing had not ended in Missouri apparently when

Pendergast went to jail. However, the St. Louis men as they rose—or hoped to rise—to power lacked Pendergast's skill in his most effective days. Others had learned how to swap and trade, too, particularly some of those southeastern Missourians who were strong for Truman.

"All this time," says Conran, who was chairman of the Speakers' Committee, "we were contacting other political figures in St. Louis to get the word to Hannegan that southeast Missouri would ditch McDaniel if St. Louis was not going for Truman. McDaniel gave us hell over that, but we stood our ground. Then we started the move over the state to keep calling St. Louis with like statements.

"Senator Bennett Clark was in on all these moves. He finally ended up in a hospital and we continued to push him even there and he kept his telephone busy. I finally contacted James Waechter, who had been helping us get our position over to Hannegan, within a few days of election day, and told him we couldn't wait any longer. If Hannegan was going with Stark we were ready to start our campaign against McDaniel. Hannegan telephoned me later that day and said he was going for Truman and would slate him in his ward. He followed this with an announcement in the papers just a day or so before the election. We were later informed that he and Dickmann had a conference and decided something had to be done. They agreed that Hannegan would make his move for Truman and Dickmann would stay with Stark—which is exactly what they did."

Even that apparently final agreement, however, seemed shaky. At the other side of the state, Truman's friend Sermon, who thought they had a clear agreement by that time with the St. Louis leaders, was badly frightened and fighting mad.

"A day before the election," he told me, "Gene Gualdoni [an important ward leader in St. Louis] called me up and told me that Dickmann and Hannegan were selling Truman out in St. Louis. I called Dickmann and asked him about the agreement on Truman and McDaniel. I told him that I was starting then to call every friend of Truman's and tell them to switch from McDaniel to McReynolds."

McReynolds was the second man in the race for Governor as it turned out in the primary and was then blowing very hot on the back of McDaniel's neck.

"It was not long," Sermon continued, "before Larry McDaniel called me, 'What's going on?' And I said, 'That's what I want to know. We made a solemn agreement. I understand it's not being carried out and we're calling Truman's friends to let them know.' He cussed and fumed but he agreed to get every ward leader in St. Louis together. I told him, 'There's no time to check. Do I have your word of honor as a gentleman?' He agreed and later called back and told me that fourteen wards would go for Truman, eight for Stark, and that six were not committed. He gave me his word of honor that that was the way it was going to be."

It turned out about that way. Politicians could count the vote in advance in St. Louis almost as well as once they had been able to do in Kansas City. Truman carried St. Louis by 8,411 votes and that covered his whole victory as the margin in the State amounted to only 7,976. In later years, that last-minute switch to Truman carried Hannegan to the National Chairmanship of the Democratic Party and carried him there at a time when he and Dickmann had completely lost out in the state. Oddly enough, also, that election which pushed Hannegan up brought down Jim Aylward, of Kansas City, who had persuaded Truman to run for the Senate in the first place.

"Aylward was a fine person," Truman told me, "but he was against me in 1940 and has never been to see me since. He knows that if he had been for me then, he would have been National Chairman in place of Hannegan."

The 8,000-vote lead in St. Louis was by no means the whole story. The election showed how broken was the Pendergast machine. Not only had the vote fraud investigations and the disruption of the organization cut the total vote from Jackson County, including Kansas City, from 146,966 in the primary of 1934 to 105,487 in 1940. Also Truman, who had carried the county by over 100,000 votes in 1934, had a margin of only 20,000 votes in 1940. Actually, his two anti-Pendergast opponents polled a larger total vote in Jackson County than he did. Significantly, however, though he carried only forty-three outstate counties to Stark's sixty-five, his outstate vote was greater than it had been in his first election by an amount practically equal to his margin of victory in the state. Those country and small-town votes were as important as his lead in St. Louis. The long rides, the many handshakes, the short speeches and the record in the Congress paid off.

The St. Louis Globe-Democrat spoke of the "calamitous result." Its editorial, which Governor Stark sent to Franklin Roosevelt, spoke also of the "lamentable apathy" of the people. A hundred thousand fewer Missouri Democrats, it said, voted than in the primary of 1936. It missed the fact that forty thousand of the missing may have been Jackson County ghosts. Stark, in his letter to Roosevelt, added this explanation:

"You will be interested to see that the machine vote, backed by Bennett Clark with every force at his command, was 100,000 less than our combined vote [Stark and Milligan]. I am sorry to report that virtually all of the Federal appointees, including Postmasters and WPA workers, were lined up with Clark and the machine against us.

"Due primarily to the severe drought, etc., about 100,000 of our rural vote, which is strong for me, did not turn out."

In his letter Stark mentioned that he had received letters from Roosevelt during the primary on July twenty-sixth and thirty-first. The letter which he got back in response to his explanation is a composition which is pure Roosevelt:

> Dear Lloyd:
> Your letter enclosing the clipping has been received and I was interested to read the analysis of the recent Primary figh⁺ I am sure you understand my personal feeling toward you. . can only say that we will all have to get behind the ticket and work for a Democratic victory.
>   With all good wishes,
>   Your friend,
>   (*signed*)   Franklin D. Roosevelt

Truman also got a message of congratulations from FDR, though he had not come forward with any explanations.

"I was not worried," he said years later, "by the Pendergast troubles. Pendergast had more friends than any other man in Missouri at that time. They thought he had been mistreated."

And Truman added: "He was a damn sight better than those who were prosecuting him. Maurice Milligan was not smart, not half as smart as his brother."

Yet, a month after the primary Truman wrote Roosevelt asking him to reappoint Milligan as District Attorney. He wrote:

"Due to legislation passed in this Congress, it was necessary for Mr. Milligan to resign in order to make a Primary campaign for United States Senator. Had this legislation not been passed, Mr. Milligan could have made the race and still held his position.

"He has made a good District Attorney, and I do not feel that he ought to be penalized by losing his job."

That letter makes interesting reading in comparison with Truman's speech when Milligan was reappointed in 1938. It is interesting also in view of Truman's refusal to reappoint him himself in 1945 after he became President. Political considerations may explain it. Some of Truman's enemies said that he had used the offer of the I.C.C. post and the possibility that he might accept it as bait to lure Milligan into the race. That seems highly improbable. It is much more probable that after the primary Democratic unity was important in the campaign against the Republicans which was still in progress. However, he had no such feeling about Stark after Stark's term as Governor ended at the beginning of 1941. A Senate committee upheld a Truman charge that Stark had required all state employees to contribute to his campaign. ("Put the lug on them," is the Truman and the American language for that process.) Obviously acting for Truman, Senator Minton, of Indiana, wrote Roosevelt protesting against the naming of Stark as a member of "the proposed Labor Mediation Board."

"This appointment," said Minton, "would be very displeasing to Senator Truman, who has always been our friend. Several of his friends have called me about it and expressed the hope that this would not be done. The appointment would give Senator Clark, whose support we never have, an excellent opportunity to work on Truman.

"I have just had occasion, in connection with the American Export Lines' appropriation, to contact Senator Truman, who very promptly agreed to support your request, and because it was a part of your program.

"I hope you will give this consideration to Truman."

Stark did not get the appointment. So far as Democrats and a Democratic President were concerned, Harry Truman was the man from Missouri.

Perhaps Truman was not worried in that primary campaign. Throughout that intra-party fight, as in the presidential election

of 1948, he gave the impression of being the only Truman man
who was not worried. Certainly, however, the primary campaign
came to its concluding days with little hope around Truman.
Sermon says that Messall kept calling him from Sedalia on election night almost ready to concede. Governor Stark had his
friends gathered with him at the Governor's Mansion ready for
celebration, but at four o'clock in the morning they went home.

"I went to bed defeated," Truman said. "I went straight to
sleep but in the middle of the night a fellow from St. Louis
called me up to congratulate me. I told him to stop bothering
me. He said, 'The Post-Dispatch says that you are ahead and
gaining.' "

Shortly before he died, Sermon told a story of a Truman the
next day who looked like a man who had gone through a sausage
mill. He was, Sermon said, depressed all day long until news
finally came late in the afternoon at the cabin of a friend on
Lake Lotawana near Independence.

"Then I saw him begin to nod, finally relaxed. He was perfectly worn out. I took him home to sleep. He was supposed to
fly back to Washington on important business the next morning
at nine."

Neither Truman nor any of his other friends recall any such
day of despair. It was, indeed, a day on which the news got
better and better. But there was plenty of work still ahead.
Furthermore, while he had won the primary election, it came at
a time when the family had lost the Truman farm. The sheriff
foreclosed on the mortgage held by Jackson County, filing the
deed on August 22, 1940. They had to find a house for old
Martha Ellen and Mary Jane. Truman's mother broke her leg
in the new house, and a little irrationally but emotionally Truman somehow blamed that on those who had sold her out of
the old Solomon Young homestead.

"Old man Montgomery, succeeding Buck Purcell, as presiding
judge foreclosed to embarrass me," Truman told me. This was
George S. Montgomery who became presiding judge in the post-
Pendergast Jackson County election of 1940 and not the Montgomery against whom Truman ran in his first race for county
judge. "They sold it under the hammer without giving us any
chance to refinance and moved Mama off the farm. She broke
her hip in the house I got for her. The county bought it in and

held it until I got to be Vice-President. Then a real estate man suggested that if Vivian and I would like to buy it back he thought it could be arranged. We paid all the taxes, interest, etc., and the county made $6,000 on the deal. We took back 279 acres, plus 100 across the road. Vivian got 15 to fill out his 80. All told 394 acres."

Certainly that year he looked at triumphs and disaster. He was Democratic nominee for the United States Senate and a man too poor to save his mother's house. Also, midway between his nomination and his election, when he was being denounced as unfit for public office, he was chosen Grand Master of the Grand Lodge of the Masons of Missouri. It was a crowded year. Even the Scottish Rite Temple in St. Louis must have seemed particularly crowded in the general election campaign when his induction as Grand Master emphasized his brotherhood with Forrest C. Donnell, Republican candidate for Governor that year who was later to be Grand Master, too. Truman had first been put in the line of Masonic offices in the state by a Mason who was also an active Republican. Later in the bitter politics of Missouri there had been an almost unprecedented fight on Truman in his supposedly automatic movement through the various chairs of the Grand Lodge. Some Republicans in the fraternity from east and north Missouri had opposed him unexpectedly. They did not succeed, but their action hurt him. He had moved forward beyond that fight in the Grand Lodge. Donnell was engaged in no such fight against him in 1940, but he was, as an energetic Republican, bearing down hard on Truman with the anti-Pendergast line. He took up where Stark had left off—or had been left off. And another Missouri Mason asked Donnell a question.

"Is Harry Truman a man of character worthy to be Grand Master of the Grand Lodge of Missouri?"

Donnell dropped his eyes to the ground.

"Yes," he said.

It was an opinion shared by the people of Missouri in the election that fall. There were scars. Truman won only by half the majority Roosevelt received over Willkie. However, Donnell defeated McDaniel for Governor in the same race.

Actually those Missouri elections seemed very unimportant that year. Truman's opening rally at Sedalia had been held on the day after the Germans entered Paris. In his final speech of the campaign, Roosevelt had emphasized that "Democracy is not just a word, to be shouted at political rallies and then put back into the dictionary after election day." Increasingly that year it looked like a word which might disappear from the face of the earth. And in the month after the election Harry Truman was listening with other Americans when Roosevelt said: "I want to make it clear that it is the purpose of the nation to build now and with all possible speed every machine, every arsenal, every factory that we need to manufacture our defense material. We have the men—the skill—the wealth—and above all, the will. . . . We must be the great arsenal of democracy."

It would need a great President to press for it. And a man, who had been riding around Missouri seeking votes and seeing the first bursting signs of defense building, knew that such an arsenal would need somebody to watch it, too. Harry Truman, in his Chrysler coupe, had already been looking at the defense progress and defense-spending with increasing concern when he came back to Washington to begin his second term in the Senate in the January of Pearl Harbor year.

CHAPTER XIV

Captain of Confusion

AFTERWARDS REPORTERS, ADMINISTRATORS, generals, contractors, members of Congress, ordinary people and Franklin Roosevelt were amazed by the mass of revealing and corrective detail which the Special Committee Investigating the National Defense Program pulled out of the camps, the Pentagon, the factories, the whole labyrinthine hurry and grab of World War II. Even in the time of astronomical spending the fifteen billion dollars it was credited with saving was impressive. Its objective, always unanimous, reports added as much in war efficiency as they saved in war cash. It was clear that the committee's work took Harry Truman to the White House. It has never been adequately understood what Harry Truman brought to that committee. Actually, the Truman Committee was not so much the start of a presidential story as the sum of the experiences and the qualities of his American career.

It was as a Missouri politician that he was first impressed with wasteful inefficiency in the defense-spending. Apparently he was primarily shocked at Fort Leonard Wood in Pulaski County, Missouri. Pulaski was one of the outstate counties which he carried in the race against Stark and Milligan. It was also a county in which the confusion, the fumbling, the corruption and the waste of the swift, first spending for defense could be seen at that time as clearly as the trees. The essence of the work of the Truman Committee was that it came to the general from the specific, from the country to the capital.

He was the man who had examined Miles Bulger's rotten macadam nineteen years before. Now, he could look at the American confusion in 1940 and 1941 as a Senator with no lingering sense of his own inadequacy. Pendergast was gone. Any basis for the office-boy legend had disappeared with him.

Perhaps more important, Truman's own sensitiveness about the adverse opinion of others had disappeared. He had as many friends as any man in the Senate, and as much respect, even if he had not yet earned any special admiration. Nobody expected the proportions that admiration would assume when, on February 10, 1941, he proposed the creation of his committee. That same day the House of Representatives passed a bill raising the national debt limit to $65,000,000,000.

Truman based his proposal upon the waste he had seen as veteran and citizen and Senator with his own eyes. He also made it as a man who had gone over the ground of old American wars. What he saw at Fort Leonard Wood added to what he had learned as Senator on a history student's holiday at Chancellorsville and Gettysburg as well.

"I had studied the Civil War battles on the map at the Staff and Command School at Fort Leavenworth," he told me, "and when I came to Washington I went down and looked over the battlefields on the ground and in person. Sometimes later John Snyder went with me."

And he did more reading about them. He was particularly interested in military maneuvers. "There is no basic difference between the maneuvers of Ramses II or the King of the Hittites and those today. I was interested in maneuvers, particularly of the leaders, Alexander, Napoleon, the perfect maneuvers like those of Hannibal at Cannae, Alexander at Arbela, Napoleon at Austerlitz, Lee at Chancellorsville."

Those maneuvers may seem a far cry from the Truman Committee in World War II but: "There was only one copy of the hearings of the Civil War Committee on the Conduct of the War. I got it from the Library of Congress."

He learned more than maneuvers from that reading. It was the record of a committee which had undertaken as the war went on to supervise the actual conduct of the Union cause in all its phases of the Civil War. It meddled in military strategy. It was the current equivalent of the Un-American Activities Committee of that time. Lincoln felt impelled to appear before it when it was dealing with wild rumors of the un-Union activities of Mrs. Lincoln. Truman understood the irresponsible and not merely political quality of its work which, as one scholar has said, was carried on with "that high moral pleasure which is to be found in the justification of a strong animosity." Obviously, neither Senator Truman nor Student Truman was interested in setting up such a committee as that.

"Lee said that committee was worth two divisions to him," Truman told me later.

In 1941, however, the waste and inefficiency showed too little sign of abating. He was impressed with the necessity that something be done then. He was not impressed by the statement of General Brehon B. Somervell, of the Army Service Forces, and his associates that "it's axiomatic that you can't save time and money at the same time."

"I had known Somervell in the Army and I knew he cared absolutely nothing about money," Truman told me.

If the Civil War Committee on the Conduct of the War had been dangerous, the 116 committees set up to make investigations after the fact and after World War I were futile. As soldier-citizen-Senator he wanted something done when it would do some good. He would have opposed any committee set up by himself or any other Senator which would undertake to have anything to do with the selection of commanders, the shaping of strategy or the disposal of munitions and men. He could see no objections to one which would, as the defense program and the war after it proceeded, disclose waste, open bottlenecks and point out inefficiency and graft. No real objections were ever discovered while he headed the committee.

Before he watched the money go at Fort Leonard Wood, he had, as a member of the Senate Appropriations Committee, followed the hearings on rising defense requirements in 1940. Then he had driven in his car not only to Leonard Wood, but also to camps in Maryland, Pennsylvania, New Jersey, Tennessee, South Carolina and Georgia. Through the year, beginning in the summer of 1940, he drove many thousands of miles looking and asking questions. Almost everywhere the waste was the same.

It was important and not merely political that the center of that wide traveling was in his own state. He not only saw the waste first at home. At home, also, he saw the results of the big grabbing for big contracts. Missouri, like many other states, was left out of the biggest spending. In Missouri he saw that little companies were left largely out of it, too. He saw the same sort of concentration of war business as the bigness of credit and business power of which he had complained in peacetime in that speech which old Brandeis had liked so much. He had faith in the back places and the many small men as the components of American power.

In January 1941, he predicted the failure of the defense effort unless thousands of small manufacturers were given a part in it. Later he pointed out that "more than three billion dollars in defense contracts have been let to just four companies." Also he said, "I am reliably informed that from seventy to ninety per cent of the contracts let have been concentrated in an area smaller than England." (The United Kingdom is only, he knew, a third larger in area than Missouri.)

"It undoubtedly is the plan to make the big manufacturers bigger and let the little men shift for themselves," he said.

Raymond P. Brandt, the correspondent of *The St. Louis Post-Dispatch*, in his story of Truman's speech asking the creation of the committee, emphasized that Truman, as one basis for the investigation, charged favoritism in the granting of contracts in Missouri and to Missouri. *The Post-Dispatch* also quoted Truman, after the committee was set up, as saying that the reason Missouri lagged in defense contracts was a belief in the East and in Washington that all Missouri politicians were crooks. If his resentment of that remained, his intimidation was gone. He was clearly irritated about his own state situation as late as July 1941, nearly five months after his committee had been set up. He tried to telephone Roosevelt but, as he wrote a presidential Secretary, "was informed that he had so many things to do that he couldn't talk to me, and I know that is true." He then wrote Roosevelt about a TNT plant at Malta Bend, Missouri, on the Missouri River about one hundred miles east of Kansas City, which had been approved by the Ordnance Department but: "The matter was referred to the OPM Plant Site Committee for confirmation. A young man was sent out there who made a cursory investigation and reported a shortage of labor which doesn't exist."

Truman went on:

The matter has been held up by the Site Committee of OPM because they can't reach an agreement. I understand that it has finally been referred to a committee consisting of Mr.

Hillman, Mr. Knudsen, the Secretary of War and the Secretary of the Navy.

A plant in that location will, in my opinion, solve the labor situation in Western Missouri. It will also assure the establishment of a bag-loading plant in the area of St. Joseph, Missouri, which is the only town in that part of the country between Omaha and Dallas and St. Louis and Denver with a labor problem that hasn't been solved by National Defense. That solution is absolutely vital to Congressman Duncan of Missouri, who is our member of the Ways and Means Committee of the House and, I think, one of our ablest Congressmen.

I have never attempted to bring any pressure to bear on the Ordnance Department or the OPM for plants or plant sites, or for any other matter in relation to National Defense because I think that the people authorized by you to do these jobs are much more competent than I am to make the necessary decisions. The only reason I am vitally interested in this decision is that the Ordnance Department believes this site to be the best one in the United States for the purpose, and of course I want the plant in Missouri if there is any way it can be done.

The only reason I am writing this letter to you is because I am informed that you are going to have to make the decision.

This will solve a serious labor problem in Missouri, and I hope that the Ordnance Department's finding can be carried out.

Roosevelt sent the letter straight over to the Office of Production Management:

MEMORANDUM FOR

MR. KNUDSEN:

For preparation of reply.
Dear Harry:

F.D.R.

The reply both denied the request and contradicted the Senator: "The site was considered but due to an admitted labor shortage and the fact that the land was rich and expensive farm land, another location was chosen in another State." The letter said, however, that the Senator would "be interested to know" that four defense projects were in the course of construction or completed in his state. He was treated as a politician to be disregarded in a nation making ready for war.

That was just six months before the Truman Committee, a few weeks after Pearl Harbor, drafted a 190-page document on the chaos and indecision in OPM under its two-headed management by Knudsen and Sidney Hillman, who themselves at that time were subject to the control of the Supply Priorities and Allocations Board which had been created in August 1941. This report of the Truman Committee was quietly given to the President in advance of its publication. It was an unanswerable indictment of administrative confusion.

"The result," Truman told the Senate later, "was the appointment of Donald Nelson and the creation of the War Production Board."

The result also indicated the coming to prestige and power of the Truman Committee. The "you will be interested to know" technique disappeared from letters prepared for dispatch to Senator Truman. The clearly emerging fact was that he knew probably more about the over-all war effort, its complexities, its fault and its failures, than anybody in Washington with the exception of the President himself. Certainly, as the chairman of his committee, he made such a study of big government under great pressure as had hardly ever been made before. That meant that when he came to the Presidency he had had opportunities for studying and knowing that government hardly equalled by any other President. It was big, sprawling, complex. Also, around it and in it, beside many patriots, were the same sort of contractors, the same sort of dull power, the same business men and politicians he had known in Jackson County and Missouri. The frame was multi-magnified; in people and purposes the picture was not strange. Chairman Truman was County Judge Truman watching the spending of the biggest nation in the greatest war.

He was qualified by long experience for the watching, even if he seemed to two sympathetic observers, as the committee began its work, "just another obscure Junior Senator with no visible political future." Also then, too many misunderstood his past. He had observed the confusion as the artillery captain who had made an effective battery out of undisciplined human materials. He had watched the billions spent in carelessness at a time when he lacked the money to save even his mother's farm from foreclosure. He was still the honest, careful road builder. He was the railroad investigator who could be both fair and determined upon the facts. Perhaps it was most important that he was the politician.

That was basic even if a good deal of pious talk about the Truman Committee has been devoted to the fact that politics did not enter into its work. Americans always forget that the word "politics" does not merely mean the artifice of doing the people out of something but the art of doing what the people require as well. Politics in Truman's case loomed, even in 1941, as the image of Pendergast. It was an appropriate image at that time though its appropriateness was not always understood. The county judge who could stand up to Pendergast and his contractor companions was equipped by experience not to be intimidated by power. After Tom Pendergast in Jackson County, big brass, big money, big labor were not terrifying in the United States.

Perhaps in that flood of spending he did look also like the boy ready to put his finger in the dike. In the United States, as in Jackson County, he was, to use Pendergast's word about him, "contrary" enough to try. He had come back from all his riding and looking early in 1941 with the determination to make a speech describing the waste and confusion which he had seen. And while he was writing that speech a newspaperman suggested that he embody in it a request for a committee to investigate. The probability is that Truman himself had been thinking toward that ultimate end all the time.

"Early in February 1941," Truman recalled, "I was in my office thinking about a speech on heading scandals off before they started and Bill Helm suggested that I introduce a resolution. I couldn't get Jimmy Byrnes to act. Everybody thought I wanted to set up a headline business like the Dies Committee. Finally they gave me just $15,000."

At another time when friends of Mr. Byrnes, then chairman of the Committee on Audit and Control, were suggesting that Byrnes had done much for Truman as Senator, including setting him up in the war investigating committee, Truman's patience wore out.

"The only favor I ever asked of him while I was in the Senate was to approve a $25,000 allowance for the Committee to Investigate the National Defense Program—afterwards shortened to the

Truman Committee. After much haggling and delay he recommended that I be given the magnificent sum of $15,000 with which I started the activities of that committee. Some people, who should know, say that committee prevented the waste and unnecessary expenditure of fifteen billions of dollars in the war of 1941-45. After the committee became known I always asked the Senate as a whole for expense money and the Committee on Audit & Control had to approve it."

Byrnes was very close to the Administration at that time. Roosevelt appointed him Supreme Court Justice three months later. One reason for Byrnes' delay, it has been suggested, was that the Administration was afraid that Truman might be attempting to set up over Roosevelt another such Committee on the Conduct of the War as plagued Lincoln. However, Helm says that he asked Roosevelt at a press conference what he thought of the idea and Roosevelt said he favored the investigation and hoped that it would be thorough. Roosevelt later told politicians discussing Truman as a vice-presidential candidate that he had approved Truman as the chairman of the committee. There was actually no great interest in the matter at the beginning. Only sixteen Senators were on the floor when the resolution, as cut and altered by Byrnes, was approved without objection on March 1.

After some consultation among leaders the original committee named, with Truman as chairman was: Tom Connally, of Texas; Carl Hatch, of New Mexico; James Mead, of New York; Mon Wallgren, of Washington; Joseph Ball, of Minnesota; and Owen Brewster, of Maine. Connally was the only old-timer in the crowd. Those chosen finally by Truman and agreed to by Senate leaders had, however, as it turned out, the one common characteristic of "a sort of unspectacular competence," according to some of those who closely watched them work. Four of them were from very small towns in widely separated parts of the country. Later additions to the committee during the war included: Homer Ferguson, of Michigan; Harley M. Kilgore, of West Virginia; and Harold H. Burton, of Ohio.

"I went to see Attorney General Jackson," Truman recalled, "and told him what I was going to do. 'If we find anything wrong I'll leave it to you to prosecute, but I want the best investigator you've got.' In a few days he phoned me that he had the man. He had just convicted a Federal judge of fraud. He sent Hugh Fulton to see me.

"He came in," Truman remembered, "wearing a derby hat, a big fat fellow with a squeaky voice. I said to myself, 'Oh shucks!'

"However, I paid him more than half of the money I had, $8,500 a year which was $500 more than he was getting. We took the members of the committee to the first investigation we made of Camp Meade. The Senate was so impressed by the report of our first investigation that we got $100,000 on the strength of it. All the time I was there the committee spent only $360,000 but saved the nation fifteen billion—$250,000,000 on the Canol project alone."

As counsel of the committee, Fulton had a good deal more equipment than a derby hat and a squeaky voice. He was a careful investigator who had not only secured the conviction of a corrupt Federal judge. He had also been the government attorney who had sent Howard C. Hopson, of the Associated Gas and Electric Corporation, to jail. He had infinite capacity for work. Moreover, he strongly shared from the beginning Truman's determination that the committee not constitute either a "witch hunt or a whitewash." As an early riser who did not care for breakfast, Fulton was ready in the early mornings for conferences with Truman who still maintained farm hand hours. Many of the committee's accomplishments were worked out in such morning conferences with only the chairman and the counsel on hand. More was done in informal meetings in a Truman office, called "Harry's Doghouse," with just one or two members on hand. By all accounts Fulton did an excellent job. Afterwards some wondered why he did not, as seemed indicated when Truman went to the White House, become an important figure in his Administration. He was the victim of bad timing and poor sense of propriety. His announcements of his entry into private practice had engraved upon them the fact that he had been counsel to the Truman Committee. They were sent out so that they arrived, among other places, at the White House after Truman had been President only a few days. There may have been other earlier incidents which irritated the relationship. Fulton clearly, however, went off the Truman preferred list at that time.

The chief of the investigating staff under Fulton was Matthew J. Connelly, who later became Secretary to the President. An able and charming young Irishman from Massachusetts, who could be close-mouthed and conversational at the same time, Connelly had had much experience as an investigator in New Deal relief agencies and for several Congressional committees. He was, indeed, at that time making a career as one of the committee investigators who are colloquially referred to as "Committee Dicks." Other members of the staff were chosen from those with experience in Congressional investigations.

It would be a mistake, however, to attribute the success of the committee to the idea that its investigators were picked on a strictly non-political, civil service merit system basis. Truman picked men whom he knew, some from Missouri. Canfil, who had been his most devoted political aid in Jackson County, became an implacable Congressional investigator. He even got into the hush and double-hush atomic bomb projects. Truman brought from Missouri, also, William M. Boyle, later Democratic National Chairman, whose mother had been as helpful as Canfil when Truman ran for the Senate for the first time. Boyle, who was no kin to the Pendergast contractor of the same name, had been director of police and street commissioner of Kansas City. He became assistant counsel and investigator for the committee. Altogether there was a good political infusion in the objective, non-political Truman Committee.

(Other changes were taking place in Truman's own office which was committee headquarters at the time. When Canfil came to Washington, so also did Colonel Vaughan, the campaign treasurer. Vaughan became Truman's secretary in March 1941 when Messall, who had managed the Truman campaign of 1940, resigned to go downtown and make some money in the private practice of his governmental know-how.

"They were both jealous of me," Messall says of Vaughan and Canfil, "and bitterly jealous of each other.")

The committee went very seriously to work. Perhaps if it had not begun its work immediately after an election instead of before one, it could not have been so non-partisan in the mountain-high problems it faced. Pearl Harbor lifted higher the basic patriotism of them all, Republicans and Democrats alike. Their chairman was both as convivial and as stubborn as the relentless investigation of the mass of stupidity, greed and confusion, perhaps inevitable in such rush and spending, required.

In his work on the committee he gave clear emphasis to the hard-headed idealism which his mother had taught him on the Middle Border. His committee proceeded under the declared conviction that "inefficiency and self-interest have always existed." Yet, in a speech, as chairman of the Truman Committee, at a labor-management meeting in Philadelphia he suggested that the needs of both management and labor included "more time reading the twentieth chapter of Exodus and the fifth, sixth, and seventh chapters of St. Matthew." Not all who listened that day may have recognized from his citations that he was talking about the Ten Commandments and the Sermon on the Mount. But his speech along with his work emphasized the need for "trusting the other fellow" and watching him carefully at the same time.

"We started out with five members," Truman said, "then seven, then ten. We never had a minority report. Wallgren was head of a sub-committee on light metals and airplane plants. Hatch, Kilgore, Ferguson, Brewster, Burton—everybody got a chance to head an investigation. But I read every report that came into the committee. We held committee meetings only about once every two weeks. Once Connally threatened a minority report on synthetic rubber but he changed his mind. When the committee held hearings I sat as a court judge. I would not let anybody browbeat witnesses. I permitted witnesses to have counsel though not to ask questions. Once I had to give John L. Lewis a real dressing-down.

"We let any interested Senator attend and take part. It got so Senators would ask me, 'Harry, won't you investigate this for me?'"

Perhaps the main accomplishment of the committee was not the fine result it obtained in the war effort in better organization or greater production in aluminum or rubber, steel or planes. Its lasting product was the example it provided "of the results that can be obtained by making a factual investigation with a good staff." It demonstrated the effectiveness of intelligent investigation by a committee of Congress. Perhaps such objective, non-partisan fact-finding and fact-reporting as a basis for wise Congressional action would have been impossible at any other time. Maybe only a war makes such an operation possible in this country. Perhaps only a remarkable chairman can assure it. When Truman left the basic idea did not depart but the committee's accomplishment was completed.

Three months after Truman left, according to a man above all others who should know, "it had gone to the dogs."

Truman was in charge of its work for more than forty months. And looking backward, it appears that the public appreciation of the committee's work came very quickly. At the time the appreciation seemed to come only on the other side of a tunneling through a mountain of detail. There was an insistent opposition by the chairman to any grabbing at headlines for public attention. A young man named Walter Hehmeyer, who later collaborated on a Truman biography, combined investigation with publicity work for the committee. Its publicity bristled with facts and findings but studiously avoided, other reporters said, "the synthetic fireworks which characterized some other Congressional investigations."

That turned out to be not only information useful to the Congress and the country but the best publicity, too. Yet, the first major publicity came at a time when the question was dramatically raised as to whether there should be any publicity at all. The committee was shaping its first annual report, filled with criticism of the defense program, when the Japanese bombed Pearl Harbor. There was some feeling that such criticism had no place in a nation which was closing ranks in a war which had begun with a catastrophe. There was serious consideration given even as to whether the work of the committee should continue. The committee decided on both continuance and publicity. In a later report it stated of an American hush policy about submarine losses which had given credibility to enemy propaganda: "Certainty is always better than rumor." The reports came out in a steady stream, forty of them while Truman was chairman, every one of them with the unanimous approval of all the members. In many controversial particulars the committee became the one dependable report of the war effort itself. Newspapermen in search of dependable facts very suddenly, it seemed, discovered the dependable Senator. In a poll of Washington correspondents conducted by *Look* magazine, Truman, of Missouri, who had been a Senator almost tiptoeing tentatively into Washington one term before, was named one of the ten most valuable men in Washington in the war. He was the only member of Congress among the ten.

The nation's discovery of Truman, however, seems less significant than the rediscovery of Truman in the Missouri country from which both he and his investigation had grown. That rediscovery was demonstrated dramatically within the first year of war by *The St. Louis Post-Dispatch* which had editorially screamed its disappointment and chagrin when Truman was first sent to the Senate.

In *The Post-Dispatch* of November 8, 1942, the day after the American landing in North Africa, Marquis Childs wrote the rediscovery. The Truman he described should have been as surprising to *Post-Dispatch* readers as that trained and well-equipped Army which reached Africa from the camps which had risen in confusion from the cornfields. Childs wrote as a member of the St. Louis paper's Washington staff that among Senators Truman had become "one of the most useful and at the same time one of the most forthright and most fearless of the ninety-six."

"There is no doubt," Childs wrote of the Truman Committee for The P-D, as Missourians call that paper in anger or admiration, "that it has saved billions—yes, billions—of dollars."

Watching that spending seemed to Harry Truman in his middle fifties a remote participation in great war in his time. Hehmeyer, the committee publicity man, wrote later that Truman went immediately to see General George C. Marshall, Chief of Staff, and offered his services. He had been on his last duty a full colonel in the Field Artillery Reserve. Their meeting must have been the beginning of the great affection and admiration which Truman held for Marshall in later years. He did not, however, Hehmeyer suggests, care for General Marshall's comment at the time.

"Senator Truman, you've got a big job to do right up there at the Capitol, with your Investigating Committee. Besides, Senator, this is a young man's war. We don't need any old stiffs like you."

"I am younger than you, General Marshall."

"Yes, but I'm a general and you'd be only a colonel. You stay right where you are."

He did. Harry Vaughan went off to Australia. Vivian's boys went from Grandview into service. The committee work went on and Truman spoke more and more in a greater variety of places. If he was no orator, people listened with increasing attention to what he said. The year in which he set up the Truman Committee he also worked at his job of Grand Master of Masons in Missouri. He spoke in lodge halls from Illinois to Kansas. Also, he talked about the war, and increasingly he talked about the peace. He told boys at a military school, "I'm for Russia. They're killing Germans every day and saving American lives." Also, in August 1943, when Roosevelt and Churchill were meeting at Quebec, Truman found time to go back to Shelbyville, Kentucky, to speak at the Old Settlers Reunion. Just a hundred years before his people had been moving from Shelby County to Missouri. It had been a long century and was worth remembering even in the midst of war.

That August when he looked back with the old settlers was an important month for Harry Truman. It was the beginning of his last year as chairman of the Truman Committee. Also, as Roosevelt pointed out, the second anniversary of the Atlantic Charter that month was the birthday as well of the American Social Security Act, which was a charter, too. The war seemed well in hand. Roosevelt still seemed strong and well.

In spite of Truman's work there were still bureaucratic conflicts, bottlenecks, basic differences in government. It seemed pertinent to Truman's concern for war efficiency, but not personally important to him as a politician and a Democrat when Roosevelt sharply knocked together the heads of Jesse Jones, Director of the Reconstruction Finance Corporation, and Henry Wallace, who was not only Vice-President but Chairman of the Board of Economic Warfare, too. The feuding of Wallace and Jones, which Roosevelt condemned with barbed impartiality, was not only the major example of the bureaucratic collisions which often disturbed the Truman Committee more than crookedness or waste. It was also the collision of the irreconcilable right and the irreconcilable left in the Democratic Party and the New Deal. It did not seem Truman's task to investigate that and settle it, too. No senatorial committee, however objective, could hope to deal with any American conflict of such dimensions in government or outside it.

The true nature of the quarrel was not so clear to some observers. At a distance it seemed merely another Washington row. Such a stout old Republican as William Allen White was satisfied with no such settlement as Roosevelt's rough "a plague on both your houses" plan. Roosevelt ought to decide and swiftly, he thought, between the right and the wrong. He wrote Wallace:

"One of you men was wrong and one was right. It was the President's job to find out which and stand by him. I have upheld the President probably more often than any other Republican editor in the country. But when he is wrong, I am free to say so. And I don't wish to be pharisaical but I thank God I have never been bitter about him and have great respect for what he has done and the great war job that is going on under his administration. But between you and me, twelve years is going to get him. I mean, get his keen sense of justice, get his quick reaction to evil. I know personally from experience that there is a certain zone which when a man has walked through it, he has got to be careful. Maybe Time was the scissors that Delilah used for shearing Samson! After which, 'Samson wist not that God had departed from him!' I am afraid—deeply and morally afraid—because I love my country and want it to go right, that I can hear Delilah's scissors clicking. . . ."

Perhaps Mr. White was right. But at seventy-five Time had clipped some of his perspicacity, too. His great collisions were far behind him. Theodore Roosevelt was dead and William Howard Taft, too. William Jennings Bryan, in 1943, was as dead as Grover Cleveland. Governmental conflict was not all confusion, nor necessarily waste. Simple choices between right and wrong were—and are—easier to contemplate in Emporia than in the White House. But some scissors in 1943 were already clicking. Roosevelt was sick after he came home from Teheran that December and, though those who watched closest to him may differ, he seemed to me, as one of his assistants, to be never quite well again. There were people around him seeking political decisions which sometimes, in Time's weariness, he seemed to wish only to avoid or postpone.

Obviously, as 1943 passed and 1944 lengthened across the spring, Truman was concerned with such collisions. His new stature as chairman of the Truman Committee suggested him to some as a solution to them. His friend Lowenthal had been one of those strongly urging him to run for the Vice-Presidency. And on one of the last Sundays before the convention in Chicago he called Truman's secretary, Bill Boyle, about it.

"He told me," Lowenthal remembered, "that Truman had decided not to do it and that he was leaving town."

Lowenthal went up to the Senate Office Building to see Truman. They talked in the Sunday quietness of that huge building.

"Truman said he had talked it over with the Mrs. and had decided not to be a candidate. Also, he had a daughter and the White House was no place for children."

That statement suggests that there was a time before the convention when Truman was thinking and thinking hard about the nomination. The statement Lowenthal remembers about the child and the White House emphasizes the current political calculation that the Democratic vice-presidential nominee that year would probably become President of the United States.

"He drove me home," Lowenthal said. "We stopped at his apartment on Irving Street to get his bags, then he dropped me at my house in Chevy Chase."

Somewhere along the way Truman told Lowenthal that he was too poor to think about running. And he used an earthy American expression about the lack of both a pot and a window. Lowenthal was still arguing, reluctant to agree, when he got out of the car at his own house. He did not return Truman's easy, good-natured grin. He watched the back of Truman's car as he drove off toward Missouri—and Chicago—in the late Sunday afternoon. He stood in the street and watched the car until it disappeared up the road.

CHAPTER XV

As Far as the Bridge

HARRY TRUMAN WAS tired on Tuesday afternoon of convention week, when Robert E. Hannegan knocked on the door of his room on the seventeenth floor at the Stevens Hotel in Chicago. As Missouri's member of the Resolutions Committee which was working on the platform for Roosevelt's fourth term campaign, he had arrived in Chicago the previous Friday. The Resolutions Committee had held sessions through the days and long into the nights. Also, Truman had been at work for the nomination of James F. Byrnes, of South Carolina. Hannegan knocked and the worn Truman let him in. Hannegan told him that Roosevelt wanted him as his running mate. Truman answered him very briefly.

"Tell him to go to hell. I'm for Jimmy Byrnes."

He got back on the bed and the very pale Irishman who was that year, on the recommendation of Truman, National Chairman of the Democratic Party argued with him. Truman grinned at Hannegan.

"Bob, look here. I don't want to be Vice-President. I bet I can go down on the street and stop the first ten men I see and that they can't tell me the names of two of the last ten Vice-Presidents of the United States." Then he grinned at Hannegan. "I bet you can't tell me who was McKinley's Vice-President."

Truman laughed later remembering that.

"By golly, he couldn't and that one became President of the United States."

Stubbornly he told Hannegan to go away, but Thursday afternoon he went reluctantly when Hannegan asked him to come to his suite across the street in the Blackstone Hotel for a conference. Hannegan, Postmaster General Frank Walker and the Big Bosses—Kelly of Chicago, Flynn of The Bronx, Hague of

Jersey City—were there, and individually and in a body they began "raising hell with me to be Vice-President."

"The President wants you to be Vice-President," Walker said.

"I don't believe you," Truman told him.

The phone rang. It was four or five o'clock in the afternoon of Thursday July 20, the second day of the Democratic National Convention of 1944. Truman was sitting on the bed by the telephone and he could hear all that Hannegan said and most of what Roosevelt on the other end of the line said to him.

Hannegan said, "No. He hasn't agreed yet."

Roosevelt replied loud enough for Truman to hear him. "Well, tell him if he wants to break up the Democratic Party in the middle of a war, that's his responsibility."

Hannegan turned to Truman. "Now what do you say?"

"My God," said Truman.

Kelly remembers beyond the expletive that Truman said he was a soldier and would carry out his leader's command.

They turned immediately to the question as to who should make the nominating speech. Truman said that he supposed that it should be Bennett Clark. It was very late when he finally located a hide-out room which Clark had at another hotel. Even then Clark was sleeping so soundly that the only way Truman got in to ask him to make the speech was to follow into the room a valet who had come to bring back a suit of clothes. Truman came down out of the hotel and went home to get a little sleep himself.

Some mysteries still surround the events in that convention and before it. Men differ as to the exact time of that call and even whether any such single phone call can be set apart in decisiveness as Truman remembers it. There were undoubtedly many calls. FDR talked several times to Hannegan, Flynn, Walker, Kelly, and others. There was talk from Washington. The convalescing Harry Hopkins was operating from his Georgetown house. White House switchboard operators remember calls over those lines involving Hopkins and Niles, Walker, Hillman, Hannegan. One call, even a decisive one, from Hannegan's suite to Roosevelt's train is lost not only in history but in the busy lines of the past. Truman and Walker remember the time as late Thursday afternoon. Others are not so sure.

Sometimes Truman has seemed in the confusion the product

of a "conspiracy" to push the Democratic Party after Roosevelt sharply back toward the conservative side of the American debate. Truman himself was not a part of any such conspiracy, which at the beginning was much less concerned about his promotion than the demotion of Henry Wallace. He was nominated by some of the same machine forces in the party which, at the direction of Roosevelt, had pushed Wallace through a reluctant convention in 1940. Roosevelt's part in that convention is still historically confused, yet he got what he wanted. Truman's story is clear, but he came away from the convention with the nomination which he is still certain he did not want at all. As time passed it became increasingly clear that this was not only an important convention in American history but one which qualifies as almost the cream of the American political jest. Truman was nominated by men speculating beyond the death of Roosevelt who knew what they wanted but did not know what they were getting.

Perhaps the man who understood best what had happened was not even there. He made his report after the convention to Henry Wallace, whom Truman had defeated. Senator George W. Norris, in rejection and retirement at McCook, Nebraska, after forty years. of carrying the Middle American banner of progressivism, suggested that he might be puzzled but what he wrote was clear. Was the fighting based on the idea that Roosevelt would not live through his next term? And so was a final decision made as to Democratic directions?

He said in that letter: "I am wondering if the gambling chances are that he is going to die before he serves out his next term if he is re-elected. . . . Is this why the machine was so anxious to defeat you? . . . Cold-blooded politicians are not moved by any patriotic sentiment. These are the gamblers of the world of politics."

But old Norris, who unexpectedly outlived Roosevelt, saw that some gamblers had bet wrong on Harry Truman. In that same letter he said of Truman: "He has done a very fine progressive work . . . steered a very fine progressive course . . . done a wonderful work, I think, in the Committee of which he is chairman, investigating our various war efforts. Such a man would not be the selection of the machine which nominated him."

The machine was there undoubtedly, sweatily, even ruthlessly at work on the floor and in the smoky hotel rooms, just as it had been when it carried out its orders in 1940. Perhaps in 1944 with a tired and preoccupied President, "the machine" felt and thought it was more independent. It was dealing with a weary man who wanted to divest himself of any pain in personal relationships which he had disliked when he was well and almost deviously dodged when he came to the profound fatigue of 1944. The clear thing in the confusion is that Roosevelt did get what he wanted and, in terms of the continuation of his New Deal, what he believed the country required. There was more reluctance than Harry Truman's about him that year. Henry Wallace was nobly reluctant to get out of the race. Jesse Jones at the other extreme in the diverse forces Roosevelt had led was a sulking old man. Roosevelt in politics understood the maxim which he had quoted for war: "My children, in time of trouble it is given to you that you may go with the devil as far as the bridge." The clear political result is that he found the bridge for the politics of his long purposes.

At least as early as August 1943, just after Roosevelt had sharply divested both Jesse Jones and Henry Wallace of their duties and powers in connection with foreign economic matters, there was talk at the White House that Henry Wallace would not do as vice-presidential candidate again. In my own diary I made an entry about that time:

> Talked with David Niles who said I could bet any money that Henry Wallace would not be the Vice-Presidential candidate next time.

Niles was then an astute and well-informed politician on Roosevelt's staff as he continued to be later on Truman's. Also, at that time around Roosevelt, and increasing, like rings on a pond, away from Roosevelt, the talk grew about Roosevelt's health. Practical politicians began six months before the convention of 1944 to make their decision that the next vice-presidential candidate would be President of the United States.

In January 1944, *The St. Louis Post-Dispatch,* which was no longer under any illusions about Truman as a puppet pushed up impudently by a boss, stated that the selection of Hannegan as Democratic National Chairman boosted Truman's stock for the vice-presidential nomination but that Truman himself was unwilling to talk about the Vice-Presidency. That was not only news but history in *The Post-Dispatch*. It had not only snorted at Truman. In 1942, when Truman and Clark had agreed upon the endorsement of Hannegan as Collector of Internal Revenue in St. Louis, The P-D had strongly dissented on the grounds that Hannegan had tried to get a Democratic Missouri Legislature to grab the governorship for McDaniel after he had been defeated by Donnell in the same 1940 general election in which Truman won. That was a complicated piece of local political finagling. Truman, however, had told Brandt of *The Post-Dispatch,* which had called the Hannegan appointment a "disgraceful example of plum passing,' that Hannegan would be collector or there would be no collector in St. Louis. He became collector. Also, in 1943, he became with Truman's pushing, United States Commissioner of Internal Revenue. Those eight thousand last minute votes in the 1940 Missouri primary were worth at least as much per vote in gratitude as any ever cast or counted in the United States.

Then a vacancy occurred in the Democratic National Chairmanship—or rather Postmaster General Walker, who had reluctantly taken on the job after Edward J. Flynn, of New York, in January 1943, was anxious to create a vacancy. Walker and Roosevelt had first offered the job, Truman says, to him but he recommended Hannegan. Certainly Hannegan owed his entire political status to Truman since he and Dickmann had lost out not only in the McDaniel race in the state but in the St. Louis city hall as well. Hannegan once told me, however, that he had only reluctantly in succession taken the jobs of collector, commissioner and chairman. His sponsor, Truman, was equally reluctant about talk of the Vice-Presidency for himself, but both of them were opposed to the renomination of Henry Wallace.

Wallace's biographer, Russell Lord, says that Hannegan and other politicians told Roosevelt that Wallace would divide the liberals, labor and the city machines and cause a bolt of Southerners, at an informal caucus in his White House study "very early in January." It seems improbable that that could have been anything more than a very informal conversation if such a caucus took place at all. Roosevelt was not well in January. He spent a week in Hyde Park that month trying to shake off the succession of colds and the bronchitis which had wracked his winter. If Truman was expecting or hoping to get his nod, he left Roosevelt in February to back Barkley when Barkley, as Democratic Majority Leader angrily resigned after Roosevelt had sent to the Senate a peculiarly sharp veto message on a tax bill. At the same time, Truman was telling Kansas Democrats that failure to re-elect Roosevelt would imperil the peace.

If Truman did not want to be Vice-President, however, there were men at work making a way for him. One of them was Edwin Pauley, then treasurer of the Democratic National Committee, who has frankly described himself as "a conspirator" to that end. Hannegan, he said, "was a most willing conspirator, but was afraid to push Truman because they were both from Missouri and very good friends.

"My own intensive activities in this regard were occasioned by my conviction," Pauley said later, "that Henry Wallace was not a fit man to be President of the United States; and by my belief, on the basis of continuing observation, that President Roosevelt would not live much longer."

In the pre-convention months he says that his slogan was: "You are not nominating a Vice-President of the United States, but a President.

"At first," he said, "I found it difficult to recruit accomplices." Most people near Roosevelt "were afraid, for one reason or another, to oppose Roosevelt in his wishes." Exceptions to the rule, he says, were: former Chairman Flynn; Charlie Michelson, the veteran publicity director of the Democratic Party; George Allen, Secretary of the party; and General Edwin A. (Pa) Watson, devoted and politically minded Military Aide to the President. Watson died early in 1945 while on his way home with the President from the conference at Yalta.

"Pa Watson," Pauley said, "was the most active accomplice in my plot to change Roosevelt's sentiments from pro- to anti-Wallace. He was as anti-Wallace as anyone. I had a huddle with him during one of my visits to the White House, and entered into a conspiracy with him to arrange appointments with Roosevelt for all potential convention delegates who were opposed to Wallace. Most of their stories were like this:

" 'Mr. President, we are all for you, but we cannot take Wallace, and Wallace will be a liability on the ticket.'

"This went on for month after month. These callers were

generally the National Committeemen, or the State Chairmen, or the Governor of a state, and so were well known to Roosevelt.

"At first, these interviews made little difference in Roosevelt's thinking. Then slowly, and little by little, they began having their effect. At the end of about three months, I could sense that the President had begun to change from an enthusiastic Wallace supporter to a man who had sincere doubts concerning him. Pa Watson finally told me that this constant barrage was having a definite effect."

One certain thing is that Pa Watson loved Roosevelt and would not have entered any conspiracy which he did not think was for Roosevelt's good. In 1940, he had similarly "conspired" to convince Roosevelt of the necessity of running for a third term. In such dealings with Roosevelt, however, it was often difficult to be sure who was the conspirer and who the conspiree. But that spring he had been sick. He was overwhelmed with the war load. He put off political matters. When he came back from a month's rest at Bernard M. Baruch's South Carolina estate and a reporter told him that it was only seventy-one days before the Democratic Convention, Roosevelt told him that counting on the calendar was a bad habit. He did not even announce that he would run for a fourth term until July 11, and, counting on the calendar, that was just eight days before the convention. It was also the same day, according to Pauley, when the politicians met with him at dinner and extracted from him his choice as to his vice-presidential running mate.

Harry Truman was busy that spring. He and members of his committee crossed the continent to hold hearings on various aspects of the war effort. Also, that spring Truman was called on with increasing frequency to speak at Democratic money-raising dinners, which in wartime were given the euphemistically non-partisan name of "George Washington Dinners." Pauley, who had charge of the dinners, says that the most sought-after speakers were Truman and Speaker of the House Sam Rayburn.

"I very carefully planned," he said, "that there would be a minimum of Wallace participation in any of these events. As a matter of fact, he was seldom sought as a speaker; and, when he was, we discouraged it. He was no good at raising money, and, beyond this, he usually provoked an argument within the party ranks."

In March, Pauley accompanied Rayburn to a series of party banquets on the West Coast, and on March 30, Truman with Senators Wallgren and Kilgore, who had been in the Northwest investigating "ship fractures," joined them before the dinner in San Francisco. Pauley and Rayburn had cocktails before the dinner with the Senators in Truman's rooms.

"We got to kidding about the Vice-Presidency," Pauley said, "and one of the Senators—I forget whether it was Wallgren or Kilgore—mentioned that Harry Truman was a candidate. I said that he was fine with me, but that I was already committed to Rayburn.

"The fact is, I believe that the cocktail party preceding the San Francisco dinner marked the first time that Truman and Rayburn realized that both of them were candidates for the Vice-Presidency. At the cocktail party, Truman proposed a toast to Rayburn as the next Vice-President of the United States. Later, in an unprepared speech at the dinner, he said the same thing and got a tremendous ovation. Just a week later, speaking at a dinner in St. Louis, Rayburn proposed Truman for the Vice-Presidency, and evoked thunderous applause."

On April 30, Truman continued the bowing out for Rayburn at a rally in St. Joseph. Missourians were pleased by the mutual politeness of the two candidates, but like the rest of the country they were a little puzzled, too. Everybody was puzzled, not the least some of those closest to Franklin Roosevelt who was expected to make the choice. There is some contest among the remembering politicians as to who helped him make up his mind and when. One newspaper reporter quoted Hannegan as saying before he died in 1949: "When I die, I would like to have one thing on my headstone—that I was the man who kept Henry Wallace from becoming President of the United States."

Flynn has reported that Roosevelt asked him to "make certain inquiries" about the opposition to Wallace. After travel and inquiry, he told Roosevelt that what he learned convinced him that, even with labor support, if Wallace were nominated the Democrats could not carry New York, Pennsylvania, Illinois, New Jersey or California. Then together he and Roosevelt went over the potential candidates. Truman "just dropped into the slot. It was agreed that Truman was the man who would hurt him least."

After reaching that agreement, Roosevelt told Flynn to get together a group of political leaders at the White House and "inject Truman into the picture." That was the meeting of July 11, attended by Hannegan, Walker, Mayor Edward Kelly, of Chicago, George Allen, Flynn, Pauley and after dinner by Anna and John Boettiger, Roosevelt's daughter and son-in-law.

Flynn had brought together an interesting dinner company. He himself was Roosevelt's old friend in New York politics and one in whose character and political intelligence Roosevelt put great confidence. He was dressed, however, as usual in a flashy vividness. It made him look too much like the kind of boss he was said to be the year before. Then the Senate had been so clearly opposed to his confirmation as Minister to Australia that Roosevelt was forced to withdraw his name. Walker, who had come into politics after making a fortune in movie theaters, had the same single-minded devotion to Roosevelt as General Watson had. Hannegan was a handsome Irishman whose paleness even then indicated the condition from which he died a few years later. Kelly of Chicago looked like an Irish priest, strong and benign; later his Illinois votes in the convention went to Roosevelt's vice-presidential choice only after they were no longer needed. Allen was that evening the shrewd money-maker and politician who wore his obesity like a clown's suit, but was never quite pure clown; he traveled with Truman during the campaign that year, laughed loudly at the quality of Truman's speeches but gave him some good advice, too; Truman made him Director of the Reconstruction Finance Corporation. Pauley, that evening as always, covered the terrific energy which carried him through oil speculation to politics with almost somnolent quietness; later the combination of oil politics, money-raising and Harold Ickes prevented his confirmation when Truman wished to make him Under Secretary of the Navy.

Flynn said later that the dinner proceeded according to plan so that "everyone thought he had suggested Truman and that the President had taken his suggestion." George Allen believed that he, Hannegan and Pauley brought Roosevelt reluctantly to the Truman decision and not that Flynn and Roosevelt met them on it. They held their breaths, he said, until Roosevelt finally said, "Let's make it Truman." And when Boettiger raised some question as to Truman's age, before any change of mind could occur,

"Pauley wigwagged the company that this was the time to go."

Pauley's memory is closer to Allen's than to Flynn's. His memory is that he talked to Flynn some time before March and that Flynn brought practical political objections against Byrnes, Barkley and others, leaving only Rayburn and Truman. At that July dinner, apparently, everybody was feeling a little nervously conspiratorial. It will be hard for a historian to decide who was fooling whom. Roosevelt, after a familiar Roosevelt fashion, put the impatient politicians on a conversational rack.

"At dinner, nothing was said about the Vice-Presidency," Pauley said. "Roosevelt reminisced clear through his terms as President. He got on the subject of food and food poisoning, and on attempts to poison the President through food. He entertained us all by telling of the many attempts that had been made on his life, most important of which was the time Mayor Cermak, of Chicago, was fatally wounded by a bullet aimed at Roosevelt, who was riding in the same car.

"After dinner, we adjourned to the President's study in the blue oval room on the second floor, where we all went over the various candidates one by one, and, for various reasons eliminated them; Rayburn because of the split in the Texas delegation; Byrnes because of coming from the Deep South; Barkley because of his apparent lack of loyalty to President Roosevelt, and coming from the South, too.

"Much to my amazement, Roosevelt injected the name of John Winant, at that time Ambassador to Great Britain; and William Douglas, Justice of the Supreme Court. He said that, in the first place, Douglas had the following of the liberal left wing of the American people; the same kind of people whom Wallace had; that he had practical experience from the backwoods of the Northwest as a logger; that he looked and acted on occasions like a Boy Scout, and would have, in his opinion, appeal at the polls—and, besides, played an interesting game of poker.

"When President Roosevelt had finished this, there was dead silence on the part of everyone. No one wanted Douglas any more than Wallace. The President sensed this.

"The next person discussed was Truman. Roosevelt recalled the occasion when he approved the naming of Truman as head of the War Investigating Committee, and said that Truman had

done a good job; that he had not known him too well, and that
he had been trained in politics."

It was at that point that Boettiger, the son-in-law, asked the
question about Truman's age. Truman was exactly sixty years
old, just two years younger than Roosevelt himself. That was
an age which made him when he became President a year later
older than any President on his entrance into the White House
since the arrival of Buchanan. It was not a popular question
with the assembled politicians and apparently they got out of
the White House without anybody answering it. Roosevelt did
not press it. On their way home in the taxicab Pauley said that
George Allen told him, "Ed, this is the greatest personal victory
you will ever obtain." Flynn believed that he and Roosevelt
had won it before Pauley arrived or dinner was served.

Yet, fifteen days before that dinner Roosevelt was still uncertain what he wanted to do or was playing, as he was quite capable of playing, a very "interesting game of poker" himself,
even with his own staff. On June 27, I made a diary entry about
a conversation around his big desk in which he talked to Niles,
James M. Barnes and myself about the matter. We three were
all Administrative Assistants to the President at that time. That
entry reads:

> Then we got to talking about the Vice-Presidency. I told
> him that the three of us realized that we might be sticking our
> necks out in asking him, but that we felt we should be more
> useful in the Vice-Presidential situation and that we thought
> a fight at the last minute might be bad. He said, "Of course,
> everybody knows I am for Henry Wallace." Then he went on
> to say that he had thought the feeling against Wallace had
> been largely that of politicians but he was beginning to believe
> that it went down below. Some people told him that it meant
> forty per cent of the vote in their precincts. He said that
> if you cut that in half and then half again, it still might mean
> the loss of a million or two votes. He asked when Wallace
> was coming back. [He was then on a trip to China.] Dave
> told him that he is arriving on the 9th and was planning to
> speak on a nation-wide hook-up. The President said, "Well,
> I told him what to say—it is going to be perfectly banal, point-
> ing out the great trade possibilities for America in China and
> Siberia after the war." At one point, however, he said, "I
> think one or two persons ought to go out and meet Wallace
> and tell him about this feeling about his political liability."
> Dave said he thought Wallace had said he did not want to

run if he was going to be a drag on the ticket. Then the President began to talk over possibilities. Dave asked him about Truman and the President said he didn't know about him, but we all agreed that he had done a magnificent job and had a good press. Then the President mentioned Winant who, he said, had great ability and made the rottenest speech in the world but when he got through people thought he sounded like Lincoln. Then he said, "There is one we have got up our sleeve and that is Henry Kaiser. He is talking about great plans in employing five million people by building jitney airplanes for everybody. He would make a great appeal." I said, "Do you think you can trust him politically, Mr. President?" and he said, "I don't know."

He said, "You know how the nomination of Wallace came about before. My first choice was Cordell and he sat in my room while I was in bed for three hours and just said he wouldn't be Vice-President. My second choice was Jimmy Byrnes but I talked with Archbishop Spellman * and others in the church and they said that the feeling against a renegade Catholic would be such that any Catholics in doubt would resolve the difference against us—and so at the last minute it was Wallace." The President seemed convinced of the doubts of Wallace's candidacy.

If he was wavering on Wallace then, he had not swung over to the Jesse Jones side of the governmental or Democratic debate. If the insistence of both Wallace's friends and Wallace's enemies troubled him before the convention, he was also irritated with the split in the Texas delegation to the convention in which there seemed a close connection between the anti-Administration Democrats and Texas associates of Jones. Many anti-Wallace Democrats at the time were close to Jones. Talking politics that month, Roosevelt spoke contemptuously of "Jesus H. Jones."

"There is going to be a period between the seventh of November and the twentieth of January," he said of the election and the inauguration. Then he swung his big forefinger from ear to ear across his throat. He clearly was planning to get rid of Jones even then.

On the day of the dinner with the politicians, I made another diary entry about another conversation at the President's desk involving Eugene Casey, who had the title of Special Executive Assistant to the President though his duties were very nebulous

* In 1950 when the matter was called to his attention Cardinal Spellman informed me that he made no such statement to President Roosevelt.

and his judgment was sometimes questionable. The diary entry
reads:

> Gene Casey said, "There is one other question, Mr. Presi-
> dent. What about the Vice-Presidency?" The President asked
> "Did you ever know Charlie Murphy?" Casey said he had not
> but that he knew he was a great friend of Ed Flynn's.
> "Charlie was a wise man," the President told him, "when they
> asked him who was going to be Lieutenant Governor, he
> would always say, 'The convention will decide,' and he got
> away with it for years." Casey said, "Mr. President, do you
> mean that the convention will decide, period?" The Presi-
> dent laughed and said, "Yes." "Of course," he added, "there
> are some people I wouldn't run with."

When Roosevelt said that to Casey on the day of the dinner
with the politicians, Truman had already ended his drive from
Washington to Missouri on his roundabout way to the convention.
He had made up his mind. He had told the boys in his office,
Matt Connelly remembered, that he was going to Chicago to
work for the nomination of Byrnes, that he was not personally
interested in seeking the nomination and that, if the nomination
was offered to him, he would be forced to decline. Before promising his support to Byrnes, he had been for Rayburn, but when
Texas came up with two contesting delegations Rayburn had
phoned him that he was not a candidate.

Truman had been notified that he was to be Missouri's member on the Resolutions Committee as he had been in 1940. In
order to attend the committee hearings, he had made his reser-
vations for early arrival and prepared to leave Independence for
Chicago in the car with Bess and Margaret at eight o'clock on
the morning of Friday, July 14. The first session of the convention itself was scheduled for Wednesday noon, July 19. Just
before they were ready to get in the car the telephone rang. It
was Byrnes in Washington.

"Harry," he said, "the President has given me the go sign and
I'm calling up to ask you to nominate me."

Truman told him he would be delighted and that he would
also do what he could about lining up the Missouri delegation.
He started for the car again and the phone rang again. It was
Barkley. He also wanted Truman to nominate him for the Vice-
Presidency. Truman told him that he was sorry but that he had

promised Byrnes. He went on to Chicago as a Byrnes man and a man working at the job.

As a Byrnes man, Truman called up Sidney Hillman, who was there as the head of the CIO's new Political Action Committee working for the renomination of Wallace. Later he was the figure in the phrase which the Republicans attributed to Roosevelt concerning that convention, "Clear it with Sidney." Hillman asked Truman to come around and have breakfast with him. That was on Sunday morning, July 16, Truman remembered later, at "that fancy hotel," the Ambassador East. They had, of course known each other in Washington when, with Knudsen, Hillman had been co-chairman of the OPM. Truman's committee had been sometimes sharply critical of their work. Hillman, however, knew Truman's labor record. Truman told him that he was going to nominate Byrnes and that he hoped that Byrnes would be acceptable to Hillman.

"No," said Hillman. He did not look like the dangerous character he was described as being that year by the Republican press. He had worked with Brandeis. He was fifty-seven years old and still spoke with a slight accent after nearly forty years in America and almost as many in the American labor movement. His expressive Jewish face was by turns completely smiling or wholly grim. He could talk with persuasive earnestness and laugh with a quick sense of humor. He was serious that morning.

"No. We're for Wallace, but we might accept two other men. Our second choice after Wallace would be Douglas. I'm looking at our first choice now."

(Hillman died not long after Roosevelt, but it seems in retrospect at least a remarkable coincidence that the two men he put into his conversation with Truman were the same two names which Roosevelt, to the surprise of both Hannegan and Pauley, put into the letter which they expected to mention Truman alone. In the summer of 1945, I had luncheon with Hillman in New York and was surprised to learn his poor opinion of Wallace as an American political leader.)

Truman protested across the breakfast table: "I'm not running. Byrnes is my man."

Hillman smiled as he went with him to the door. Truman told Byrnes about the conversation and Byrnes was not disturbed.

The South Carolinian had come to Chicago in a marching, if not a strutting, self-confidence. He had taken the big Skyway suite on the twenty-third floor which Thomas E. Dewey had triumphantly occupied when he was nominated a few weeks before. Some Californians, including Pauley, who thought they had it reserved believed that Byrnes as Director of War Mobilization used some sort of wartime priority to take it away from them. He had come into it with the conqueror's air. Indeed, when Flynn arrived a few days after Byrnes, he said that even Hannegan rushed him into a corner and told him, "It's all over. It's Byrnes." Flynn's story is that as an angry politician insisting that other politicians keep their word to the President he had to get Roosevelt, then in the midst of a transcontinental train trip, to reiterate on the telephone, to Walker, Hannegan and Kelly that his choice was Truman.

Byrnes obviously thought, or like an Irish actor made others think, that he had the Roosevelt blessing. He joined in that illusion a company which extended during the Roosevelt years from James A. Farley to perhaps even Lloyd Stark. Some who did not get such a blessing felt slighted. Alben Barkley, who renominated Roosevelt at that convention, was an angry man, before he made the speech, when he learned that Truman had got the blessing and he had not. How Byrnes got the idea that he was Roosevelt's choice in 1944 is difficult to understand. It is quite possible that Roosevelt did not say, "No," when Byrnes said his friends were urging him to run. It was the essence of Roosevelt that he could charmingly fail to say, "No," in a manner which sounded to the hopeful like the practical equivalent of "Yes." Yet he had made no secret of the check on Byrnes with the Catholics which he made in 1940. After that he never considered him.

Apparently the only person around the White House who thought that Byrnes might be the Roosevelt choice was able but non-political Admiral William D. Leahy, who says in his memoirs that Harry Hopkins told him that Byrnes would be a strong contender. Hopkins did not get back to the White House after a six-months siege of illness until a few days before Roosevelt left for the Pacific. Also, Robert E. Sherwood, in his *Roosevelt and Hopkins*, says that Hopkins told him on the day of Roosevelt's funeral that "I'm certain that the President made up his mind on Truman long before I got back to the White House last year." Whatever Hopkins said to Admiral Leahy at the time, however, lay behind the Admiral's exclamation when Roosevelt told his train companions over drinks that Truman was to be Vice-President.

"Who the hell is Harry Truman?" the Admiral demanded. It was the oft-repeated question, but this time only the outburst of an old sea dog's surprise in the midst of high strategy in a conflict puzzling to him.

At that moment Truman was a man still working hard for Byrnes. He had breakfast Monday morning with Philip Murray of the CIO and got the same answer he had received from Hillman. The railroad labor leaders, A. F. Whitney and George Harrison, told him much the same thing Monday afternoon. William Green, of the American Federation of Labor, telephoned Truman and fed him another breakfast and the same words. Truman realized that they were talking to each other and about him. There was a remarkable unanimity in the things they said. He told all of them that Byrnes was his man.

Yet it was not only labor who pressed him. Senators Millard Tydings and George Radcliffe wanted to present him to the Maryland delegation which tentatively was supporting Governor O'Conor as a favorite son. There was open, comic, and affectionate revolt against his reluctance as a candidate in the Missouri delegation, led by Sam Wear whom Truman later made District Attorney. There were anti-labor Southerners who wished only to be sure to beat Wallace. They talked earnestly to Truman in Deep South accents. Also, strenuously active among Democrats was Kansas City Republican Editor Roberts of *The Star*. Truman stubbornly told them all that he was for Byrnes.

"I kept Byrnes informed," Truman said later, "but what I told him did not seem to bother him."

The convention formally convened, after much informal politics on the days preceding, on Wednesday, July 19. That day, after Hannegan talked again with Truman and showed him a Roosevelt note, Truman went to the Byrnes suite. It was not an easy occasion for either of them but Truman made it a completely honest one.

"I'll call the President up," Byrnes said. He tried. Roosevelt was in San Diego waiting to speak to the convention the next night, but Byrnes could not get him on the telephone. It was quite obvious then what Truman said later.

"Roosevelt would not talk to him."

The story was by no means over, though after Byrnes on Wednesday withdrew "in deference to the wishes of" FDR, the Skyway suite was big and empty. Byrnes' name was never presented to the convention. He seemed, as he sat afterwards in the White House box, a small tragic Irishman even to those who opposed him. The tumultuous fight, dramatized by the PAC, began when Wallace came into town with his long arms swinging on the day the convention began. Wallace claimed not only the Roosevelt blessing but that he was the leader of the Rooseveltian cause. He had a cryptic blessing in writing which had been released and was in the hands of the chairman of the convention.

In later years, after Hannegan's death, Truman was under the impression that after the dinner at the White House on July 11, Roosevelt had given Hannegan a little penciled note: "Bob, I think Truman is the right man." On the second day of the convention, Thursday, July 20, however—the day after Wallace arrived as the insistent symbol of the Roosevelt spirit, and the day when Truman reluctantly agreed to be Roosevelt's running mate, the Permanent Chairman of the Convention, former Senator Samuel D. Jackson, read the Wallace letter to the delegates:

> Hyde Park, New York
> July 14, 1944
>
> My dear Senator Jackson:
>
> In the light of the probability that you will be chosen as Permanent Chairman of the Convention, and because I know that many rumors accompany annual conventions, I am wholly willing to give you my own personal thought in regard to the selection of a candidate for Vice President. I do this at this time because I expect to be away from Washington for the next days.
>
> The easiest way of putting it is this: I have been associated with Henry Wallace during his past four years as Vice President, for eight years earlier while he was Secretary of Agriculture, and well before that. I like him and I respect him, and he is my personal friend. For these reasons, I personally would vote for his renomination if I were a delegate to the Convention.
>
> At the same time, I do not wish to appear in any way as dictating to the convention. Obviously the convention must

do the deciding. And it should—and I am sure it will—give
great consideration to the pros and cons of its choice.
                    Very sincerely yours,
(*signed*)   Franklin D. Roosevelt

It was dated as of the day Roosevelt left Hyde Park on the
trip which would take him by Chicago to San Diego and the
Pacific bases.

That date was the day preceding the stop in Chicago during
which Hannegan and Pauley came aboard his train to see him
about a letter indicating an entirely different feeling. At that
secret conference, Pauley says, the President wanted to know
how the convention was going, and what the reaction was. Hannegan told him that Byrnes and others were refusing to get out
of the race, and said that he wanted a letter which he could use
if necessary. Pauley, who in 1950 was the only one of the three
still living, says that Roosevelt replied, "Sure," he would give
them a note, and he took an envelope and wrote on it in long
hand, saying that he would have Grace Tully, his secretary, follow with a letter on White House stationery. Pauley says that
neither he nor Hannegan knew what was in the letter until after
they got off the train and then discovered to their chagrin that
they had a letter "we could not use . . . with that man Douglas,
confronting us again." A newspaperman, who under security
regulations could not write anything about the presidential trip
at the time, remembers that Hannegan used a *National Geo-
graphic Magazine* in lieu of a brief case in which to carry the
letter.

Miss Tully, the secretary, has a very different memory of the
incident. Her memory is that the letter was first written before
Roosevelt left Washington but that in it Roosevelt had said that
he would be glad to run with "Douglas or Truman." After a
"lengthy palaver" in the Chicago yards, she says, Hannegan came
out with directions from the President that she switch the names
so as to make it read "Truman or Douglas." The copy of the
letter among the Roosevelt papers at Hyde Park, marked "file
very confidential" is as follows:

                                        July 19, 1944
Dear Bob:—
    You have written me about Harry Truman and Bill Doug-
las. I should, of course, be very glad to run with either of

them and believe that either one of them would bring real
strength to the ticket.

Always sincerely,

Honorable Robert E. Hannegan,
Blackstone Hotel,
Chicago,
Illinois.

Truman himself had difficulty afterwards in tracing and placing the Roosevelt letters blessing him as his running mate.

"Hannegan was very specific," he said, "in his statement that
the memorandum was written in the study at the White House
on the Thursday night before the Chicago convention. Pauley
says no such memorandum was written that night but it was
written on the train in Chicago. Frank Walker is equally certain
that a memorandum was written at the White House and that
the photostat copy of the document in Mrs. Hannegan's safety
deposit box is the one written on the train going to Chicago.

"I am very certain that Hannegan told me that he obtained a
memorandum from the President at the White House the night
of the conference and Walker thinks he obtained one, and I
remember his showing me a pencil memorandum on a little slip
of paper about two inches wide off the bottom of a scratch pad
at Chicago on Wednesday afternoon before the convention. It
had only one name mentioned in it and that was mine. That
memorandum seems to have completely disappeared, if it ever
existed. I have a hazy recollection that such a memorandum did
exist."

Under any circumstances, it is clear that the "Truman or
Douglas" letter was written at least four days before the date on
it. During those four days Hannegan and Pauley used the Truman authority without publishing the Douglas alternative. Indeed, they made the letter such an exciting mystery that when
they finally turned it loose, grabbing newspapermen scattered
the mimeographed copies all over the room. Douglas was never
active. His forces were not organized but Truman supporters
always believed that at the last minute they were the ones who
began an energetic re-emphasis of the Pendergast legend.

Pauley said that he and Hannegan, who controlled the organization of the convention, planned to bring about Truman's
nomination on Thursday evening. That was the evening also

on which Roosevelt was to accept the nomination in a speech
from San Diego just before he boarded a cruiser for Hawaii.
Kelly does not remember it that way. It would have meant a
tight schedule for Truman to have found Clark and for Clark
to have prepared for his speech. It certainly did not work out
as Pauley remembered the plan.

"I had gone back to my hotel for dinner and conferences,"
Pauley said, "and, while I was there, I got a call from Neale
Roach, whom I had put in charge of certain of the physical arrangements. He told me that the hoodlums and the Wallace
people had counterfeited tickets and had already gained entrance
to the stadium."

Pauley went on with the story:

"They had pushed down a guard at one of the gates, and
people who were not delegates were seated in the delegates' seats.
The gallery was packed with people carrying Wallace banners;
and the organist, who was not supposed to start playing for another full hour, was already playing 'Iowa—That's Where the
Tall Corn Grows.' Unauthorized banner-bearers were already
marching around, shouting for Wallace.

"I rushed to the Stadium as fast as I could; and, by the time I
got there, I found complete pandemonium. I knew there was
nothing we could do to bring about a Truman vote that
evening. We could not even seat the delegates in their proper
places. I telephoned Hannegan and got permission to call off the
vote, suggesting that we might find some excuse to adjourn until
we could get the delegates seated.

"Mayor Kelly came to my office about that time, and I told him
my idea. He said he had complete authority to speak for the Fire
Chief, and to call off the session because of the fire hazard involved. By that time, the Stadium already was occupied by one
third more people than its lawful capacity."

(Kelly told me that the Wallace people did not force their
way into the convention that night. They were deliberately let
in, he said, to "give them their fling.")

Pauley's memory is vivid and detailed: "The organist seem-
ingly would never quit playing 'Iowa' from the time I got to
the Stadium, and I sensed that it was an organized plan to
stampede Wallace through the convention. In fact, if a Wallace

man, instead of myself, had happened to be in charge of the convention, the result might have been different.

"I finally sent for Neale Roach and told him to get a fire ax and sever all wires leading to the amplifiers carrying the organ music. The threat of doing this caused the organist to follow the schedule of music provided for him.

"And, so, ultimately, the evening ended—without a vote on the Vice-Presidency. It ended, also, without our ever being able to reach George Allen, who was in charge of program arrangements, despite continuous telephone efforts.

"Next day, it was different, but still there were troubles to be surmounted. Once a favorite son was nominated, or presented to the convention, he seemed to feel that, in some way, the lightning might strike, and he would be the fair-haired boy when it came to changing on the second ballot.

"Hannegan's office and mine were below the platform, and we had delegated the work of contacting the various delegates to swing them in line for the second ballot.

"I had been given the handling of the Alabama delegation, Tennessee, Oklahoma and Maryland. We naturally wanted to start off with Alabama, the first alphabetically and the first up, and have them change their entire vote from Bankhead to Truman. We had instructed Senator Jackson to hold the second roll call until this could be accomplished.

"In my office, I had Bankhead, Congressman Boykin, Governor Sparks and Pitt Manor, and I told them that now was the time to go for Truman, or otherwise Wallace would be nominated. But, Bankhead was stubborn and wanted to go for another ballot.

"At that time, I heard the call for the next roll call being announced, and Alabama was called. Suddenly, Bankhead stated he would change and was ready to go for Truman if I would hold the roll call.

"I rushed up to the platform—but, by the time I got there, Alabama had answered the roll call, for Bankhead. I told Bankhead and the Alabama delegates that they had missed their great opportunity to start the bandwagon.

"In the meantime, O'Conor, of Maryland, had agreed to go for Truman if someone would yield, or as soon as Maryland was called. This was a substantial block of votes, and was psychologically good at the time.

"Soon thereafter came the turn of Governor Kerr, of Oklahoma. At the given sign, I pointed my finger at Kerr and gave the signal for Truman, and I must say that Kerr looked a little pale at the moment. He had done a magnificent job as keynoter, and had sensed his popularity among the delegates.

"The rest was relatively easy."

Wallace had led on the first ballot by 429½ to 319½ for Truman. But the work had been done. On the second, Mississippi tried to shift to Truman out of turn. Iowa moved that the nomination be made unanimous, but was ruled out of order. By eight o'clock Friday night it was all over. Truman had come to the platform and spoken with his habitual humility, but in speaking of the great responsibility he said that he was "perfectly willing to assume it." There were perfunctory resolutions to be passed. They were adopted in a careless tumult. The platform was overwhelmed. The crowds roared into the streets. Bess Truman, who had sat primly all day in the box next to the cold dignity of the Byrnes group, found Harry. There were hands reaching toward them, people pressing around them. The police fell into line. Secret Service men walked beside them. They went out of pandemonium into the Chicago night. Bess was not smiling.

"Are we going to have to go through this all the rest of our lives?" she asked. He did not answer. The car roared them through the crowds to the Stevens Hotel. There in the bars were conservatives and Southerners, regulars and old-timers celebrating their victory over Henry Wallace. An hour after Truman was nominated, Franklin Roosevelt went on board the U.S.S. *Baltimore*. Before the celebration in Chicago was really begun she was heading into the swells of the Pacific.

Roosevelt had secured what he wanted though he had left behind many puzzled people—and some shocked ones. No sensible friend of Roosevelt will try to make neat, punctilious logic out of Roosevelt's political behavior at that convention. There will be no easy explanation of his various letters, his apparently vacillating positions. He was tired. The scissors of Time had cut at his strength. No conspirators or merely angry men ever pushed him away from his purposes for America. He understood Truman better than Wallace did, better even than Pauley, better than the bosses, better than the delegates who voted for him from Mississippi. He was content as he headed out to sea.

CHAPTER XVI

Brief Interlude

TRUMAN TOOK HIS old Battery D sergeant, Edward McKim, with him to the White House reception for the cast of the movie *Woodrow Wilson* on September 7, 1944. McKim, then an insurance executive, was in Washington making plans to accompany Truman on his long vice-presidential campaign tour. For him the reception was a well-remembered event. Democrats hoped the motion picture would impress Americans with the idea that if the Democrats lost the election, Americans would lose the peace again. Also, as a man from Omaha, the visit to the White House was a very special occasion for McKim. He stood in the crowds during the hour and a half they were there and looked as much as he could at Roosevelt.

They came out of the East Entrance where Hopkins had his office, and Leahy and Byrnes. And on the sidewalk in the very late afternoon, McKim stood still and halted Truman, too.

"I stopped in the street," he recalled, "and said, 'Hey, bud, turn around and take a look. You're going to be living in that house before long.' "

They looked back at the great building, the people coming out and the cars rolling up to get them.

"Eddie, I'm afraid I am," Truman said.

They went on to a party at the Statler Hotel, to the movie at the theater on F Street where McKim had to "bulldozer" Truman through the crowds. Later the conversation on the sidewalk was resumed as if it had been only momentarily interrupted.

"And it scares the hell out of me," Truman told McKim.

Then, McKim remembered, Truman sketched in all their disturbing proportions the problems which he expected the peace to bring.

He did not seem a frightened man. There was a gay, informal, second-string quality about the two cars attached to regular trains in which he circled the continent that late summer and fall. There was the high-spirited meeting in Texas with John Nance Garner whom most New Dealers did not like. There seemed to be an almost rural roughness about the way in which he spoke sharply of the isolationism of Democratic Senator David I. Walsh in Massachusetts. The Democratic high command sent shrewd, fat George Allen to ride with him to keep him out of trouble. And Allen was sweating when he rushed to Truman in the last days of the campaign with the news that the Hearst papers had just printed a story that he had belonged to the Ku Klux Klan. Truman grinned at that old lie, but he nailed it four times in three days. He played the piano on the first of his election night sessions at the Muehlebach Hotel penthouse while McKim and Fulton, Connelly and Allen kept record of the returns.

He enjoyed being Vice-President. He and Bess went to parties and dinners, and dinners and parties which sometimes in Washington seem almost the only business of the social second man. Bess Truman kept her sense of humor and Margaret, a student at George Washington University, was blonde and young and gay. Mrs. Truman has had to guard Margaret from the indulgences of her father. He likes to go off and buy them dresses and other such gifts which most husbands and fathers would fear to buy. Essentially they make a family with strong senses of both humor and unity. No hurly-burly of Washington society or officialdom has much changed them. Bess Truman was a lady in the old tradition of Independence before she came to Washington, and she knew Washington society well for ten years before she became First Lady. She is reticent and shy but forthright and quickly amused by pretentions. Margaret is their one world. She is seriously interested in her music, merry, unpretentious, hard-working and determined to make a well-deserved career of her own.

It was not all gaiety. Early in 1945 Harry and Vivian were able to buy back part of the lost family farm. Truman organized his office, with some contempt for the way Wallace had run his, to be effective for the Administration. Harry Vaughan was back from the war with jokes which appealed to the senatorial sense of humor. Also, after the inauguration when Roosevelt was getting around with going-away haste, but with not much of his usual skill, to "Jesus H." Jones' throat, he called Truman in. He told him he was going to make Henry Wallace Secretary of Commerce.

Truman dropped two words from the New Testament. But he went to work.

"I told him I'd see every Senator I could. Wallace was almost beaten at one point when Barkley was not paying attention and Taft asked to be recognized. He was going to bring up the question of Wallace's confirmation and Wallace would have been beaten right then. Finally, Barkley woke up and I recognized him. I broke two ties to get Wallace confirmed."

Truman was not given many other tasks. Roosevelt left Washington for the Yalta Conference two days after Truman became Vice-President. FDR was not in Washington a month altogether during the eighty-two days that Truman was Vice-President. (Only Tyler and Johnson were Vice-Presidents for shorter periods.) Roosevelt was at sea on the U.S.S. *Quincy,* four days before his sixty-third birthday, when Tom Pendergast died, on January 26, in Kansas City. It was news which Truman read very seriously. He called an Army bomber to take him to the funeral. Some people in Washington grimaced when they heard of the flight.

Nothing would have kept Truman away from the Visitation Church that day. And many other people seemed to feel the same way. The church was crowded to overflowing. There were people who at the last believed what Pendergast had said of himself a little while before he died: "I've done a lot for Kansas City—for the poor of Kansas City. I've done more for them than all the big shots and bankers, all of them put together. We used to take care of our poor, with coal and wood and food and rent, and we helped them in their trouble." That could be debased but, if times had changed in Tom's lifetime, that was still the meaning of politics and of humanity everywhere in the world.

After the funeral Truman hurried back to the bomber. He had to speak in Philadelphia, before going back to Washington, at a dinner for Francis John Myers who was a freshman in the Senate that year. It had been just ten years since Truman had come, lonely and uncertain, to take his own seat. Yet, somehow it seemed like a very long time.

CHAPTER XVII

President in the Dark

IT WAS GROWING dark in Washington, that night of April 12, at 7:09 P.M., when Harry Truman very solemnly took the oath. Bess Truman beside him looked like a woman in pain. Margaret was tense and drawn. It seemed dark in the world outside the ring of the klieg lights, the cameras and the Cabinet. Indeed, people everywhere, men in the streets, women who got the news by radio as they were cooking supper, soldiers in the Pacific, Ed Flynn in London on his way home from Moscow, old Bernard M. Baruch whom Flynn met there, Harry Hopkins in a hospital room in Minnesota, all had an individual and collective sense of the light going out like that at no other time in America since Lincoln had died in April exactly eighty years before. Each person was so suddenly aware of his own sense of darkness, that there was scarcely any realization of the almost complete darkness in which Truman found himself as President of the United States.

In his hands immediately were all the decisions which had been piling around his predecessor in the months in which the American forces had been moving to and beyond the Rhine and in the weeks in which the agreements with the Russians at Yalta had been quickly slipping into suspicion and disintegration. The San Francisco Conference to set up the United Nations Organization was only two weeks off. The physicists were only three months away from the first successful explosion of an atom bomb at Alamogordo, New Mexico. Harry Truman knew practically nothing about any of these things. Yet, the final decision about all of them and the complex problems involved in each of them was in essence his alone. In the darkness which surrounded him he was suddenly Commander-in-Chief of a nation at war and

President of a nation facing the swiftly growing problems of the peace.

"I don't think I saw Roosevelt but twice as Vice-President except at Cabinet meetings," he told me. Also: "Roosevelt never discussed anything important at his Cabinet meetings. Cabinet members, if they had anything to discuss, tried to see him privately after the meetings."

The Roosevelt files at Hyde Park bear out Truman's memory of their meetings. He saw the President by appointment only on March 8 and March 19. Indeed, according to those files, as candidate, Vice-President-elect, and Vice-President, Truman saw Roosevelt only eight times during the whole year before Roosevelt's death. There may have been other meetings off the record, but not many of them. When they met, Roosevelt was not taking time to instruct his Vice-President in all the problems which were crowding in upon his weariness. There is not the least evidence that he was divesting himself of the estate of his leadership, though some around him, notably his daughter Anna Boettiger, were working to reduce the pressures upon him. There were too many little pressures. Also, the greatest problems of big government in a world war had been handled as the personal dealings of one man. Admiral Leahy, who loved Roosevelt and learned to respect and admire Truman, said after FDR's death that Roosevelt would rewrite a policy proposed by the State Department without telling them he was going to do it. "He'd get Harry [Hopkins] and me to help him." His great knowledge of the many details of a high purpose was closely guarded and shared only in small pieces with specific men who served him whether they were bosses or ambassadors. He had a special task for Truman and he counted on his help in connection with it. Two days after Truman became President, fragile Harry Hopkins in bed at his Georgetown house spoke of it.

"People seem to think," he said, "that Truman was just suddenly pulled out of a hat—but that wasn't true. The President had had his eye on him for a long time. The Truman Committee record was good—he'd got himself known and liked around the country—and above all he was very popular in the Senate. That was the biggest consideration. The President wanted somebody that would help him when he went up there and asked them to ratify the peace."

The job of making that peace beyond the winning of the war was now to be Truman's alone, and his in months during which he had to try to acquaint himself with all the complex background matters which, in many cases, Roosevelt had carried in his own head. Truman had been devoting his time to building the support among his friends in the Senate for his job on the Hill. He was at work at that job on Thursday afternoon, April 12, 1945.

Speaker Rayburn, who had been down in Texas, that afternoon asked a few friends to come to see him about five o'clock in his first-floor hideaway office in the Capitol which was referred to as the "Board of Education." Lewis Deschler, Parliamentarian of the House, was among them and suggested to the Speaker that there were a few matters they ought to take up with the Vice-President. They called first at Truman's office and found that he was still in the chair in the Senate. They got him out of the chair and asked him to come over. He arrived a little after five. Deschler had got out a bottle and some ice.

Truman had barely arrived when the telephone rang and the operator said that the White House was calling the Vice-President. Truman took the phone and said hello. His face turned hard and white.

"I have to go to the White House immediately, as quietly as possible," he said.

Somebody said, "What is it?"

Truman raised his hands and did not say a word. It was not long before the men in the room learned the news. Some of them followed quickly to the White House. And one of them remembered how shocked he was standing in the Red Room when Howell G. Crim, the White House usher, announced: "President and Mrs. Truman, Mrs. Roosevelt." That was protocol. The man who remembered the incident and the words liked Harry Truman. But only Roosevelt had been President of the United States for twelve years before that moment. It seemed almost impious to attach the title to Truman's name.

The nation swung into line "to help Harry." Not since the first three months of Andrew Johnson had there been so tumultuous a helpfulness of a man who had stepped unexpectedly into the shoes of greatness. Also, it was a period in which, despite his almost quarter of a century in politics, the country seemed to

know as little about Harry Truman as he did about the complex
and secret problems which were suddenly pushed into his hands.
He seemed all things to all men, and all men including New
Dealers and anti-New Dealers, Roosevelt friends and Roosevelt
enemies, old friends and new ones, members of the 129th Field
Artillery, old-time Pendergast politicians, Truman Committee
members, the eager and the ambitious, seemed to expect that he
would be all things to them. His insistent modesty at that moment seemed almost designed to help the thinking of those who
hoped to be bigger than he was, underestimating the stubborn
Middle Border strength behind the modesty.

Truman tried to keep his appointment list, on the first day in
the Presidency, restricted to the men close to the tremendous
military and diplomatic jobs which had become his responsibility. So far as his official appointments were concerned he was
able to do that. Mourning gave him some brief protection from
those who welcomed change. But there were both pressure and
confusion in the White House lobby. Some of the old authority
was relaxed; new authority was assumed sometimes without
right. There was tug and pull for place even among those who
guarded the security of the President. Some people got in who
looked and acted less like mourners than looters. Other more
dignified invaders took what they wanted to find in Truman's
trip to the Capitol for luncheon with old Congressional colleagues. They seized it as the sign of change from a strong,
independent Presidency to a lonely and perhaps subservient one.
Old Roosevelt people were confused, and new Truman men were
overwhelmed. The funeral of one President and the future of
another were mixed up in a dark, crowded, confused but decisive
American day. The man least confused but most aware of the
proportions of his job as he was honestly concerned about his
power to meet it was Truman himself. He met the war, the
peace and old insistent friends with the same magnified modesty
but also with clear self-possession. His first day in the Presidency
was not a Missouri political picnic for him. Indeed, perhaps
strangely that day the only Missourians who got on his official
appointment list (though some others marched, almost without
knocking, into his offices) were Editor Roberts of the Republican *Kansas City Star* and his Washington correspondent, Duke
Shoop.

As the first official Missouri caller, though a Republican, Roberts appeared to have the best right to explain to the country what had occurred. He wrote that this new President had "the innate, instinctive conservatism in action of the Missouri-bred countrymen." The meaning to America of his arrival he compressed into one central phrase: Power in America had shifted from the Hudson to the Missouri Valley. That meant, Roberts said, "the shift from personal government back to what is called, for lack of any better term, constitutional government, or government by consultation." Also, he sounded the "average man" note which seemed so comfortable somehow after the departure of Roosevelt whom Roberts called "the patrician." He wrote: "The sheer fact he is this average man, understands the average man and his quality, is probably Truman's greatest asset as he undertakes these new overpowering responsibilities."

Truman's certainly was no average task. He had the personal problem of finding his way into the closely guarded knowledge essential to presidential leadership in time of rushing war and hastening peace. Even years later he lifted his hand higher than table level to indicate the pile of documents, agreements, conference minutes, cables which he had to read in trying to understand the problems and the responsibilities he had assumed. That first day he saw the Secretary of State twice, once with C. E. (Chip) Bohlen, expert on Russian matters, who had been appointed by Stettinius as liaison officer between the White House and the State Department. (This was an effort, Admiral Leahy said later, to get the department in closer contact with the President "who had been handling much foreign affairs business without consulting the Department of State.")

Just sixteen hours after he had been sworn in, Truman met for the first time with the Joint Chiefs of Staff, Leahy, General George C. Marshall, Admiral Ernest J. King, and General Barney Giles, deputy commander of the Army Air Force. Also present at that first conference were Secretary of War Henry L. Stimson and Secretary of the Navy James V. Forrestal. It was a brief meeting. Truman told them that he was sure they understood the terrific burden which had been unloaded on him and how much help he would require. Admiral Leahy stayed behind after the others filed out. He suggested that his relations with

Roosevelt had been very close personal ones and that Truman should let him go and get someone whom he knew.

"Admiral," Truman said to him, "I should like very much for you to remain in the office for so long as it is necessary for me to pick up the strands of the business of the war with which you are familiar, and with which I am not."

The Admiral, whom some New Dealers regarded as a reactionary influence close to the Presidency, told Truman very seriously that when he had disagreed with Roosevelt, he had told him so very frankly, and that Roosevelt had seemed to like that way of doing business.

"If I am to remain as your Chief of Staff," he said, "it will be impossible for me to change. If I think you are in error I shall say so."

"That is exactly what I want you to do," Truman agreed. "I want you to tell me if you think I am making a mistake. Of course, I will make the decisions, and after a decision is made, I will expect you to be loyal."

The Admiral, who was almost seventy then, stayed with Truman for four more years with increasing respect on both sides of the relationship. That day, Leahy began to get together the papers which he knew the President would require in understanding the decisions he had to make, particularly some of the summary papers of the Joint Chiefs of Staff.

"They made a sizeable stack when placed on his desk," he said. In a few days—and those few days in which the world and Missouri were pouring in upon him—the Admiral realized that Truman had digested them and was rapidly catching up on the "strands of the business of war."

"I soon discovered," Leahy said, "that he was amazingly well informed on military history, from the campaigns of the ancients such as Hannibal and Caesar down to the great global conflict into which he suddenly had been thrust in virtual supreme command. He absorbed very quickly the gist of the dispatches brought to his attention in our daily conferences and frequently he would go to the Map Room to discuss some particular development."

However, the old Admiral who has little gift for flattery added: "Everyone, including Truman himself, knew that in the field of international relations he had much to learn."

At 2:30 P.M. on that first presidential day he saw the man who was personally most eager to teach him. Byrnes had left Washington just five days before Roosevelt died. His resignation was given, Byrnes had said, on the basis of an understanding that he would only stay through the war effort and in terms of his feeling that whoever administered the reconversion program should take over at its beginning. Also, Byrnes had said in his letter to Roosevelt that he had attempted to resign twice before, once just before the Democratic Convention and once right after the election in 1944. Undoubtedly he was tired. Undoubtedly, also, after that afternoon in Chicago on which Truman had to tell Byrnes that Roosevelt did not want Byrnes but did want Truman, the diminutive South Carolinian was a disappointed man.

Through the fall after the election of 1944, it was understood around the White House that Byrnes was unhappy. There were reports of bitter things he had said to old friends on the Hill about Roosevelt and the validity of his promises. There were reports that he asked to be made Secretary of State but that Roosevelt, who wanted to be his own chief of foreign affairs, preferred the handsome but amenable Stettinius in that job. No one doubted Byrnes' great ability in those months as in the months before, but there seemed to be signs of increasing irascibility. He showed signs of pain inside and outside Roosevelt's door. When his feelings were hurt he could be an articulately emotional man. He himself says that it was a "complete surprise" when, during Christmas week in 1944, Roosevelt looked up suddenly from a memorandum he was reading and told Byrnes he wanted him to go with him to the Crimea. Byrnes realized the domestic problems were his primary concern and told Roosevelt so, he has reported. There were some indications during and after Yalta that Roosevelt took him, as he did Ed Flynn on the same trip, because he realized that the feelings of both had been lacerated: Flynn in his failure to secure the Ministry to Australia, and Byrnes in the loss of the Vice-Presidency. Byrnes took no very significant part in the discussions at Yalta (though both he and Flynn were greatly disturbed by the agreement to give Russia extra votes in the United Nations Assembly). However, he did make careful (and Leahy thinks) accurate stenographic reports of the conference. He had begun his long public career as a court stenographer in South Carolina.

When Truman became President five days after Byrnes had gone back to Spartanburg to live, it was clear that at Chicago Byrnes had missed not only the Vice-Presidency. Truman understood that and Byrnes' probable feeling about that, too. One of Harry Truman's important gifts is his sensitive understanding of the feelings of others. He still remembered the hour in the Skyway suite when he had to tell Byrnes and Byrnes could not get Roosevelt on the phone. He did not, however, call Byrnes to Washington after Roosevelt died.

"The Secretary of the Navy, James V. Forrestal," Byrnes said, "telephoned that he was sending his plane to Spartanburg to bring me to Washington because he thought I might be of some service during the next few days and he knew I would want to attend the President's funeral."

He was not only on the appointment list at 2:30 on the first day. He saw Truman twice by formal appointment on Saturday, once with Henry Wallace and once with Leahy, and on other less formal occasions as well. He was eagerly helpful. That night as the funeral train was departing for Hyde Park, Grace Tully, by pathetic habit, went on to the rear presidential private car of the train "only to find that I had intruded on President Truman, his wife and daughter, and Jimmy Byrnes. I remember how surprised I was to see him and at first I didn't realize I was bursting in on the President of the United States."

Byrnes has stated that on that funeral train, returning to Washington, Truman said that he would like for him to attend the San Francisco Conference as his representative, but he thought it would be a mistake as the delegation had already been appointed and that a personal representative of the President would cause dissatisfaction in the delegation. Then on Monday, Byrnes has reported, Truman told him that he wished to make him Secretary of State and that he accepted. They agreed that there would be no announcement until after the San Francisco meeting.

"He almost jumped down my throat taking me up," Truman himself said later.

With longer and greater knowledge of Roosevelt's conduct of foreign policy, Harry Hopkins came from his bed in St. Mary's Hospital in Rochester, Minnesota, and stayed to help Truman, too. But he told Sherwood, and probably in other words told Truman, too, of a strong conviction which he held.

"Truman has got to have his own people around him, not Roosevelt's. If we were around, we'd always be looking at him and he'd know we were thinking, 'The *President* wouldn't do it that way.' "

Within the first week after Truman took the oath, old, able Henry Stimson, for whom Truman had great respect, came in to tell him all about the bomb. The last time Stimson had seen Roosevelt had been just a month before, when some unnamed "distinguished public servant" had sent FDR a memo that they were pouring out billions on "a lemon." Others around Roosevelt, including Admiral Leahy, had little faith in the project. Stimson told Truman the whole history and the whole hope. That was three months before even the scientists could be sure on the great gamble.

"Now I understand why you didn't want us to investigate," Truman told him. He remembered the time when his investigator, Canfil, had got into the project and come back with word of great and costly goings on.

"If it explodes as I think it will," he told some of his associates that summer while he was at the Big Three Conference in Potsdam before the final test, "I'll certainly have a hammer on those boys."

He seemed to be referring not merely to the still unconquered Japs but to the Russians with whom he was having difficulty in shaping a collaboration for lasting peace.

Also, he knew when Stimson talked to him that if it did not explode, he would be the Democratic President who would have to explain the greatest and most costly fizzle in the history of the world.

There was a swift pushing in of men of smaller dimensions than the Chiefs of Staff, or Byrnes or Hopkins or Stimson. There were the secret celebrants of Roosevelt's death, some of whom put foot in the White House for the first time in years and liked the feel of its floors under their feet. Most of Truman's old friends merely wanted a handshake, a well-known hand on their shoulders, and a presidential word from the man who had so suddenly and so greatly ceased to be "Harry." There were others almost droolingly ready to help and be helped. Some acquaintances—and men who had made themselves useful in little things to Truman as a Senator or to his staff—presumed on their relationships to move in with a show of new power.

Some such supposed friends—and a few actual friends, too—later helped embarrass Truman as members of a so-called Missouri Gang. There was, for instance, John Maragon, who once shined shoes in Kansas City and later sold railroad tickets at the Capitol in Washington. Also, later he got involved on the basis of magnified White House connections in an investigation of petty and disreputable lobbying in Washington.

Maragon's only contact at the White House at the time of the Congressional hearings which led to his conviction for perjury was General Vaughan who sometimes seemed too free in sharing his White House association with old acquaintances. Ross, the Press Secretary, developed a saying when adverse publicity appeared, "Cherchez le Vaughan." Truman valued Vaughan's old friendship and believed in his basic integrity. Sometimes, however, he felt that Vaughan still acted as if he were secretary to a Senator, more eager to please constituents than to guard presidential prestige. Even in those first days some of Truman's own staff gave Maragon a rebuff any more sensitive man would have understood. He was out to grab the position of Dewey Long, expert White House transportation man. He did not get it. But in the confusion, when the Roosevelt staff were relinquishing the reins and the Truman staff had not completely picked them up, he did coolly occupy Compartment D in Car No. 4 on Roosevelt's funeral train, between the compartment of Admiral Leahy and one which had been originally reserved for Mr. Baruch. Quite different in their character and influence, Pauley and Allen, who had labored for Truman's nomination long before Chicago, shared Compartment I in Car No. 9. They spent most of their time in the new President's private car.

There were others on that train, in the White House lobby, in Mayflower Hotel rooms who assumed new powers and took presidential time. The man who "looked like any other man on the street" was swarmed over and surrounded when he went on the street. And that swarm is remembered. What was forgotten once again was the student of history and of facts, who had read the dullest documents about railroad finance and investigated the biggest war plants. He had to accomplish a greater learning in less time than almost any other man in our history. If the number of the eager visitors grew, also each day he realized with increasing understanding how vastly greater was the job he had assumed than even he realized when he was first called to the White House.

"I don't know whether you fellows," he said to the newspapermen, "ever had a load of hay or a bull fall on you. But last night the moon, the stars and all the planets fell on me. If you fellows ever pray, pray for me."

There was no secret about the size of the presidential job that April. Actually, however, it was more seriously beset with problems involving American security than any but a very few insiders understood at the time.

Years afterwards there were those who said that, if Roosevelt had lived, there would have been no such breakdown with the Russians as plagued and imperiled any real hope of peace after World War II. ("If Roosevelt had lived" became a drumbeat with many who did not understand the dimensions of the difficulties Roosevelt was already facing when Roosevelt died.) What Truman discovered quickly was that almost before Roosevelt got home from Yalta, the Russians were already acting very strangely about the agreements they had made. Both Byrnes and Stettinius used the phrase "high tide" of the unity at Yalta. When Harry Truman came to the White House he found the tide already rapidly ebbing.

Even while Roosevelt was reporting to Congress on the success of the conference on March 1, a crisis was growing around reports that American prisoners being liberated by the advancing Russian armies were being shabbily treated. Stalin denied it but turned down a request that, in dealing with the situation, American relief planes be allowed to operate in Poland. This was in the face of the Yalta promise of joint action by the Allies in liberated areas. By March 16, Molotov was sharply charging that the United States was breaking its agreements in connection with the surrender of German forces in Italy. Ambassador Averell Harriman had cabled from Moscow: "The arrogant language of Molotov's letter, I believe, brings out in the open a domineering attitude toward the United States which we have before only suspected. It has been my feeling that sooner or later this attitude would create a situation which would be intolerable to us." The disintegration continued as it had quickly begun. Before the end of February, Vishinsky had arrived in Bucharest where, despite the Yalta pledge of Russian, British and American joint action, he began to force the creation of a Rumanian government with Communist leadership. An American protest was bluntly rejected. There were other incidents. Finally, FDR told Stalin directly that he felt "bitter resentment" toward his informers for their "vile misrepresentation of my actions or those of my trusted subordinates." That message drew a disclaimer from Stalin that he ever distrusted Roosevelt's honesty and dependability. Roosevelt hoped such incidents could be minimized. The day he died at Warm Springs, he sent a message to Churchill hoping that such incidents would pass but containing the four words: "We must be firm."

Five days after he became President, Truman answered a question at his first crowded press conference as to whether he expected to see Foreign Commissar Molotov before the San Francisco Conference: He did. Molotov was going to stop and pay his respects to the President of the United States. Molotov had been sent by Stalin at Ambassador Harriman's suggestion after Roosevelt's death as an indication of Russia's continuing desire for cooperation.

Molotov arrived on Sunday, April 22, just ten days after Truman became President. In that time Truman had read the stack of papers Admiral Leahy had brought him, more that had come from the State Department, and the White House copy of the minutes of the Yalta Conference. Also, on the day after Molotov's arrival but before his conference with him, he called his principal advisers together. While they talked it was evident that Truman had studied his papers and that he also had made up his mind.

When Molotov, accompanied by Ambassador Gromyko and Pavlov, the Soviet interpreter, arrived at the White House in the late afternoon, he was ready for them. Stettinius, Leahy, Bohlen remained with Truman. One of those who was present remembered that Truman used "blunt language unadorned by the polite verbiage of diplomacy." It was the natural language of a direct politician to men whom he recognized as politicians, too. Perhaps not much was accomplished by that conference. Truman stressed the Yalta agreement as to the character of the government of Poland and intimated strongly that he meant to see the creation of a union of peace-loving nations at San Francisco whether Russia became a member of it or not. Molotov insisted that the Russians were adhering to the proper interpretation of the Yalta agreements but declared that his government was anxious to solve all problems which might disturb post-war collaboration with the United States. That first meeting, indeed, was chiefly important as Truman had in it a chance to evaluate the Russians and as it gave the Russians a feeling of the new American President. His purpose already was to follow the Roosevelt line of trying to get along with the Russians, of strictly abiding by our agreements with them, and of firmness in all. Before Molotov arrived Truman had turned down a Churchill proposal for a modification of a pre-Yalta agreement on Allied zones involving the distribution of German foodstuffs. The old Jackson County political emphasis on the keeping of a word given seemed to Truman to be pertinent in foreign affairs —the politics of the world.

Afterwards he realized that in some cases he had tried to learn too much too fast. There was very little time. On April 28, in one of its increasingly familiar news dispatches quoting an unnamed high authority, The Associated Press flashed a statement to the world that Germany had accepted unconditional surrender to the Allied Powers. It turned out that Senator Tom Connally had talked too big and that AP man Jack Bell had taken him too literally. The flash, however, threw the White House in a turmoil, nevertheless, and Truman had to tell the crowd of newspapermen which gathered that the report was false. There were other false and premature reports during the next ten days and the general atmosphere around Truman was hardly that to be chosen by a student with much work to do. And when the final news was arranged it was so tangled up in agreements for a mutual release by the British, Russians and Americans that Churchill telephoned querulously from a London already celebrating the news which he could not give out.

"What is the use," he demanded, "of me and of the President looking to be the only two people in the world who don't know what is going on?"

Truman insisted, however, that the agreement with the Rus-

sians, even as it approximated insanity, be kept. It was, though
a request for postponement from Marshal Stalin was not accepted. The news was almost anti-climactic when Truman made
the announcement at 8:15 A.M., on May 8. It was his sixty-first
birthday. It was his twenty-sixth day in the White House.
Twenty-seven years before he had been a soldier studying war on
his birthday at Chatillon-sur-Seine.

It was not so easy even for a President to see it then, but there
was a confusion in victory almost like that which had disturbed
him as Senator when the defense boom began. Four days after
the surrender he approved a paper put before him by Leo Crowley, Director of the Office of Economic Warfare, terminating all
lend-lease to Russia. Crowley had succeeded to the direction of
foreign economic matters when Roosevelt sharply divested both
Jesse Jones and Henry Wallace of their responsibilities in August
1943. Wallace's friends were troubled then because they regarded Crowley as "a friend and admirer of Jones."

Perhaps the ending of the aid to the Soviets was the tech-
nically correct position to take. The European war was over.
Moscow did not announce until August 8 that a state of war
existed between the Soviet Republics and Japan. (That was
three days after the bomb was dropped on Hiroshima.) Admiral
Leahy thought that Crowley was "carefully guarding American
interest in all lend-lease matters." But in May, the Russians felt
that the termination without warning, the emptying of ships
already loaded, the "scornful and abrupt manner" in which it
was done, as Stalin told Hopkins later that month, was designed
"as pressure on the Russians" in the post-Yalta debate. The
withdrawal, or the manner in which it was done, clearly sharpened Russian suspicions at a difficult time. Truman afterwards
thought it was a mistake and blamed Crowley for leading him
into it.

"Crowley was as anti-Russian as Wallace was pro-Russian,"
Truman said.

The lend-lease error was only one item in a swarm of great
troubles. It was increasingly clear that the victory had brought
no release from pressure. Truman and Admiral Leahy went
over the problems two days after the lend-lease decision had been
made. Stalin was suspicious. Churchill was bitter, for the war
had left the Empire weak and the victory brought Churchill

himself to a difficult domestic election. Rebellion was growing around Chiang Kai-shek. The United Nations Conference at San Francisco seemed headed for failure. Eden and Molotov were both heading homeward. The whole situation around Truman seemed more serious than when he had come to the White House that dark Thursday afternoon.

Leahy brought up the question of a new meeting of the Big Three. Truman discussed it with him, with Britain's Foreign Minister Anthony Eden, with his own State Department people. On May 20, he cabled Stalin that he was sending Harry Hopkins as his personal representative to Moscow to talk with him about the problems which seemed to be causing increasingly poor relations between their countries. Also, before Hopkins arrived in Moscow on the evening of May 25, Truman suggested to Stalin a meeting of the great powers that summer. When Hopkins saw Stalin he had already agreed to the meeting and suggested that it be held in the region of Berlin. In Washington, Truman believed that somehow, together there, the three nations could put the world together again after war in a cooperation which would insure the peace.

Early that summer, when he flew back from the ceremony at the signing of the United Nations Charter, he told his Jackson County home people of the flight from Salt Lake City to Kansas City that it was no further "than it was from here to Lone Jack in Eastern Jackson County, when we used to go to the picnics there on the sixteenth of August to celebrate the beginning of the Democratic campaign in the fall.

"I am anxious to bring home to you that the world is no longer county-size, no longer state-size, no longer nation-size," he said. "It will be just as easy for nations to get along in a republic of the world as it is for us to get along in the Republic of the United States."

Peoples were different, but people were the same. Even Presidents were people, and he understood, also, Presidents' wives and Presidents' daughters. Perhaps Roosevelt's grandson, young Johnny Boettiger, helped teach him that in the swift learning weeks and it may be that what young Johnny taught him was as important to his appreciation of his job as the things old, dour, bushy eye-browed but deeply humorous Admiral Leahy told him. He felt comfortable in the sincerity of the old sailor and the child.

Johnny had been sick when his grandfather died at Warm Springs. He had been at the Naval Hospital when his grandmother and his mother had been moving out of the great house. Somehow in the process some of his cherished possessions had been overlooked. He wanted them. He came to find them. It is not clear whether his grandmother, Eleanor Roosevelt, or his mother, Anna, brought him back to the White House. It is certain that when he came Harry Truman insisted upon helping him with the search. They went around and looked in closets. In one of Mrs. Truman's closets he parted the hanging dresses and looked on the floor at the back. When he emerged, he looked up at the President.

"Her closets," he told him, "are as messy as Grandma's."

Harry Truman laughed like a tickled boy. Nothing that had happened since he came to the White House had pleased him more. It became a standard joke with Bess. It delighted Margaret. But there was a parable in Johnny's report which went beyond Eleanor and Bess. The problems which he faced in the world were not more messy than those Franklin Roosevelt had left behind.

CHAPTER XVIII

The Rubble and the Flag

STALIN WAS LATE in arriving. The opening session of the Potsdam Conference on July 16, 1945, was postponed, and so that afternoon Truman, Byrnes and Leahy drove as sightseers from their residence in suburban Babelsberg to look at the ruins of Berlin. On the autobahn they passed the American Second Armored Division with its double row of armored vehicles stretching as far as they could see. Also, they passed the even longer procession of old people, women and children, moving aimlessly and hopelessly with their small possessions. They went on to the center of ruined Berlin, along the old streets, Bismarck Strasse, Berliner Strasse, Unter den Linden, Wilhelm Strasse to Hitler's New Chancellory. They stopped at the broken remains of the balcony from which Hitler had so often spoken. Truman spoke a little sententiously there, as apparently was expected of him, about a man overreaching himself, about whether the Germans had learned anything in the rubble. Also, he made a statement of fact: "I never saw such destruction."

It had not ever been equalled in the world until that day. Yet, that very morning all the destruction Truman saw in the afternoon had become out of date.

Winston Churchill, Anthony Eden and Sir Alexander Cadogan, British Permanent Undersecretary of Foreign Affairs, had come to call on Truman at eleven o'clock. They stayed about two hours in the "Little White House" at No. 2 Kaiser Strasse in Babelsberg, which had been the residence of the head of the German movie colony before he was sent to a labor battalion somewhere in Russia. The British officials had many things to talk about in advance of the conference. This was the first meeting of Truman and Churchill as leaders of their nations. They had some knowing of each other to accomplish as the leaders of

274

the greatest democratic nations and as men, too. Also, they were politicians together at a time when Churchill faced an election just ten days off. Labor Party men, led by Clement Attlee, were already at Potsdam, ready to take over. Churchill was worried about the election, though the Labor Party then had only 163 seats of the 640 in Parliament. Two hours in the summer morning was not too much time for Churchill's and Truman's first talking. But while they talked in that big stucco house, with too few bathtubs and inadequate screens, scientists and soldiers in a state of almost hysterical tension set off the first test atomic blast in New Mexico, near Alamogordo.

The sound was heard a hundred miles away. The light was seen at Albuquerque, Silver City, El Paso, in other towns 180 miles away. The Army covered its huge secret quickly with a false communiqué about the explosion of a "remotely located munitions magazine." Not only the public, however, was kept in darkness about what was happening that day and the month that followed: so apparently also, in many particulars, were the biggest men in the world, Harry Truman with the rest. Not any of them could know that the month which began with the detonation in the desert would include the dropping of the bomb itself, the surrender of Japan, the defeat of Churchill and the beginning of the Labor Government in England, the ratification of the charter of the United Nations by the United States Senate, and, though obscured by some small agreements at Potsdam and the mushrooming elation over victory in the Pacific, the clear beginnings of the cold war between communism and democracy in the world.

Truman had, of course, been expecting the news of the test. While he talked to Churchill, Secretary of War Stimson, an effective patriot at seventy-seven, was waiting near Babelsberg to receive the news and bring it to the President. Truman had been aware as he crossed to the conference on the U.S.S. *Augusta,* the cruiser on which Churchill and Roosevelt had shaped the Atlantic Charter, that the chances of success seemed good. As a born optimist, he did not share the salty skepticism of Admiral Leahy that the whole thing was "a professor's dream." It was not for him a skeptical time. He translated the almost unanimous good wishes of Americans for his leadership at the time into American good wishes for the world. When he had slipped out of Washington on the evening of July 6, two days after the anniversary of American independence, he was speaking the overwhelming, native American feeling in saying that "the all-important thing which confronts us is that the unity, mutual confidence and respect which resulted in the military victory should be continued to make secure a just and durable peace." He was less Calvinistic in his purposes than Wilson had been when he sailed on the *George Washington* for Paris, in 1918, to secure a covenant for peace. He lacked at the other extreme the inspired flexibility with which Roosevelt might have sought, not a covenant, but a bargain as the basis for the hopes of mankind. He was the Middle American still who believed without contradiction in loving his neighbor and steadily watching him at the same time.

Admiral Leahy and Secretary Byrnes, who later disagreed over arrangements with the Russians, have each published detailed stories of the Potsdam Conference. Byrnes called it "the success that failed." Admiral Leahy was impressed by the grim pun implicit in the code word chosen for the conference: TERMINAL. It was the conference which covered the widest range of subjects. It lasted longer than any of the others. It was the last conference by the Big Three in the war and in some respects, Leahy felt, the most frustrating. Roosevelt was gone. Churchill appeared less well prepared than he had been at earlier conferences and showed an irritation in his collisions with Stalin which may have reflected his fears about the elections before him in England. Stalin there began to show the sharper stubbornness which either he concealed at Yalta or which was insisted upon after Yalta by his associates in Moscow who began quickly trimming down the Yalta agreements. It was at Potsdam that he asked in hard humor, "How many divisions has the Pope?"

Clearly Harry Truman set out for that conference in high spirits. He enjoyed almost boyishly, in those first presidential days, the physical, palace aspects of the Presidency. This was his first trip abroad since he had gone packed in a troopship. He had men around him whom he trusted. Many of them were Missourians at a time when Missouri appointments were both a joke and a charge. Some of them lacked the qualities he required. One or two of them failed afterwards even in the loyalty which he expected. Also, there were the unquestionably loyal men who sometimes seemed more to hurt than help his prestige, though two of them had been unpublicized items of the Truman effectiveness in the Truman Committee days. Vaughan, the treasurer of the 1940 campaign, was along as Brigadier General and Military Aide. Truman's old-time political man Friday, Canfil, went as a Secret Service man. (The Russians clicked their heels when Canfil, as United States Marshal for the Western District of Missouri, was introduced as Marshal Canfil. Also, in some of his dealing with the Russian guards and secret police, he undertook to show them that police methods in Missouri could sometimes look as tough as those in Moscow. He could smash cameras, too, and put American guards beside Russian guards.) Charles G. Ross, of *The Post-Dispatch,* who had the confidence of Washington newspapermen, went as Press Secretary.

Actually, however, there was not a Missourian, except Truman himself, in the staff which prepared for the conference. Ambassador Harriman and Chip Bohlen, both of whom had been with Roosevelt at Yalta, were waiting in Berlin. Truman's chief assistants on the cruiser were Byrnes, of South Carolina, who had been sworn in as Secretary of State just three days before they sailed, and that deep-water sailor from Iowa, Admiral Leahy. Byrnes' chief assistants in the studies on the way to the conference were Benjamin V. Cohen, Indiana native of the old Rooseveltian team of Corcoran and Cohen, whom Byrnes made Counselor of the State Department, and H. Freeman Matthews, Maryland man and a veteran foreign service officer, then Chief of the European Division.

Byrnes has fully emphasized the work they did in preparation. Indeed, in his book about his services, he has made direct comparison of the work on the way to Potsdam with his observation that when he made the trip to Yalta "a very complete file of studies and recommendations prepared by the State Department" was not even considered by Roosevelt on the way. However, Byrnes pointed out that Roosevelt was sick and that all the problems were familiar ones to him. There was much work on the *Augusta.* Also, before Byrnes was sworn in as Secretary of State, Truman in Washington had had the government files combed for background material and had discussed it with his diplomatic and military advisers.

It was a journey of drama and pageantry as well as study,

nevertheless. The big victorious brass, led by Eisenhower, were at Antwerp to meet the *Augusta*. Stimson and more generals, Admiral King, ambassadors, including Pauley who had been given that rank as head of the Reparations Commission, met the President at Berlin. They moved on the autobahn twelve miles to the presidential residence in Babelsberg on Griebnitz Lake, which was not only lovely but provided the mosquitoes which emphasized the lack of screens. Churchill's house was two blocks away, at 23 Ringstrasse. Stalin's quarters were nearer the former Hohenzollern estate of Cecilienhof, three miles away, which was the seat of the conference itself. They arrived in time for early dinner on a still bright afternoon. During the long northern summer days around Berlin, darkness does not come until nearly midnight.

It was the next day that Truman saw Churchill and the ruins of Berlin. Stalin did not arrive to call until noon on July 17. Then he and Foreign Minister V. M. Molotov and their interpreter, Pavlov, stayed for lunch and Stalin liked the California wine. From the beginning Truman liked Stalin, as he liked Churchill but in a different way. Indeed, the record is that almost all of our representatives, great and small, who have come in contact with "Uncle Joe" have found him attractive as a person. Roosevelt had liked him. Yet, in the Big Three Roosevelt and Churchill had been men of similar backgrounds and interests. Perhaps the word "patrician" is exact in description of both of them even though they disagreed on many things. It is equally clear that Truman and Stalin seemed men grown straight out of their diverse soils. Truman recognized Stalin's type the moment he saw him.

"Stalin is as near like Tom Pendergast as any man I know."

There was a physical similarity. Stalin was built close to the ground. He carried none of the surplus weight Pendergast acquired in his later years but both he and Pendergast had huge hands—hands, Harry Hopkins said of Stalin's, "as hard as his mind." Stalin gave Truman the impression, afterwards increasingly difficult to understand, that, as Tom Pendergast always insisted about himself, he meant to stand by his word when he gave it.

"I got the impression," Truman said later, "that Stalin would stand by his agreements, and also that he had a Politburo on his hands like the Eightieth Congress."

It was easier, with no language bar, to become friendly with Churchill. Truman felt his great charm. Also, sometimes the lesser difference between himself and the British Tory gave an amused turn to his affection for Churchill. He was amused when the blunt and direct Stalin, who could "see straight through any question quickly," twitted Churchill for his long speeches at the conference table. Their antagonism was clear. Later, the Americans noted that when Clement Attlee took Churchill's place at the table, Stalin clearly liked him less and was noticeably cooler in his attitude toward the Labor Premier than to his Tory predecessor.

Churchill insisted early that since he and Roosevelt had operated on a first name basis that he and Truman should do the same. Later they became friends of poker-table intimacy. That was when Truman took Churchill to speak at Vaughan's alma mater Westminster College in Fulton, Missouri, in March 1946. On that occasion when Churchill, in Truman's presence, in effect proposed an English-speaking alliance against Russia and received a $4,000 lecture fee, Truman and his companions got Churchill in a small poker game on the train. It is not certain whether in it Churchill was pulling Truman's leg or Truman Churchill's. There are reports that Churchill as a reporter was playing poker at least as early as the Spanish-American War. However, Truman remained afterwards amused by Churchill's remarks in that twenty-five-cent limit game.

"Harry, what does a sequence count?"

And, "Harry, I think I'll risk a shilling on a couple of knaves."

There was not much time for card playing at Potsdam, though there is official record of at least one session on the *Augusta* at sea. At Potsdam, the extracurricular competition was in music, and it may sound as loud in history as the music for the waltzes played at the Congress of Vienna. Stalin and Truman were the competitors in the classical music they provided at their dinners. Churchill was bored by it and at length undertook to combat it with a band. The contest began at Truman's state dinner for Stalin and Churchill on Thursday evening, July 19. There had been sharp talk back and forth at the third plenary session that day about ships and Spain, Bulgaria and the Macedonian fron-

tier, but that was also the well-fed evening on which the General-
issimo got up to toast the American sergeant pianist and Truman
himself played Paderewski's "Minuet in G Minor." Stalin
imported two huge lady violinists as special talent from Russia
for his dinner two nights later. The music went on and on. At
one o'clock that evening Churchill, who had an election coming
up five days later, confided to an American that he was "bored
to tears" but Stalin and Truman were still listening. Monday
night, three days before the British would go to the polls,
Churchill retaliated at his dinner with the full orchestra of the
British Royal Air Force playing long and loudly through the
whole dinner. It was his last entertainment as War Prime Minister of Britain, but it was a finality full of flourishes.

The pianist who started it all was Sergeant Eugene List, who
played for the small dinner on Tuesday, July 17, the day after
the blast in New Mexico. Stimson, General Marshall, Admiral
King and General Arnold were at the "Little White House" as
guests that evening. That day Stalin had suggested Truman as
the chairman of the conference and old Admiral Leahy made a
note in his records that Truman had "handled himself very well."
Stimson brought the details of the news about the bomb to the
dinner.

That July night in Potsdam, Stimson did not have General
Leslie R. Groves' highly theatrical full report on the atomic
explosion, which was not dispatched until July 18, but enough
news had come to make it clear that energy had been cracked
out of the atom. The military men at dinner, however, could
not have been too much impressed. On July 19, they set the
target date for the unconditional surrender of Japan for November 15, 1946. It was more than a week later at a conference
session on July 28, that Stalin said that he had received a request
from Japan to mediate for the ending of the war. It is clear,
however, that at that dinner and after it, the bomb became a
portentous reality in Truman's thinking as an item of great
hope in terms of both war and peace.

"There at Potsdam the decision to use the bomb was made,"
he told me. In speeches and in conversations he has emphasized the proportions of that decision as both a war leader and
a humanitarian. Years after the bomb had been dropped he still
remembered his feeling as the man who had to make the final

decision as to the use of a weapon the effectiveness of which was in exact ratio to its frightfulness.

"I know FDR would have used it in a minute," Leahy told me, "to prove that he had not wasted two billion dollars."

Stimson thought later that there was never any real question about the bomb being used if the bomb were developed.

"At no time, from 1941 to 1945," he said, "did I ever hear it suggested by the President or by any other responsible member of the government that atomic energy should not be used in war."

It troubled Truman, nevertheless, though he did not hesitate to make the decision which disturbed him. He has had no regrets since. It is his memory that this decision was made at a session attended by Stimson, Eisenhower, Marshall, Byrnes, Leahy "and another Naval officer, probably King." All of those officers were available around Berlin during the days after the test. There was, Truman remembers, a discussion of the pros and cons of using the bomb but that "all at the conference urged using it." He asked Marshall and Eisenhower specifically, he told me later, how many American casualties a landing on the Tokyo plain would involve. Marshall, he said, told him it would take a million men for the landing and a million to hold it and that he thought such a landing would involve half a million casualties.

"They thought that Japan was weakening and that such an explosion might push them over."

That hope and prospect were clearly in Truman's mind when he rode with Generals Eisenhower and Omar Bradley on Friday following the blast on Monday to speak briefly at the raising of the American flag over the United States section of the City of Berlin. He was in familiar company. The two generals and the President all came from the Missouri-Kansas country; Eisenhower from the town of Abilene, Kansas, which is smaller than Truman's Independence; Bradley from the tiny village of Clark, in Randolph County, Missouri. Members of Congress who were politicians like Truman had sent the country boys to West Point where Truman had wanted to go, too.

"This is an historic occasion," Truman said in his brief speech that day. The flag which they raised was the same one which had flown over the Capitol in Washington on the day war was declared against Germany. Truman had been a restless Senator, thinking of his own uniform, that day forty-four months before he spoke. He was not then chairman of any committee except one which he had created himself. Eisenhower had had some waiting to do before that time, too. He did not become a permanent lieutenant colonel until 1936, twenty-one years after he graduated from West Point. Truman had ranked him then as a colonel in the reserve.

"We are here today," Truman said, "to raise the flag of victory over the capital of our greatest adversary."

That was nearly three years before the cold war brought the blockade of Berlin, the airlift and new ideas about adversaries. But that same day there was argument in the conference at Cecilienhof about difficulties with the Russians in the zones of occupation around Vienna. Truman, of course, did not refer to them. He made a very simple, impromptu speech but a strong one in its implicit comparisons of totalitarianism and freedom. At the base of the flagpole in the courtyard of the building which had been the headquarters of the ineffectual Berlin Air Defense Command, he was aware of both powers and dangers never equalled before in war or peace.

"We must remember that in raising this flag," he said, "we are raising it in the name of the people of the United States who are looking forward to a better world, a peaceful world, a world in which all the people will have an opportunity to enjoy the good things in life and not just a few at the top. Let's not forget that we are fighting for peace and for the welfare of mankind."

He restated for emphasis a position which was more important than any of the papers prepared by the State Department, as it was the policy which underlay them all.

"We are not fighting for conquest. There is not one piece of territory or one thing of a monetary nature that we want out of this war. We want peace and prosperity for the world as a whole. We want to see the time come when we can do the things in peace that we have been able to do in war. If we can put this tremendous machine of ours, which has made this victory possible, to work for peace, we can look forward to the greatest age in the history of mankind. That is what we propose to do."

The flag ran up in Berlin over that purpose and, above the walls of the courtyard, it whipped out in the breeze. It was not clear how many even of the Americans in the courtyard understood all he had said. There in Germany, however, like Luther, he was ready to nail them on a door as the things in which he believed. He drove back to Babelsberg where his old friend of the 129th Field Artillery, Colonel L. Curtis Tiernan, then Chief of Army Chaplains in the European Theater, had come to visit him for several days. Tiernan had grown older and balder, a little more plump since he had shown up at the auditorium in Kansas City in 1917 to tell a methodically cursing Headquarters Company captain that he wanted to join up as chaplain. Tiernan came as another important Missourian departed. Young Sergeant Harry Truman, son of Vivian, had been taken off the *Queen Elizabeth* as it was about to sail for home so that he could see his uncle. It was fine to see Uncle Harry but the sergeant got permission to head home again three days later. All he asked of the peace at that moment was to get back to Jackson County. And that was not a unique attitude in the European Theater of Operations. Truman himself had been in that sort of hurry a quarter of a century before.

Next day Colonel Tiernan went with the President to Protestant church service at ten o'clock, and an hour later Truman attended mass celebrated by his old friend Father Tiernan. Sunday was no day off, however, and it was at the sixth meeting of the conference that evening that Stalin, confronted with the rights of Catholics in Poland, stroked his moustache and asked his question about the number of the Pope's divisions. That came up directly with regard to Poland. It related to other satellites such as Rumania, Bulgaria, Hungary which had seemed safeguarded at Yalta. It involved the suggestion that only divisions would move the Soviets from their purposes in the states around them. It pointed the basic impasse of the conference and the fundamental conflict of the developing cold war. Truman told Stalin directly across the table that the United States had no intention of recognizing Rumania, Bulgaria, Hungary until each should have a "free government established by themselves without pressure from beyond their borders." That was a position which applied in Truman's thinking not merely to the specific satellites but to "all the people" of the world. It was the position which later, altered without his knowledge, began the break with Byrnes.

There were fourteen days of talk, interrupted on two days by

the sickness of Stalin and split in the middle by the substitution
of Attlee for Churchill. The agreements (some of which were
later repudiated by the Soviets) seemed afterwards less important
than the clear stubborn impasse which in so many fields was
evident. Truman was disappointed at the failure of the Russians
to agree to many of the proposals which he thought would serve
the future peace of Europe. While it was not his greatest disappointment and he did not regard it as the most important proposal, Truman, as a man who had devoted so much of his
thinking to transportation, was regretful of the blunt Russian
unwillingness to consider a plan for free navigation of waterways
—the Rhine, the Dardanelles, the Kiel Canal, and the Danube
which they controlled. It was a new suggestion among the old
battered questions. Even afterwards he liked to trace out its
possibilities with a blunt finger on his map. In conversations at
Potsdam he went beyond the official suggestion as to European
waterways.

"I suggested that the Rhine, the Danube, the Black Sea Straits,
the Suez Canal, the Panama Canal, the Straits of Gibraltar be
made free waterways for international traffic except that the
people along the shores would have the same riparian rights that
Missourians do in the Mississippi River. The United Nations
would make such charges as to maintain them, but no warships
allowed except for police purposes. The Russians would not
agree."

He had the same enthusiasm about the suggestion as Roosevelt did when he talked about the possibilities of TVA's for
Europe—and even for China.

Apparently no one was elated by the results of the conference.
It had set up machinery in the Council of Foreign Ministers
which might provide for settlements or only for longer debate.
The principles established with regard to German reparations
were to be repudiated by Molotov later. Perhaps the greatest
achievement seemed to be in the field of Russian assistance in
the Japanese war, which was to end six days after the Russians
entered it. What was not so clear but was clearer than ever
before was the open conflict between democracy and totalitarianism, the cold war, had already begun. However, while the
suspicions stiffened the feeling of fixed enmity had not come.

Indeed, the conference ended in good spirits all around. There was a feeling among even the most conservative Americans that Stalin, though less yielding than at Yalta, had been arguing sincerely for what he thought were the best interests of his government. Leahy, who would not have used the phrase that he had "a Politburo like the Eightieth Congress behind him," did suggest that if he had taken a more conciliatory attitude he "undoubtedly would have been in trouble when he returned to Moscow." Edward Stettinius suggested that that is what had happened to him and the agreements he had made when he returned from Yalta.

Truman came away with the same feeling. As in so many other aspects of his life he found himself able to act afterwards intelligently on the basis of seeing for himself. He had seen Stalin and he thought he understood him. He looked at him as at another politician. A President, he is sure, cannot act in foreign affairs even in a cold war on the basis of the reports of either ambassadors or other agents. His understanding must be based upon his own experience in dealing with the smaller politics which includes the same human attributes and problems as the politics of the world.

"You can understand the Russian situation if you understand Jackson County," he believes. "But you have to recognize that the people of Jackson County came out of the dark ages in 900 A.D., while Moscow emerged from the dark ages only in 1917."

He came away from Potsdam unimpressed with any ideas of absolute power unrelated to politics in the government of a nation or a people.

"A dictatorship is the hardest thing in God's world to hold together because it is made up entirely of conspiracies from the inside."

He had had some experience with that in the days when people said that Tom Pendergast was the absolute power in Jackson County. If he was, Truman had seen his organization from the inside. He had also seen that organization fall apart, not because of Milligan and the Federal judges and Stark, but because of a disintegration which began in Pendergast himself. And when Pendergast did fall he had seen other smaller politicians scurrying for their own cover or even joining the pack against Pendergast—and had been unwilling to be one of them.

The conspiracies had always been there, the jealousies, the betrayals, the greeds and the ambitions, also the hungers and the needs. He remembered that when the "good citizens" opposed Pendergast, they offered nothing to the masses they needed and who needed government concerned for their welfare. It was necessary to understand men in Russia or Jackson County to have faith that somehow more would be decent than would always be afraid. But that all required a confidence that leaders were building for them and their needs.

Truman still wanted the collaboration of Russia for a decent, free peace. He kept a grinning admiration of "Old Joe" which some dull patriots in America later decided was strange if not somehow disloyal. When the bomb for Hiroshima was in the making he got up and walked around the table and quietly told Stalin that we had developed a weapon more powerful than anything yet seen in war. Stalin did not seem to be interested or even quite to understand what Truman was talking about. He hoped the weapon would be used effectively, he told the President.

The packing for the trip home had already begun before the last and thirteenth session of the conference at Cecilienhof. The communiqué went out which did not entirely reassure the fraying hopes of men. Before Truman left the palace, a woman, who was the housekeeper there, gave him the almost perfect gift: *Battles and Leaders of the Civil War,* edited by Robert Underwood Johnson and Clarence Clough Buel. The Hohenzollerns had not even cut the pages but it was easy for Truman to read on them that though weapons might change, maneuvers remained the same from Lee and Grant to Eisenhower and perhaps also to Truman and Stalin.

Everybody had to get up as early as Truman himself next morning for the departure from Berlin on the flight to rejoin the *Augusta* at Plymouth. Fog made them land a little short of St. Mawgans Airport at Plymouth but they were safe aboard the *Augusta* in Plymouth Roads before noon. The President called upon the King for lunch on the British battle cruiser *Renown,* and after lunch the King returned the call to the *Augusta* and brought a present from Churchill who was Prime Minister no more. (Also, he asked for presidential autographs for his collecting daughters.) The *Augusta* stood out of the harbor at four o'clock.

There were movies that night in the Secretary of State's cabin but the President turned in early and did not attend. Byrnes had more movies the next night but not the President. On Saturday, August 4, Truman was up by five. He worked all day and had no time for the movies in the Secretary's cabin that night. On August 5, he went to church services in the crew's forward mess hall and spent the afternoon going over voluminous conference reports. That night at dinner in the wardroom he seemed preoccupied. It was hot on Monday; the *Augusta* had slipped into the Gulf Stream off the coast of New Jersey. The crew was in white uniforms when the President sat down for lunch with them in the after mess hall. He sat at the table with sailors from Thomasville, Connecticut; Woodhaven, Long Island; San Francisco; Northville, New Jersey; Bald Knob, Arkansas; and Two Harbors, Minnesota. While they ate, Captain Frank H. Graham, the Map Room watch officer, brought Truman the telegrams he had been expecting. The first message from the Navy Department a few minutes before noon said:

HIROSHIMA WAS BOMBED VISUALLY WITH ONLY ONE TENTH COVER AT SEVEN FIFTEEN P M WASHINGTON TIME AUGUST FIVE. THERE WAS NO FIGHTER OPPOSITION AND NO FLAK. FIFTEEN MINUTES AFTER DROP CAPTAIN PARSONS REPORTED "CONDITIONS NORMAL IN AIRPLANE FOLLOWING DELIVERY. RESULTS CLEAR CUT SUCCESSFUL IN ALL RESPECTS. VISIBLE EFFECTS GREATER THAN IN ANY TEST."

Ten minutes later another wire from Stimson added:

COMPLETE SUCCESS, EVEN MORE CONSPICUOUS THAN IN EARLIER TEST, IS INDICATED BY FIRST REPORTS.

Truman showed his excitement. He called to the crew to listen. The sailors cheered and the President carried the news like a boy running to the officers in the wardroom. The new weapon, he told officers and men, carried a charge twenty thousand times as powerful as a ton of TNT.

"This is the greatest thing in history," he told Captain Graham who had brought the message.

"It's time for us to get on home," he said to his Secretary of State.

It was home-coming time. Three days after he got back to Washington the Japanese government offered to surrender. Four days later the terms were met and the surrender accepted. The restraint, which Americans had shown when only half a war had been won with German surrender in May, disappeared completely. This was victory. This was hilarity, and men coming home, and America free of strain and strangeness, restrictions and fears. The popularity of Harry Truman was flag-high. He had the dignitaries beside him in his office for the announcement. He grinned like a boy when he made the expected statement to the press. It was time for peace.

Yet, even then he was the American with personal memories of the meaning of peace before—the peace of the Trumans and the Jacobsons, of the Irishmen of the 129th Field Artillery, and the farmers of Washington Township, and of Kansas, Texas and Kentucky. This was the peace of the old people, the women and the children on the autobahn, of the soldiers like young Sergeant Harry who wanted to come home. The President stood back of the big desk, with the summer twilight in great windows behind him while celebration began, a man still much aware of the maneuvers of Potsdam. The new weapon had won a war, but the maneuvers were ancient and unchanging. Even in victory men were already talking of the new, growing conflict of Russian communism and American democracy. In the conflict and maneuver of those forces, it was Truman's business to lead in the clear and actual demonstration of the meaning of that American democracy. It was his duty to prove that it was not frayed, old-fashioned, even obsolete in terms of men's needs and men's hopes. It was his office to work out in detail and in example the purposes to which he had given impromptu outline at Berlin in the rubble and by the flag: "A world in which all the people will have an opportunity to enjoy the good things in life and not just a few at the top."

When he walked home that early evening of victory the little way, under the arcade by the rose garden, from his office to the White House, he could hear the tumult of celebration. It went on long into the night.

CHAPTER XIX

Rejected Honeymoon

The Message of the President of the United States to the Congress, on September 6, 1945, amounted to the termination of a presidential honeymoon by the man who was enjoying it. The end of the honeymoon was not immediately apparent. The trajectory of his popularity had shot up in May, according to the polls, higher than Roosevelt's had ever been. A little over a year later it seemed to be completing its curve in widespread lack of public confidence. It followed in that year almost exactly the course of Andrew Johnson's popularity after Lincoln died. Even more significantly, his popularity was beaten down in the same struggle between the Congress and the Presidency which broke Wilson and all but ejected Johnson from the White House.

Yet, probably no President has so publicly seemed, as he entered the White House, to be ready to accept the legislative branch's estimate of its paramount position in the American system. As an old Senator, hastening to the Capitol for the comradeship of his companions there on the first day of his Presidency, he gave color to hopes that he would regard the executive not as a branch undertaking to drive the Congress but as a man administering Congressional decisions. In the Washington confusion after Roosevelt's death on Thursday afternoon, his quick Friday visit to the Capitol with reporters running after him and Senators smiling welcome to him seemed a gesture deliberately designed to demonstrate that he regarded himself as only one among equals in the government of America. It proved to those whom it pleased that he was habituated in the legislative concept. Not only was Roosevelt dead but so also was presidential government.

The luncheon at the Capitol that day was important. A rigid Constitution in the United States has always been the machinery of a very human and flexible people. Its operators are seldom theorists. Truman had the luncheon arranged in the Capitol by the Secretary of the Senate, who is as much a permanent civil servant in the American political system as any who works under the British Constitution. He remains in the Capitol regardless of Republican or Democratic control, though he may change his title and his offices, if his party loses, from Secretary of the Senate to that of Staff Director of the Minority Policy Committee. The Secretary when the new President called was his old friend Leslie Biffle, who had come as a boy to Washington from Piggott, Arkansas, as secretary to a Congressman. He had been too young to vote when he came, but he had been in the Senate and in politics ever since. He was a close friend of Truman's, and his offices have always been at least as much of a club as the Vice-President's. Yet, they are also offices which keep the machinery of the Senate and the party in the Senate running as smoothly as Senate diversities will permit.

The men Biffle got together for lunch with the new President were all his old friends. It was a solemn occasion on a solemn day and in many respects a sentimental one, too. Twelve of the guests were Democrats, four Republicans, one a Progressive. Thirteen were Senators and four were members of the House. They represented the party chiefs in each house. They represented the leaders of the two parties in the two houses. With the President they constituted at that troubled midday the mastery of American power in both the legislative and executive branches. Their home towns pointed out their diversity: Truman, Independence; Barkley, Paducah; Rayburn, Bonham; White, Lewiston; Connally, Marlin Falls; Austin, Burlington; Hill, Montgomery; Vandenburg, Grand Rapids; LaFollette, Madison; Wheeler, Butte; George, Vienna; Magnuson, Seattle; Hatch, Clovis; Pepper, Tallahassee; O'Mahoney, Cheyenne; McCormack, Dorchester; Martin, North Attleboro; and Ramspeck, Decatur. They had, Barkley said after the luncheon, "a heart to heart talk."

As sensible men they realized that differences would divide them but at that time their unity as Americans indicated the effectiveness of the American system to work quickly when there is clear need for quick working. No sensible person expects it to work always with smooth speed in a combative and argumentative land. Only those who wanted to be fooled thought that day that Truman, if he would, could have ended the conflict implicit between a President who represents the whole people and a Congress which represents the competitive, combative, determined places and differences of a continental Republic. There would be a lapse in vigor if there were a lapse in strain in the working of such a machine.

Yet, there were other gestures by Truman as a former Senator who understood legislative feelings. Between Truman and Mc-Kinley only Harding had had experience in Congress; it did not save him. Yet, when Roosevelt died not a single member of his Cabinet had ever served in Congress. More important to the politicians in the Capitol, no member of that Cabinet had ever successfully run for major public office except Wallace as Roosevelt's running mate. (Claude Wickard had been elected to the Indiana State Senate; Stimson had been an unsuccessful Republican candidate for Governor of New York.) When Truman named four former members of Congress to his Cabinet that summer, that seemed to make sense in Congress.

More important, however, than his overtures to Congress was Truman's immediate understanding of where he should stop. That understanding was demonstrated quickly though without immediate publicity when he told David Lilienthal that he would reappoint him as Chairman of the Tennessee Valley Authority. That reappointment was passionately, even feverishly, opposed by Senator Kenneth McKellar of Tennessee, who had quarreled with Lilienthal over both jobs and dam sites. McKellar, then, was not only President of the Senate but Chairman of the powerful Senate Appropriations Committee. He could make many things easy or hard for the executive branch. And Roosevelt, who seemed the very epitome of expanded presidential power which Truman seemed almost designed to end, had as a practical presidential politician been weighing the virtue of the reappointment against the value of McKellar's appeasement as Appropriations Committee Chairman.

On the morning Roosevelt got back from Yalta, he had spoken quite incidentally about the possibility of naming Lilienthal to another job, taking him out of Tennessee, and taking McKellar off his presidential neck. McKellar, apparently, was willing to let Lilienthal be confirmed as anything else if he could get him out of TVA Over his breakfast in the combination dining and sitting room at the west end of the second floor of the White House, Roosevelt spoke of the transfer only tentatively but it was clearly in his mind. There were protests around him. He listened but he went on with his eggs and made no further comment. That reappointment was one of the pieces of unfinished business when he died.

Truman made up his mind promptly. The actual reappointment was not announced until later, but he made his decision before May 4, less than a month after he had been in the White House. I remember his grinning in understanding of both senatorial ideas of prerogatives and his visualization, from association with him, of McKellar's pain.

"Old McKellar is going to have a hemorrhage," he said.

The idea amused him. Yet, he understood such senatorial pain as clearly as he already understood his presidential duty and purpose in such a matter. The essential relationship between patronage and policy in the operation of party government in the United States was no distasteful secret from him. He had a politician's strong instinct for easy personal and political relations in the intricate processes by which policies are converted into programs with appropriations to support them. He named Lilienthal and took his chances with McKellar.

From the beginning, eagerly and earnestly, he wanted to get along with Congress. Indeed, even in the eighty days he was Vice-President he had set that up as his special job as the Capitol member of the Administration team. However much he may have disagreed with Henry Wallace on ideas, his publicly expressed low opinion of Wallace as Vice-President was based on Wallace's lack of political skill as the Administration's man on Capitol Hill.

"While Garner was Vice-President," Truman said when he succeeded Wallace, "there was hardly a day when at least half of the members of the Senate did not see him in his office or talk to him somewhere around the Capitol. In the past four years, I doubt if there are a half a dozen Senators all told who have been in the Vice-President's office. You can draw your own conclusions."

It was not difficult to understand Truman's conclusions. He demonstrated them in his plans as Vice-President. Perhaps, as some of his critics were saying before Roosevelt died, he made his office too much of a political club. Colonel Vaughan, back from war service in Australia, served as club steward and comedian, ready with small talk or sustenance for any Senator. Without that club and without Truman's promise to Roosevelt, Wallace would not have been confirmed as Secretary of Commerce by the Senate over which he had presided for four years. If in those congenial offices some blows were struck for liberty, some effective ones also were struck for the support of the Administration.

Truman understood long before he moved to the White House the confusing complexity of men and their views which are supposed to be contained only in the two-party division in Congress and the United States. The Wallace-Jones fight which started there before Truman was Vice-President perhaps dramatized it better than any in his time. It became his job, as Vice-President, to try in that fight to deal with the irreconcilable right and the irreconcilable left. Truman was personally friendly with Jones. Wallace, even when Truman admired some of his work, always seemed to him an odd character. But he helped to get Wallace confirmed. And in 1948, both Wallace and Jones were equally opposed to his re-election. Jones, who had come to Washington with Hoover, went to Dewey. Wallace went his own unraveling way.

By coincidence, Wilson was writing his *Congressional Government* in the year of Harry Truman's birth. Also, though he later somewhat modified his scholar's ideas after a politician's experience, Wilson was pointing out the evils resulting from the separation of the executive and legislative branches of the government. As Truman came into the White House, some intellectuals went home from Washington in wartime to urge again some change in our government to bring it closer to the British parliamentary cabinet system. One Democratic United States Senator, who had been overtrained at Oxford in the virtues of the English system, was to suggest when the Democrats lost the 1946 Congressional elections that Truman ought to resign and let the Republicans into executive as well as legislative power. Woodrow Wilson, who understood American constitutional government at least as well as this suggestor, Senator William Fulbright of Arkansas, had not considered resigning when the same thing happened to him in 1918. Cleveland had not resigned when he not only lost party control of both houses of Congress in 1894 but also lost control of the remnants of his own party in it, too. Truman's comment was that a little more United States land grant college education on the United States Constitution and what it meant would do Fulbright a lot of good. He did not think of resigning. Indeed, he counted that defeat later as the basis of his triumph.

"There is always a let-down after every war," he told me in 1949, "and the Eightieth Congress was the luckiest thing that ever happened to me."

Few men have come to the White House with more knowledge about the Congress than Truman. He understood it not as theorist but as technician, not as professor but as politician, and he understood it well. He believed in party government. He had accepted the disciplines of party organization under Pendergast. He accepted them in exactly the same way under Roosevelt. He had run for the Senate as an Administration Democrat. He served and voted as one. He never undertook any such "purge" as Roosevelt tried in 1938. He did get angry and determined, too, when Roger C. Slaughter, the Democratic Congressman from his own county helped bottle up his legislative program in the Rules Committee. Truman's enemies charged that he used Pendergast machinery to defeat him in the primary. His own candidate who beat Slaughter was afterwards defeated in the general elections. Truman may have been tough in this case. Slaughter clearly, however, was as a Democrat from Truman's own county undertaking to fight his party leader. Subsequently the Administration's charge of illegal lobbying against Slaughter was dismissed on the grounds that he was serving as an attorney, not as a lobbyist.

Truman believed in the party organization system as as much a part of the organization of the American government—and as essential a part—as any of the devices, checks and balances, limitations and powers in the Constitution itself. Indeed, as a practical American he recognized that across the American years only such ingenious American political machinery as the party system informally beside the Constitution made it possible for the constitutional system to work. He was under no illusions, however, that it would always work to please everybody or always seem as neat as some political scientists (dully ignorant of politics) would have liked it to seem.

"I have not been disillusioned about it," he told me. "I have not been surprised."

Undoubtedly, however, he surprised some Congressmen when he sent his post-war program to the Capitol on September 6, 1945. It seems a little odd now that he sent so important a document by messengers and did not take it in person. He had made a good impression when he spoke to Congress four days after Roosevelt died. He had been applauded, also, when he appeared again before the Senate early in June to urge the ratification of the United Nations Charter. But there were relatively few listeners and no cheers when the clerks read the September sixth message, which in history must be recognized as Truman's own charter for the United States. His failure to appear in person might possibly have been another gesture of his recognition of the right of the legislative branch. Thomas Jefferson had felt that he should not go in person, and when Woodrow Wilson came as the first President in 130 years to deliver a message in person some of his own most devoted supporters were shocked. John Sharp Williams, of Mississippi, quoted Jefferson's reasons for discontinuing the practice and referred to it as "the speech from the throne." Some found the speech sent by messengers in September, shocking all the same.

The message was the substance of the New Deal which had gone before and the Fair Deal which would be ratified in the presidential election three years later. Those who had buried Roosevelt deep under their conservative hopes in Truman found quoted *in extenso* in the message that Economic Bill of Rights which Roosevelt had enunciated in his State of the Union message to Congress in January 1944. As a preamble to the Economic Bill of Rights, Roosevelt had then put the goal of an American living standard, higher than ever known before, in equal conjunction with that of a lasting peace.

"Let us make the attainment of these rights," Truman told the Congress, "the essence of post-war American economic life."

It is essential that the statement of rights on which Truman joined Roosevelt be repeated and remembered:

> In our day these economic truths have become accepted as self-evident. We have accepted, so to speak, a second bill of

rights under which a new basis of security and prosperity can be established for all—regardless of station, race, or creed.

Among these are:

The right to a useful and remunerative job in the industries, or shops or farms or mines of the Nation.

The right to earn enough to provide adequate food and clothing and recreation.

The right of every farmer to raise and sell his products at a return which will give him and his family a decent living.

The right of every businessman, large and small, to trade in an atmosphere of freedom from unfair competition and domination by monopolies at home or abroad.

The right of every family to a decent home.

The right to adequate medical care and the opportunity to achieve and enjoy good health.

The right to adequate protection from the economic fears of old age, sickness, accident, and unemployment.

The right to a good education.

All of these rights spell security. And after this war is won we must be prepared to move forward, in the implementation of these rights, to new goals of human happiness and well-being.

America's own rightful place in the world depends in large part upon how fully these and similar rights have been carried into practice for our citizens. For unless there is security here at home there cannot be lasting peace in the world.

These rights constituted, Truman understood, the pattern of independence in our time. His message set out to strengthen it in proposals for the extension of unemployment compensation to millions who were not protected; a higher minimum wage; full employment legislation; the operation of the employment service by the Federal government; stronger machinery for farm price supports; a private and public housing program; a scientific research program; more TVA's on the Columbia, the Arkansas and the Missouri rivers, and in the Central Valley of California. He urged a permanent Fair Employment Practice Committee. He promised other messages on a national health program, expanded social security, and aid to education. Also, he thought that Congressmen should get better pay.

The message, however, also carried some negative suggestions to a nation headlong in its will to put the war behind it. Many controls would be removed but some must remain. He emphasized the necessity that the line be held against price and wage increases which would threaten inflation. He urged that the draft be continued for young men between eighteen and twenty-five. Taxpayers were notified that he felt that any reduction program would have to be limited. In the whole message there was no suggestion of a retreat in presidential powers or presidential leadership.

"Maybe I moved too fast in removing wartime controls," Truman said to me later, in reflective reminiscence. Then he grinned over a stubborn chin. "But that September the sixth speech was made to let the Hearsts and the McCormicks know that they were not going to take me into camp." He used the names of the big publishers as generic nouns for the whole body of American conservatives who had that summer of 1945 been telling him persuasively that he was a conservative, too.

Conservatives should not have been surprised by that speech. Truman's purposes were not new. That had been well understood—or at least well stated—in the first Truman summer, not by New Dealers but by Walter Chamblin, Jr., who became that year vice-president of the National Association of Manufacturers in charge of all governmental relations.

"Those groups," said Chamblin, "which feared government because of fear of one-man rule now have nothing to fear unless they fear the will of a majority of the people speaking through the Congress and the Chief Executive."

He also said with more wisdom than was then generally shown that Truman faced "fifty-year-old problems in the light of today." The issues which "Mr. Truman must settle were born long before he took office." The problems and the political cleavage about them went back, he said, at least as far as the six-cent cotton and the ten-cent corn which followed the Civil War.

Mr. Chamblin laid down the situation as he saw it with almost brutal frankness to the members of the NAM:

"The man who was feared by his enemies as seeking to portray himself as the indispensable man, as the superman, and the only man capable of guiding the Nation during this critical period is gone.

"In his place there is not a superman, not an indispensable man, but a man whose greatness lies in a realization of his own limitations.

"So just an average citizen takes over the greatest office in the world and just an average citizen will demonstrate that he is capable of handling the job.

"This will break down the idea of one-man rule, or of one-man government and demonstrate again that the strength of the country lies not in the man who runs it but in the people themselves."

Mr. Chamblin was a better reporter than even he himself realized at the time. Truman had grown beside the average American and through all the problems in the years since six-cent cotton and ten-cent corn. He had been for Bryan before Roosevelt was out of Groton. As a young Missouri farmer he had liked Wilson's New Freedom long before, as a politician, he supported Roosevelt's New Deal. And he did have, as Chamblin wrote, a sense of his limitations. Indeed, that spring and summer his sense that the weight of the moon and the stars had fallen upon him raised his old modesty from a becoming humility to what seemed almost the insistent expression of his own ineptitude. Some old friends like Speaker Sam Rayburn protested to him about the proportions of his self-depreciation. Truman listened almost bashfully. What even some of his friends missed was that his stubbornness overmatched his modesty. He believed what he believed. And five days after the formal Japanese surrender, which he had ordered sentimentally to be staged on the deck of the *Missouri,* he let the country and the Congress, the Hearsts, the McCormicks, and the people have that all in one piece.

"The 1948 platform," he said, "was written on the basis of the twenty-one points I laid down then."

Perhaps, as Truman thought later, he moved too fast in removing wartime controls. At the time, however, those which remained seemed more irritating to those whose profits they curbed than pleasing to those they protected. The continuation of Selective Service was not popular at a time when the American will to get home and stay home was measured by piles of mail on the desks of Congressmen. The "let-down" which Truman mentioned after every war was a resurgent "back to normalcy" in 1945. As a design for the time, the message was full of irritants even if it was also full of liberalism, wisdom and courage. Politically, it turned out to be wise to lay down the whole program, the restrictive with the expansive. He asked for more than he could hope to get. He made some mistakes in the administration of the complex price control and other powers which he secured. There was debate within the Administration as well as in the Capitol. Undoubtedly that message began the ending of the honeymoon. The clear fact in history is that it would have ended anyhow. Also, the clear fact in history is that that message and its meanings cost him the Congressional elections of 1946. In a greater sense, however, he became President, not on April 12, but on September 6, when he let the country and the Congress see not the modest man but the stubborn and purposeful politician who understood in a rich and restless post-war land, as well as the National Association of Manufacturers, that the American cleavages were at least as old as ten-cent corn—and as determined as the possibility of ten-cent corn or its equivalent for people again.

The honeymoon did not seem to disintegrate quickly. Party government in America so far as the Democratic Party is concerned never seemed more like a beautiful unity than it did a couple of weeks after Truman sent the post-war message. Certainly, the relations of the executive and legislative branches looked like a love affair on Jefferson Island, on September 23. The occasion was a party given by some of his friends for Jim Barnes, now a Washington lawyer, who had been one of Roosevelt's Administrative Assistants. But the real guest of honor was Truman. He was the well-loved center of Democratic Party government at play.

The Jefferson Island Club in Chesapeake Bay was a sort of private bastion of the Democrats and a Missourian, former Senator Harry B. Hawes, was one of its principal founders. It was established "for the purpose of supporting, defending and advancing the fundamental principles of government enunciated by Thomas Jefferson." There is, of course, no subject upon which Democrats more violently disagree than the meaning of Mr. Jefferson's ideas in the second century after his death. There were no signs of disagreement on the island that day. Liberal and conservative Senators were pitching horseshoes together. New Dealers stood in the clubhouse in affectionate conversation with Deep South States' Righters. Old Chairman Bob Doughton of the Ways and Means Committee in the lunch tent looked like a cattle farmer at a stock sale. Swarthy Senator

Chavez, of New Mexico, munched his lunch with spruce, bald Lister Hill, of Alabama. Every Democrat in Congress seemed to be there, and all the old and new executives in the Administration. It was a political picnic of a political party united, confident and having a very good time.

Harry Truman was having a good time. He held court for a constant and changing body of Democrats in the informality of brashly new-looking sports clothes. He wore an oversized tweed cap and a sports jacket made half of leather and half of brown tweed. He told a few stories himself, but he demonstrated his great gift for amusement at other men's jokes. Big Chief Justice Fred Vinson, then Secretary of the Treasury, contributed both his Kentucky stories and his Kentucky mountain laughter. Secretary of State Byrnes' face lit up like an Irish boy's with a candle in his hand. It was a good day in rich early autumn weather. It was holiday and in the sometimes strange-seeming American system it was government, too. Perhaps under the Constitution in the American two-party system all the pieces of power, the checks and balances, men and powers can only be seen together in fear or frolic, in hilarity or mourning. That day on Jefferson Island the cold war and the Congressional elections both seemed a long way off. It would be two weeks before Harry Truman had been President half a year.

CHAPTER XX

The Head of the Table

"I DON'T KNOW how I ever got out of that mudhole," Truman said. He shook his head in wondering remembrance. He was talking about the Cabinet—or many members of it—which he inherited from Roosevelt.

"I had to get their information and do the best I could."

He had known most of them as Senator. He had sat at the long, coffin-shaped Cabinet table with them at the few meetings held between the inauguration and Roosevelt's death. Almost the first thing he did on the evening of April 12 was to call a meeting of the Cabinet and ask its members to carry on with their work. Nobody thought that meant that the Cabinet would indefinitely continue. In less time than he had been Vice-President, he completed the swift first realignment of his own Cabinet.

Apparently the first new member was Tom Clark, of Texas, who, upon the urging of Rayburn and Connally, of Texas, was made Attorney General in place of Francis Biddle. Reluctantly, as a man already in questionable health, Truman's old Senate friend Schwellenbach left a judgeship to succeed Frances Perkins as Secretary of Labor. Bob Hannegan took over the duties of Frank Walker as Postmaster General on the same day that it had been agreed before Roosevelt died that he would do so. Clinton Anderson, who as a member of the House had been making some not always complimentary studies of Administration food policies, took Wickard's place as Secretary of Agriculture. The two outstanding members of the new Administration, however, were clearly Byrnes and Fred Vinson, of Kentucky, who in late July moved into the Treasury Department.

By the end of July, only the heads of the armed services, For-restal and Stimson, and Wallace in Commerce and Ickes in Interior remained. (Stimson at seventy-eight was retiring in

301

September when his war job was done.) The great days of Cabinet reshuffling were those between June 29 and July 3, when Clark, Hannegan, Anderson, Schwellenbach and Byrnes moved in. Vinson did not take office until July 23, but, according to the official log of Truman's Potsdam trip which began July 7, "Vinson dropped out of the party on the eve of the President's departure to become Secretary of the Treasury." The appointment was already made and Vinson only waited for Henry A. Morgenthau, Jr., to take his pictures down and his papers away.

Theoretically Truman had his governmental organization already arranged then before he took the train to the cruiser. Also, he had the pattern of his Presidency in his mind. Not only in the place of Stettinius but in every other case, he expected to find the Cabinet chieftain and leave the operation of the department to him. It took him some time to discover that while he could delegate every duty he could escape no responsibility. He was to find the same sort of Cabinet contentions which began with Jefferson and Hamilton at the table of George Washington. He was to discover that some who accepted places as his subordinates did so with no lapse of their sense of superiority. No other President in history ever had at his table two men who so deeply felt that somehow they had been cheated out of his chair.

On a number of occasions, Presidents have selected party leaders, supposedly subordinate in stature only to themselves, as their Secretaries of State. Not all of them have agreed that they were subordinate. Seward never lapsed in his remembrance that he had led Lincoln 173½ to 102 on the first ballot at the Republican Convention of 1860. Benjamin Harrison and James G. Blaine did not get along. As Wilson's Secretary of State, William Jennings Bryan found it difficult to forget that he had been the "peerless leader" of the Democratic Party when Wilson was only a professor. There are other cases of conflict.

Truman was to discover that whether he wished it or not the President is the whole executive and above his subordinates, must bear the weight. He must be the chief in actual command of the government or the clerk of a contentious Cabinet. Above all, what Truman found was that with many assistants but with no equals the President himself must make the policy of his Administration in the United States. And in no field did he find that to be so true as in that of foreign policy about which he was so little informed when he became President of the United States. It took him many papers and more time than a few months to discover that.

It was in Vinson more than any other man that he found the statesmanship he required. When Truman arrived in the Presidency, Vinson was already in the White House as Byrnes' successor as Director of the Office of War Mobilization and Reconversion, which under Byrnes had carried with it the prestige of Assistant President. Vinson, who had started out as a commonwealth's attorney in the murderous mountains of Kentucky, had come through Congress to the Federal Judiciary as a member of the United States Court of Appeals for the District of Columbia. Like Byrnes, he had resigned from a lifetime court appointment in wartime to become Director of Economic Stabilization. He followed Byrnes and finally, as Chief Justice, went further, and oddly enough he was tracked by another gentleman, too, Truman's old friend John Snyder. Roosevelt made Vinson Federal Loan Administrator in March, then moved him, in April, to Byrnes' old place in the White House as Director of Mobilization and Reconversion. Truman put Snyder in the vacancy as Loan Administrator. When Truman moved Vinson to the Treasury, he moved Snyder after him to the Mobilization and Reconversion position. When Vinson was made Chief Justice, Snyder became Secretary of the Treasury. Snyder had a good man to follow.

Vinson was in the Cabinet less than a year, but in that time he was the kind of Cabinet officer Presidents seek and do not often find. He was a politician who could talk the language of politics with the President. He was a poker player whose bets Truman respected. As a mountaineer he could match even the sea-going toughness of Admiral Leahy who sided with Crowley on the lend-lease matter which long afterwards troubled the President. Leahy was supporting the position of Crowley and the American Joint Chiefs of Staff that after the German surrender there could be no more lend-lease except in the war with Japan. The State Department and the Army wanted to continue giving lend-lease material to Europe, particularly to France for use by French forces of occupation in Germany. Vinson, as Director of the OWMR, sided with the State Department and asked the Admiral by what right he had advised the President. It was one occasion on which the Admiral spoke his piece and then left the field. What Vinson and the others realized was that the abrupt termination of lend-lease created the dangerous gap which afterwards had to be bridged by the British loan, the Truman Doctrine and the Marshall Plan. Hopkins had already found the bitterness over the abrupt termination in Russia. There were similar feelings in the sudden "peace" among our other allies. It was the sort of problem with which Vinson was admirably qualified to deal. And it was his wisdom in such dealings which Truman had in mind when he considered sending Vinson to Moscow during the political campaign in 1948. Nobody in Washington had greater skill in solving the differences which were inevitable in government and which, in 1946, were reaching open-row proportions on the Supreme Court. Truman's appreciation of his qualities suggested his promotion to the Chief Justiceship when Stone died in April 1946, but the elevation deprived the President thereafter of probably his wisest counselor.

Vinson's departure by promotion emphasizes the impermanence of Cabinets. Only two members of the Cabinet which Truman completed before he departed for Potsdam remained when he ran for the Presidency in 1948. There had not been much pain involved in the changes he made. Perkins and Walker had been planning to depart before Roosevelt died. Biddle, Wickard, Stettinius and, later, Perkins, took other appointments from the Truman Administration. Morgenthau went out with irritation showing on his side and on Truman's, too.

The real rows came later, and the first dramatic one was when Harold L. Ickes, as Secretary of Interior, in effect walked out over the dead body of Ed Pauley, the effective California politician, in February 1946. Ickes had been combative even under Roosevelt. Indeed, just before Roosevelt left for Yalta, Ickes had threatened to let loose a public blast against Lilienthal of TVA in an ancient feud between them over public power. He took pride in his character as a curmudgeon and liked to see himself publicized as "Honest Harold." He made his exit dramatic with an attack on Pauley when the latter's nomination by Truman as Under Secretary of the Navy was being considered by the Senate. Pauley was vulnerable. Later, at his own request, his nomination was withdrawn. He had combined his energetic collection of Democratic campaign funds with an equally energetic campaigning in Washington to keep tideland oil fields from control by the Federal government. There was nothing new about either. Ed Flynn, as Democratic Chairman, had put Pauley in charge of the far western presidential campaign in 1940. He was treasurer of the committee long before Roosevelt died. Truman had first appointed him his special representative on the Reparations Commission with the rank of ambassador. He was successful in dealing with the Russians in that operation. (Indeed, one of his associates said that he "got too good a bargain.") When Truman named him to the Navy post, Ickes came up to him after Cabinet meeting and said he had been asked to testify.

"Well," Truman said to him, "don't tell anything but the truth but be as nice as you can be to Ed, I like him."

(Ickes' quotation of the President at the time was: "You must tell the truth, of course. But be as gentle as you can with Ed Pauley.")

Ickes told the committee that Pauley had suggested to him that the filing of a suit by the Federal government to claim control of the tideland oil fields might cost several hundred thousand dollars in campaign contributions. Similar testimony was given by Norman Littell, former Assistant Attorney General, who dated the "pressures" as far back as the week before the 1940 election. Boss E. M. Crump, of Memphis, joined them in opposing the confirmation of Pauley. Ickes resigned and Truman promptly accepted his resignation. That was, some commentators said, the end of the New Deal revolution. Actually, Ickes himself realized better than that later. He had a glorious day of retirement in 1946, one month before he was seventy-two, but he was in the campaign speaking for Truman in 1948.

Truman told me his version of that well-dramatized row.

"I wanted the hardest, meanest so-and-so I could get as Secretary of Defense," he said. Obviously, he was thinking ahead. The unification of the armed services was being fashioned then and was formally put into effect in September 1947. "Roosevelt had told me that he was going to make Pauley Secretary of the Navy. Forrestal understood that. If Pauley had not been as tough as he is, we would never have got any reparations policy. He made the Russians agree. I don't agree with all Pauley's policies but he is a tough, mean so-and-so who might make sense of this defense policy. Ickes was a good Secretary of the Interior and he has made up since he left."

The old man's departure made more news but in some ways it was less dramatic than the story of Bob Hannegan. He was the youngest member of the new Cabinet. Despite his paleness, he seemed Irish young and Irish gay. Schwellenbach seemed sick almost from the beginning, but Hannegan who was nearly ten years younger only outlived him for a year. He seemed at least as much the precinct politician as Pauley. Indeed, he undertook to extol the virtues of the precinct politician as the essential infantryman of democratic action. The strange thing about him was that, though he wanted it on his tombstone that he kept Henry Wallace from being President of the United States, in the Cabinet of the man who did become President in Wallace's possible stead he was almost left wing in his insistence upon the New Deal emphasis in the Truman Administration.

He had got where he was by reluctantly accepted last-minute luck in Truman's 1940 campaign, and what he got killed him. In his ornate office in the Post Office Department, four years before he died, he told me that he had not wanted any of the offices which in swift succession had come to him. When Truman had endorsed him as Internal Revenue Collector in St. Louis, he was making much more money than the job paid and would have turned it down if *The Post-Dispatch* had not started a campaign to the effect that he was unfit for it. He had not wanted to be National Chairman, he said, and had declined it until they took him to FDR and he said, "How's the new chairman?" When he had taken the job of United States Commissioner of Internal Revenue and then that of chairman he had explained to his pretty wife that it was like going to war.

"I'm just killing myself," he said. It seemed the comic complaint of an Irish politician in the center of his delight. In October 1947, he resigned all the jobs he did not want and two years later he was dead. It was not then unexpected. Somehow the deaths of politicians and public officials never seem unexpected after they occur. When James Forrestal plunged out of the Naval Hospital window in 1949, two months after he had left the post of Defense Secretary, men at the White House recalled that long before he was succeeded by Louis Johnson there were strange signs. He talked with power and lucidity but in the afternoon might have no memory of a conversation in the morning.

With Hannegan's death Truman began to show one of his most marked characteristics in Cabinet selections. He named, as Hannegan's successor as Postmaster General, not a politician as had been the American custom for at least half a century. He picked Jesse M. Donaldson who had been a career Post Office Department employee since he was twenty-three. When Anderson resigned to run for the Senate, he picked as Secretary of Agriculture Charles Brannan, who had come into the department as an assistant regional attorney in 1935. Julius A. Krug, who succeeded Ickes, had been in government service, notably TVA, for a decade. Krug's successor, Oscar Chapman, had come into the Department of Interior in May 1933. Averell Harriman and Charles Sawyer, who in succession followed Wallace in Commerce, had been ambassadors concerned with the increasingly difficult problem of European trade. Howard McGrath, who succeeded Clark as Attorney General, had already served as Solicitor General. Robert Patterson and Kenneth Royall, the last Secretaries of War with Cabinet rank, had both been promoted from within the Department. Louis Johnson, who followed Forrestal as Secretary of Defense, may have got the post because of his services in the difficult job of Democratic finance chairman in the 1948 campaign. He had served, however, three years as Assistant Secretary of War under Roosevelt.

Under the Truman plan the escalator within the government was at work. Of the nine men at his table in 1950, six had held subordinate posts in the departments which they headed. Two others had had other and considerable service in the Federal government. Only Secretary of Labor Maurice Tobin had come to his Cabinet post as his first job in the Federal government, and he had been the mayor of a city and governor of a state before he arrived in Washington.

Truman used fewer free-lance assistants than Roosevelt. He had divested himself of those who came in with lightning-like or maybe just hit-and-run wisdom. There is no man approximating either the Harry Hopkins or the Colonel House of the Truman Administration. Truman seems, indeed, to have a predilection for not very dramatic but industrious men in his Secretariat.

The Cabinet was—it always is—a body of very human men, ambitious, contentious sometimes, acutely aware of their prerogatives and their prestige as well as their purposes. But they are not very different from the members of a county court, a Senate committee, any body of politicians and officials anywhere. The one difference is that the business of all of them is primarily the business of the President. Truman had known much about such men before he came to the White House. He has learned much since. He learned most and quickly and painfully in the greatest field of their activity, the security of the United States. He learned first of all that he need not be his own Secretary of State, as Roosevelt appeared to wish to be, but that always and eternally he must be the chief of the foreign—as of the domestic—affairs of the United States.

Truman began to learn the inescapable responsibility of the President for foreign affairs in dealing with the first man he asked to take his first job as Secretary of State. Byrnes had many of the talents of Vinson. He was able, persuasive and, when he rushed to Washington after Roosevelt's death, clearly anxious to serve not merely himself but his time. Perhaps he lacked a certain restraint in ambition which Vinson seemed to have as he moved steadily forward. The probability, however, is not only that no man could at that time have succeeded as he hoped to succeed by argument or diplomacy in the conflict with the Russians which Byrnes undertook, but also that it was impossible in terms of the characters of the men and the personal histories behind them for Truman and Byrnes to have got along on a permanent basis. Politically Truman owed Byrnes nothing; as a man who had received what Byrnes thought was to be his, he felt oddly in Byrnes' debt. In the complicated psychology of American politics, Byrnes could not escape the feeling that he should be President, not Truman. Unquestionably his opinion was that he was better qualified for the Presidency. He was, he felt, doing Truman a favor by taking on his toughest job and, while Truman did not want a Stettinius as Secretary of State, he was, as every President is, acutely aware of the fact that the President alone is chief of American foreign policy. Perhaps not Byrnes but some of his subordinates did not keep that constantly enough in remembrance.

That was not a unique mistake by Byrnes or members of his

staff. Wallace and Wallace's friends had much the same feeling and were preparing the same mistake. Wallace, who after his defeat in 1944 made himself increasingly the first apostle of Roosevelt, must have been deeply disappointed when Roosevelt's "Truman or Douglas" letter was released in Chicago. The mantle which Roosevelt had declined to give him Wallace wrapped tighter and tighter around himself after Roosevelt died. Also, both Byrnes and Wallace had worked under Roosevelt who seemed often to like contentions in his Cabinet. Even Secretary Morgenthau had been actively undertaking to shape foreign policy with particular regard to the fate of Germany. The Truman Committee had had to push Roosevelt to end spattered and divided leadership in war production. Certainly part of the presidential estate which he left Truman was a precarious balance in which Wallace was not only Secretary of Commerce but the well-loved of many groups which felt a peculiar loneliness in the Democratic Party when Roosevelt died. Ickes had some of the same support which Truman was presumed to lack. Among the new members, Byrnes gave to Truman both real ability and something of the awkward feeling John Alden must have always had for Captain Miles Standish after he carried the message of Priscilla, the Puritan maid, back to him.

As boss and subordinate their relationship was probably doomed from the beginning. The clear fact is that that relationship had begun to fray before 1945 was over. While even presidential memories as to dates are sometimes tricky, Truman afterwards recalled that before General Marshall went to China as American envoy, he said to him, "If Byrnes quits me, I want you to be Secretary of State." And that Marshall told him he would do anything he wished him to do. Marshall left for China on December 15, 1945, the same day Byrnes arrived in Moscow for the meeting of the Foreign Ministers. There seems a possibility that the President's proposal to Marshall may have been made when Marshall visited the United States during his Chinese Mission. There is no doubt that Truman dates the break with Byrnes to that Moscow Conference where Byrnes, he believed, went much too far in accepting Russian positions with regard to the governments of Bulgaria and other satellite states. Truman had directly refused any recognition at Potsdam which did not insure real free governments for these countries.

"Byrnes lost his nerve in Moscow," Truman believed later.

And the real break, as Truman remembers it and Admiral Leahy recalls, too, came on the President's yacht, the *Williamsburg,* down on the Potomac River the day after Byrnes returned. Apparently they felt that Byrnes had given support to Stalin's contentions with regard to those states which Truman had repeatedly rejected in Potsdam. Also, the first news about it which got to Truman was in the newspapers. Truman was in Missouri when the press reports came through and from there phoned or wired Leahy asking him what he knew about the matter. Leahy only knew what he had seen in the papers. When, therefore, Byrnes wired Truman that on his return he would like to report on his mission by radio to the American people, Truman told Byrnes to join him on the *Williamsburg.*

"He was angry," Leahy said of the President.

The log of the *Williamsburg* shows that at five o'clock on the afternoon of December 29, 1945, Byrnes came aboard where she was anchored off Quantico "and reported to the President of the Foreign Ministers' Conference at Moscow. The Secretary was invited by the President to stay overnight but declined as he felt he should return to Washington to work on the radio speech he is to deliver on December 30th." Byrnes, who wrote later that he had returned from Moscow "thoroughly exhausted," said that he initiated the visit to the yacht. He said also: "After I reported to the President on what had happened at the conference, he expressed wholehearted approval of my action." At dinner, he said, at the President's request he repeated what he had told the President to his staff and "there was no expression of disapproval or approval by any other except Admiral Leahy who said that my report made him feel much better about the situation but that he did not approve of the agreement on Rumania and Bulgaria." The Moscow agreement, he said he told Leahy, was simply one more effort to achieve the objective of the Yalta and Potsdam agreements.

Truman does not remember it that way.

"Byrnes got the real riot act after Moscow. I told him our policy was not appeasement and not a one-way street."

Also he told Byrnes, he said later, that he did not mean to have a policy announced to the public before he was even informed of it.

"He didn't even communicate with me from St. Petersburg—
that shows I'm a man who learned about Russia unders the czars
—from Moscow. Jim blamed the State Department for not in-
forming me."

Certainly Truman's memory is that there was stern talk when
Byrnes came up into the President's lounge, which is top side on
the *Williamsburg*. Admiral Leahy remembers it that way, too.
Yet, some of the other members of Truman's staff who were
present do not remember any signs of sharp differences in the
general company on the yacht.

George Allen, the business man-politician, who was then Director of the RFC, wrote: "While there was no disagreement,
Truman was more determined than Byrnes to put an end to
the hold-over policy of Russian appeasement, and the substitute policy that finally emerged was accordingly more his than
Byrnes."

Clark Clifford, then Assistant Naval Aide to the President,
remembers no signs of a break, though he thought that Byrnes'
behavior toward the President in the Moscow Conference had
been inexcusable. "All through dinner," he recalled, "Leahy, in
a really effective and gentle manner to which Byrnes could not
take exception, had the needle in him."

Whatever Truman may have said that night, it was clear to
those around him that he resented both Byrnes' modification of
the American position in agreement with the Russians and his
failure to inform him of it at the time. There was no open
break. There was an uneasiness of relationship, however. Three
months later, in April 1946, "on the advice of a physician"
Byrnes gave Truman his resignation and it was agreed that the
resignation would take effect upon the completion of the pre-
liminary peace treaties. Truman was troubled over the whole
design of his foreign policy. He had gone to Potsdam eager to
preserve, in the peace, the good relationship between the Soviet
Union and the United States which had existed during the war.
He went there also determined to be firm in his insistence upon
agreements already made. He had been particularly insistent on
the free governments of the central European States which had
been agreed to at Yalta. It disturbed him deeply when he felt
that Byrnes at Moscow had weakened that position.

That feeling may have had something to do with the first of

two world-resounding speeches on foreign policy with which he was popularly and unpopularly connected. A feeling against appeasement undoubtedly entered into the fact of his presence on the platform at Westminster College, in Fulton, Missouri, in March, when Private Citizen Churchill spoke of the "expansive tendencies" of the Soviets and called for an Anglo-American alliance to halt them. Truman still insists, however, that his relationship to the Fulton speech was based upon neighborly impulse and not international relations. He was joining in a build-up for Westminster, the alma mater of his lively Military Aide Vaughan, and not on a pattern for foreign affairs. Vaughan had brought Franc McCluer, then president of the college, to see him about it.

"I knew what he was going to say," Truman said afterwards of the Churchill speech. "I didn't read his speech but he talked to me on the train about what he was going to say. What happened was that Harry Vaughan and McCluer came to see me and said they had about $4,000 in their lecture fund and they wanted to get Churchill to make a speech. Churchill was then in Florida taking a rest. Would I ask him? I told Churchill that I would like for him to come to my state and make a speech. He jumped at it. It was not intended to be a policy speech at all. I didn't care what he said. We pretend to believe in free speech, don't we?"

Undoubtedly, however, his presence on that platform seemed to many to have carried him beyond the middle ground between firmness with Russia and steady desire for such agreements with Russia as would serve or save the peace. Clearly his relationship with and his dependence on his Secretary of State at that time was not entirely satisfactory. It did not displease him to have the eloquent bluntness of Churchill sound from the platform on which he sat in Missouri.

"Churchill had tried to get me not to withdraw our troops from Prague," he said of the last days of the war. "I told him we were bound to do that by our agreements with the Russians. But if I had known then what I know now, I would have ordered the troops to go to the western boundaries of Russia."

He had been increasingly uneasy also about the much softer policy toward Russia which Henry Wallace was urging in the Cabinet and elsewhere. He realized—or thought then—that Wallace represented the views of a large segment of Americans. He hoped to bring Wallace's views closer to his own. For some reason, apparently, he thought he was succeeding as the summer passed. It was that idea, apparently, plus his always awkward feeling with Wallace which involved him in the other speech and in the naked blunder with regard to it. The Wallace speech in Madison Square Garden, on September 12, 1946, was the extreme opposite of the Churchill speech six months before. And after the Wallace speech Truman appeared to be lost in uncertainty and ineptitude between them.

The Wallace speech was afterwards quite naturally interpreted in the light of his further swing in politics toward Russian appeasement in a campaign for the Presidency, in which he had the support of American Communists. Wallace's friends have insisted that then some other politics was involved in the speech and Truman's advance approval of it. Bob Hannegan, they said, looking toward the tough Congressional elections (which turned out to be disastrous) hoped that such a speech would provide Administration support among liberal Democrats and Independents who had been troubled by the growing mood of toughness in Russian relations. (Governor Dewey's man, Irving M. Ives, badly defeated James Mead for the Senate that year.)

The greater probability is that Truman, who had always wanted to get along with this man Wallace who seemed odd and strange to him, let that desire lead him into grievous error. The clear thing is that at that time he was dealing in his Cabinet with the two men, Byrnes and Wallace, each of whom felt that he ought to be sitting in the presidential chair which Truman occupied.

It is difficult to read the speech today free from the color of Wallace's further movement left in the months and years which followed. Anyone who does now bother to read it, however, may be amazed at the number of sharply uncomplimentary things about Russia which it contained. Basically, however, it was a vigorous dissent against the "get tough" policy and an almost direct reply to what Churchill had said in Fulton six months before. The speech sharply answered any proposal to bind Britain and America together in an alliance against Russia which Wallace thought would lead to war. The trap for Truman, however, was in the lines:

"I am neither anti-British, nor pro-British—neither anti-Russian, nor pro-Russian. And just two days ago, when President Truman read these words, he said that they represented the policy of his Administration."

Truman had been asked about that quotation by newspapermen who had seen advance copies of Wallace's speech at his press conference the afternoon before the speech was delivered. He verified it. Did that apply to the whole of Wallace's speech? It did. Didn't that represent a departure from the foreign policy Byrnes was carrying out? It was in accord with that policy, Truman said.

Clark Clifford, who had by then been made Counsel to the President, was one of those who helped Truman in this matter.

"Then Wallace spoke," he said, "and hell broke loose next morning. Oh, boy, it really did!"

The incident led to a revisal of all White House speech-clearance procedures, but that did not help the situation at the time.

"The President told me about the Wallace speech," Clifford remembered, "after the press conference. Wallace had come in a few days before he spoke. He handed the President a copy and he kept a copy. The whole purport of Wallace's comments was that he was in process of coming around to the view that we could not deal with the Soviets as he thought we could. The President was very much gratified. He does not like differences around him. So he thumbed through the speech while Wallace told him that he was taking a sort of tough line with the Soviets."

When the speech was delivered, Truman felt imposed upon.

"First after the speech," Clifford remembered, "the President said he was going to let Wallace go. Somehow that got out. The next day or so Wallace saw the President and came out and said he was not going to make any more speeches on foreign policy. That seemed like a tap on the wrist for Wallace. The next day the Boss told me he was going to have a teletype conversation with Byrnes. I was beside him during the conversation in the Map Room. It's claimed some place that on the basis of Byrnes' representations Wallace was fired. That's not so. Byrnes said that his position was made infinitely more difficult. He needed to know if any more speeches were coming. The President assured him that they were not. I remember that the President ended up,

'I look forward to your returning so that together we may strike a blow for liberty'—meaning have a drink together.

"There was no sharpness on either side. When the Boss talked to Byrnes the only arrangement with Wallace was that he was not to speak while Byrnes was in Paris. I remember that well because I thought that settled the matter. Then the next day the President had completely changed his mind and said that Wallace had to go. This was not the result of his talk with Byrnes. I don't know what changed his mind."

Byrnes has published in *Speaking Frankly*, the story of his years as Secretary of State, his part in that teletype conversation. He did most of the talking (Truman 338 words; Byrnes 1,295) demanding that Wallace cease criticism of the foreign policy of the Administration of which he was a part not only during the conference but after it. Byrnes said that he realized "that in reaching the agreement announced by Mr. Wallace you were trying to reconcile the differences in views held by us on the one hand and by Mr. Wallace on the other," but that it had raised a doubt as to whether "the American people have a foreign policy." Byrnes did not specifically threaten to resign but he stated that, if after the Paris Conference, Wallace was permitted to return to such criticisms he would have "to insist upon being relieved.

"I do not want to ask you to do anything that would force Mr. Wallace out of the Cabinet," he said. "However, I do not think that any man who professes any loyalty to you would so seriously impair your prestige and the prestige of the government with the nations of the world."

In the conversation the President made it clear that Wallace would not again as member of the Cabinet make any speeches in dissent from the foreign policy of the Administration of which he was a part. And, as Clifford remembered, the conversation ended in an exchange of compliments and good wishes:

> *Mr. Byrnes:* I greatly regret that you have had trouble in the field of foreign affairs but my conscience is clear and I have done my best to minimize your difficulty.
> *The President:* You have done an excellent job. Nobody appreciates it more than I do and I shall continue to support you with everything I have.
> *Mr. Byrnes:* You certainly have done it up to this time and your statement makes me feel good.

The President: Keep on feeling good and I'll be doing something I think you ought to be doing in an hour.
Mr. Byrnes: I still believe in liberty and am willing to strike a blow for it.
The President: Go to it and I am with you.

The whole incident was badly handled. Obviously no President should clear any speech on such a basis and without any staff check. Obviously, also, Truman, who always felt a trifle ill at ease with Henry Wallace, trusted the man he had beaten too far with a blank check. It is equally clear, however, from a reading of the Wallace speech and from some of the hisses as well as some of the cheers which his left wing audience gave him that Wallace probably really thought he was getting tougher with the Russians than he had been before—or was afterwards. The clearance of the speech was a mistake. The effort to explain it away as a clearance of Wallace's right to speak rather than what he said was in the face of the record a worse mistake still.

"I called Wallace in," Truman said of the final incident in the fiasco. "Charlie Ross was present. We made an agreement as to what he would say to straighten the thing out. In the conversation I remember Wallace saying, 'I think there are times when the end justifies the means.' I said, 'What did you say?' and he repeated it. I knew I could not get along with him. He went out and gave out an interview diametrically opposed to what he had agreed to do. The next day I fired him."

That was September 20, 1946. Byrnes retired in January 1947, and was succeeded by Marshall who was in China. The Truman-Byrnes relationship, broken then, has steadily deteriorated since.

"He failed miserably as Secretary of State," Truman said, "and ran out on me when the going was very rough and when I needed him worst. His 'bad heart' has now left him when he has found that he made a bad guess. So he and old Baruch have joined the McCormicks, Hearsts and Scripps-Howards to discredit me. They will not succeed."

Truman had, when he appointed him and afterwards as well, more confidence in Marshall than in anybody in the government and probably anybody in the world. Sometimes, indeed, he acted when some members of his staff thought that Marshall was being a little stuffy, as if Marshall were his walking equivalent of George Washington and Robert E. Lee. Some others who admired the General's great abilities as a war leader were not so confident of his abilities as a diplomat or foreign minister. As a Secretary of State they thought he depended too strictly on the proposals which came up to him in the line of command in a field with which he was less familiar than he had been as a professional soldier.

Beside the adoring Truman, old Admiral Leahy, who had also tried his hand at diplomacy, was not so sure about Marshall.

"I was present when Marshall was going to China," he told me. "He said he was going to tell Chiang that he had to get on with the Communists or without help from us. He said the same thing when he got back. I thought he was wrong then, both times." I suggested to the Admiral that in taking China the Communists had an historically indigestible land. "Yes, I've heard that since I was an ensign and I still don't believe it."

Truman completely trusted Marshall. Marshall, he told me, started cleaning the dead wood out of the State Department, not Byrnes. It would have been difficult to see how the commuting Byrnes could have had time for much cleaning. Some dull bureaucracy remained after Marshall. But in Marshall, Truman had a Secretary of State whom he trusted sometimes, some of his staff felt, to the point of his own injury. Marshall, they believed, stood by his subordinates even when what seemed to be their prejudices reversed the policy of the President himself. The clear case they felt was Israel. Some White House men still believe that a number of the positions taken by career men on this matter were based on anti-Semitism, not diplomacy. And there were men in the State Department who believed that some of the presidential staff were clearly more concerned about Israel in terms of American politics than in terms of American security. It will take time and perspective to untangle the difficult mass of American and Middle Eastern politics, oil, prejudices, from the story. It is a dramatic story in any event.

Truman himself had long been an advocate of a homeland for the Jews. He had a personal part behind the United States support of the resolution of November 30, 1947, providing for the partition of Palestine. There were and are men in the State Department who opposed the idea and, within a month after the resolution had been passed, members of his staff told Truman that these men were working to undermine his policy. He did not believe it.

"I know how Marshall feels and he knows how I feel," he said.

His policy for partition as a basis for a Jewish state seemed to be moving satisfactorily in the United Nations when, at the request of his old business partner Eddie Jacobson of Kansas City, Truman saw, "off the record," Chaim Weizmann, first President of Israel at 12:15, on March 18, 1948. Weizmann had seen the President before and got from him, he believed, direct and personal intervention to prevent the slicing of the region called the Negev from the Jewish state which had been designated under the original partition plan. In March, when Weizmann came again, he had noticed increasing weakness in American support of the partition plan in the Security Council.

"The President," he said, "was sympathetic personally, and still indicated a firm resolve to press forward with partition."

"You can bank on us," said Truman. He liked old Weizmann as a decent, simple man. "I am for partition."

The very next day, Friday, March 19, Senator Austin, as the American representative on the Security Council, in "a surprise move" proposed suspension of the plan to partition Palestine and that pending a decision on its permanent status the Holy Land be placed under U.N. trusteeship. Truman called Clifford at 7:30 Saturday morning.

"Can you come right down," he said. "There's a story in the papers on Palestine and I don't understand what has happened."

In his office Truman was as disturbed as Clifford had ever seen him.

"How could this have happened? I assured Chaim Weizmann that we were for partition and would stick to it. He must think I am a plain liar. Find out how this could have happened."

Marshall was in San Francisco. Under Secretary Lovett who was in Florida was as surprised, he told Clifford, as Truman had been. He said, however, that there had been an understanding that, if they could not get partition, in order not to leave a vacuum, they would try trusteeship. Marshall in memorandum had approved the procedure. Actually, partition had not failed, though one resolution had not passed. The failure of that resolution and the Marshall memo, however, gave a chance to those who had opposed partition all along.

"I reported to the President," Clifford said. "He talked to Marshall in San Francisco. So Marshall gave out a statement along lines we suggested which alleviated it a little. But every Jew thought that Truman was a no-good."

Weizmann apparently did not. He telephoned Jacobson in Kansas City: "Eddie, I'm seventy-three. All I have left seem to be disappointments. This is another. But I don't believe Truman knew on Thursday what was going to happen on Friday."

The next chance for Truman to indicate his good will toward Palestine came in the middle of May when the British mandate was terminated. Weizmann wrote a letter urging the President to grant immediate recognition. Truman liked the idea but wished to talk to Marshall. Marshall was opposed but his opposition, Clifford, David Niles, and other members of the White House staff thought, actually only represented the views of those same members of the State Department organization who they thought had messed up the matter of partition. Clifford finally persuaded the President to call a conference on the question. Those present included: Marshall, Lovett, a State Department Palestine expert (McClintock, Clifford thought), Niles, Clifford and Truman. Truman stated the question of recognition. Marshall said it was inadvisable and called on Lovett to state the reasons. Then Truman turned to Clifford who had prepared himself for a fifteen-minute argument on the subject. He pointed out that Truman was already on record for an independent Jewish state and that it was unrealistic to pretend that there was no such state.

"Marshall's face flushed," Clifford recalled. " 'Mr. President,' he said, 'this is not a matter to be determined on the basis of politics. Unless politics were involved, Mr. Clifford would not even be at this conference. This is a serious matter of foreign policy determination and the question of politics and political opinion does not enter into it.' "

And Clifford added: "He said it all in a righteous God-damned Baptist tone."

Truman closed the matter, "I think we must follow the position General Marshall has advocated."

Apparently that closed the matter. However, late that day Under Secretary Lovett called Clifford up.

"Clark," he said, "I've been uneasy about the decision made today. I'm going to get my boys together tomorrow and talk about it."

Lovett met with his Middle East staff the next day. Then he suggested that he and Clifford meet for lunch at the 1925 F Street Club the next day, which was Saturday, May 14. At the luncheon table he said that he had concluded that Israel should be recognized. Marshall had agreed but the State Department wanted to wait a few days to take the matter up with the British and French. On the basis of the agreement to recognize, Clifford got the President to insist that the recognition be immediate. There was work to be done, but at 5:16 Israel, which had become a state at five o'clock, was recognized by the United States— a full day ahead of recognition which came in from the Soviet Union and Poland.

Even if he did not always please Truman's political advisers, so far as Truman himself was concerned Marshall was the Secretary of State he had been seeking and needing from the beginning. He had a soldier's distaste for politics. But he had magnificent presence, great prestige and a deep loyalty to Truman. Having resisted politics at a time when he had been put in command of a bi-partisan foreign policy in a hotly partisan country, Marshall was one of Truman's Cabinet ministers who came to tell the President good-by when Truman set out on his 1948 presidential campaign. Also, if some career subordinates in the State Department, in that campaign and before and after, undertook to suggest that the American foreign policy was something independent of the President who constitutionally is its chief, they got no support or sympathy from Marshall in that undertaking. He was the man with whom and through whom Truman could work. Truman did not need Marshall as a political assistant. He knew that both he and Marshall were imposed upon in some cases. Above all, however, he knew that Marshall could be depended upon in both spirit and act to carry out a policy designed under the responsibility of the President for the security of the United States.

Within less than two months after Marshall succeeded Byrnes, the aggressive Truman foreign policy for peace and freedom began to emerge in the instruments which have since become familiar. It was shaped to combine the prevention of Communist aggression against states not already under Communist dictation with aid in the reconstruction of other states so that want and insecurity might not invite the spread of communism to them. It has seemed to be composed of separate pieces, the Truman Doctrine, the Marshall Plan, the Atlantic Pact. Actually, all were the steps in one plan and parts of the policy of one man.

Its inception, of course, was the Truman Doctrine which Truman announced himself in a message to Congress, on March 12, 1947, in which he asked Congress for aid for Greece and Turkey against the Communist threats to those countries. The threats were not new. In the teletype conversation with Byrnes after the Wallace speech, Byrnes had spoken of the disturbing messages from Turkey and Greece. It was six months later, months in which the messages became increasingly more urgent, however, before Truman himself announced the Truman Doctrine. He had postponed and cut short a vacation, on which he planned to witness the fleet maneuvers off Culebra Island, to speak to the Congress. Perhaps he was unduly warlike in his message. Certainly afterwards the Truman Doctrine seemed to some, in the sharp statement of its purposes, contradictory to the later Marshall Plan. Actually, one was the complement of the other and both were the instruments of the same man.

Formally, the Marshall Plan was announced by Marshall at Harvard University, on June 5, 1947. Actually, it was outlined and enunciated in a speech, in essence dictated by Harry Truman, which the then Under Secretary of State Dean Acheson delivered in the little town of Cleveland, Mississippi, on May 8. Truman was to have made that speech to the Delta Council in the Teachers College at Cleveland where every year from seven to ten thousand farmers and their wives gather to hear new speeches and meet old friends. Later, as Secretary of State, Acheson remembered that there were also "sisters, cousins, grandparents, and children down to babes in arms." When Truman could not go he called Acheson to the White House and outlined what he hoped he would say.

Truman had adequate excuse for not going himself. The vote on the appropriation for the Truman Doctrine aid to Greece and Turkey was pending. (The House approved it 287 to 107 the day after Acheson spoke.) Also, he was standing by, troubled about the condition of his ninety-four-year-old mother. He knew, however, as a small-town man himself, the excitement of Cleveland about the coming of the President and the disappointment which would follow the announcement that he could not come.

"The President, therefore, wished," said Acheson, "to have a speech of broad character and of some importance in the international field made and asked me to do it."

Truman had more on his mind than the disappointment of Delta farmers. Aid to Greece and Turkey was only an item in meeting the predicament which the United States and Western Europe were approaching.

"We had at that time," Acheson recalled in connection with the speech which Truman wanted then, "a tremendous export surplus, as we still do, but there was then very little likelihood of the recipient nations being able to fill the dollar gap. It was also clear that if our exports did not continue, the political consequences in the battle of resistance against the spread of Communism in Europe would be lost."

For this occasion in the little town in the cotton country, Acheson said, Truman "wished to have the most complete and thorough clearance of the speech, so that it would not be a personal utterance but one on behalf of the Administration.

"The speech was, therefore, prepared, submitted to all the Departments of Government having concern with its subject matter, and then reviewed by the President in the light of the total commitments. It received his approval and was made."

Afterwards Acheson was modest about having the speech labeled as the original announcement of the Marshall Plan. In it, however, to the farmers in the college auditorium, to those listening from loud speakers under the trees outside, to their wives and cousins and children and beyond them to the whole world, Acheson said for Truman:

> Since world demand exceeds our ability to supply, we are going to have to concentrate our emergency assistance in areas where it will be most effective in building world political and economic stability, in promoting human freedom and democratic institutions, in fostering liberal trading policies, and in strengthening the authority of the United Nations.
> This is merely common sense and sound practice. It is in keeping with the policy announced by President Truman in

his special message to Congress on March 12 on aid to Greece and Turkey. Free peoples who are seeking to preserve their independence and democratic institutions and human freedoms against totalitarian pressures, either internal or external, will receive top priority for American reconstruction aid. This is no more than frank recognition as President Truman said, "that totalitarian regimes imposed on free people, by direct or indirect aggression, undermine the foundations of international peace and hence the security of the United States."

There in essence in the spring of 1947 was the whole Truman foreign policy in which the Truman Doctrine and the Marshall Plan and the logical steps beyond them were all parts of the same piece. It made sense that day to the congregated cotton farmers of the Mississippi Delta. But its impact came slowly on other minds.

"Its reception," Acheson said later of the speech, "was interesting, but not unexpected. The local audience was most receptive, and a few papers in the South printed parts of it and commented upon it. But for a week or ten days it was received with rather monumental indifference and silence in most of the papers. It came back to the American press via the British and European. *The* (London) *Times* printed it almost in full, and the Continental press published considerable parts of it. It became the subject of lively comment abroad. As these papers and dispatches came back here, the columnists began to look at this speech which was creating so much interest in Europe and so little in the United States, and gradually, two or three weeks after it was made, it began to be talked about."

Secretary Marshall made his full-dress speech about it at Harvard one month after the Acheson address in Mississippi. In Washington and in the world then it was clearly the essential, fully grown post-war policy of the Truman Administration. Truman himself was in Kansas City when Marshall spoke in Cambridge. He was practically a commuter between Washington and Grandview that spring and early summer. Old Martha Ellen seemed to be showing her stubborn strength after a fall in February. But on May 17, the President flew there hastily after news that she had suffered a relapse. In his emergency offices in the penthouse of the Muehlebach Hotel where he had received the news of his election as Vice-President in 1944, he signed with ceremony, on May 22, the bill which embodied the assistance promised in the Truman Doctrine. The hotel proprietors put up a plaque in the penthouse to commemorate the event. It was an historic event in the city of Jim Reed.

Martha Ellen died on June 26. Her death received the attention of a nation which did not universally like her son but recognized her as a strong and good tie with the American past. When she was born, young Victoria had been Queen fourteen years. Karl Marx as a political exile in London was about to become correspondent of *The New York Tribune*. Jenny Lind was singing in America. Abraham Lincoln was an ex-Congressman who had unsuccessfully tried to get the job of Commissioner of the General Land Office. Millard Fillmore was President of the United States which was a Republic sixty-two years old containing 23,191,876 people.

The nation had changed some and the world around it, too. But power in America still lay in the representatives of the people. It was Truman's purpose to keep it that way in the world. On the day of Martha Ellen's funeral her son said that he would "well and faithfully" administer the Taft-Hartley labor law which Congress had overwhelmingly passed over his protest and his veto. It was the kind of law which seemed to him to misunderstand the mood of the times and the design of freedom required in America as a pattern for the world. The basic American foreign policy must always be, he understood, America itself. That had not changed in all Martha Ellen's years nor the lengthening years of her son.

CHAPTER XXI

If a Fight Seems Required

THE MOVEMENT OF Truman's foreign policy proceeded from no vacuum. What happened in America made the American impression and example. When strikes threatened to bind United States strength, Truman pointed out that not only was the domestic economy threatened but that trains and ships were halted, stopping our aid to a hungry and restive world.

"I got them in before the strike and all agreed not to strike except Johnston and Whitney."

Truman spoke of A. F. Whitney, president of the Brotherhood of Railroad Trainmen, and Alvanley Johnston, chief of the Brotherhood of Locomotive Engineers, in connection with the railroad strike of 1946. He talked, in 1950, with a still stubborn sense of his determination at that time.

"I sent for them and talked to them like a Dutch uncle, 'If you think I'm going to sit here and let you tie up this country, you're crazy as hell.' "

Truman said this to the two men at the end of months of fruitless negotiations. He had started talking to them in February. The abortive strike came late in May. He knew the two men well. He never had any great affection for Johnston. "A damned Republican," he called him. But he and Whitney had been friends from the days of his service on the sub-committee investigating railroad finances. There was no yielding in either of them.

Whitney said, "I've got to go through with it."

Truman looked at him steadily through the thick lenses which magnify his eyes.

"Well then," he said, "I'm going to give you the gun."

Around the White House then the American economy was in the midst of those stresses and strains which have always been most apparent after the wars. Truman, who had himself been caught in the squeeze before, was involved then in the long, complicated fight over price controls in a country in which the fears of general inflation were matched by demands for an end to any price and profit limitations. Post-war readjustment was plagued, as it always has been in America, by a wave of strikes. The no-strike pledge and wage limitations both seemed to restive workers to have lost their meaning with the peace. The demand for higher wages rose with the insistence upon the removal of the lid from prices. Some economic historian may some day precisely prove which came first, the higher wages or the higher prices. It was clearly the time when a variety of post-war irritations was producing the Eightieth Congress.

There was nothing new or strange about the strikes. There was in America nothing new about stubbornness and arrogance in industrial disputes. When in Truman's youth Theodore Roosevelt had, with strong presidential leadership, settled the coal strike of 1902, he had faced the self-righteous immobility of the mineowners whose chief spokesman said: "The rights and interests of the laboring man will be protected and cared for—not by the labor agitators, but by the Christian men to whom God in His infinite wisdom has given the control of the property interests of the country. . . ." Whitney and Johnston did not (nor even John L. Lewis) assert any divine right of labor. But there did seem a resurgence and transfer of the primitive position: The public be damned.

Franklin Roosevelt had faced a coal strike in the middle of the war. Wilson had faced a railroad dispute on the eve of war, late in 1916. Either such strike could disrupt the nation. But, as Truman pointed out, the rail strike in 1946 also stopped the movement of 100,000 tons of grain to the hungry and unhappy world. In Truman's case the coal and rail strikes came simultaneously. As he entered his second year in the White House he also entered a seven-months period of unprecedented labor problem as both the old friend of labor and as President of all the people of the United States.

When Truman spoke at Roosevelt's grave on the first anniversary of his death, on April 12, 1946, John L. Lewis' miners were already out on strike. Truman seized the coal mines on May 21. He stopped the railroad strike on May 25. Actually, however, the end of this period is best dated on December 7, 1946. On that day a chagrined, if not chastened, John L. Lewis ordered his men back into the mines after Judge T. Alan Goldsborough, in the case brought by the Truman Administration, fined Lewis $10,000 and his union $3,500,000 for contempt.

One clear thing is that Truman did not come to his attitude toward labor on any theoretical basis. As both county judge and as Re-Employment Director in Missouri he had hired men and sought jobs for men with a practical attitude in both hiring and finding jobs. He had stated his willingness long before he was a Senator to cut the working day to any necessary extent to make sure that there were jobs for all. Also, once in 1934, when there seemed to him to be an unjustified strike of union workmen on the new courthouse in Kansas City he had told them to go back to work or "the job will be thrown open to the employment of labor on the basis of competence and skill at NRA wages, which are much lower than union wages." In the Senate, he had found facts which made him believe that railroad management had been readier to cut wages than to reform their own costly and profitable practices. He could not regard as a principle any situation which required him to be impractical. Indeed, his patience was thin when he felt that the impractical was insisted upon.

As a practical American at a time when as always after American wars the effort was being made to confuse labor protest with foreign agitation, Truman understood that he faced a traditional American conflict. No foreign ideologies or ideologists entered into it. It was as native as brass knuckles and bowie knives. At the long, finally impatient last, he met it in that spirit. The theorists in history will have to debate as to whether any other course would have sufficed.

His principal antagonists, Whitney, of the Engineers, and Lewis, of the Miners, both came from Missouri's next neighbor state, Iowa. Lewis was born and lived (except when his father, blacklisted by the mines for union activity, had to leave to find other work) in the coal village of Lucas, which is only 150 miles from Independence. Both Lewis and Whitney grew up in the Middle Border in the years of its angry revolt. Lewis' wandering father lived for a time in Colfax, Iowa, the home town of General James B. Weaver, who led Populism to the top of its disturbance to Wall Street and the East. Whitney was a brakeman when

Cleveland smashed the great rail strike of the 1890's with Federal troops. Both as union leaders had learned to fight not at any foreign ideological barricades but in the backyard of American protest. Truman was the product of the same American backyard. Also, Truman had the same stubborn Middle Border willingness for a fight if a fight seemed required.

After Truman's lawyers had won the case before Judge Goldsborough, Lewis' biographer, Saul Alinsky, said that "Lewis was so accustomed to dealing with a subtle, brilliant, wary Roosevelt that he could not anticipate the directness of a politically insensitive Truman." Truman was in such a situation politically insensitive. Labor and other groups were to find out that the strange thing about this Missouri politician is that when he gets his "Show Me" Missouri spirit up he always is. Throughout his career from the Pendergast contractors to the union leaders, his stubbornness when he knows he is right has always been his most marked political characteristic. That and one other thing: his willingness to fight. In this summer of industrial strife, he was not always consistent. He sometimes, indeed, seemed vigorously inconsistent. The important thing to him was that he believed he was right even against old friends, and what he looked for in that fight was not a sensitive show of political consistency but whatever weapons he could use in his hand.

When Truman came to the White House in 1945, labor had not been disturbed by the celebrations of the conservatives. If Truman had suited the bosses and the Southerners at Chicago, he had also clearly suited, and in succession, Hillman, Murray, Whitney and Green. They had already energetically helped him win his Senatorial renomination fight in 1940 because by that time he was regarded as "the best friend labor ever had in the Senate." The railroad union men were his particular friends. He had the highest regard for George Harrison, president of the Brotherhood of Railway Clerks. He liked David Robertson, of the Brotherhood of Locomotive Firemen and Enginemen. On the other hand, he did not have a high regard for Lewis, who had shown less admiration and more arrogance to the Truman Committee than any other individual during the war. Truman did not care for the fine art of his arrogance.

On Thursday, April 25, 1946, Truman came back to Washington from Naval maneuvers off the Virginia capes to the funeral of Chief Justice Harlan F. Stone. He came also to meet the news that the two railroad brotherhoods of Whitney and Johnston, which had rejected a presidential fact-finding recommendation, had called a strike for May 18. On May 14, Truman called representatives of all the railroads and brotherhoods to the White House. He talked straight to them across his big desk and they agreed to resume negotiations and report to him. But on the same day the negotiations in the coal strike ended in deadlock. The railroad negotiations collapsed again on May 16, and on May 17, Truman ordered seizure of the railroads by the government. The next day he announced that a five-day rail truce had been arranged but only after confusion had been caused by workers following the original strike call. On May 21, the President ordered the seizure of the coal mines. Then on May 22, all the railroads and all the unions except those led by Whitney and Johnston accepted a compromise proposed by the President. If necessary, he was ready then to give those two "the gun."

The next day, May 23, at 4:00 P.M., the two railroad leaders precipitated the most complete transportation tie-up in history. That was Thursday. Clark Clifford, who was Naval Aide then, remembered later the stiffening stubbornness of the President. On Friday, a Cabinet meeting discussed the crisis and that afternoon Truman called a meeting of the government officials most concerned. There were about twelve people present including, Clifford remembers, Patterson, Schwellenbach, Krug and Byrnes. When the conference was over everybody filed out after deciding that the President should go on the air that night and announce that he would take a special message on the subject to Congress the next day. There was not much time to prepare a speech and Truman asked Clifford, still in Naval uniform, to go to work on it. It was the first such work which Clifford did for the President.

Truman had asked Fred Vinson, who was to leave the Cabinet and become Chief Justice, to come in at eight o'clock. Truman was to go on the air at ten. A first draft of the speech had just been completed when the conference began. There was not much time for any revision. A girl outside the door of the President's office copied the pages as they were revised and approved. Truman's secretary, Rose Conway, worked on Truman's reading copy as soon as she got the sheets from the girl. Clifford afterwards claimed credit for the shillelagh sentence comparing the action of Whitney and Johnston with that of the Japs at Pearl Harbor. The last pages of the speech had not been typed when Truman went on the air, a clearly angry and determined man. Many thought the speech was mistaken in its tone and the attack on the labor leaders. It was almost the first of his presidential speeches in which his strength came clearly over the radio. Truman's words came like blows:

"The crisis of Pearl Harbor was the result of action by a foreign enemy. The crisis tonight is caused by a group of men within our own country who place their private interests above the welfare of the nation."

Even while the President was speaking over the radio, plans went forward for his message to Congress the next day. Its controversial center, which the House accepted quickly but which the Senate rejected with Robert Taft leading the opposition, involved a proposal "to draft into the Armed Forces of the United States all workers who are on strike against their government." It was Truman's steady insistence that, since the roads had been taken over by the government the strike was not against the railroads but the nation itself. Obviously such a draft was a questionable weapon for use even in a crisis. Truman himself as a Senator had opposed proposals for a labor draft in wartime.

Only members of Truman's own staff were at the conference the next morning when the message to Congress was considered and the final decision on the labor draft proposal was made. John Steelman, who had come in as Special Assistant to the President and seemed a sort of extra Secretary of Labor, was at the Statler trying desperately to work out some settlement with the two angry labor leaders.

"I remember very distinctly," Clifford told me later, "the argument as to whether or not we should keep the suggestion that the strikers be drafted. The President said the situation was so acute that the speech had to be as stiff as it could be made and that this suggestion should stay in.

"Then word came from the Statler that there was a possibility that the strike might be settled. That was going to put us in a hell of a fix if it were settled at the last minute and we had this speech. So Sam Rosenman and I went into the Cabinet room and wrote three or four alternative pages. The President did not know the strike was settled. He had got into his car to go to the Capitol when I carried him the alternative pages. I remember that although I was still in the Navy then, I went to the Capitol without a hat.

"I stayed in Rayburn's office to try to talk to Steelman at the Statler and had trouble in getting him. Finally I got him. He said, 'We are awful close but it is not signed yet.' He said they had orally agreed to the points which had to be put into writing but that there was no knowing whether they would finally sign.

"I told him, 'I'll wait in Rayburn's office. Phone me as soon as it is signed.' I sat there while the President started his original speech in the House Chamber. The phone rang. Steelman said, 'It's signed.' I wrote a note, 'Mr. President, agreement signed, strike over' and gave it to Biffle. The President read it and said, 'Gentlemen, the strike has been settled.'"

The Congress broke into cheers. Afterwards, however, Senator Wayne Morse, liberal Republican from Oregon, said that Truman knew before he started speaking that the strike was settled and that his speech was just "ham acting." Truman did not know. But in the American language he was determined to keep Whitney's and Johnston's feet to the fire until the strike was formally and finally called off. Also, he wanted then, and for the future, powers to deal effectively with such situations. He got the strike precipitately settled but he also got from the infuriated Whitney a statement that his union would use its entire $47,-000,000 treasury if necessary to defeat him if he ever ran for office again. At a CIO conference in New York City, an attack on Truman as "the No. 1 strike breaker of the American bankers and railroads" was loudly cheered. Also, at a Sunday conference on the day after the speech with John L. Lewis at the White House, he got nowhere. Lewis walked out, never to be welcomed again.

Lewis won again that May, getting a contract with Krug which granted his major demands. But two weeks before the Congressional elections that fall he put new demands up to Krug and set in motion the process by which a tough and insistent Truman carried him into the courthouse in November to give him the first real set-back he had had in more than a decade. Lewis never forgave Truman. A month before the 1948 election, Lewis spent an hour telling the delegates to the United Mine Workers Convention his opinion of Truman. He packed it all into a few final lines: "He is a man totally unfitted for the position. His principles are elastic, and he is careless with the truth. He has no special knowledge of any subject, and he is a malignant, scheming sort of an individual who is dangerous not only to the United Mine Workers, but dangerous to the United States of America." Truman laughed when he got that report on his campaign train. (This was the same Lewis who opposed Roosevelt, too, and who said that Roosevelt "disregarded the ordinarily recognized virtues" and connived "for no objective except the unholy satisfaction of connivance.")

Labor in general, which did not like the stern tactics by which Truman stopped the rail strike, was not in agreement with Lewis then nor actually with Whitney when he blew off after the rail strike speech. Its leaders noted Truman's veto of the harsh Case labor disputes bill two weeks after he stopped the rail strike. Also, both Lewis and Whitney were known and not always trusted in their leadership by other labor leaders. Not long after Whitney's death in July 1949, I spoke to a man in the labor movement about the collision of Whitney and Truman who had been friends before the 1946 strike. It seemed to me that that had been the collision of two strong, stubborn Americans. I was surprised to find him not sympathetic with the position which Whitney had taken.

"Whitney was a man of violent temper," he told me, "and he found it difficult to 'get along' with the other chiefs of railroad labor organizations. This was revealed early in the New Deal, when Whitney was asked to resign as chairman of the Railway Labor Executives' Association and get out of the organization. He never came back, although he sometimes cooperated with the other chiefs in wage movements, and once in a while in political drives. However, you could never tell when he would 'blow up.'

"Naturally, Truman's strike decision infuriated Whitney and he went completely off the beam, probably encouraged by some Republican 'liberals.' He talked indiscreetly with newspapermen. But after he got home and had a chance to confer with some of his associates—many of them extremely shrewd men—he began to cool off and came to realize that, in the circumstances, he probably couldn't control his own men in a fight against Truman.

"That didn't mean the railroad boys approved what the President had done," he added, "but they couldn't overlook the fact that 'Bob' Taft and men like him led the Republican Party. So, Whitney effected a reconciliation with Truman. He liked publicity and it gave him the spotlight. I have no doubt he supported Truman fervently in the last campaign, but at least half a dozen of our chiefs were individually more effective."

Truman's idea that the Republican Congress which was elected in the fall after the strike was a lucky thing for him certainly was true in the case of labor. If not all labor was ready to follow Whitney and Lewis, large segments of it did not like Truman's action in the rail and coal strikes. . The strong differences which Truman tried to emphasize between "strikes against the government" and strikes against private employers was not easily understood. In the Lewis case particularly, while many labor men had no love for Lewis, they did not like the use of government injunctions in labor disputes which they thought had been outlawed by the Norris-LaGuardia Act years before.

Old Senator Norris himself, who was proud of his part in that law prohibiting the use of court injunctions against strikers, did not think it gave labor unlimited rights. Of Lewis' wartime strike, Norris in retirement wrote that nothing in the law "justified anyone in staying the hands of government in its glorious, noble attempts to save a civilized world from European dictatorship." Truman believed that such a limitation extended into the making of the peace.

No man, however, was more opposed than he to the punitive restrictions put into the Taft-Hartley Act. Undoubtedly his requests for legislation to help him deal with such situations as faced him in 1946 contributed to the development of the labor legislation which followed. His fighting mood at the time of the rail strike seemed to suggest a repressive spirit. He helped dramatize the recklessness of Whitney and the arrogance of Lewis which were made by the enemies of labor to seem typical of labor as a whole. But the Taft-Hartley Act which emerged from the Eightieth Congress distorted his purposes and met his stern rejection. Students of the labor movement have regarded this act as the most extensive piece of legislation dealing exclusively with labor-management relations ever passed by any Congress. It was conceived in the same spirit of slapping labor down after war as that which William Allen White said dictated the financial policies of the Federal Reserve in the first years of the Harding Administration. In that case it hit not labor but many farmers and some haberdashers. In the Taft-Hartley case it did not hit labor as hard as it did the Republican Party.

When Truman vetoed it as "a shocking piece of legislation" which was "bad for labor, bad for management and bad for the country," Senator Taft said that his message closely followed a memorandum prepared by Lee Pressman, counsel of the CIO. Though Pressman later supported Wallace, Taft was right to the extent that Truman and organized labor were seeing eye to eye again so far as this particular piece of legislation was concerned. Truman took that position although less than a third of the Senators and less than a fifth of the Representatives had opposed the bill which was sent to him. He must have anticipated that his veto would be quickly overridden. It was overridden by more votes in both the Senate and House than it had received when it was originally passed. If Truman acted, not as labor's old friend, but as a new presidential politician, his judgment of the mood of the country differed from that of an overwhelming majority of the members of both houses of Congress. When he received the bill a majority of the members of his own party in both houses had voted for it. Also, a majority of the members of his party in the two houses voted to override his veto. He seemed very lonely politically in the veto action which he believed to be right. He was clearly the old friend of labor and not its angry enemy. And he was a lonely man as such.

His reconciliation with Whitney did not come quickly. Truman's memory about it fits into the story of the reconciliation with his many old friends in the labor movement. About a year after the rail strike, Truman sent Steelman to tell Whitney that he thought he was right about some labor question which had come up.

"But tell the so-and-so," he told Steelman, "that I don't want to make up with him."

Truman accompanied such hard talk with a smile. Apparently Whitney had been waiting for such a message.

"Later," Truman said, "when the Eisenhower for President

thing got going Whitney called John and asked to come in to see me."

Whitney came to the White House on January 23, 1948, three days before General Eisenhower issued a statement that he could not accept the presidential nomination "even under the remote circumstances that it were tendered to me." As he came out, the old brakeman, who was nearly seventy-five, told the reporters that his organization's 220,000 members would support Truman for re-election.

In the President's office he had said to Truman, "Mr. President, I'm a third generation Irishman who's part Scotch and you know they are kind of hot-headed sometimes."

"I'm made up on the same plan," Truman said.

It pleased Truman after Whitney's death in 1949 to recall Whitney's visit.

"He was my friend when he died," he said.

There was never any reconciliation with Lewis.

"I never had anything to do with John L. Lewis until the wartime coal strike," Truman said. He was referring to the time when the Truman Committee ineffectually sought to be useful in that strike in 1943. "Next in the 1945 coal strike, I sent for him and suggested that he settle. He wouldn't and we took the mines over. Finally we got them together with the best contract the miners ever had. He broke it just before the election of 1946. I've never let him into the White House since."

CHAPTER XXII

Civil Rights and Civil Liberties

"THE TOP DOG in a world which is over half colored ought to clean his own house."

If the metaphors were confused Truman's meaning in the American language was very clear. He said it with determined earnestness. It was a matter about which he felt very strongly and a matter in which he had been much misunderstood. The world aspects of the situation in a cold war with the Communists, who everywhere make propaganda of any mistreatment of Negroes in the United States, have been impressed upon him in the Presidency. But his feeling for the rights of people regardless of their color is old and fixed in his heart and mind.

Yet it seemed new. Indeed, some of the anger in his own party in the South was the feeling that presidential politics quickly built his great interest in the colored people—and particularly those who vote in the concentrations of Harlem, Chicago and Philadelphia. Mississippi politicians, who turned furiously Dixiecrat in 1948, remembered that their delegation at Chicago in 1944 tried to vote out of turn to switch its twenty votes to Truman. Louisiana and Arkansas cast solid votes for Truman against Wallace on the first ballot that year. Then the man in the White House came out with this civil rights business. It seemed both hypocritical neo-abolitionism and political betrayal.

It has been difficult even for some less emotional men to reconcile Truman's concern for human liberties with his tolerance of the roughneck invasion of civic liberties by the Pendergast machine in Kansas City elections. That may not be consistent but it can be understood. America did not relinquish its love of liberty in the years in which so much of it clung tenaciously to slavery. Indeed, the insistent devotion to American liberties was nowhere greater than in the South. On the Middle Border,

John Brown committed cold-blooded murder for human freedom. And those Missourians, who defended the Constitution from such fanatics by force and arms and numbers, packed the Legislature of Kansas. Liberty in America has been steadily attended by both lawlessness and idealism, hypocrisy and hope. It was of the Missouri-Kansas country that Lincoln was speaking when he said:

> As a nation we began by declaring that "all men are created equal." We now practically read it "all men are created equal except negroes." When the Know-nothings get control, it will read "all men are created equal, except negroes and foreigners and Catholics." When it comes to this, I shall prefer emigrating to some country where they make no pretense of loving liberty,—to Russia, for instance, where despotism can be taken pure, and without the base alloy of hypocrisy.

In Russia in Truman's time the hypocrisy had risen with the new tyranny. But some American conflict between faith and act remained. Indeed, sometimes in contemplation of Russian tyranny there seemed almost the suggestion that the United States in defense should dispense with liberties. That idea had risen while Woodrow Wilson was sick after World War I. There had been then what his Assistant Secretary of Labor called a "deportations delirium." It had returned sharpened by a greater reality of fear under Truman. It echoed the old cry against the Jacobins after the French Revolution. But in Truman's time the liberties which were sometimes disregarded made the only basis of the good choice which America offered to mankind.

Free men understand roughneck and even rough boss politics. There remained in free men's minds always and increasingly, however, the less formal feeling about liberty than is stated in the Bill of Rights that individuals are not to be kicked around by cops, Congressmen or anybody else. It was as native in Missouri as Truman or the trees. Truman built on it from books and talks with men like Justice Brandeis. But it was a faith long before he insisted that men who appeared before his Truman Committee be treated with fairness and consideration and before he emphasized in his civil rights message that even Negroes in America, and everywhere in America, be treated with decent consideration. In neither case was he a radical but a conservative insisting on the preservations of the freedoms which

America emphasized as the basic superiority of its democratic doctrine in the cold conflict of the modern world.

There has been no presidential change in Truman. If delegates from Mississippi, Arkansas, Louisiana misunderstood their man, they had not informed themselves about him. Indeed, it was at a Democratic National Convention, in 1940, before anyone thought of him as a President and when Missouri was not sure about him as a Senator that one of his first recorded declarations on civil rights came. He and Barkley and Minton and Guffey went out on a hot July night before that convention and spoke to an audience of Negroes which crowded the Eighth Regiment Armory in Chicago. There Truman laid down his views. Any Mississippians who were not in that hall could have read his speech when it was reprinted in the *Congressional Record* shortly afterwards. It did not seem radical then. It represents his views now.

"I wish to make it clear," he said, "that I am not appealing for social equality of the Negro. The Negro himself knows better than that, and the highest type of Negro leaders say quite frankly they prefer the society of their own people. Negroes want justice, not social relations."

Then he emphasized his feeling that the civil rights of Negroes are an essential part of the civil liberties of Americans: "I wish merely to sound a note of warning. Numberless antagonisms and indignities heaped upon any race will eventually try human patience to the limit and a crisis will develop. We all know that the Negro is here to stay and in no way can be removed from our political and economic life, and we should recognize his inalienable rights as specified in our Constitution. Can any man claim protection of our laws if he denies that protection to others?"

That was a public speech. It was a significant speech, too, as it pointed out the indivisible quality of freedom. The civil rights of Negroes, he felt then and afterwards, were essential to the civil liberties of all Americans. It was a problem which perhaps most of all had disturbed Southerners from Jefferson forward. Yet, forward from John Mason, of Virginia, who wrote the Bill of Rights, there had been almost a clearer understanding of the meaning of liberty in the South than anywhere else— even beside slavery until not slavery, but the fears around it, all but overwhelmed the native freedoms of white Southerners, too. Truman understood that as a man of Southern tradition. The warning which he spoke that night in Chicago had increasingly worried him as a man.

"We had no real trouble at home," he told me later of Negroes and civil rights. I did not take that as a statement of the perfection of Missouri. Some ardent civil rights advocates may be disturbed to learn that segregation in the schools is the old and standard practice in Independence. There had been there few dramatic instances of discrimination which disturbed him or the community. There was not a drop of abolitionist blood in his veins. On the Middle Border his people were always on the other side.

"But in the railroad cases," he told me, "we came upon the situation where in Louisiana and Arkansas and Mississippi in the old days coal shovelers were Negroes, but when the railroads turned to oil burners white men wanted the jobs and shot the colored firemen off the engines. Then (and this was later) there was the case of the boy that got his eye knocked out in South Carolina."

Cases like these troubled his conscience long before he became President. His interest was not radical. It never involved any proposal even approximating the mixing of the races. It does, however, involve the determinations of a man who takes very seriously both the Bill of Rights and his unparaded Christianity. He spoke his feelings again in 1940 to his Missouri home folks when he opened his campaign for renomination as Senator. At that Sedalia rally, with his mother, sitting on the platform before the courthouse, approving what he said, he gave his views on the racial question.

"I believe in the brotherhood of man," he said, "not merely the brotherhood of white men but the brotherhood of all men before law.

"I believe in the Constitution and the Declaration of Independence. In giving the Negroes the rights which are theirs we are only acting in accord with our own ideals of a true democracy.

"If any class or race can be permanently set apart from, or pushed down below, the rest in political and civil rights, so may any other class or race when it shall incur the displeasure of its more powerful associates, and we may say farewell to the principles on which we count our safety.

"In the years past, lynching and mob violence, lack of schools, and countless other unfair conditions hastened the progress of the Negro from the country to the city. In these centers the Negroes never had much chance in regard to work or anything else. By and large they went to work mainly as unskilled laborers and domestic servants.

"They have been forced to live in segregated slums, neglected by the authorities. Negroes have been preyed upon by all types of exploiters from the installment salesmen of clothing, pianos, and furniture to the vendors of vice.

"The majority of our Negro people find but cold comfort in shanties and tenements. Surely, as freemen, they are entitled to something better than this. . . . It is our duty to see that the Negroes in our locality have increased opportunity to exercise their privilege as freemen. . . ."

The story of Truman and civil rights, however, is presumed apparently to have begun abruptly on December 5, 1946—the day before Lewis brought the coal strike to an end after Golds-borough had fined him—when Truman appointed his Committee on Civil Rights. For some time before that Dave Niles had been working to assemble an impressive group of citizens as members of the committee. Undoubtedly there had been a certain feeling of leaderlessness among the Negroes since Roosevelt died. The committee as finally named was an impressive-seeming body of industrialists and clergymen, labor leaders and educators. Its chairman was C. E. Wilson, president of the General Electric Company, who had also served as vice-chairman of the War Production Board. Only two Negroes were on the committee. There were two women. Franklin Roosevelt, Jr., was a member. Altogether it was a distinguished group. It was not a packed jury though there were no representatives of those who later became Dixiecrats on it. The two Southerners, Dr. Frank Graham, president of the University of North Carolina, and Mrs. M. E. Tilly, of Atlanta, were known for their liberal views. They balked, however, at the extreme views of the others. On the committee they were only a minority. Clearly, however, in most respects their more moderate views were those which were accepted by Truman as his basic proposals for the Congress and the country.

Nearly ten months later the committee made its report on October 29, 1947. Such a report on the civil rights of minorities came at a significant time. Four days before it was made public, Eric Johnston, Republican, former president of the Chamber of Commerce of the United States, and then president of the Motion Picture Association of America, sent letters to leaders of both Houses of Congress, urging reform of the procedure of investigations by Congressional committees in order to safeguard the rights of individuals. The day after the civil rights report was made, Dr. Colston E. Warne, an Amherst College economist serving as an unpaid consultant to the Council of Economic Advisers, refused to sign the loyalty questionnaire sent to all Federal employes. He called President Truman's loyalty check order "an unconstitutional insult to Government employes."

Clearly for good or ill, America was back at the familiar business of internal loyalty suspicions which have recurred in American history since the Federalists passed the liberty-curbing Alien and Sedition laws in 1798 against which Jefferson and Madison drew up the famous Kentucky and Virginia Resolutions. However liberty-loving may have been the Amherst professor, he misunderstood his man in condemning Truman's loyalty checks. Truman, in the great care for fairness with which he conducted the hearings of the Truman Committee, indicated his understanding of the dangers to innocent people of careless publicity-seeking Congressional investigations. Also, as citizen, veteran and President, he understood the necessity that real loyalty checks be in the hands of serious and professional investigators. He understood that the protection of America required the safeguarding of liberties as well as the discovery of enemies and enemy agents.

At the very moment when the Civil Rights Committee was proposing new safeguards for Negro citizens, Truman and such a conservative as Johnston were with many other Americans disturbed about precedures which sometimes seemed not only careless of the rights of individuals but even irresponsible in dealing with the national security. In both the loyalty excitement and the civil rights matter, Truman showed that basic conservatism which is concerned with the preservation of the American promise. He refused to let publicity-seeking Congressmen use for publicity purposes the secret files of the F.B.I. and other government agencies except in one or two crucial cases.

(J. Edgar Hoover of the F.B.I. testified that such publicity would endanger the sources from which his agency systematically sought information.) At the same time he refused to join those members of his own Civil Rights Committee who wished, with excellent intentions, to undertake to eliminate prejudice by force of Federal law and Federal appropriations.

The majority report of the Civil Rights Committee not only proposed a better and stronger Civil Rights Division in the Department of Justice, the strengthening of some civil rights statutes, an anti-lynching law, a Fair Employment Practice Commission, the ending of Jim Crow practices in interstate commerce. It went further and proposed the use of Federal grants and Federal sanctions to force the states to put an end to all segregation in public services and even in private schools and colleges. It proposed that those Southern states which most needed the Federal grants in aid in education, housing, public health "or other public services and facilities generally" be denied them so long as they persisted in segregation. Led by Dr. Graham, who was later defeated as Senator by angry misunderstanding and distortion of his racial views, the minority wrote its protest in the report to the President:

> A minority of the Committee favors the elimination of segregation as an ultimate goal but opposes the imposition of a federal sanction. It believes that federal aid to the states for education, health, research and other public benefits should be granted provided that the states do not discriminate in the distribution of the funds. It dissents, however, from the majority's recommendation that the abolition of segregation be made a requirement, until the people of the states involved have themselves abolished the provisions in their state constitutions and laws which now require segregation. Some members are against the non-segregation requirement in educational grants on the ground that it represents federal control over education. They feel, moreover, that the best way ultimately to end segregation is to raise the educational level of the people in the states affected; and to inculcate both the teachings of religion regarding human brotherhood and the ideals of our democracy regarding freedom and equality as a more solid basis for genuine and lasting acceptance by the peoples of the states.

The publication of the report itself let loose a Southern storm. Intelligent Southerners were disturbed by what seemed to them to be reckless and punitive proposals. The report was of particular service to those Southerners who were Democrats by geography and not conviction and whose ideas of freedom were as limited as their faith in a nation founded upon the premise of the promotion of the general welfare. When, after three months of study, Truman, on February 2, sent a very much more conservative civil rights message to Congress, a wrathlike rebellion roared up from Mississippi where ten days later four thousand "all true white Jeffersonian Democrats" joined to oppose his proposals. There was scarcely any notice given by anybody to the fact that in his message Truman had disregarded all those proposals to end segregation by force which the Civil Rights Committee had proposed. He had gone further than that. In his recommendation that self-government be granted to the people of the District of Columbia he had urged that they be given opportunity themselves to "deal with the inequalities arising from segregation." That stated the Truman faith that that problem should be left to the people primarily concerned. He proposed in the racial field only the three basic and familiar items: elimination of the poll tax, an anti-lynching bill and a Fair Employment Practice Commission. All three had been repeatedly urged by Roosevelt before him.

Truman did not duck the storm. Actually, indeed, I have the impression that despite the shock of many Southerners and the almost obscene screaming of some others who became Dixiecrats, Truman was never as disturbed by the attack on his civil rights program as he was by some of the invasions of civil liberties in the Capitol itself. Some of them seemed to him not only to hurt Americans but to serve the Russians. He recognized some of the wilder and more irresponsible activities of publicity-seeking committees which pilloried innocent people as they pretended to be protecting America as a part of a recurrent American hysteria after all the wars which would have to—as he knew it would—scream itself out. Clearly, however, he did not mean to stand idly by. His own melodramatic-seeming request for $29,000,000 with which to check the loyalty of government employes represented, I believe, not merely determination to keep the government clean of any disloyal people but also to put the checking into the hand of officials more concerned about real security than scare headlines or political scarecrows. Also, I know that quietly he assigned a member of his staff to the job of collecting the record on past American efforts to invade American liberties and the declarations of the real patriots in repudiation of such invasion of other men's liberties.

Truman understands that the cold war is a resistance against the very methods which some head-long politicians would use in a pretended defense of a free America. He has been at the business of civil liberties, as well as civil rights, for a longer time than most Americans realize. Truman had not only known Brandeis but the spirit of the old man. In dissent in a famous wire-tapping case in prohibition days, Brandeis had said:

"Our government is the potent, the omnipresent teacher. For good or ill, it teaches the whole people by example. Crime is contagious. If the government becomes a lawbreaker, it breeds contempt for law; it invites every man to become a law unto himself; it invites anarchy. To declare that in the administration of the criminal law the end justifies the means—to declare that the government may commit crimes in order to secure the conviction of a private criminal—would bring terrible retribution."

Truman put his own statement into clearer, sharper language: "We are not going to turn the United States into a right-wing totalitarian country in order to deal with a left-wing totalitarian threat."

This was no new position with him. Four or five years after he met Brandeis, as the chairman of a sub-committee to which all wire-tapping bills were referred in the Senate, Truman killed them all. He did it quietly as his nature causes him to do most such things. But he killed them effectively. Once when Cordell Hull was Secretary of State, Truman wrote him asking whether a wire-tapping law would help or hurt the operations of that department, setting forth his own ideas that such a law would create a danger to the very security of this country and its allies. The letter brought an answer from Hull that he did not think such a law would be in America's interest.

Truman did not learn his devotion to liberty from Brandeis or Hull or any other person in Washington, however. He grew in it. I remember the man who had introduced him to Brandeis talking in realization of that.

"What I think is deep in him," said Max Lowenthal who had discovered Truman's integrity on the railroad committee, "is a sense of the atmosphere of the American tradition. That sort of atmosphere was pervasive and a part of men's feeling for America in the eighties and nineties and 1900's when Truman was growing up. I know it of the Middle West where my own childhood and youth were spent in that atmosphere. While there was much economic injustice at the time, there was a quality of freedom—an absence of any aspect whatever of the modern police state—that some of the younger generation today may not know of except in a limited way through their reading.

"Besides this feeling," Lowenthal went on, "Truman has undoubtedly acquired much from his reading—you know how night after night, while he was in the Senate, he was taking books home to read until midnight."

He read biographies, histories, reports and old American debates. Once when I was waiting to see Truman, I talked to a man in his big anteroom who remembered in the noise about both civil rights and civil liberties the old fighting in his time about freedom in America. Sometimes in the new fight Truman disturbed him, more often surprised him.

"I would give a lot to know how Truman came to denounce so immediately," he said, "the proposal made by Mundt and Nixon for a sedition law. And you remember his speech saying that the way to prevent the spread of communism in America was to provide economic justice. As one reads the debates back in 1918 and 1920, and in 1798 also, one sees in the remarks of the Truman of this period the same ideas as were spoken on the subject of the American political way of life in 1798 by Jefferson and Nicholas of Virginia, by Woodrow Wilson in condemning the anti-alien sedition features of an immigration bill.

"About a year after Lister Hill had publicly broken with Truman, I was having a chat with Lister. I asked him what he thought of Truman. Lister said that he was out of the soil of America."

And out of its record, too. The old liberal went on talking quietly in the big room.

"Nothing is more important," he said, "than the grasp of fundamental American principles shared by such liberals as Truman and old-time conservatives, too. I think we find it in Truman, not because he is for liberalism in economic matters, but because he senses the spirit of the American political system.

That has something to do with the way he ran his big investigations. It is an innate part of his personality to be fair and to know what is fair, and to exercise restraint when he possesses great power, particularly the power to investigate and detect, and the power to police."

Perhaps such talk is out of date. It sounded almost romantic in America in the midst of the cold war in 1950, even in the President's anteroom, perhaps especially there. Not even liberty seemed simple. There were prominent or at least noisy people who insisted that liberty had to be sacrificed if liberty was to be preserved. Sometimes there seemed more American anger than American faith around both civil liberties and civil rights. There seemed in the United States much more emphasis on the material things to guard than the faith America had had so long to give. The same day on which Truman sent his civil rights message to the Capitol, the Eightieth Congress passed for a third time, and this time with enough votes to override the President's veto, a $6,500,000,000 tax reduction bill. It was a lot of money even in a rich land. It would have certainly seemed like the full cash payment of the American dream not many generations before. It was going to be less easy to pass any civil rights bills or even maintain the old protections of civil liberties.

Later that month Truman went south and to sea on a rest trip to Key West, Puerto Rico, and the Virgin Islands. On St. Croix he rode with William Hastie, the American Negro Governor, past the shop in which young Alexander Hamilton had worked as clerk and bookkeeper before he went off to help make America. That night on the *Williamsburg* he studied the speech Senator Austin was to make next day before the Security Council on Palestine. For three days he rested in the sun at Key West while the South between him and Washington seethed and snorted in revolt. At the Washington Airport, coming home, he was met by Mrs. Truman and Margaret, and by Marshall and Forrestal, Harriman and Krug, Anderson and Clark. But the log of the journey noted that the presidential party "was jolted by the sub-freezing weather that greeted them in Washington." It was going to be colder still.

CHAPTER XXIII

The Everyday Man

TRUMAN MADE TWO speeches on the night of April 17, 1948, at the annual banquet of the American Society of Newspaper Editors, where he had only been expected to make one. The first speech that evening was almost a perfect example of the sort of official but uninspired address which obviously had been prepared for him and for a precise presidential purpose. He said in too many words which reflected none of his human personality that inflation was a grave danger to the economy of the United States and the world, and once again he urged a ten-point anti-inflation program. What he said was undoubtedly very important. It was a part of the most serious post-war adjustment problem. The problem itself had been dramatically disastrous to him when it was expressed before the 1946 election in a rich America's hunger for more meat regardless of price. There were neither meat nor juices nor votes in the anti-inflation speech which he gave the editors. Before he finished there was a perceptible movement among the molders of public opinion at the back tables from the banquet room to the bars. It was the fashion then to walk out on Truman. New Dealers, party bosses, young Roosevelts, and the incipient Dixiecrats had all announced their departure from Truman before that night.

There was polite applause when he finished. But he did not sit down. Instead he began an entirely different, extemporaneous, and off-the-record speech of his own, in his own vocabulary, out of his own humor and his own heart. He told the newspapermen about his difficult dealings with the Russians. He spoke of "Old Joe." He made the story of his problems seem one told in earnestness and almost intimacy with each man in the hall. He was suddenly a very interesting man of great candor who discussed the problems of American leadership with men as ᴗᴧᴅors. He spoke the language of them all out of traditions common to them all. When he finished there was long and loud applause. His friends were delighted. In a reception room after the speech, Truman was grinning, too. He liked the appreciation of persuasive leadership which he had received.

As the record of the press in the election which followed showed, he won few final converts that night. (In terms of their circulation that year the newspapers were eight to one for Dewey. This was not strange. Claude Bowers says that when Jackson ran in 1828 he was opposed "by two thirds of the newspapers, four fifths of the preachers, practically all of the manufacturers and seven eighths of the banking capital.") He made one important convert, however: himself. He knew as well as anybody in the hall what a tough, sales-resistant audience he had in the editors of the American press, which during the three past presidential elections had shown a steady and increasing preference for the Republican Party. As a sample group set up to test Truman, it could not have been tougher. But the occasion indicated that the native, natural Truman had a gift of speech which was all his own and full of unexpected power.

The "non-political," whistle-stop, do-nothing-Congress tour began forty-seven days later. It ended just a month before the divided, defeatist Democrats held their national convention in the City of Brotherly Love where the Declaration had been framed and the Constitution put together. The trip, as it was reported in the American press, sounded less like a presidential procession in a Republic than a barn-storming tour of a one-ring, even one-man, circus. The train itself was made to seem more like a branch line local than a presidential special. But despite a well-publicized mix-up resulting in a half-filled hall at Omaha, there were the crowds and the listening people and Truman talking over the rail on the back platform of his special like a farmer talking to neighbors over a fence. It was a good, though slightly comic-seeming, show.

It was not comic. Truman was deadly serious. The "non-political" pretenses of the tour did not prevent him from meeting politicians, some of them reluctant and some distinctly unfriendly, in the various cities. In California he "told off" James Roosevelt, two of whose brothers had already come out for Eisenhower, and who himself was even more noisily anti-Truman on the eve of the convention. Truman got Jimmie, who was then Democratic National Committeeman, into a corner.

"Here I am," Truman said, "trying to do everything I can to carry out your father's policies. You've got no business trying to pull the rug out from under me."

The Democratic politicians wanted a winner. Franklin Roosevelt had made them accustomed to one. And Truman did not remotely resemble one early that summer from the point of view of any politician or pollster. Only he noticed that the people seemed to be interested. He got on increasingly well with them at the stops. Yet, increasingly as the summer moved on toward July, he was in terms not of the people, but of the politicians, increasingly left alone. The left and the right slipped noisily away. Young Roosevelts and some older, very self-conscious Roosevelt friends publicly divested themselves of political faith in Truman. Increasingly, in terms of political counsel, he was left to Harry Truman himself. And that was Harry Truman of Independence, farmer, small business man, veteran, politician, local government official, Senator, the whole man and the man alone. He had to be President of the United States and candidate for President of the United States by himself.

Undoubtedly there had been great plans from the beginning of his Presidency for him to be something else. He was, of course, the heir of Roosevelt. But there were always men standing by, as Harry Hopkins on the day of Roosevelt's funeral had understood there would be, saying, "The *President* wouldn't do it that way." Probably no man ever tried more conscientiously than Truman to be a loyal heir. The simple fact was that he was not Roosevelt. But there were some men who stayed in Truman's Administration who in emotional ways felt that their own opinions were Roosevelt's legacy. Some of them did talk as Harry Hopkins had known they would.

Also, undoubtedly there were other, different men ready to give different color to his Administration. Some New Dealers perhaps dreamed up out of their own sadness the idea that somehow Truman had been imposed upon Roosevelt in 1944 as the architect of the liquidation of his New Deal. They named names. Undoubtedly, Pauley was no idealistic reformer. Allen was not a starry-eyed New Dealer. Hannegan was a devoted Missouri politician. There is even a story in Kansas City that Roberts of the Republican *Star* went to that convention in Chicago to help stop Wallace and put Truman in.

"After the nomination," a Kansas City newspaperman told me, "Roberts arranged the big Kansas City blow-out in Truman's honor. It was entirely an affair of the Republicans and anti-New-Deal Democrats. I wondered then if Truman wasn't somewhat shocked at the fawning and flattery showered on him by Roosevelt's deadliest enemies. They were so blatantly trying to play Harry for a chump."

Beside any such plutocratic collaborators, the Truman "cronies" to whom so much publicity had been given seemed innocent if not elegant in democracy's battle. Also, there were able and loyal conservatives among his friends, like John Snyder who had been one of the right-hand men of Jesse Jones. Truman himself listened to Snyder but was not, he thinks, much moved by his conservatism—a good deal too little, he sometimes gathered Snyder thought. He had also listened to Bob Hannegan. And Hannegan, not as idealist but as practical politician, believed in the necessity of New Deal directions. Around him, Leahy was a military conservative and Vinson was a practical New Dealer but not embittered as Byrnes was. Truman had listened to Ickes and, though sometimes uncomfortably, to Wallace. He had in his inheritance from Roosevelt a rainbow of opinion which stretched across the Washington sky from horizon to horizon. In terms of some of his counselors he could have followed Roosevelt in any direction he chose. Roosevelt had had to be Roosevelt among them. From the beginning Truman had to be Truman. The President's choice is always between personal leadership and confusion.

Truman himself believed that he made his own position clear —perhaps too quickly clear—with his message on September 6, 1945, after the Japanese surrender. Part of his purpose in that speech had been to let the big publishers, who had been praising him as Republicans had flattered him at Roy Roberts' party, know that they had not taken him into camp. The one unquestioned fact is that in trying to be true to a trust which he had inherited and to his own eagerness to do as good a job as he could for America, he had been badgered and harassed, tugged and pulled in the Presidency. For one or two men who hurried him into decisions, which he afterwards believed to be wrong, when he first came to the White House, he cherished long resentment. In general, however, he had made his own policy from the beginning. It was, based upon his Senate service and on his association with Roosevelt, a New Deal policy but grown in his own life and not inherited from one man. Indeed, he knew that the New Deal was not Roosevelt's invention but his inheritance, too, from the people and traditions, purposes and needs of America.

In 1948, however, his very political loneliness made his policies and his political purposes more clearly than ever his own. He was as alone as any President, who was to be successfully renominated and re-elected by his party, had ever been when the divided and defeatist Democrats in July moved on Philadelphia. Also, in a world in which many of them were saying Truman did not seem adequate in leadership, there was hardly even any suggestion that any other Democrat filled the requirements. Indeed, the extreme left and the extreme right among the delegates at Philadelphia looked outside the Democratic Party to try to get a candidate in General Dwight Eisenhower whose views on all subjects were as unknown by the right as by the left. (Later the people did not think the man produced by the Republicans was an adequate substitute either.) If Truman was not adequate the fault, apparently, was not his stature but America's.

Despite the noise made by reporters and politicians, there was never any question about his nomination. There was no serious trouble about the selection of a running mate, though Justice William O. Douglas, who had been coupled with his name in Roosevelt's letter in 1944, declined Truman's personal request that he run with him. He got an excellent substitute in Alben Barkley, who has probably been the most popular Vice-President in our times. By the time the Democrats began to gather, the convention situation was well in hand, even if it was turned into tumult over a new civil rights and states' rights row while Truman waited in a guarded room of the big hall to make his speech accepting the nomination. His task then was tougher than most of the tired delegates suspected. He had found anew, that spring, his faith in his own ability to speak to the people. He had come alone to confidence in his policies which he believed were the people's policies, too. But that night in the convention he had a more difficult job to do.

The queer quality of the American combination of dedication and circus in the most important occasions of its democracy was clearly shown that hot night in Philadelphia. Destiny is generally worked out by sweating men. The convention seemed to have no resemblance to the debate 172 years before in the same Philadelphia when Jefferson sensed the aspirations of ordinary men and embodied them in a Declaration to mankind. The occasions are not only far separate in the American years. The revolutionaries who composed the Continental Congress seem elegantly different from the crumpled delegates who sat waiting for Harry in the convention hall in 1948. It must have been hot in Philadelphia in 1776. There could have been smoky rooms. The Declaration of Independence was a political platform, too. Actually, Philadelphia in 1776 was vastly more remote from the people than the convention in 1948, when the listening millions whose votes had to be secured made what happened there almost an American community meeting. Also, though it may seem to unduly dignify the sweaty delegates and Truman, too, in the first National Democratic Convention after Roosevelt died, after World War II, and after the beginning of the cold war, decision was significant as it was significant in 1776. That convention began the campaign in which it was made very clear to the world that America was not turning away from the expansive spirit for the happiness of all the people expressed in that Declaration.

Above the small room where Truman waited, the convention was in Speaker Sam Rayburn's tough Texas hands. They were needed. No Democrat had been more loyal in party government in the United States under difficult circumstances to both Roosevelt and Truman. He banged his gavel on the lectern as if it were an anvil. The convention was tired and hot, angry and uncomfortable. Also, that was the time when some of the female dignitaries of the Democratic Party undertook to be prettily dramatic. They brought an ornate floral offering to the platform and from it turned loose bewildered pigeons which flew out over the speakers and the delegates. Perhaps they were supposed to be doves of peace. They flew about desperately and blindly. One went perilously close to Rayburn's bald head and he warded it off with his free hand. Another flew at full speed against a balcony and dropped to the floor as if it had been shot.

"A dead pigeon," said an Irish delegate from New York. "Some damn newspaperman will use that as the symbol of this convention."

It was long after midnight when word went down that the time had come for Harry Truman to come up and accept the nomination which he had won 947½ to 263 from Senator Richard Russell, of Georgia, the last-minute choice of the last-ditch South. The cheers were louder than the grumblings when he came up to the rostrum in an almost dazzling white suit to speak to his rumpled and sweaty fellow Democrats. The actual job he had to do was not to accept the nomination. He had that night the business of recreating a Democratic Party which stretched in the weary fragments of its angry factions before him. Alben Barkley and others had done a good job of stating the party's past and trying to stir its enthusiasm for the future. Rayburn had his gavel in his hand. But despite the noise of welcome there were not many who thought that Truman could put the raveling remains of Roosevelt's Humpty-Dumpty party together again.

FDR, it was clearer than ever that night, had left Truman an inheritance both of greatness and of trouble, like that Lincoln had left Johnson. The summer in which Truman was called to the rostrum in Philadelphia, Republican Senator Homer Ferguson, of Michigan, had used the sharp word "impeachment" on the floor of the Senate about Truman, too. In the convention Truman faced his own party which, if it had had any choice except Truman or repudiation of its own record, might have been ready to reject him. He spoke to the delegates, but very clearly also he spoke to the Democrats and to the country. There was no humble Harry Truman on that rostrum. Whatever else he may have been he was a fighting man. It is a Truman trait to be more humbly troubled in victory than disturbed before the promise of defeat. He believed as Roosevelt believed that the people out there at the radio sets were with him.

What Truman undertook to do was not merely to put himself before the delegates who had nominated him but before the people who must elect him. He felt instinctively as a politician

from Missouri and personally as a man who had just talked to
them on a continental tour that the people were out there listening and waiting, eager for clear declaration in the fulfillment of
their purposes, and also that somehow they trusted him as a
man. He was not Roosevelt. He did not appear to possess great,
almost paternal-seeming leadership. Perhaps the people sensed
more fellowship than leadership in him. He was not the average
man but step by step he had come up the average man's way. He
knew that the business of leadership is to give the people not
merely a free choice but an unconfused choice. That is always
the basic problem in democracy.

"Great men go, but the average man is immortal," Gerald
Johnson, the critic and historian, said of Roosevelt's death.

Sam Rayburn banged his gavel. And Truman looking almost
starch white under the lights began to speak. It was a fighting
speech. Actually there was not much that was new in the recital
of his program and the opposition to it of the Eightieth Congress. But it was the first speech made by Truman as the leader
not by inheritance but by choice of the political party of Jefferson, Jackson, the New Freedom and the New Deal. What he
stated in such first speaking was clearly his own message made
out of his purposes for his country.

Essentially what he stated in terms of the two American
political parties was the issue not merely of plans for people in
America but the pattern of democracy which America, at a time
when it felt somehow besieged, would present to the world.
What he faced, what the Democratic Party faced, what the people faced, he knew as one of them, was not merely division but
confusion. He meant to make it perfectly plain that his program
was the straight unconfused program of a President meaning
to use the full power of government for the general welfare of
the people and all the people. But he knew also that no such
issue would be clear unless he made it clear. That was the tac-
tical problem. He dealt with it as a student and a master of
maneuver.

The Republican Party in that same hall three weeks before
had not only nominated Thomas E. Dewey, it had also adopted
along with Dewey a platform almost paralleling the New Deal
achievement. Dewey had promised in 1944 that he and his party
would do the same things for people only they would do them

better. Perhaps that was not cynicism. Perhaps it was not, as even some Republicans called it, a "me-too" policy. It was, Truman thought and Roosevelt before him, a clear unwillingness to face the issues upon which modern men differed in the United States. It paralleled the process by which more than a hundred years before, when Truman's people had been moving to Missouri, the American conservatives had won. Then they had adopted the vocabulary of frontier democracy to halt that democratic movement itself. In that way they elected the first conservative since John Adams had been elected in 1796. Log cabins and hard cider, Tippecanoe and Tyler, too, had seemed to end the Jacksonian revolution and terminate the forty years of control in increasing democratic faith from Jefferson's election in 1801.

In 1940, 1944 and 1948, it was proposed to end the New Deal by a similar process. Truman's achievement was that on that night he stopped at its confident moment the return of Old Guard government by such methods at a time when an appealing democratic alternative to communism was essential to the masses of the ordinary average free men in the world. Truman's phrase is the good, traditional American "everyday man."

It may be, as history student and artillery officer Truman likes to say, that the science or art of maneuver has not changed from Alexander to Eisenhower. There was, perhaps, a more blunt approach to political maneuver in Truman than in Roosevelt, as there was in Jackson after Jefferson. In 1948 it was required. He used the constitutional machinery to give the people an opportunity to escape the confusion made by the New Deal promising of those whose purpose was to destroy it. He made his strategy sharp and clear.

"There is a long list of these promises in the Republican platform," he said. "If it weren't so late I would tell you about them. I have discussed a number of these failures of the Republican Eightieth Congress. Every one of them is important. Two of them are of major concern to nearly every American family. They failed to do anything about high prices, they failed to do anything about housing.

"My duty as President requires that I use every means within my power to get the laws the people need on matters of such importance and urgency."

He paused and then he ran his words together as if there were hyphens between them all.

"I am, therefore, calling this Congress back into session July twenty-sixth."

He grinned beyond the surprise and the cheers.

"On the twenty-sixth of July, which out in Missouri we call 'Turnip Day,' I am going to call Congress back and ask them to pass laws to halt rising prices, to meet the housing crisis—which they are saying they are for in their platform.

"At the same time, I shall ask them to act upon other vitally needed measures, such as aid to education, which they say they are for; a national health program; civil rights legislation, which they say they are for; an increase in the minimum wage, which I doubt very much they are for; extension of the social security coverage and increased benefits, which they say they are for; funds for projects needed in our program to provide public power and cheap electricity. By indirection this Eightieth Congress has tried to sabotage the power policies the United States has pursued for fourteen years. That power lobby is as bad as the real estate lobby which is sitting on the housing bill.

"I shall ask for adequate and decent laws for displaced persons in place of this anti-Semitic, anti-Catholic law which this Eightieth Congress passed.

"Now, my friends, if there is any reality behind that Republican platform, we ought to get some action from a short session of the Eightieth Congress. They can do this job in fifteen days, if they want to do it. They will still have time to go out and run for office."

It was crude politics, the Republicans said. Of course, it was politics and effective politics, tough and native. It did, however, in a fashion as colloquial as "Turnip Day" draw the issue between the President and the Republican Congress, between the New Deal and its opponents, which left no doubt where Truman stood and was designed to leave no doubt about the Republican position. The issue of the meaning of democracy was drawn not only in the world but clearly at home.

Truman took his final text in that convention speech from Roosevelt's words in 1932: "This is more than a political call to arms. Give me your help, not to win votes alone, but to win in this new crusade to keep America secure and safe for its own people." The meaning of words like "secure and safe" had altered and sharpened. Truman, whatever had been the hopes of any who put him into office, had taken his stand firmly on the New Deal not merely as a pattern for America, but also as the measure of possibilities of government by free men everywhere.

Quickly after Truman finished at 2:20 in the morning, the Democrats poured into the night. If there was no confidence of victory among them there was consciousness of a fight. Truman's waiting train hurried him back to Washington. His special session of the Eightieth Congress accomplished, as he had in effect predicted, practically nothing. It sat less than the fifteen days he had suggested. It was, he said, at its conclusion the do-nothing session of a do-nothing Congress. He was content. He began his preparations for a campaign he had already patterned by taking one of the quietest cruises he had ever made while President. The *Williamsburg* moved by easy stages, down the Potomac, up the Chesapeake, through the Chesapeake and Delaware Canal, out to sea and back to Chesapeake Bay again. The President went to the movies shown on the yacht, which was noted in the log as unusual. At sea off York Spit, Virginia, he watched "a small yellow and black bird" which hovered over the fantail and then disappeared. Time was not pressing him. The *Williamsburg* moved in the sun and the fog around the neck of land which holds Delaware and the Eastern Shores of Maryland and Virginia. It was an easy nine-day cruise to no where. And that was the general impression of where he was going. Yet he seemed as free in spirit as the Sunday crowds of picnickers who lined the Potomac shores, on August twenty-ninth, when he came home to start his circling of America. He had hardly begun his campaign before Elmo Roper, the public opinion expert, announced that it was so clear that Dewey would be elected that any further polls would be scarcely worth attention.

Speeded, magnified, multiplied and clearly, vigorously political, the journeys he took that late summer and fall duplicated the shorter, testing, "non-political" journey he had made in June. It took him more than thirty thousand miles to make 351 speeches to more than twelve million people. But the lines had been drawn. The trip was a continental castigation of that "do-nothing, good-for-nothing, worst Eightieth Congress." Not even that phrase, a "do-nothing Congress," was new though he made it the drumbeat of his campaign. His fellow Missourian, Champ Clark, had used the phrase in his autobiography with regard to the Fifty-fourth Congress which sat in the two years before Bryan frightened the conservative East at the head of Southern and Western revolt in 1896. Truman's speeches were made to seem by sophisticated reporters as out-of-date as warmed-over Bryanism. Some of the phrases he used—"Wall Street," "the special interests"—did seem dated. As a matter of fact, all of them were. They dated back beyond Bryan, to the uncouth language of the Jacksonians, and even to the words used in the rout of the Federalists by Jefferson's men. They represented the ancient American understanding that there is and always has been a contest in America between those who want government by and for the benefit of the few and those who conceive of government in terms of Lincoln's inclusive prepositions. They were phrases worn and battered in a long fight.

In the history of American politics, too, he and his train were given familiarly condescending description. His whole campaign was given a sort of rube reputation by a self-consciously streamlined press. His crowds were not exactly the mobocracy of Jackson's. A shrewder Toryism did not fall into Hamilton's error of describing the people as a great beast. It was confidently assumed, indeed, that the Truman crowds were not Truman's followers but the curious, looking at a President and following the spectacle of a really very nice man on a spectacular flight not to world leadership but into oblivion. Truman in that campaign was not even accorded respectful enmity. The pattern of his detractors was almost that of affectionate contempt.

The people came to listen. Increasingly the Democratic candidates came aboard. There was, however, a remarkable absence of Democratic statesmen guiding his campaign. The elder counselors had departed. The break between Truman and Bernard Baruch was not typical but it was significant. Truman was undoubtedly sensitive about departures when Baruch declined to serve as a member of a money-raising committee. Even under Roosevelt, Baruch had stayed out of the publicity of politics, preferring appearances on his "economic dunghill" to the "political cockpit." Truman mistook, I think, an old preference for a new desertion and wrote a sharp letter to the effect that politics was not a one-way street. The quick pride of the old counselor met the pride, too, of a beset President. Also, as often happens in politics, there were people to give each of them aid and comfort in their irritation.

No misunderstanding or sensitiveness was involved in the case of Jesse Jones. He began to put Dewey editorials in his newspaper in Texas, even before Truman asked him to help. Also, after he had tried to beat Truman for President, and had failed, he telephoned in as an old Truman friend. The late call stirred no affectionate Truman response. Even some members of Truman's own Cabinet were too preoccupied with their official duties to be noticeably active in the political campaign. The Democratic Party and the democratic people around the train and around the country came together behind Truman long before even his party leaders began to come together at the top.

Also, in hardly any other campaign was there more contemptuous description of the staff which did stay with him. Newspapermen who moved back and forth between the trains of Dewey and Truman wrote stories of the glittering efficiency with which Dewey was surrounded in comparison with the ineptitude of Truman's men. Actually, one of the things that campaign showed was that Truman was not surrounded merely by cronies sharing with him the pleasures of the palace. None of them had come out of the advertising agencies or from the staffs of the "mass circulation" magazines. They had come diverse ways into his service. One of the most active directors of the President's personal campaign was his old secretary, Bill Boyle. He deserved his promotion later to the Democratic National Chairmanship. Clifford, his counsel, had arrived almost by accident so far as Truman is concerned, as an Assistant Naval Aide. ("I was a stinking lieutenant," Clifford recalled in his more eminent days.) He was industrious. He was intelligent. His influence as an assistant to Truman was always toward the traditional, liberal Democratic position. Truman's secretary, Matt Connelly, was able, shrewd and devoted. He combined the affability of an Irish politician with training in government both in the Capitol and in Federal agencies before Truman found him as a member of the staff of his Truman Committee. Charles Ross, his Press Secretary, came to him with the endorsement of the entire Washington press corps. He dealt with a press corps which had already made up its mind. In many ways he had the toughest job on the train.

Young George Elsey, who had begun as a Naval officer in the Map Room under Roosevelt, did excellent work in speech preparation. William D. Hassett, whom Truman had inherited from Roosevelt as his able Correspondence Secretary, remained on duty in Washington. Also in Washington, and as the central man in the collecting, preparation and design of the Truman speeches, was Charles J. Murphy, whom Truman later made Clifford's successor as Special Counsel. Truman had found him in the office of the legislative counsel at the Capitol.

Many others helped in the preparation of some speeches, including Sam Rosenman who had been FDR's most consistent draftsman. On the long trips, the only outsiders were William Bray, who had learned his politics as assistant to Jim Farley, and myself. No man on the train, except the President, had more skill in dealing with the diverse politicians of America than Bray. He did a little-known but efficient job in that campaign.

The train did have advance agents like a circus—and circus advance agents may rejoice that they have easier jobs. Under Secretary of the Interior Oscar Chapman (now Secretary) took leave without pay from his job to ride far ahead of the presidential special, making arrangements and smoothing the often difficult way. The same job in some other sections was done by Donald Dawson, who found his way to the Truman staff as one of the most competent personnel men in the government service. He was—and is—one of Truman's Administrative Assistants. Probably no men on the train were more devoted to the President politically and personally than the members of the Secret Service detail who are not supposed to be in politics at all. Indeed, they were very interested when their big boss in Washington, James J. Maloney, decided that he would take his place with the Dewey detail on election night.

The Truman train was not a Toonerville trolley. It did make the milk stops. It was in effect a one-man train, but it had been put together for political competence by a man who understood politics at least competently. He understood before he started where he expected to arrive. Not once, locked up in the confidence of a compartment on that train, did he express a doubt to any one of his confidential staff as to his destination. He occasionally had some sharp things to say to wavering Democrats. Once or twice he frightened his own staff (as when he spoke to a group of Jewish leaders in New York) by the forthrightness of his statements. The remarkable thing about both that rolling train and the man seemed to me his ability to take his campaign easily and confidently. When the going was toughest and the rolling over the roadbeds was roughest, he could make a "give 'em hell, Harry" speech at one whistle stop and then go sound asleep before he was roused to make another, thirty minutes later. He spoke at midnight and at dawn. Strain seemed only to make him calmer and more firm.

The Vinson incident was the final perfect example, I think, of both his judgment as President and his unwillingness to be pushed as candidate. If he was confident of his re-election, those around him, even after they were encouraged by the crowds, were not. The Vinson plan was proposed as a dramatic gesture if not a desperate one. It originated with two brilliant and energetic men, David Noyes and Albert Z. Carr, who had been brought in to work in Washington on speeches. They were disturbed about the people's fear of war. They were disturbed, as were others, by suggestions which seemed to emanate from the State Department itself that Truman had really very little to do with the foreign policy of the United States. The Republicans were very carefully trying to prove that the bi-partisan foreign policy had two halves, the Republicans and the State Department, and that Truman did not enter into the fractions.

Noyes and Carr had written a speech in which Truman was to announce on a national radio hook-up that he was sending Vinson to Moscow to make a last effort to find some common ground with the Russians. It was an idea which they believed would make good sense as well as good politics. Vinson had agreed that if it seemed the wise thing to do he would accept the assignment. Arrangements had gone further than the tentative Vinson agreement. On a Monday morning in October, Ross was instructed to see about arrangements for such a non-political broadcast. He went out of the room to make those arrangements at almost the same time that Truman went down to the communications room in the White House to discuss the idea with Marshall. Unfortunately, Ross felt that he had to explain to the radio people in confidence what it was all about at almost the same moment that Truman was agreeing with Marshall that he would not do it. Truman came back and firmly vetoed the whole proposal. The story of the abandoned plan appeared in the press on October 8, while Truman was campaigning in the rain in upstate New York.

Rain and shine, night and day, he went on. He used the same words worn so long in American conflict and in the world conflict of people, too. He met the same and greater crowds, and the insistence on the certainty of his defeat seemed to grow as the crowds around his train, on the streets, in the great halls grew, too. Even the perceptible affection for him and the response of the people to their old worn political words seemed irrelevant. Once during the long riding, Richard H. Rovere, of *The New Yorker*, after making one of the big laps of the great journey, wrote that the people of the United States were ready to give Harry Truman anything in the world except the Presidency of the United States.

Truman was sure that they would give him that, too. He believed that the free people given an unconfused choice would make what he believed to be the right choice, not merely for himself but for the old native revolution for people. He believed he had helped them to that choice in a country which sometimes seemed scarcely less confused, harassed and badgered in its thinking and its choices than he had sometimes seemed.

It had been, even before victory, a wonderful year. It had freed him from any last acceptance of the old criticism that he lacked the gift of speech to people. In San Antonio one night in that campaign, he spoke of people and peace and his purposes with an eloquence close to presidential poetry. He also spoke day after day with a slap-bang, colloquial, understandable vigor. He was no longer the trustee of a political estate inherited from Roosevelt but, with Roosevelt, one of the keepers of an American faith older than the Republic and as always new as the needs of man.

He was alone in victory. He went to bed and soundly to sleep in a hide-out hotel in Excelsior Springs, Missouri, before the decisive returns began to come in. He was tired. The Secret Service men, grinning and excited themselves, woke him when the victory began pouring in in the early morning, and he went to the penthouse of the Muehlebach Hotel where he had played

Mozart and Chopin while he waited in 1944 for his and Roosevelt's election.

Now he and the people themselves together had done it. No politicians nor powers could claim to share substantially the victory with them. He had made contact as one of them with his countrymen. They still had together a Declaration for mankind. He and they understood that they still had together the tasks of a revolution in freedom and abundance. It provided the dynamic way forward still for the average, the common, the "everyday man" in America and in the cause of freedom everywhere.

CHAPTER XXIV

Men of Independence

THE ROAD OF revolution at midcentury still lay down the American way. No other radicals had yet proposed any such startling determinations for men on earth as those old plotters at Philadelphia in 1776, who came up with the Declaration that men in equality were not only capable of governing themselves but that the only purposes of government were protecting them in their basic individual rights including their individual and common quest for happiness.

The revolution remains. It has met counter-revolution before. Indeed, the whole history of America has been the effort of some to prevent the fulfillment not of any hazy American Dream but of the emphatic American promises made when the revolutionaries at Philadelphia realized that the security of independence required the good opinions of mankind. The Communist counter-revolution is only a more direct and brutal attempt to destroy the liberties and the dignity proposed for all men so long ago. Reaction does not become radicalism because it wears red.

The American Revolution is not spent. Indeed, it is still fighting its way toward fulfillment. Generally, though not always, that fight has been made in the Democratic Party. And its aim has been always that government which served most men best, even if Mr. Jefferson when he began it said something to the effect that the government was best which governed least. Yet, even Mr. Jefferson, in a doubtful exercise of great governmental power, he thought, bought Louisiana which happened to contain Missouri. Jackson came out of the turbulent demanding West to talk anti-statism while making the central government stronger than ever before and for the purposes of the great masses of the people. When the Democratic Party split in its hard and angry confusion over liberty, Mr. Lincoln built the Federal and the presidential power to serve freedom with greater strength. That was at a time when some said that it was infringement of a man's liberty not to be able to keep another man as slave. (That was a counter-revolution, too.)

The counter-revolutionists succeeded in operating under the false face of Lincoln's human purposes after he died. It was thirty years before they were even frightened in reaction. William Jennings Bryan accomplished that. In a real sense, too, he and the protest which had been behind him aroused the indignation which came through Theodore Roosevelt briefly into the Republican Party. TR and Woodrow Wilson joined in creative debate about a growing and changing America in which the hopes of "everyday men" seemed lost in American bigness in business and industry. Old TR believed in bigness. He would have permitted bigness under control. Wilson, along with Justice Brandeis, opposed bigness as such. Franklin Roosevelt borrowed from the philosophies of both. Harry Truman was the man listening to that debate and inheriting it, too. The certain thing clear to him and to the people, by his time, was that the purpose of government, however big in a land of forces however powerful, was the guarding of the people in their lives, liberties and pursuit of happiness. Wars have slowed it and depressions have hurried it forward. But, in 1950, the American Revolution was back on its track. It provided the most revolutionary program for people in the world.

Its strength was a surprise not only in the United States but everywhere else. At midcentury, Truman himself was surprising no longer. The old differences about him emerged. There were many once again who questioned his capacity for American leadership at a time when nobody doubted the proportions of the tasks of his leadership in America and on the earth. President Harry S. Truman had ordered the scientists to proceed with their development of the hydrogen bomb. But Harry Truman was only the man of Independence who had come up through politics, which somehow seemed very different from rising through democracy. Against the dimensions of his problems and his countrymen's fears, he seemed to many quite too evidently that average man again about whom so much was said when he moved into the White House. That was not a strange idea in

American history. Lincoln told that in a dream someone said of him, "He is a very common-looking man." And Lincoln's famous reply was, "Friend, the Lord prefers common-looking people. That is the reason he made so many of them."

In 1950, that did not seem a particularly encouraging tale. It was easy to smile over Lincoln's depreciation of himself. Truman was not Lincoln, but the greater counter-revolutionary question was whether the American—that average American in the White House or elsewhere—was the man he had been when an ex-Congressman named Lincoln entered into the average at midcentury before. And that lifted a greater question still. It was not whether Harry Truman provided adequate leadership but whether the old revolutionary faith in the capacity of ordinary men to govern themselves still made sense in the modern world. In such a testing it is good fortune if Truman did seem the symbol of the common, ordinary, "everyday man" in the leadership of democracy in the divided world. Such a symbol was never so much needed before.

He suffices. He is not overwhelmed.

"County Judge, Chairman of a Committee, President of the United States," he said. "They are all the same kind of jobs. It is the business of dealing with people."

He has not lost his county-size or his state-size understanding of people wherever they are, however. He has not lost his faith, shared with other average Americans wherever they are, that in terms of its meaning to the earth America must be a New World still and forever.

That is not a small idea. Diplomats as world statesmen, Roosevelt used to say and grin and bear it, were often lost at home. Once, indeed, before he had thought of a Missourian as Vice-President, Roosevelt said in joke but not quite joke either, that every ambassador ought to be required at intervals to come home and serve in some such job as Collector of Internal Revenue at St. Louis. (By coincidence, Bob Hannegan held that job then.) What Roosevelt understood and Truman, too, is that not even with jet planes or atomic motive power will the diameters of the earth ever grow so short that the central problem of the governance of men will not be the understanding of their needs, their rights and their security where they are. Our frontier is not the Volga. It might be more nearly located on the Missouri.

It is not isolationism to understand that the fight for freedom more than ever before in the history of the world is today centered in the "everyday man" wherever he is. And that the world leadership which he requires cannot lose its center in concern for a widening circumference of security. The American defense —and much more than the American defense—lies in the radical New World that America set itself up to be.

There is not any question in Truman's mind of the continuing quality of the average Americans. The only American danger could come from the possibility of their failure to believe in the essence of their own Revolution. There has been effort from the beginning to make them forget its meaning. Jefferson's name has been used to deny the spirit of Jefferson's Declaration. The governmental devices he found useful for his time have been emphasized above and against his spirit and purposes for all men in all time. His fear of "a government of wolves and sheep" after his revolutionary experience with the faults of a distant British monarchy has hidden his conception of the purposes of all government.

"The only orthodox object of the institution of government," he wrote from Monticello, "is to secure the greatest degree of happiness possible to the general mass of those associated under it."

And he meant all associated under it. "We of the United States, you know," he wrote to Monsieur Dupont de Nemours, "are constitutionally and conscientiously democrats."

In our times those statements mean that the average men who believe themselves worthy of freedom and capable of government in America must show themselves creatively ready to believe in the possibilities also of other men everywhere on earth. That is the Truman faith. He believed in the capability of men given a fair and unconfused choice to make a wise choice. Once I asked him about his almost incredible confidence that he would win in his 1940 and 1948 election campaigns.

"I knew my record was good," he said, "and that they would vote for me."

That was not a tribute to his own record. There were some in both cases who loudly insisted that it was bad. But it was the expression of his faith that given a free opportunity and an unconfused choice, men are capable of good will and good sense.

Once in a speech to a group of Negroes long before he was considered for the Vice-Presidency he indicated his feeling about the indivisible quality of freedom, that none were safe when some were denied. His whole foreign policy, built on the sound example of the effectiveness for democracy in his domestic program, lies upon that idea. His hopes for democratic action for world order and peace by all nations great and small in the United Nations has not faltered though one nation, he believes, has by anti-democratic action prevented its effectiveness. The basic ideal of both the Truman Doctrine and the Marshall Plan is aid to nations in the creation of such stability as makes a free choice possible. He has no notions that a part of freedom is standing back while freedom is violently destroyed.

His basic faith in both the possibilities of all people and the necessity for an expansive American faith was best expressed in that "Point Four" of his foreign policy which he stated on that clear, cold day in January 1949, after Vinson had sworn him in as the President and leader of the American democracy. In it he proposed that America "embark upon a bold program for making the benefits of our scientific advances and industrial progress available for the improvement and growth of undeveloped areas." It was a program which he had initiated himself in the preparation of his Inaugural Address. That address, he knew, would be listened to expectantly by common men and average men everywhere.

"I got to looking at the big globe in my office," he said of that Point Four conception. "I was talking with T. V. Soong one day about the food situation in China and I asked him if the Yangtze and the Hwang Ho rivers could be harnessed like the Columbia to stop floods, provide power and irrigation to increase the food supply of China. He said, 'Yes,' it was possible. Then I talked to a man who had been out to Arabia—I forget his name—if it wasn't possible to do something to increase the food supply there. Ibn Saud heard about that conversation and asked for an adviser. He's there now.

"There are so many other places," he told me in talking of the plan, "the Valley of the Euphrates, the Parana in Paraguay and Brazil, the Zambezi and the Congo in Africa. That's in a section of Africa which is a plateau like our central west plain only it is infested with the tsetse fly. There is twice as much potential power on the Zambezi as at Niagara. The plateau in Brazil is like our West before it was opened up. It could support two hundred million people in luxury if properly opened up.

"The development of our country was all on the basis of British, French and Belgian capital. But what happened to it? They have spent all that capital in two world wars. Now we have two hundred billion dollars in savings in the banks and the insurance companies, two hundred billion in cash in the banks, and an annual income of two hundred billion. Is there any use letting that lie there doing nothing if we can develop these bread baskets? All this, as I plan it, would be private risk capital. The assets in these valleys would ten times overpay for these investments. It would only be guaranteed from confiscation by the governments of the lands in which it would be invested."

That might not always be easy. Already any such possibilities on the Yangtze and the Hwang Ho were gone. Capital was often timid in an uncertain world. Men were less ready to pour out across any unknown, strange wests than once they had been. But the possibilities were there. The need was there. And the people. Perhaps most important of all, the idea was there.

A decent, developed world could sustain the possibility of liberty and the faith in freedom's fulfillment.

"The initiative is ours," Truman said.

And perhaps the greatest need was ours, too. The measure of the ordinary men who built this nation could never be merely resistance against the counter-revolution of communism. Ordinary Americans had shown courage, ingenuity, confidence on every beachhead of the world. There was required of them a new expansive spirit in freedom—the re-emphasis in their own hearts of their own great revolutionary faith.

"A dictatorship," as Truman said, "is the hardest thing in God's world to hold together because it is made up entirely of conspiracies from the inside."

He did not minimize the danger of its old tyrannies. The stresses and strains of democracy were all around him. Also, he went on working at the American purpose for peace and freedom everywhere.

"They told me that we would never get the Palestine thing settled and the Indonesian. They are settled. We will get the Chinese thing settled, too, and not as a Communist State. Of course, it will take time. We are in too big a hurry. All we can do is set the spark that may bring it about."

The spark is lit. Actually, it is a torch now. It will not go out. There can be no long triumph for any brutal movement which pretends to be radical in the reactionary enslavement of human beings. To the freedom of all men Americans have pledged their lives, their fortunes and their sacred honor. The fulfillment of the pattern of independence is the task of ourselves and our leadership. Our passion in that purpose is the measure of our own capability for freedom, the symbol of our security, and the example for all men of good hope and good will in this world.

The challenge to the capabilities of "everyday men" in world leadership belongs to us all.

BIBLIOGRAPHY

No BIBLIOGRAPHY COULD encompass the number and variety of books consulted in putting this story together. It seems unnecessary to list old Kansas City and Independence telephone books and city directories though they were very useful in tracing a forgotten story through skimpily remembered years. Other such books like the *Official Manuals* of Missouri, the census reports and the *Proceedings* of various Democratic National Conventions were similarly useful, as were countless contemporary magazine and newspaper articles. I list, however, the books which piled up around my office and were needed in my office while I wrote this book:

Agar, Herbert. *The People's Choice*, 1933
Aikman, Duncan, editor. *The Taming of the Frontier*, 1925
Alinsky, Saul. *John L. Lewis*, 1949
American Guide Series. *Missouri, A Guide to the "Show Me" State*, 1941
—— *The Oregon Trail*, 1939
Barker, John T. *Missouri Lawyer*, 1949
Bellamy, Edward. *Looking Backward*, 1888
Bergh, Albery Ellery, editor. *The Writings of Thomas Jefferson*, 1907
Bower, Claude. *The Party Battles of the Jackson Period*, 1922
Brandeis, Louis D. *The Curse of Bigness*, 1934
Brashear, Minnie. *Mark Twain, Son of Missouri*, 1934
Bryan, William Jennings. *The Memoirs of*, 1925
Bryce, James. *The American Commonwealth*, 1888
Bundschu, Henry A. *Harry S. Truman—The Missourian*, 1948
Burch, John P. *A True Story of Charles W. Quantrell and His Guerilla Band*, 1923
Byrnes, James F. *Speaking Frankly*, 1947
Chamberlain, John. *Farewell to Reform*, 1932
Clark, Champ. *My Quarter Century of American Politics*, 1920
Clemens, Cyril. *The Man from Missouri*, 1945
—— *Truman Speaks*, 1946
Coffin, Tris. *Missouri Compromise*, 1947
Coleman, J. Winston, Jr. *Slavery Times in Kentucky*, 1940
Crane, Milton, editor. *The Roosevelt Era*, 1947
Douglas, Robert. *Boise Penrose, Symbol of an Era*, 1937
Ernst, Morris L. (and David Loth). *The People Know Best*, 1949
Farley, James A. *Behind the Ballots*, 1938
Flynn, Edward J. *You're the Boss*, 1947

Ford, Worthington Chauncey. *Letters of Henry Adams 1858-1891*, 1930

Fowler, Richard B. (and Henry C. Haskell, Jr.). *City of the Future*, 1950

Garwood, Darrell. *Crossroads of America*, 1948

Goddard, Frederick B. *Where to Emigrate and Why*, 1869

Goodman, Jack, editor. *While You Were Gone*, 1946

Haskell, Henry C., Jr. (and Richard B. Fowler). *City of the Future*, 1950

Hehmeyer, Walter (and Frank McNaughton). *Harry Truman, President*, 1948

Helm, William P. *Harry Truman—A Political Biography*, 1947

Helms, E. Allen (and Peter H. Odegard). *American Politics*, 1938

Herrying, Pendleton. *The Politics of Democracy*, 1940

Hill, Edwin C. *The American Scene*, 1933

Howe, E. W. *The Story of a Country Town*, 1884

Howe, S. Ferd. *Commerce of Kansas City*, 1886

Hutton, Graham. *Midwest at Noon*, 1946

Johnson, Gerald W. *Incredible Tale*, 1950

Johnson, Icie F. *William Rockhill Nelson and The Kansas City Star*, 1935

Kansas City Chamber of Commerce. *Where These Rocky Bluffs Meet*, 1938

Kansas City Chapter, Daughters of the American Revolution. *Vital Historical Records of Jackson County, Missouri, 1826-1876*

Kansas City Star, staff of. *William Rockhill Nelson*, 1915

Kent, Frank R. *The Democratic Party, A History*, 1928

Leahy, William D. *I Was There*, 1950

Lee, Jay M. *The Artilleryman*, 1920

Leighton, Isabel, editor. *The Aspirin Age*, 1949

Lord, Russell. *The Wallaces of Iowa*, 1947

Loth, David (and Morris L. Ernst). *The People Know Best*, 1949

McNaughton, Frank (and Walter Hehmeyer). *Harry Truman, President*, 1948

—— *This Man Truman*, 1945

Mason, Alpheus Thomas. *Brandeis—A Free Man's Life*, 1946

Miller, W. H. *The History of Kansas City*, 1880

Milligan, Maurice M. *The Inside Story of the Pendergast Machine by the Man Who Smashed It*, 1948

Minor, Henry. *The Story of the Democratic Party*, 1928

Mitchell, Ewing Young. *Kicked In and Kicked Out of the President's Little Cabinet*, 1936

Myers, William Starr. *The Republican Party—A History*, 1928

Norris, Frank. *The Pit*, 1903

Norris, George W. *Fighting Liberal, An Autobiography*, 1945

Odegard, Peter H. (and E. Allen Helms). *American Politics*, 1938

Orth, Samuel T. *The Boss and the Machine*, 1919

Parkman, Francis. *The Oregon Trail*, 1849

Parrington, Vernon L. *Main Currents in American Thought*, 1926
Pollard, James E. *Presidents and the Press*, 1947
Powell, Gene. *Tom's Boy Harry*, 1948
Pyle, Ernest. *Home Country*, 1935
Roosevelt, Elliott, editor. *FDR His Personal Letters, 1905-1928*, 1948
Roosevelt, Franklin D. *The Public Papers and Addresses of*
Roosevelt, Theodore. *Thomas H. Benton*, 1886
Schauffler, Edward R. *Harry Truman—Son of the Soil*, 1947
Schlesinger, Arthur M., Jr. *The Age of Jackson*, 1945
—— *The Vital Center*, 1949
Schnapper, M. B., editor. *The Truman Program*, 1948
Seitz, Don C. *They Also Ran*, 1928
Sherwood, Robert E. *Roosevelt and Hopkins*, 1948
Smith, Merriman. *Thank You, Mr. President*, 1946
—— *A President Is Many Men*, 1948
Shoemaker, Floyd C., editor. *Missouri Day by Day*, 1942
Sinclair, Upton. *The Jungle*, 1906
Slaughter, J. L., editor. *Public Men in and out of Office*, 1946
Spencer, Cornelia. *Straight Furrow*, 1949
Steffens, Lincoln. *The Shame of the Cities*, 1904
Stettinius, Edward R. *Roosevelt and the Russians*, 1949
Street, Julian. *Abroad at Home*, 1916
Sullivan, Mark. *Our Times*
Truman, Harry S., as county judge supervisor of publication. *Results of County Planning Jackson County, Missouri*
Tully, Grace. *FDR My Boss*, 1949
Turner, Frederick Jackson. *The Frontier in American History*, 1920
Twain, Mark (and Charles Dudley Warner). *The Gilded Age*, 1873
Van Devander, Charles W. *The Big Bosses*, 1944
Vestal, Stanley. *The Missouri* (American Rivers Series), 1945
Wector, Dixon. *When Johnny Comes Marching Home*, 1944
Weizmann, Chaim. *Trial and Error*, 1949
White, William Allen. *A Puritan in Babylon*, 1938
—— *The Autobiography of*, 1946
Williams, Walter, editor. *The State of Missouri*, 1904

INDEX